CW00549867

London's Night Buses

Volume Two 1984–2013

Philip Wallis

Capital Transport

ISBN 978-185414-372-3

First published 2013

Published by Capital Transport Publishing
www.capitaltransport.com

Printed by Parksons Graphics

Front cover. The N41 was a most elusive route in its original form with its two allocated buses scheduled to be in service for less than three hours of the night between 01.33 and 04.29. Route N41, which formed a 24-hour service between Tottenham Hale Station and Archway Station with daytime route 41, had been introduced on 1/2 December 2000. Arriva London North's Wrightbus Eclipse Gemini-bodied Volvo B7TL VLW 119 was photographed at Turnpike Lane in the early morning hours of Saturday 29 January 2005. One week later the N41 was extended beyond Archway Station to Trafalgar Square. *Philip Wallis*

Back cover: The night-time elements of most existing 24-hour bus routes lost the distinctive N-prefix to their route numbers in 2003/2004 and new route introduction since then have been publically identified with plain route numbers. Only one 24-hour route has ever gained an N route number prefix. This occurred from 30/31 August 2013 when the night-time element (only) of 24-hour Paddington Station to Bow route 205 was extended beyond Bow to Leyton. Stagecoach East London's Scania OmniCity 15121 was photographed in the bus station at Euston Station. *Philip Wallis*

Introduction: The majority of all-night bus routes introduced from 13/14 April 1984 by London Transport Executive have prospered and grown in frequency. Route N14 has developed from a nightly hourly frequency service between Liverpool Street Station or Farringdon Street and Roehampton to have become the night-time element of 24-hour route 14 between Warren Street Station and Putney Heath with a 15 minute week-night and 10 minute weekend night frequency service. Go-Ahead London General's Wrightbus Eclipse Gemini-bodied Volvo B7TL WVL 17 was seen in Putney High Street during the early morning hours of Sunday 28 March 2004. Route N18 operated just three nightly return journeys along a route axis between Liverpool Street Station and Sudbury when introduced. It has been progressively developed to give a nightly 30 minute frequency service between Trafalgar Square and Harrow Weald combined with a 15 minute week-night and 10 minute weekend night frequency service out as far as Sudbury. First London's Plaxton President-bodied Dennis Trident TN 956 was photographed at Baker Street Station bus stop in Marylebone Road early on Saturday morning 1 November 2003. *Philip Wallis*

Title page. The demand for all-night bus travel in London was demonstrated by Arriva London North's Wrightbus Eclipse Gemini-bodied Volvo B7TL VLW 88 as it neared full capacity loading for its outbound route N73 journey at Tottenham Court Road Station in the early hours of Saturday morning 7 June 2003. *Philip Wallis*

CONTENTS

ACKNOWLEDGEMENTS

A number of people have helped with aspects of content and research for this book for which I am most grateful.

London commentator the late Dennis Cox and the late David Ruddom, former Chairman of the London Historical Research Group of the Omnibus Society, gave staunch support to me throughout the preparation of both volumes of *London's Night Buses*. Their reviews of draft manuscripts, with resultant informed criticisms and helpful suggestions on matters of content, based upon their extensive knowledge of London's bus operations, have enhanced the accuracy and scope of both books. I am saddened that neither gentleman survived long enough to read this finished second volume.

Dennis Cox's deep knowledge of fare-related matters assisted with the preparation of Appendix 1, Fare Policies. Appendix 2, Changing the Clock, was formed as a composite piece from comprehensive Notes supplied by both John Bull and Chris Holland and I wish to extend my thanks to both of them. Both gentlemen also kindly assisted with many other aspects of research. Dick Halle, former Strategy Director of London Bus Services Ltd, gave much helpful advice on operational and policy matters. Dean Sullivan, Managing Director of Sullivan Buses, provided me with a comprehensive account of his company's operation of Watford area night bus routes N1 and N2. Clive King, Business Development Manager of Arriva the Shires and Essex, and Robert Williams, Commercial Manager of Stagecoach in Oxfordshire, kindly elaborated upon the night-time travel opportunities entirely within Greater London of Green Line route 757 and the Oxford Tube respectively.

I am most grateful to the London Omnibus Traction Society for permission to extract information from its products including *The London Bus* and *London Bus Magazine*. Dave Stewart, editor of *The London Bus*, kindly extended further personal help in resolving specific queries and providing updates on operational matters. The Omnibus Society's *The Omnibus Magazine* proved to be a valued reference source. The PSV Circle kindly gave me permission to extract information from its extensive range of publications. Other assistance was provided by David Bowker, Peter Larking and Malcolm Papes. Kevin Lane provided first class photographic services.

All-night bus photography is a challenging pursuit and I am most grateful to all the photographers who have afforded me access to their collections. It is my hope that this volume's photographic content will adequately convey the ambience of all-night service operations. Mike Harris, a key photographic contributor, prepared the specially drawn maps whilst Alexander Zalicks drew the graph of all-night bus allocations.

The full support of my wife Rosalind has been vital to the preparation of this book. She has not only accepted the time that I have necessarily spent researching, writing and taking photographs for this volume but she has also guided me in computer usage and thereby ensured the delivery of an acceptable electronic manuscript to the publisher.

Philip Wallis
Tregowris, Cornwall
August 2013

NOTES ON THE TEXT AND ABBREVIATIONS

PERIOD OF COVERAGE – VOLUME TWO
13/14 April 1984 to 30/31 August 2013.

NIGHTS OF OPERATION
Operational times of all-night bus routes often overlap either side of midnight over two successive days, with services starting in the late evening of one day and finishing during the early morning hours of the next day. Generally speaking dates quoted in the text span both days of operation, but sometimes, for brevity, the text may refer to operation as being, for example, on 'Friday night' and in such instances it is implicit that an overnight service running into the next day is involved.

VEHICLE TYPES
The author has assumed that readers of this book will have some understanding of the vehicle-type codes used by successive operators since the London General Omnibus Company Ltd. Those readers wishing to refresh or expand their knowledge of London bus-type codes, models, specifications and manufacturers are recommended to consult the great number of fleet books and vehicle-type histories that have been published over very many years.

VEHICLE ALLOCATIONS TO ROUTES
The primary reference sources for Volumes One and Two have been London General, London Passenger Transport Board, London Transport (Executive and Board) and London Regional Transport *Traffic Notices, Traffic Circulars* and *Allocations of Scheduled Buses* as appropriate published between 20 June 1915 and 14 March 1992. These sources have been supplemented by reference to listings of *Allocations to Routes* published between 1967 and 1976 by The PSV Circle and, since 30 January 1971, by the London Omnibus Traction Society, as well as by photographic evidence. Post 14 March 1992 the primary reference sources have been the London Omnibus Traction Society's monthly bulletin *The London Bus* and its *Route Working Indexes*, supplemented by the author's personal observations and photographic evidence. Readers should bear in mind that vehicle-type changes to particular routes were sometimes progressively introduced over a period of time and also that operational exigencies sometimes led to the substitution of buses other than the allocated type.

ROUTE PROFILES IN CHAPTERS 4 TO 7
Night bus routes extant at 13/14 April 1984 are listed in chapter 4 after which route introductions follow a chronological sequence through chapters 5 to 7. Routes which were either re-numbered with the loss of their N-prefix or introduced without such a prefix, as the night-time element of a 24-hour service, are identified by the prefix (N).

Re-numbering of routes has been incorporated into appropriate route profiles, in order to identify service continuity along particular route corridors. In such instance a succeeding route number and its profile has been added to follow the route profile of the preceding route number. It should be noted that in some, but not all, instances of route re-numbering identified in these chapters London Regional Transport or Transport for London regarded the prior numbered route as having been withdrawn and superseded by the introduction of a new route contract.

GYRATORY (ONE-WAY) TRAFFIC SYSTEMS
In view of the scale, complexity and sometimes-changeable nature of gyratory traffic flow systems across Greater London no attempt has been made to detail every variation. However gyratory systems, or alterations to such systems, which had a profound effect on all-night bus routes are chronicled.

TEMPORARY ROUTE DIVERSIONS OR CURTAILMENTS
Temporary diversions or curtailments to all-night bus routes due to road and utility works, construction projects, accidents, police or security incidents, sporting events, weather, natural disasters and war are not generally chronicled.

CLOCK SYSTEM
This volume adheres to the 24-hour clock system.

ABBREVIATIONS
Su – Sunday night / Monday morning
M – Monday night / Tuesday morning
Tu – Tuesday night / Wednesday morning
W – Wednesday night / Thursday morning
Th – Thursday night / Friday morning
Fr – Friday night / Saturday morning
Sa – Saturday night/Sunday morning

LBSL – London Bus Services Ltd
LCC – London County Council (Tramways)
LGOC – London General Omnibus Company
LPTB – London Passenger Transport Board
LRT – London Regional Transport
LT – London Transport (Executive and Board)
TfL – Transport for London

arr – arrive/arrival(s)
bph – buses per hour
BST – British Summer Time
dep – depart/departure(s)
GLC – Greater London Council
GMT – Greenwich Mean Time
hr – hour(s)
min – minutes
opo – one-person operation
pvr – peak vehicle requirement
RLST – Round London Sightseeing Tour
SNJ – Special Night Journey(s)
t/a – trading as
TSU – Transport Studies Unit (of Oxford University)
Weekdays: Monday to Saturday inclusive

N14
Putney Heath
THE ULTIMATE ROMANTIC COMEDY
Go-Ahead
orange
LG02 KHR

Paddington Harrow Rd
Harlesden Stonebridge
Wembley Sudbury
N18
TRAFALGAR SQUARE
GIORGIO ARMANI
UNDERGROUND
First
TN956
X956 HLT

INTRODUCTION: A BRIEF SUMMARY OF VOLUME ONE

London's public all-night road passenger transport services were inaugurated in 1899 with horse-tram routes operated by London County Council Tramways, London United Tramways and the North Metropolitan Tramways Company, along with two London County Council Tramways-operated night horse-bus routes. Conversion of all-night horse-tram routes to electrically-powered tramcar operation started in 1903 and the last regular night horse-tram service ran over the Hampstead Heath to Holborn route in April 1909.

London's first all-night motor bus-operated routes were introduced in 1913 when the London General Omnibus Company started routes 94 and 94A, between Liverpool Street and Cricklewood or Willesden respectively, operated by open-top B-type buses. Some expansion of both the all-night tram and the all-night bus networks followed in 1914 but the prospects for any further growth were stunted by the outbreak of the First World War. Wartime exigencies led to the complete withdrawal of all-night bus routes in 1916 and a reduction in both the scale and scope of all-night tramway operations.

All-night motor bus operation was restored by the LGOC to routes 94 and 94A in 1920. Modest expansion of both the all-night bus and the all-night tram route networks occurred in the 1920s and early 1930s. Schedules on all-night bus routes were speeded up by the allocation of ST-type AEC Regents and LT-type AEC Renowns to all-night duties in 1932 and 1933 when such buses superseded NS-types. These then-modern vehicles were complemented by allocations of longer wheelbase STL-type AEC Regents to some all-night routes from 1933 onwards.

The London Passenger Transport Board assumed powers from 1 July 1933 and in August of that year introduced a further four all-night bus routes. The network of all-night bus and tram all-night services established at that date formed the framework of an enduring route network which would continue to operate in a substantially unchanged and quite recognisable form for over half a century. Most all-night bus routes were re-numbered into a numerically-descending series from route number 299 on 2/3 October 1934.

A handful of all-night tram routes were converted to trolleybus operation between 1937 and 1940. A consequence of the Second World War was the withdrawal, between 1939 and 1943, of the majority of Special Night Journeys which had operated over daytime bus routes. The Inter-Station Bus Route was reinstated in December 1943 with an all-night service element. All-night tram and trolleybus routes, which had operated as unnumbered services, were given route numbers from 18/19 June 1946.

London Transport Executive converted its remaining all-night tram routes to motor bus operation between 1950 and 1952. The few all-night trolleybus routes were similarly converted between 1959 and 1961 after which London's public all-night road passenger transport services became operated entirely by double-deck diesel-engine motor buses, principally from the RT-family but the allocations also included Routemasters which vehicle-type had made its debut on all-night service in 1959. Most all-night bus routes were further re-numbered into a descending series from route number N99 on 11/12 October 1960.

The Routemaster family of buses went on to dominate allocations across the Nighters over the next decade such that all bar three all-night bus routes and Special Night Journeys had Routemaster allocations by late April 1970. The RT-type experienced a renaissance on all-night service later in 1970 and early 1971 when that vehicle-type was re-allocated to routes N87 and N95. The RT-type, which had first been allocated to all-night duties in May 1948, continued to fulfil such a role until replaced on routes N95 and N98 in May 1978, thereby setting a vehicle-type record for longevity on all-night service.

One-man operation was first introduced to mainstream all-night bus routes in May 1972 when routes N85 and N86 were converted to DMS-type Daimler Fleetline operation. Longer dwell times for fare collection and extended journey times, in general associated with early one-man bus operation in London, led to a hiatus in conversion plans and the retention of crewed-operation on many night routes, most of which latter category had their schedules speeded up in July 1973. M-type MCW Metrobuses and T-type Leyland Titans first became allocated to all-night bus routes in 1979 and 1980 respectively. The surprise allocation of LS-type Leyland Nationals to route N96 in January 1981 represented the first-ever allocation of single-deck buses to an N-prefixed (or preceding 2xx series) all-night bus route.

London's public all-night road passenger transport network had traditionally operated 'Saturday Night and Sunday Morning Excepted' to the extent that operation of all-night bus routes on that night of the week had always been rare. That long-established practice changed from 29/30 October 1983, when Saturday night operation was expanded to cover all routes bar the Special Night Journey on route 220.

London Transport's service delivery had deteriorated progressively during the 1970s when that Executive's difficulties became compounded by chronic staff shortages, increased traffic congestion, bus fleet unreliability and increasing politically-motivated interference into matters of policy by the Greater London Council. Accusations of extravagance and waste within London Transport led to reviews of that Executive's functions, including the all-night bus route operation.

CHAPTER 1
THE OXFORD REPORT

During 1980 London Transport commissioned a team of consultants from the Transport Studies Unit of Oxford University to examine the demand for a night bus service in London, appraise the operation of the existing network and make recommendations, based on their findings, about how the service offered might more closely and efficiently match demand. The Transport Studies Unit reported back to the London Transport Executive in October 1981. The Transport Studies Unit undertook its investigation on three fronts: (a) The origin and destination surveys of existing night-time passengers, which included passengers using late Underground and British Railways trains, as well as all-night buses; (b) interviews 'at home' with members of the public; (c) interviews with staff.

The TSU presented its Report to London Transport in October 1981. Through its survey results the TSU had been able to identify areas of high actual and potential demand, the times of peak demand through the night, the nature of trips being made (i.e. work/non work), the frequency of trips and much else of considerable value in appraising demand for the service. The report highlighted certain well known deficiencies of the then extant night bus network, such as the poor service on Saturday nights/Sunday mornings, the irregular times of operation and the adherence to a route network based on a demand pattern up to 50 years old. It also recommended the use of Trafalgar Square as a central London focal point for all-night bus routes, the abolition of child fares on night routes, the introduction of a 'Night Rider' ticket valid for a specified period on all-night services, including staff buses, and the increased use of one-person operation.

Having assimilated the data the TSU suggested two possible course of action, designed around the remit not to increase the existing duty requirements:

Either:

Leave the existing all-night bus route network as it was and introduce later (sic) starting and finishing times on the Underground – a solution which the Unit proposed 'not with great 'conviction'.'

Or:

Restructure services to form a core network of nine half-hourly frequency routes which crossed central London and extended only five miles from Trafalgar Square. Beyond the five-mile limit a 'demand responsive' taxi scheme would operate. The TSU's basic premise for the adoption of the five-mile limit was that 60% of all-night bus passengers did not travel more than the five miles from Charing Cross and that those who did so had trip destinations and origins too diverse for a rational network of routes to serve them efficiently.

The proposed routes were:

N1 (Fulham Broadway – Greenwich), N2 (West Ham – Shepherds Bush), N3 (Stratford – Cricklewood), N4 (Clapton Garage – Hammersmith), N5 (Stamford Hill – Tooting Bec), N6 (Turnpike Lane – Putney Bridge), N7 (Muswell Hill – Tulse Hill), N8 (Hampstead Heath – Dulwich), N9 (Willesden Garage – Wandsworth).

The TSU estimated that its proposed 'Core Network' could be operated by 40 buses. London Transport did not agree with this figure and calculated that it would require 43 buses which represented a saving of 14 buses compared with the then-extant network's allocation of 57 buses on Monday to Friday nights. *(LT had always scheduled route 9's Special Night Journey and the later of the two Special Early Morning Journeys on route 221 as elements of the daytime service.)*

The TSU also suggested possible projections of route N1 to Woolwich, route N2 to both Uxbridge and Becontree Heath, route N4 to Heathrow Airport, route N6 to Waltham Cross and route N8 to Bromley. However, the TSU did not provide London Transport with any cost estimate for these possible route extensions to its 'Core Network'.

LONDON TRANSPORT'S CRITIQUE OF THE OXFORD REPORT

London Transport did not agree to the implementation of the TSU's suggested solution, after having concluded that the 'five-mile limit + taxis' solution proposed in the Oxford Report lacked 'full consideration of the very real practical problems, both to passengers and operators, and of the large areas left unserved'. London Transport criticised the TSU for failing to produce any costing for the proposed route extensions and also commented, 'it is virtually impossible to cost the taxi-zone operation without further detailed information'.

London Transport voiced three principal criticisms of the Oxford Report's solution:

1. REVENUE-LOSS IMPLICATIONS AND IMPRACTICABILITY OF THE DEMAND-RESPONSIVE TAXIS SCHEME

The Oxford Report had assumed that all existing night bus passengers would be retained under its 'five-mile limit + taxis' solution. LT disputed this assumption since it feared that the continued custom of the 40% of passengers who travelled beyond the 'five-mile limit' would be put at risk, with consequent revenue loss implications. LT considered that the TSU had taken no account of inherent problems in the taxi system for inbound passengers starting their journeys beyond the 'five-mile limit', who might have difficulty in finding a taxi and, if successful, might eschew the option of

Opposite Upon their introduction on 1 October 1950 Farringdon Street all-night journeys on routes 168 (re-numbered N68 from 25/26 April 1975) and N88 terminated in Farringdon Avenue. Reconstruction in the area c.1960 obliterated Farringdon Avenue and the terminal point for those routes was removed to Stonecutter Street where London Transport Golden Jubilee liveried RM 1983 was photographed on Sunday morning 24 July 1983. At that time Saturday night/Sunday morning was the sole night of the week when Stockwell garage, as opposed to Wandsworth garage, operated route N68. Routes N68 and N88 would enjoy a brief renaissance at Stonecutter Street from 10/11 July 1987 when one N68 and two N88 journeys per night (by then allocated to Sutton garage) were revised to terminate there. The return N68 journey operated to Sutton garage whilst the earlier of the two N88 journeys ran to East Croydon Station and the later one to Banstead. Short working N14 journeys to Stonecutter Street had been withdrawn after operation on 25/26 April 1985 and the withdrawal of these latter-day N68 and N88 journeys, after operation on 17/18 August 1995, ended Stonecutter Street's involvement with the Nighters for good. *Mike Harris*

ALL-NIGHT BUS NETWORK PROPOSED BY TRANSPORT STUDIES UNIT OXFORD UNIVERSITY

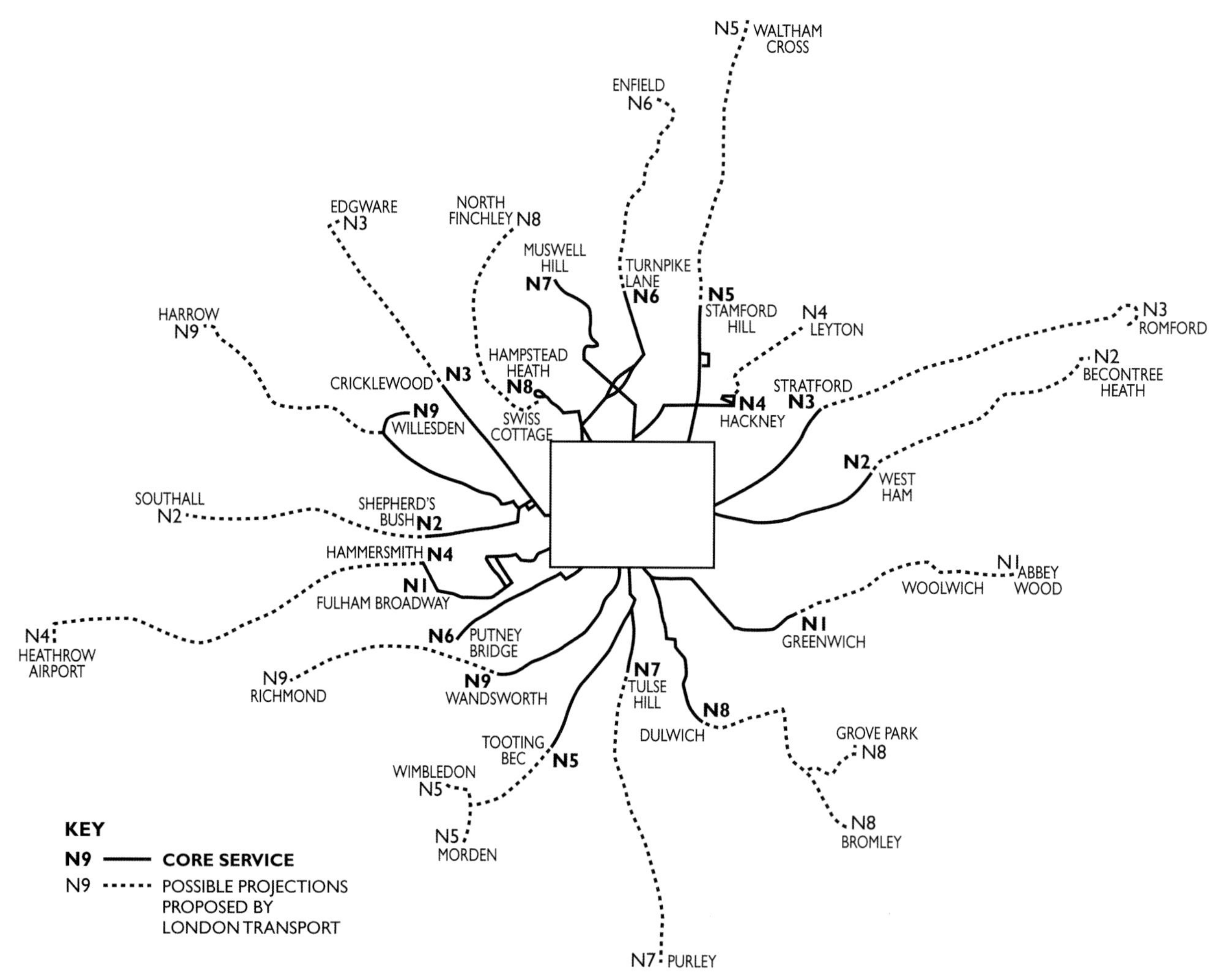

Drawn by Mike Harris

taking a taxi to transfer to an all-night bus route at its outer terminus in favour of completing the entire journey by taxi. LT also pointed out that probably 10% of all-night bus journeys comprised trips made wholly within the proposed 'taxi-zone' and that such passengers would be lost to LT.

London Transport considered that the practical problems associated with the suburban use of demand-responsive taxis had not been assessed fully in the Oxford Report. Potential difficulties highlighted by LT included the uncertainty of getting a cab late at night, the possible unwillingness of taxi-drivers to take passengers to the outer suburbs of London with little prospect of a return fare, the limited capacity of taxi cabs and the practicability of fare apportionment and payment in the event of shared-taxi use. LT also pointed out that the Transport and General Workers Union (which included both bus and taxi staff in its membership) was opposed in principle to cab sharing, which would seem to preclude the involvement of regular (black cab) taxi drivers in the para-taxi scheme. LT considered that the alternative use of minicabs late at night would cause considerable public concern.

The Oxford Report had suggested that London Transport itself might run the para-taxi network. LT considered that 'the cost of co-ordinating the operation and the resources of staff and vehicles involved suggest that it would be more efficient simply to run longer, regular standard night bus services than, in effect, 18 Dial-A-Bus networks'. Despite its arguments against the TSU's specific proposal, LT recognised that there might well be advantages in fostering relationships between LT and minicab operators, based at strategic suburban centres on night bus routes, which would be pursued.

2. LATENT DEMAND

Whilst recognising that the TSU, through its surveys, had amassed much useful data about all-night bus usage and demand, London Transport considered that the TSU's origin and destination surveys did not take into account potential demand for night bus services, citing as examples centres such as Croydon, as well as the Hertford Road corridor north of Stamford Hill. Earlier research in 1971 had revealed that 80% of night travellers (all modes) made journeys up to ten miles from Charing Cross which, to LT, indicated a sizeable, but as yet untapped, market for all-night bus services.

3. COST OF PROPOSALS

London Transport considered that the TSU had not costed its proposals properly and had failed to appreciate the marginal cost advantage gained by using buses already deployed on daytime services for all-night duties too. LT pointed out that the TSU had provided no estimate of the cost of extensions to its proposed core network and considered it virtually impossible to cost the 'taxi-fare' operation without further detailed information.

LT recognised that the routes designed by the Oxford study were based on achieving maximum efficiency in the utilisation of staff and buses. The study had been commissioned in 1980, after which London Transport's 1981 policy-shift to more one-person operation meant that most of the Unit's proposed core routes had round running times too great to achieve efficient scheduling, consistent with keeping spells of duty and duty lengths within the agreement between London Transport and the Transport and General Workers Union. However, this did provide scope to enable route projections beyond the 'five mile limit' to be included more economically as detailed in Table A and shown on the map opposite.

Table A
All-night Bus Route Network proposed by the Transport Studies Unit at Oxford University, as modified to incorporate route extensions proposed by London Transport

Proposed Route No	Termini	Nightly Duties *
N1	Fulham Broadway – Abbey Wood	6
N2	Becontree Heath – Southall	7
N3	Romford – Edgware	7
N4	Leyton – Heathrow Airport	6
N5	Waltham Cross – Wimbledon or Morden	7
N6	Enfield – Putney Bridge	8
N7	Muswell Hill – Purley	6
N8	North Finchley –Grove Park/Bromley	6
N9	Harrow/Willesden – Richmond	7

* London Transport estimate

THE LONDON TRANSPORT APPROACH

London Transport recognised many of the intrinsic faults of its present network identified in the Oxford Report but set out to resolve them by modifying the existing service, rather than adopting a more radical solution. LT's aim was to win additional traffic while causing the minimum of disruption to existing passengers. LT started by assessing demand using the current network as a base and feeding in data from the TSU's origin and destination surveys to produce a series of options, each of which took the development of the all-night bus route network a stage further.

Certain of the recommendations of the Oxford Report had already been implemented, namely:

(i) The introduction of a Saturday night/Sunday morning service across almost all the entire night bus route network from 29/30 October 1983.

(ii) The withdrawal of child fares after 22.00 on all bus services (both daytime and all-night) from 21 March 1982.

London Transport recognised the importance to passengers of an easily remembered clock face headway, highlighted in the Oxford Report, and also stated its intention to adopt one-person operation wherever practicable, another tenet of the Oxford Report.

Table B illustrates London Transport's estimate of the resource cost comparison of certain variations to the existing all-night bus route network, from which it can be seen that 20 additional duties would have been needed to achieve full one-person operation with clock face headways on all routes.

Table B
Basic Variations to Existing All-Night Bus Route Network
London Transport's Resource Cost Comparison

Option	Additional Duties
Existing Network (crew + opo). Adoption of clockface headways.	+ 15
Existing Network. Full opo conversion.	+ 5
Existing Network. Adoption of clockface headways and full opo.	+ 20

Source: Proposed Revisions to the Night Bus Network, London Buses, October 1983

London Transport then investigated ways in which the additional resources identified in Table B could be saved, or used more efficiently or economically, since certain of the route options considered were inefficient in scheduling terms. This generally entailed linking routes or introducing extensions to centres of perceived demand outside the current night bus route network, such as Bromley or Muswell Hill. LT reviewed any remaining significant gaps in the network where there was evidence of demand, shown either by the TSU's origin and destination survey or where the socio-economic nature of an area suggested that latent demand might exist, with a view to ascertaining how such areas might best be served, perhaps by entirely new routes.

LT considered that additional supervision would be required for an enhanced all-night bus route network and recommended that the number of inspectors engaged on all-night bus route supervision be increased from three to four, with one inspector based at Trafalgar Square to control services and deal with public enquiries.

London Transport's plan to launch its extended and revised all-night bus route network on Friday night/Saturday morning 3/4 February 1984 ran into trouble when the Greater London Council's Transport Committee voted to approve the plans only if no further routes were converted from crew to one-person operation. The Transport and General Workers Union was opposed to single manning on the Nighters, which it regarded as a 'social service', and also cited concerns about assaults on staff. LT produced evidence which showed that 'overall the assault rate on night buses is significantly lower than on day vehicles.' LT, the TGWU and the GLC engaged in further negotiations to break the impasse. Another planned introduction date of 2/3 March 1984 was missed before the parties reached agreement to introduce the new network on 13/14 April 1984.

MAJOR NETWORK EXPANSION 13/14 APRIL 1984

An extensive poster and advertising campaign accompanied the largest expansion to date of London's all-night bus route network, which was launched by a galaxy of West End performers, headed by Danny la Rue, at Trafalgar Square on Friday night/Saturday morning 13/14 April 1984. London Transport increased the number of N-prefixed all-night bus routes from 21 to 32, with the introduction of new routes N2, N13, N14, N18, N27, N74 and N76. Further new routes N11, N21, N77, N78 and N79 absorbed and expanded the former all-night services that had operated over daytime routes 11, 221, 177, 109 and 185 respectively. New areas served by the extended network included Edgware, Golders Green, Muswell Hill, Hammond Street, Leytonstone, Harold Hill, Dagenham, Thamesmead, Bromley, Crystal Palace, Roehampton, Richmond, Uxbridge, Sudbury and Wembley.

Clock face headways, mostly hourly, were applied to the majority of routes. All routes, bar N29, N93, Inter-Station Route and the Special Night Journeys on route 9, became one-person operated, whilst all central London services were routed to serve Trafalgar Square. In fact, the majority of pre-existing routes already passed through or terminated at Trafalgar Square, with the exception of the N89 and N96, which were substantially re-routed to serve the Square. Common pick-up points were provided at Trafalgar Square for buses travelling in the same general direction – stop C outside the National Gallery for all services to north and east London, as well as buses to Liverpool Street and London Bridge, a new stop V outside Canada House, on the Square's west side, for all services to south and west London as well as all buses to Victoria and Pimlico, except routes N76, N95 and N98 which used stop B in Pall Mall East. The Trafalgar Square to Victoria section of routes N74, N76, N77, N78, N83, N85, N86 and N93 comprised isolated journeys timed to achieve crew relief-break periods at Victoria garage. Isolated N87 journeys ran in service between Stockwell and Victoria via Vauxhall for similar purpose.

The substantial expansion of the all-night bus route network necessitated fresh bus route-blind displays for many services and the opportunity was taken to differentiate night bus routes from daytime services by creating black on yellow intermediate point blind displays for most night routes. All timetable publicity was produced with blue and yellow covers and incorporated the Night Owl logo, which had first been used with the 29/30 October 1982 timetable. New route numbers had to be displayed at hundreds of bus stops and E-plates were produced in blue and yellow, again bearing the Night Owl logo.

Be a wise Night Owl

London's Night Bus system will be dramatically improved from Friday night, 13th April. Major features include:

* More buses and more routes
* New services to many parts of London not previously served by Night Bus
* Most routes running at hourly, easy-to-remember times, every night of the week
* All Central London Night Buses to pass through Trafalgar Square, handy for the West End and giving easier cross-town connections

Left: Blackfriars Bridge is associated with the earliest years of London's all-night public road passenger transport services as well as with one of their later milestone developments. London County Council Tramways' all-night horse-bus service, which linked the tramway terminus in Blackfriars Road with Farringdon Street, first crossed that bridge on 12/13 February 1899. All-night tram services subsequently followed and culminated with the linking of the Brixton and Tooting all-night tram routes to form a cyclical working pattern via Streatham and across Blackfriars and Westminster Bridges from 27/28 July 1928. All-night tram route 1 was replaced by bus route 287 from 7/8 January 1951 which was, in turn, re-numbered N87 from 11/12 October 1960. Stockwell garage had replaced one of the allocated DMS-type Fleetlines with RML 2389 to commemorate the last night of operation of route N87 in its traditional form on Thursday night/Friday morning 12/13 April 1984 during which night that Routemaster was photographed on Blackfriars Bridge. *Mike Harris*

Above: Timetable number 6 (13/14 April 1984). The 'Buses for Night Owls' title was perpetuated on Night Bus timetables and maps until 1992.

Table C
All-Night Bus Routes and Vehicle Allocations with effect 13/14 April 1984

Route No	Termini	Allocation			Garage
		Su	M–Fr	Sa	
9	Liverpool Street Station – Mortlake	-	1 RM	2 RM	Stamford Brook
220	Willesden Junction – Tooting	1 M	1 M	-	Shepherd's Bush
N2	Trafalgar Square – West Norwood	1 DM	1 DM	1 DM	Victoria
N11	Liverpool Street Stn – Shepherd's Bush	2 DM	2 DM	2 DM	Victoria
N13	Trafalgar Square- North Finchley	2 M	2 M	2 M	Finchley
N14	Liverpool Street Station – Roehampton	3 M	3 M	3 M	Putney
N18	Liverpool Street Station – Sudbury	1 M	1 M	1 M	Willesden
N21	Trafalgar Square – North Finchley	1 M	1 M	1 M	Finchley
N27	Liverpool Street Station – Richmond	2 M	2 M	2 M	Stamford Brook
N29	Trafalgar Square – Enfield Town	2 M	2 M	2 M	Wood Green
N68	Liverpool Street Station – Wandsworth	1 M	1 M	1 M	Wandsworth
N74	Victoria – Bromley North Station	2 T	2 T	2 T	Peckham
N76	Victoria – Leytonstone	2 T	2 T	2 T	West Ham
N77	Victoria – Thamesmead	2 T	2 T	2 T	New Cross
N78	Victoria – South Croydon {	3 DMS	3 DMS	3 DMS	Brixton
		1 DMS	1 DMS	1 DMS	Thornton Heath
N79	Archway – Lewisham	3 T	3 T	3 T	Walworth
N80	Potters Bar – North Finchley	1 M	1 M	1 M	Potters Bar
N82	Kensal Rise – Woolwich	4 T	5 T	4 T	New Cross
N83	Victoria – Wood Green {	1 M	1 M	1 M	Tottenham
		1 M	1 M	1 M	Stamford Hill
N85	Victoria – Grove Park	3 T	3 T	3 T	Peckham
N86	Victoria – Crystal Palace	2 T	2 T	2 T	Peckham
N87	Trafalgar Square – Streatham Garage	3 DMS	3 DMS	3 DMS	Stockwell
N88	Liverpool Street Station – Wandsworth	2 M	2 M	2 M	Wandsworth
N89	Liverpool Street Station – Uxbridge	4 M	4 M	4 M	Hanwell
N90	Victoria – Hammond Street {	2 M	2 M	2 M	Enfield
		2 M	2 M	2M	Edmonton
N91	Liverpool Street Stn – Willesden Garage	1 M	1 M	1 M	Willesden
N92	Muswell Hill – Pimlico	2 DMS	2 DMS	2 DMS	Holloway
N93	Victoria – Hampstead Heath	1 RML	1 RML	1 RML	Holloway
N94	Liverpool Street Station – Edgware	3 M	3 M	3 M	Cricklewood
N95	Victoria – Dagenham	3 T	3 T	3 T	Barking
N96	Trafalgar Square – Chingford Station	2 LS	2 LS	2 LS	Leyton
N97	Liverpool Street Stn – Heathrow Airport	5 M	5 M	5 M	Stamford Brook
N98	Victoria – Harold Hill	4 T	4 T	4 T	Romford
N99	Chingford Station – V & A Docks	1 T	1 T	1 T	West Ham
	Inter-Station Route	1 T	-	1 T	New Cross
	Total	77	78	78	

Note. Due to an industrial dispute at Cricklewood and Willesden garages routes N18, N91 and N94 did not operate east of Marble Arch until 18/19 April 1984.

Although east London route N99 had served parts of Leytonstone since 26/27 April 1960, new route N76 provided the first-ever all-night bus link between central London and Leytonstone upon its introduction from 13/14 April 1984. West Ham garage's T 606 stands at the Green Man terminus in Leytonstone on Sunday morning 29 July 1984. *Mike Harris*

New route N27 had a two hourly headway which gave Richmond its first all-night bus service with four journeys per night. The N27's timetable was co-ordinated with that of established Heathrow airport route N97 to provide a combined 30-minute headway over a lengthy common section of routeing between Liverpool Street station and Kew Bridge station. Stamford Brook garage's M 145 is seen in Richmond bus station on Sunday morning 8 July 1984 having completed a journey from Liverpool Street station with scheduled arrival time at 04.51. This first route N27 was fated to be withdrawn after just one year's operation when alternative all-night bus facilities to Richmond were provided by an extended N93 routed via Barnes from 26/27 April 1985. *Mike Harris*

London's all-night bus route network has always used buses otherwise allocated to daytime services and has never used dedicated vehicles. The Inter-Station liveried C-type Leyland Cubs and ST-type AEC Regents used on that route at various times between 1936 and 1950 operated when the route had a daytime and/or evening service element. When the Inter-Station Route became solely an all-night service from 20/21 November 1950 Old Kent Road garage allocated standard RT-type buses which were capable of being deployed on any of that garage's daytime double-deck bus routes. When Victoria garage took on responsibility for routes N2 and N11 from 13/14 April 1984 it used buses which saw daytime service on London Transport's Round London Sightseeing Tour. Leyland Fleetline DM 2645 displayed its RLST livery when photographed outside Canada House in Trafalgar Square on Sunday morning 10 June 1984. Fleetlines were superseded by new RLST-liveried MCW Metrobuses on such allocations about one month later. *Mike Harris*

Route N13 provided the first direct all-night bus link between central London and North Finchley via Finchley Road and Golders Green. Finchley Garage's M 587 is seen at North Finchley, Tally Ho Corner, on Wednesday morning 27 June 1984 with a Routemaster in the background waiting to take up service on daytime route 13. North Finchley was also served by route N21, which had been developed from trolleybus-operated early morning journeys to Holborn introduced on 6/7 March 1938 over route 521/621, with even earlier tramway origins, and which were incorporated into bus route 221 from 7/8 November 1960, as well as much more recent Potters Bar garage route N80, introduced on 24/25 June 1983. *Mike Harris*

Route N98 was projected beyond Romford to Harold Hill with the all-night route network's expansion from 13/14 April 1984. Romford North Street garage's T 185 is seen at Harold Hill, Gooshays Drive, then the eastern extremity of Nighter operation, on Sunday morning 2 June 1985. *Mike Harris*

Peckham garage's nearly-new Leyland Titan T 980 is looking resplendent on Crystal Palace Parade as it catches early morning sunshine on Thursday 4 July 1985. The route N86 bus displays the new-style black on yellow intermediate blind display which was adopted as standard for all-night bus routes from 13/14 April 1984. This first N86 was extended to Penge from 1/2 November 1985, re-numbered N71 from 8/9 October 1993 and was partially incorporated into route N171 from 26/27 April 1996. *Mike Harris*

A notable feature of the programme was the co-ordination of timetables to give enhanced frequencies along a number of key corridors such as, for example, a combined 15-minute headway between Liverpool Street Station and Fulham Broadway provided by buses on routes N11, N14, N27 and N97.

Apart from the Special Night Journeys on route 9 only six other all-night services had no route alterations from 13/14 April 1984. These comprised routes N29, N91, N93, N99, 220 and the Inter-Station Route although, amongst these, the N29 gained an increased allocation and hourly headway whilst the N91 and N93 underwent detailed timetable changes. The 220, which simply comprised a return Special Night Journey which ran about one hour after the route's daytime service had finished, became the sole Nighter without a Saturday night/Sunday morning service.

The three mainstream all-night routes which retained two-person operation with a driver and conductor did so for varied reasons. One concern during the protracted negotiations between London Transport and the Transport and General Workers Union about changes to the Nighters had been the possibility of heavily-laden journeys being delayed by extra boarding times needed for one-person operation. This concern particularly applied to Trafalgar Square – Enfield Town route N29, on which certain journeys had been duplicated for some time prior to 13/14 April 1984, and led to the decision to retain crewed operation on that route. Pragmatism dictated the retention of crewed operation on route N93 which had a round trip running time between Trafalgar Square and Hampstead Heath of 51 minutes over which an hourly headway could be maintained using one crew-operated bus taking three minute and six minute layovers at Hampstead Heath and Trafalgar Square respectively. LT had considered extending route N93 to either Golders Green or Hendon, but opted for new route N13 as the preferred way of serving the Finchley Road corridor. London Transport decided to leave the Inter-Station Route as it was pending later review.

Whilst many areas of London gained new or enhanced all-night bus services, the network alterations of 13/14 April 1984 did break some long established operating patterns and removed, or reduced, the Nighters' presence from certain thoroughfares and districts.

The importance of Victoria Embankment as a routeing and terminus for London's all-night public road passenger transport services had been in decline ever since Archway

Holloway garage's DMS 2258 stands at stop C in Trafalgar Square against the imposing background of the National Gallery loading passengers for a journey which will run to route N92's new, extended terminus at Muswell Hill Broadway. This view dates from Sunday night/Monday morning 29/30 April 1984. *Paul Davis*

all-night bus route 292 had its outbound journeys removed from it on 9/10 September 1952. The greatest blow came on 25/26 April 1975 when the all-night services on routes 168, N87 and N88 were removed from Victoria Embankment in favour of re-routeing them between Westminster and Ludgate Circus via Trafalgar Square, Strand, Aldwych and Fleet Street. Victoria Embankment's near 77-year long association with London's all-night services, which dated back to December 1906 when London County Council Tramways had extended its all-night tram service from Clapham across Westminster Bridge to terminate on Victoria Embankment at Charing Cross District Railway Station, was severed entirely from 13/14 April 1984 when routes N85 and N86 were re-routed to terminate at Trafalgar Square, rather than Embankment Station, and the limited all-night service on route 109 was absorbed into new route N78, which reached central London across Waterloo Bridge.

Victoria Embankment did experience two fleeting night bus operations at later dates. Routes N50 and N51, which had absorbed the Inter-Station Route, were routed along the Embankment, between Westminster Bridge and Northumberland Avenue, from 26/27 April until 31 October/1 November 1985. The N50 and N51 were re-routed across Lambeth Bridge from 1/2 November 1985 but the eastbound service of route N51 continued to serve that section of the Embankment until 19/20 June 1986. A total of four buses nightly either on High Barnet route N1 or Edgware route N5, returning in service from their drivers' relief-breaks at Victoria, were routed along Victoria Embankment, between Bridge Street and Temple Place, in order to reach Aldwych, where the regular service of both routes terminated, between 27/28 October 1989 and 16/17 July 1992. It was not until 23/24 March 2001 that Victoria Embankment re-gained a sustained all-night bus service. That came about because extant East Beckton route N50 (the second-time use of that route number, which had no association with the earlier-mentioned N50) was re-routed, between Trafalgar Square and Mansion House, via Northumberland Avenue, Victoria Embankment, Blackfriars and Queen Victoria Street. Much of the N50's routeing was absorbed into Canning Town route N550 from 29/30 August 2008. The N550 continues, at 30/31 August 2013, to provide a 30-minute frequency service between Embankment Station and Blackfriars from approximately 00.30 to 05.30 nightly and is the sole contemporary TfL-contracted bus route, daytime or night-time, to serve any section of Victoria Embankment.

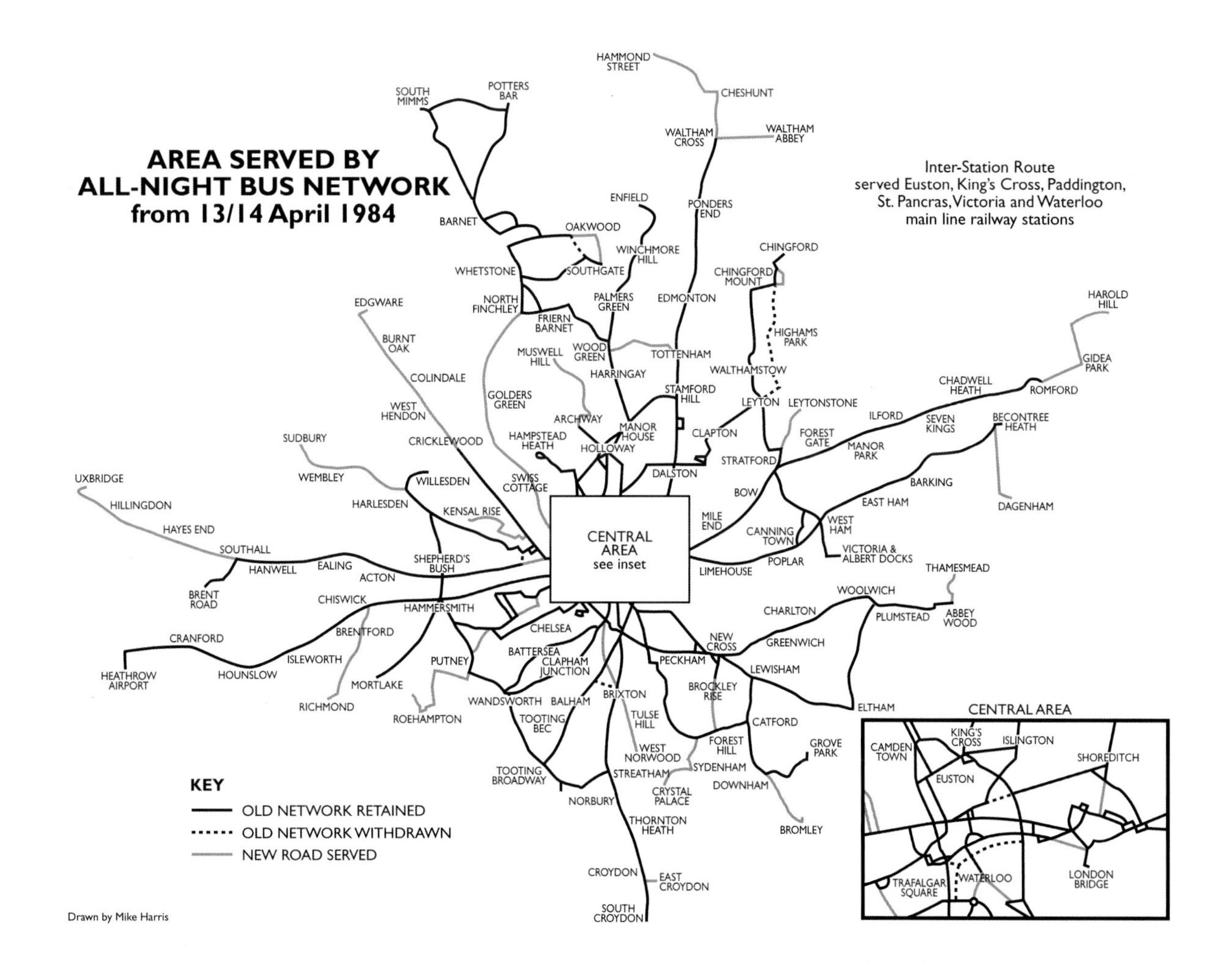

Holloway garage's crew-operated DMS 1105 is seen at Stonecutter Street in the early hours of Saturday 3 December 1977 on a short working route N93 journey to Kings Cross introduced from 14/15 July 1967. The N93 was revised to operate an hourly headway service between Hampstead Heath and Charing Cross from 27/28 July 1979 coincident with which short working N93 journeys to Stonecutter Street were withdrawn. *Mike Harris*

Stonecutter Street, another well-known all-night bus haunt off Farringdon Street, became much reduced in status. Farringdon Street had become the designated terminus for Wandsworth all-night bus routes 168 and 288 from 1 October 1950 when those services had replaced Clapham Junction all-night tram route 26 and Battersea all-night tram route 3 respectively. The 168 and 288 had actually terminated and stood in Farringdon Avenue, off Farringdon Street, upon their inception but reconstruction work in the area *circa* 1960, which obliterated Farringdon Avenue, saw their stand moved to nearby Stonecutter Street. The 288 was re-numbered to N88 from 11/12 October 1960 and the (all-night) element of the 168 became re-numbered to N68 from 25/26 April 1975. Stonecutter Street had also acted, at various times, as the terminal point for short-working journeys on routes N83, N93 and N97, the Special Night Journeys on route 221 and had even been served briefly, between 25/26 April and 21/22 November 1975, by outbound N87 buses bound for Brixton, Streatham and Tooting Broadway. Stonecutter Street almost disappeared from the Nighters' map from 13/14 April 1984 as a consequence of the N68 and N88 being re-jigged to operate through from Wandsworth to Liverpool Street Station, along with revisions to route N97's timetable, which eliminated those short-working journeys that had turned at Stonecutter Street. Only the bifurcation of three short-working journeys on new Roehampton route N14 to turn at Stonecutter Street retained a tenuous link between that street and the Nighters at that time.

Route N89 was diverted away from Paddington Station, to travel instead along the full length of Bayswater Road, whilst at its eastern end the N89 was re-routed via Cannon Street. The Highams Park and Upper Walthamstow areas lost their limited all-night bus facility as a result of route N96's re-routeing through central Walthamstow. Route N80 underwent minor re-routeing to serve Oakwood Station.

The long-established cyclical working pattern of Tooting route N87 across Blackfriars and Westminster Bridges, which had been established by London County Council Tramways on 17/18 July 1928, when operation of the formerly separate all-night tram routes to Brixton and Tooting respectively became combined, was dissolved from 13/14 April 1984. The 'eastern' Brixton leg of the N87 was largely incorporated into new route N78, which latter route also absorbed the irregular all-night service of route 109, although Purley lost its all-night journeys. The 'western' Clapham leg of the N87 continued to operate, but in a modified form, between Trafalgar Square and Streatham Garage via Westminster Bridge, Oval, Clapham, Tooting and Southcroft Road. Interestingly the traditional connection between Brixton-direction and Clapham-direction all-night buses, originally a tramway practice dating right back to 25/26 January 1901, was maintained by most outbound N78 and N87 journeys, which were timed to interconnect at Oval Station.

Route N84 (Becontree Heath – Victoria) was the only 'N'-prefixed Nighter to be withdrawn on 13/14 April 1984. The N84's origins could be traced back directly to the earliest era of London's all-night road passenger transport services when the North Metropolitan Tramways company had introduced an all-night horse-tram service between Poplar and Aldgate on 19/20 February 1899. Electrification, and extension of this route to Bloomsbury, had come about as a result London Council Tramways adoption and revival of the service from 27/28 January 1907. Under London Transport's control the service was converted to trolleybus operation from 9/10 June 1940 and subsequently, as route number 284, became the first Nighter to receive a regular Routemaster-type allocation, with effect from 10/11 November 1959. As long ago as 1/2 July 1964 a reduction in allocation to just one bus had seen the N84 contract to become a most infrequent and irregularly-scheduled service. The N84 shared a lengthy common section of routeing along Barking Road and Commercial Road with route N95, which latter route had also deteriorated to give a service pattern so erratic that only one journey was made more than once a night (Barking Garage to Victoria twice). In order to improve the general service between the East End and the West End, LT decided to combine routes N84 and N95 into an improved hourly-headway service over route N95, projected beyond Becontree Heath to Dagenham. The N95 was also re-routed between Whitechapel High Street and Bank via Commercial Street and Liverpool Street in order to cover a section of the former N84's routeing. The N84/284, and its erstwhile trolleybus and tramway predecessors, had always been worked by Poplar depot/garage, which became removed from all-night route operation as a result of the N84's withdrawal.

A further significant garage/route allocation change from

RM 1267 is seen outside Tottenham garage just before midnight on Thursday 12 April 1984 about to take up service on the last night of that garage's operation of route N90. *Paul Davis*

13/14 April 1984 affected Tottenham garage, which up until then had operated a three-bus Routemaster allocation on route N90. Coincident with the N90's conversion to one-person operation, headway expansion and route extension deeper into Hertfordshire, to Hammond Street, from 13/14 April 1984, Tottenham garage relinquished operation of the N90 in favour of two Metrobus-worked allocations from each of Edmonton and Enfield garages. This re-allocation broke a long association between Tottenham garage and route N90, and predecessor routes 290, 619 and 39D, which dated back to 17/18 July 1928, when the London General Omnibus Company had introduced all-night route 39D (Tottenham Garage – Charing Cross) with an allocation of two closed-top NS-type buses. Tottenham garage did not disappear from the all-night duty rota entirely, since it gained one Metrobus-worked allocation on route N83 (Victoria – Wood Green) from 13/14 April 1984.

LT's newest generation of production double-deck buses dominated allocations across the all-night bus route network from 13/14 April 1984, with MCW Metrobuses and Leyland Titans accounting for 78% of the network's vehicle allocation. The Routemaster became marginalised across the Nighters, with the official allocation of the vehicle-type restricted to route N93 and route 9's Special Night Journeys. Leyton garage continued to put out two LS-type Leyland Nationals on route N96, which represented the sole single-deck bus allocation to any of the Nighters. The nightly allocation of twelve DM/DMS-type Fleetlines to all-night duties was, perhaps, higher than might have been expected, given the rapid diminution in the number of that vehicle-type remaining in LT service, but was partially accounted for by the allocation of DM-types used in the daytime on the Round London Sightseeing Tour to all-night duties too.

The number of buses in service on a weekly basis increased by 29% with the introduction of the expanded all-night bus route network from 13/14 April 1984, whilst the coincident conversions to achieve one-person operation on most Nighters reduced staff requirements by 8%.

EFFECT OF THE OXFORD REPORT

Whilst the Oxford Report's proposed 'five-mile limit + taxis' solution lacked full consideration of the practical problems faced by passengers in accessing the all-night bus route network, and by London Transport in achieving scheduling efficiency, the Oxford Report unquestionably acted as the catalyst which triggered London Transport into expanding and modernising its all-night bus route network. Before the Oxford Report's publication London Transport had recognised that the network needed enhancement but seemed to lack the corporate will necessary to pursue change. Quite possibly LT's management was inhibited by impediments put in the way of change by the-then powerful trade union interests, as well as by political interference into its activities by the Greater London Council. The adoption of one-man operation, which had first impacted mainstream N-prefixed Nighters from 12/13 May 1972 when routes N85 and N86 were so converted, had been patchy, although vehicle reliability problems, notably with the Daimler/Leyland Fleetline, had compounded the problem. Immediately prior to the all-night bus route network's expansion from 13/14 April 1984, 55% of London's Nighters had remained crew-operated.

The enhancement of routes N97 and N98 during 1978, to transform them into the first ever West End serving all-night bus routes with a regular headway service on Saturday nights and Sunday mornings, clearly revealed London Transport's recognition of the potential demand for all-night bus services from the burgeoning leisure market. Yet further expansion of Saturday night services to other all-night routes had been hesitant until, quite possibly spurred on by its knowledge of, as well as its likely response to, the Oxford Report, London Transport had implemented near-universal Saturday night and Sunday morning operation across the Nighters from 29/30 October 1983.

By means of adroit scheduling London Transport further developed the Oxford Report's recommendations and so, from 13/14 April 1984, began a process of all-night route network expansion which has evolved continuously since that date.

CHAPTER 2
EXPONENTIAL GROWTH

London's all-night bus network experienced an exponential rate of growth after the expansion of that network initiated by London Transport Executive on 13/14 April 1984. The network's growth is illustrated by the graph on page 29 and detailed in Table D. It will be seen that passenger demand quickly caused vehicle allocations to rise by around 30% on weekend nights. A continuing trend towards service frequency increases on those nights of the week, accelerated upon the conversion of bendy bus-operated Nighters to double-deck bus operation during 2010 and 2011, increased Friday and Saturday night bus allocations to become around 40% higher than those on Sunday to Thursday nights. These latter nights of the week have seen no significant bus allocation growth since 2011. The number of all-night and 24-hour bus routes reached its zenith of 117 such routes upon the introduction of route (N)159 from 27/28 August 2010. Since then the withdrawal of routes (N)236 and (N)274, offset by the introduction of route N113, left 116 Transport for London-contracted all-night and 24-hour bus routes in operation at 30/31 August 2013. Operation of these routes required allocations of 635 buses on Sunday nights, 633 buses on Monday to Thursday nights, 887 buses on Friday nights and 892 buses on Saturday nights.

The bolstering of service levels on a number of all-night and 24-hour bus routes which served Olympic Games venues resulted in the highest-ever allocation of buses across London's all-night bus network. Frequency and reliabilty enhancements to routes N8, (N)10, N15, (N)25, N26, N35, N63, (N)69, N73, N74, N91, (N)108, N133, (N)148, (N)149 and (N)188, combined with upgrading of daytime route (N)238 to give a 24-hour service for the duration of the Games, resulted in allocations of 737 buses on Sunday nights, 735 on Monday to Thursday nights, 934 on Friday nights and 939 buses on Saturday nights between 27/28 July and 12/13 August 2012. Most of these routes were enhanced for the Paralympic Games too, including route (N)238. The exceptions were routes (N)10, N74 and (N)148 which did not serve Paralymic Games venues, so that allocations during those Games were not quite so high at 713 buses on Sunday nights, 711 on Sunday to Thursday nights, 909 on Friday nights and 914 buses on Saturday nights between 29/30 August and 9/10 September 2012. Increased bus allocations during both the Olympic and Paralympic Games were more pronounced on Sunday to Thursday nights when a number of routes had enhancements to match their prevailing Friday and Saturday night frequencies.

The author's original intention had been to close this book at 14/15 July 2013, the centenary of the introduction of London's first all-night motor bus operated route. It was later decided to extend the cut-off date to 30/31 August 2013 to allow the incorporation of certain operator changes and the extension of route N205. This chapter highlights trends and aspects of particular interest in the development of the Nighters. Route developments, accompanied by details of operators, bus-types used and garage allocations (including Olympic and Paralympic Games supplementation) are chronicled in Chapters 4 to 7.

Table D
All-Night and night-time element of 24-hour Bus Routes
Peak Vehicle Requirements
13/14 April 1984 – 30/31 August 2013

DATE	PVR	
	Su-Th	Fr-Sa
13/14 April 1984	77	78
26/27 October 1984	83	88
1/2 November 1985	86	109
20/21 November 1987	96	130
4/5 December 1988	101	138
9/10 February 1990	128	167
17/18 July 1992	137	177
11/12 March 1994	155	191
24/25 November 1995	170	221
28/29 November 1997	209	284
1/2 December 1998	227	308
7/8 January 2000	257	352
1/2 December 2000	285	397
30 Nov/1 Dec 2001	375	503
22/23 November 2002	436	562
12/13 December 2003	509	642
3/4 December 2004	525	665
16/17 December 2005	531	685
15/16 December 2006	543	708
28/29 December 2007	592	772
5/6 December 2008	607	801
27/28 November 2009	622	830
30/31 December 2010	623	834
30/31 December 2011	633	875
30/31 December 2012	631	886
14/15 July 2013	632	889
30/31 August 2013	633	892

SOCIAL INFLUENCES ON THE NIGHTERS

Since the inception of the first all-night tram routes in 1899, traditional custom for London's all-night routes had focused around the newspaper industry in the Fleet Street area and other late night and early morning workers, mainly in central London, such as those employed in the markets. 1986 marked the beginning of the end for Fleet Street as the capital's newspaper hub when News International moved to new premises at Wapping in order to exploit new printing technology and cut staff numbers from 6,000 to 1,000. Other newspapers moved away from the Fleet Street area between then and 15 May 2005 when Reuters, the last major news group to remain in Fleet Street, relocated. But whilst 1986 saw the ebbing away of a main source of traditional passenger demand, that same year created an even greater opportunity for London's all-night bus route network when 26 October 1986 heralded the wholesale deregulation of London's many interlocking financial markets. 'Big-Bang', so dubbed, wrenched the City's financial institutions away from a centuries-old world of gentlemen's clubs and agreements and thrust them into the maelstrom of international markets 24 hours of the day. 'Yuppies' were born, now the clock never stopped and travel demands changed radically for those in the City and its ancillary support services.

Relaxation of licensing laws, particularly in 1988 and 2005, after which licensees could apply for 24-hour drinking licences, not only stimulated demand in the West End but also fostered the development of inner London and suburban entertainment centres in once unlikely places such as, for example, Camden Town and Shoreditch. Demand for all-night bus travel became stimulated to and from central London as well as along intermediate sections of routes and along non-radial and suburban routes, which developed rapidly from 1997 onwards. A larger than expected growth in London's population has also contributed to an increased demand for bus travel.

OPERATIONAL AND POLITICAL INFLUENCES ON THE NIGHTERS: LONDON REGIONAL TRANSPORT

The London Transport Executive was superseded by London Regional Transport on 29 June 1984, when policy and political control passed from the Greater London Council to the Government in the form of the Secretary of State for Transport. London Regional Transport set up three subsidiary companies on 1 April 1985, one of which, London Buses Ltd, assumed control of six bus operating districts previously established on 2 January 1984. A tender process for selected bus routes was introduced under which other operators could compete with London Buses' own districts for London Regional Transport contracts and the first tranche of such (daytime) routes was taken up by successful bidders on 16 July 1985. Only one all-night service was ever awarded to an independent operator under this system, which continued to be used until 1993, when Ensignbus gained the London Regional Transport contract for marginal route N99 which operated between Romford (later Chadwell Heath) and Cranham, on Friday and Saturday nights only, from 27/28 March 1987.

London Buses restructured its districts in November and December 1988 to form twelve operating units, which were transferred into wholly-owned London Buses subsidiary companies in 1 April 1989. These companies were named Centrewest, East London, Leaside, London Central, London Forest, London General, London United, Metroline, Selkent, South London, Westlink and London Coaches, of which all bar the latter two companies were involved in all-night bus route operation at that time. Whilst much contemporary public relations material emphasised the autonomy of the subsidiary companies, and extolled the virtues of their local decision making ability, in reality their establishment did not engender true competition amongst them since London Regional Transport still pulled their strings, as witnessed by all-night route changes and introductions on 27/28 October 1989 when the number of all-night routes jointly operated between two London Buses' subsidiary companies increased by three. London Forest foundered during 1991 and its operation of routes N6 and N96 passed to Metroline and East London respectively from 22/23 November 1991. The Debden terminus of the N96 was in Essex and that route was one of a number of London Regional Transport all-night bus routes which projected beyond the Greater London boundary into neighbouring counties. During the 1990s all such routes were trimmed back, mostly to termini within Greater London, due to lack of revenue support from the appropriate shire counties. London Central, a thrusting operator on the LRT-contracted all-night scene at this time, expanded weekend nights commercial bus operation into Kent from an established LRT-contracted all-night service from London to Kent, and also developed commercial weekend all-night bus routes into Hertfordshire which, at various times, linked central London with Hemel Hempstead, St. Albans and Watford.

From 1 April 1993, London Regional Transport replaced the block grant system, under which groups of routes had been offered for tender as a block, and replaced it with a new system under which individual routes were put up for tender. In this new context, daytime and all-night services along similar route corridors became linked in the tender process, with the aim of establishing 24-hour services run by a single operator. The first four tranches of the new system accommodated daytime routes only but the fifth tranche included all-night bus routes. The most dramatic outcome of that round of tendering was the loss by incumbent operator Metroline of route N6 (Aldwych – Kensal Rise Station) when it was awarded to independent operator London Suburban Bus, from 28/29 January 1994. From the same date Metroline also suffered the loss to Centrewest of routes N59 (re-numbered as N139 and revised to operate between Trafalgar Square and West Hampstead) and N99 (the third reincarnation of this route number, used for a service between Trafalgar Square and Stanmore Station), as well as its majority share of jointly operated route N18 (Trafalgar Square – Watford Junction), which was revised to be operated solely by Centrewest between Trafalgar Square and Harrow Weald. In addition, Metroline-operated marginal routes N17 and N66 were withdrawn. Only the retention of route N16 (Victoria – Edgware Station) let Metroline maintain a presence on London's all-night bus route network at that time.

The serious competition which had now developed for the award of London Regional Transport's bus route tenders was intensified by the privatisation of London Buses' bus operating subsidiary companies, in a process that lasted about one year, between the sale of the first company, Westlink, to its management on 20 January 1994 and the last sale, of South London to the Cowie group, on 10 January 1995 – London Coaches having previously been sold to its management in May 1992. Some subsidiaries, such as Centrewest and London General, were sold to their managements whilst others, such as East London and Leaside, passed straight into group ownership, in those instances the Stagecoach and Cowie groups respectively. Within six years those subsidiaries sold to their managements had passed into group ownership too, the last being Metroline when it was sold to Singapore-based Del Gro group on 18 February 2000.

A dynamic new force appeared on the all-night bus scene on 31 January/1 February 1997 when Capital Citybus, successor to Ensignbus and an established operator of daytime London Regional Transport bus routes in the Romford and Walthamstow areas, secured the tender for route N91 (Trafalgar Square – Cockfosters Station), previously operated by MTL London Northern. Within the span of 2½ years Capital Citybus, acquired by FirstGroup on 8 July 1998, had gained contracts for key central London-serving routes N1, N20, N25 and N50, thus displacing previous incumbents London Central (N1), MTL London Northern (N20) and Stagecoach East London (N25 and N50).

Connex Bus UK Ltd, subsidiary of the French-owned group destined to attract notoriety for its operation of the South Central train franchise, gained the LRT contract for route N3 (Oxford Circus – Bromley North Station) from 3/4 February 2000, displacing London Central.

OPERATIONAL AND POLITICAL INFLUENCES ON THE NIGHTERS: TRANSPORT FOR LONDON

Elections for the new office of Mayor of London and the London Assembly took place on 4 May 2000 when Ken Livingstone, standing as an Independent candidate, was elected Mayor. Mr Livingstone was re-elected as Mayor in May 2004 having, by then, aligned himself with the Labour Party. The Mayor's Office has been empowered with wide-ranging authority over the administration of Greater London which has come to include responsibility for inland transport, the police, fire services, planning and economic development, the arts, housing, climate change, noise and air quality. Transport for London assumed powers from 3 July 2000 in respect of transport functions. TfL's portfolio is much broader than that of its predecessor, London Regional Transport, and includes responsibility for all trunk roads in Greater London, except motorways, along with associated infrastructure such as traffic lights. TfL's regulatory authority for bus service contracts is London Bus Services Ltd, which had superseded London Buses Ltd on 1 April 2000.

Towards the end of October 2000 Mayor Livingstone issued his Draft Transport Strategy, which included a commitment to introduce 'more off-peak and night services'. With this mandate in mind, TfL oversaw the biggest-ever increase in London's all-night bus routes when 42 new routes were introduced in little more than three years, between TfL's vesting date of 3 July 2000 and 30/31 August 2003, at which latter date 98 TfL-contracted all-night bus routes operated, which represented an increase of 75% compared with 56 such routes extant at 3 July 2000. The pattern of route development over this period increased the density of all-night bus route coverage across Greater London. 22 of the new routes served inner London or suburban areas only, whilst only 11 of the 20 new routes which entered central London served the West End. Many of the new routes bolstered existing services to create all-night bus hubs at centres such as Croydon (extant: N68, N159, new: N75, N119, N213 (from 12/13 December 2003), N250, N264), King's Cross (extant: N73, N91, N279, new: N10, N63, N214) and Liverpool Street (extant: N8, N11, N23, N26, N35, new: N133, N149, N214, N242, N271). Three new operators entered the all-night bus route scene during this period of growth:

- Sovereign London: Part of the Blazefield group, on route N13 (Aldwych – North Finchley) from 31 August/ September 2000, displacing previous operator Metroline London Northern. Sovereign London passed into the control of the Transdev Group on 3 November 2002.
- East Thames Buses: LBSL-owned subsidiary company on route N108 (Stratford – Lewisham), introduced from 28/29 September 2001.
- Metrobus: A Go-Ahead group company on route N119 (Bromley North – Purley Way, Croydon Airport), introduced from 29/30 August 2003.

Transport for London's far reaching control over transport policy within Greater London was demonstrated on 1 September 2002 when the north side of Trafalgar Square, outside the National Gallery, was pedestrianised and two-way traffic flows were reinstated in the vicinity of the Square – a traditional focal point for the Nighters. It is questionable whether or not this scheme could have been implemented had the functions of bus operation, highways and infrastructure remained under the control of differing agencies. Similarly, the introduction of congestion charging on 17 February 2003, further emphasised the power of the Mayor's Office through Transport for London.

The influence of the Mayor of London on transport matters was shown again following the election of Conservative candidate Boris Johnson in May 2008. His mandate included a pledge to rid London of articulated Mercedes-Benz Citaro bendy buses, which he maintained worsened congestion, increased road accidents and so constituted a traffic hazard. Thus the transport professionals of Transport for London, who had selected the articulated Citaro only a few years earlier as an efficient means for the mass movement of passengers along heavily-used traffic corridors, were ordered to replace them with an increased number of fixed chassis buses in an expensive exercise, considered by some to be a political stunt. All articulated Mercedes-Benz Citaro-operated all-night and 24-hour bus routes were converted to double-deck bus operation in just over 13 months, between the conversion of route (N)149 on 15/16 October 2010 and that of route N29 on 25/26 November 2011. Boris Johnson was re-elected in May 2012 for his second term.

Between 2004 and 2010, all-night bus route growth

progressed at a steady, but slower, pace than in the three preceding years. 23 new Nighters were introduced, net of re-numbering N36 to N136, N50 to N550, N159 to N109 and (N)369 to (N)EL1. Some of these newer routes replaced sections of existing night bus routes, predominantly in outer London. Over the same period four routes were withdrawn entirely, comprising routes (N)58, (N)75, N101 and N106. The pace of route innovation slowed down markedly from 2011 onwards, with only the introduction of route N113 and the withdrawal of routes (N)236 and (N)274 to record between then and 30/31 August 2013.

The higher demand pattern for Friday night and Saturday night travel has persisted, on which nights of the week route N29 has a three/four-minute frequency over its section of route between Trafalgar Square and Wood Green – the highest frequency of the contemporary Nighters, with 18 journeys per hour. The N29's frequency only reduces to 7½ minutes on Sunday to Thursday nights but this is applied over its entire route length, between Trafalgar Square and Enfield Town. Routes (N)25 and N38 each have 6-minute frequencies on Friday and Saturday nights, in the case of route (N)25 over its entire route length between Oxford Circus and Stratford and over the Piccadilly Circus to Wathamstow Central section of route N38. The N8 and N207 enjoy 7½-minute frequencies over their sections of route between Oxford Circus and Stratford and between Holborn and Hayes By-Pass respectively on Friday and Saturday nights, on which nights of the week route N155 has an eight-minute frequency over its entire route length, between Aldwych and Morden. A significant number of other routes enjoy 10, 12, 15 or 20-minute frequencies – often nightly – whilst the standard 'minimum' frequency on any all-night route nowadays is 30 minutes, with only two exceptions remaining – the N28 and N31 which each have a 60-minute frequency on Sunday to Thursday nights, although a co-ordinated timetable for those two routes gives a 30-minute headway over a lengthy common section of routeing, between Camden Town and Kensington High Street. The N28's and N31's frequencies each increase to 30 minutes on Friday and Saturday nights.

Connex Bus sold its London operations to National Express on 26 September 2004. Trading as Travel London Ltd, tender successes built up Travel London's portfolio to six TfL all-night routes before the operation was sold to Dutch-owned Ned Railways on 9 June 2009, who first rebranded the operation as Abellio and subsequently as Abellio London from 1 June 2010. Stagecoach sold its London bus operations East London and Selkent to the Australian Macquarie Bank on 30 August 2006 which traded the operation as East London Bus Group. Docklands Buses, part of the Go-Ahead group, assumed the TfL contract for a new all-night service on route (N)474 (Canning Town – Manor Park Station) from 2/3 November 2007, whilst another Go-Ahead company, Blue Triangle, assumed operation of route (N)EL1 (Ilford – Thames View Estate) on 19/20 February 2010. LBSL-owned East Thames Buses was sold to the Go-Ahead group on 2/3 October 2009, when routes N1 and (N)108 passed to London General with the (N)108 subsequently becoming a London Central responsibility. Most of Arriva's UK bus and railway interests passed into the control of German state railway Deutsche Bahn on 27 August 2010. East London Bus Group was re-acquired by Stagecoach on 14 October 2010. Transdev transferred London United to the ownership of Paris-based RATP DEV from 3 March 2011. London Sovereign, contracted operator of route N13, remained within the Veolia-Transdev combine. FirstGroup sold most of its London bus interests on 22 June 2013 when all bar one of its night-time routes passed to either Metroline West or Australian-owned Tower Transit. First Capital East retained 24-hour route 365 with operation expected to be transferred to Stagecoach East London upon LBSL-contract renewal on 27/28 September 2013.

Competition for TfL all-night bus route contracts appears to be keen. An attraction for operators is that no extra buses are needed for all-night service since the same vehicles can be deployed on both daytime and all-night operations. Thus all-night bus route contracts allow operators to spread overhead costs, such as vehicle finance, depreciation and maintenance, over a broader revenue base. Pressure on expensive garage space, at a premium in London, is also eased.

Table E
Market Share by Numerical Vehicle-Allocations
TfL All-Night Bus Route Contacts at 30/31 August 2013

Operator	Market Share
Abellio London	5.51%
Arriva	23.66%
Comfort DelGro Metroline	19.61%
FirstGroup	0.43%
Go-Ahead	21.59%
RATP London United	9.01%
Stagecoach	11.10%
Tower Transit	8.08%
Veolia-Transdev	1.01%

THE DEMISE OF THE INTER-STATION ROUTE

When considering its response to the recommendations of the Oxford Report, London Transport had harboured reservations about the viability of the Inter-Station Route but had decided to let its Saturday night and Sunday night crew-operated service continue as it was until the impact on it of universal Saturday night/Sunday morning operation, introduced on 29/30 October 1983, along with the packet of changes to the all-night bus route network from 13/14 April 1984, could be assessed. Separately, a new nightly Railair Link service, sponsored by British Rail and operated by London Regional Transport, which linked Euston Station with a non-stop service to Victoria Station and Heathrow Airport, was introduced from 13/14 May 1984. The Railair Link was modified from 26/27 October 1984 to serve Waterloo Station also.

The traditional Inter-Station Route, which had provided a non-stop all-night service between most of London's main line railway termini since 20/21 December 1943, operated for the last time on Sunday night/Monday morning 21/22 April 1985. Its function was absorbed into new routes N50/N51, introduced on Friday night/Saturday morning 26/27 April 1985. These routes were fully integrated into the all-night bus route network, served its hub at Trafalgar Square and, on request, observed all bus stops *en route*. The N50/N51 operated between King's Cross Station and Ladbroke Grove via Euston Station, Holborn LT Station, Aldwych, Waterloo Station, Trafalgar Square, Victoria Station, Marble Arch, Paddington Station and Westbourne Grove. Route numbers N50 and N51 designated westbound and eastbound journeys respectively 'to avoid confusion to passengers at Victoria and Waterloo stations where buses in both directions serve the same stop'. From the same date, the Railair Link service was absorbed into the all-night network too, as route N56. Essentially comprising one return journey, the N56 operated to the same routeing as the N50 between King's Cross and Hyde Park Corner, whence it ran non-stop to Heathrow Airport where it served all three terminal buildings. The N56 then returned non-stop to either King's Cross Station (weekday mornings) or Victoria Station (Sunday mornings) and ran one further journey from King's Cross to Trafalgar Square. The N50/N51's partial role as replacement for the Inter-Station Route ended on 20/21 June 1986 when the section of route between King's Cross Station and Trafalgar Square was withdrawn, with LRT citing poor usage and the withdrawal of British Rail's suburban night train service from King's Cross as reasons. In a compensatory move the July 1986 *Buses for Night Owls* timetable included, for the first time, a timetable of alternative all-night bus route links between main line railway termini.

A last vestige of the former Inter-Station Route was retained by route N56 which, from 3/4 October 1986, was revised to operate a single nightly journey which departed from Paddington Station at 04.41 bound for Heathrow Airport via Euston, King's Cross, Waterloo and Victoria stations. The N56 continued to operate as an element of the all-night bus route network, although its sections of route between Waterloo Station and Trafalgar Square, between Trafalgar Square and Victoria Station and between Cromwell Road, Earls Court Road and Heathrow Airport ran non-stop. The N56's return journey left Heathrow at 06.10, whence it ran non-stop to Paddington Station and thence continued via Euston Station to terminate at King's Cross Station. An identical timetable was maintained when LRT switched operation of the N56 between London Buses' subsidiary companies, from London Forest out of Ash Grove garage to London United out of Shepherd's Bush garage, on 27/28 October 1989, at which time the non-stop restrictions between Waterloo Station and Trafalgar Square and between Trafalgar Square and Victoria Station were lifted. The N56 continued in this form, with a final operator and allocation change to Centrewest out of Westbourne Park garage, from 26/27 March 1993, until its last night of operation on Thursday night/Friday morning 20/21 May 1993, after which it was withdrawn without replacement because it 'has been little used'.

New Cross garage sometimes substituted a Routemaster towards the end of the Inter-Station Route's existence. RM 1940 demonstrated that most-immediate road to rail interchange afforded by this route at Paddington Station in the early hours of Monday morning 15 April 1985. The last night's operation of the Inter-Station Route, on Sunday night/Monday morning 21/22 April 1985, was undertaken by New Cross garage's Leyland Titan T 863. *Mike Harris*

NIGHTERS WHICH CROSSED CENTRAL LONDON

Prior to the network's expansion from 13/14 April 1984, no all-night bus route had ever worked a service right across central London. Two lengthy cross-London routes, the N79 between Archway and Lewisham and the N82 between Kensal Rise and Woolwich Arsenal Station, were formed from 13/14 April 1984. A number of other routes subsequently formed services which worked across central London, sometimes with very lengthy routeings. Many of these routes were subsequently modified to terminate in central London. Six all-night bus routes or 24-hour services – routes N19, (N)27, (N)36, (N)88, (N)148 and (N)390 – continue to form cross-London services at 30/31 August 2013.

POTTERS BAR GARAGE

Outlying Potters Bar garage (PB) in Hertfordshire's initial presence on London's all-night bus route scene lasted between 1983 and 1998. PB's first involvement came about when private staff bus garage journeys were made 'live' in the form of route N80, which operated three or four journeys nightly between Potters Bar garage and North Finchley between 24/25 June 1983 and 19/20 June 1986. Most subsequent involvement was in the form of garage journeys which ran in service between Potters Bar garage and Barnet, Cockfosters Station, North Finchley or Oakwood Station at various different dates. The N80 was replaced by an extension to route N92 from 20/21 June 1986 which introduced a PB allocation to that route as well as, between then and 24/25 September 1987, providing the only instance of a garage other than PB working an all-night journey in service to Potter Bar when a Holloway garage-allocated bus worked the nightly 03.55 journey from Trafalgar Square to Potters Bar Garage and return 05.21 departure back to Trafalgar Square. PB's involvement with route N92 ended from 24/25 February 1994 when that route was truncated to terminate at North Finchley. Earlier, on 3/4 December 1993, PB had gained allocations on both route N13 and N21. Most Potters Bar journeys were positioning runs from/to the garage that operated in service to either Barnet (N13) or Cockfosters Station (N21) but on Friday and Saturday nights the N21 provided a regular hourly frequency service between Trafalgar Square and Potters Bar Garage, which was maintained when route N21 was replaced by route N91 from 23/24 June 1995. PB's involvement with route N13 ended on this latter date when that route's main service was cut back from Barnet to North Finchley but, simultaneously, the garage did gain a single bus allocation on route N20 (former N1 re-numbered). Tendering successes for Capital Citybus/First Capital saw the loss by Metroline of route N91 from 31 January/1 February 1997 and route N20 from 23/24 July 1998. Thus ended Potters Bar garage's involvement with LRT all-night bus services at that time.

Potters Bar garage's second and, at 30/31 August 2013, current presence on London's all-night bus route operations dates from 25/26 July 2003 when Metroline regained the TfL contract for route N20. PB garage's position on the Nighters was consolidated with the award of the TfL contract for route N91 to Metroline from 6/7 February 2009. Operation of both routes N20 and N91 is joint with Holloway garage but, unlike in earlier times, Potters Bar garage buses run 'dead' from their garage before taking up service at either Barnet Church (N20) or Cockfosters Station (N91).

Route N59 formed a lengthy 1½ hour journey time cross-London route from Stanmore Station to West Dulwich between 25/26 September 1987 and 26/27 October 1989. Westbourne Park garage's MCW Metrobus M 886 was seen at Stanmore Station in the early hours of Sunday morning 4 October 1987 ready to work one of three nightly through journeys to West Dulwich. *Roy Waterhouse*

LRT acquired 50 Alexander-bodied Volvo Ailsa B55-10 double deckers from West Midlands Travel in 1987 and a number of these 11 year old buses entered service from Potters Bar garage. V 22 was photographed at Mutton Lane, Potters Bar during 1988 when working route N92 although PB garage's official allocation to this route remained one M-type Metrobus. *JGS Smith*

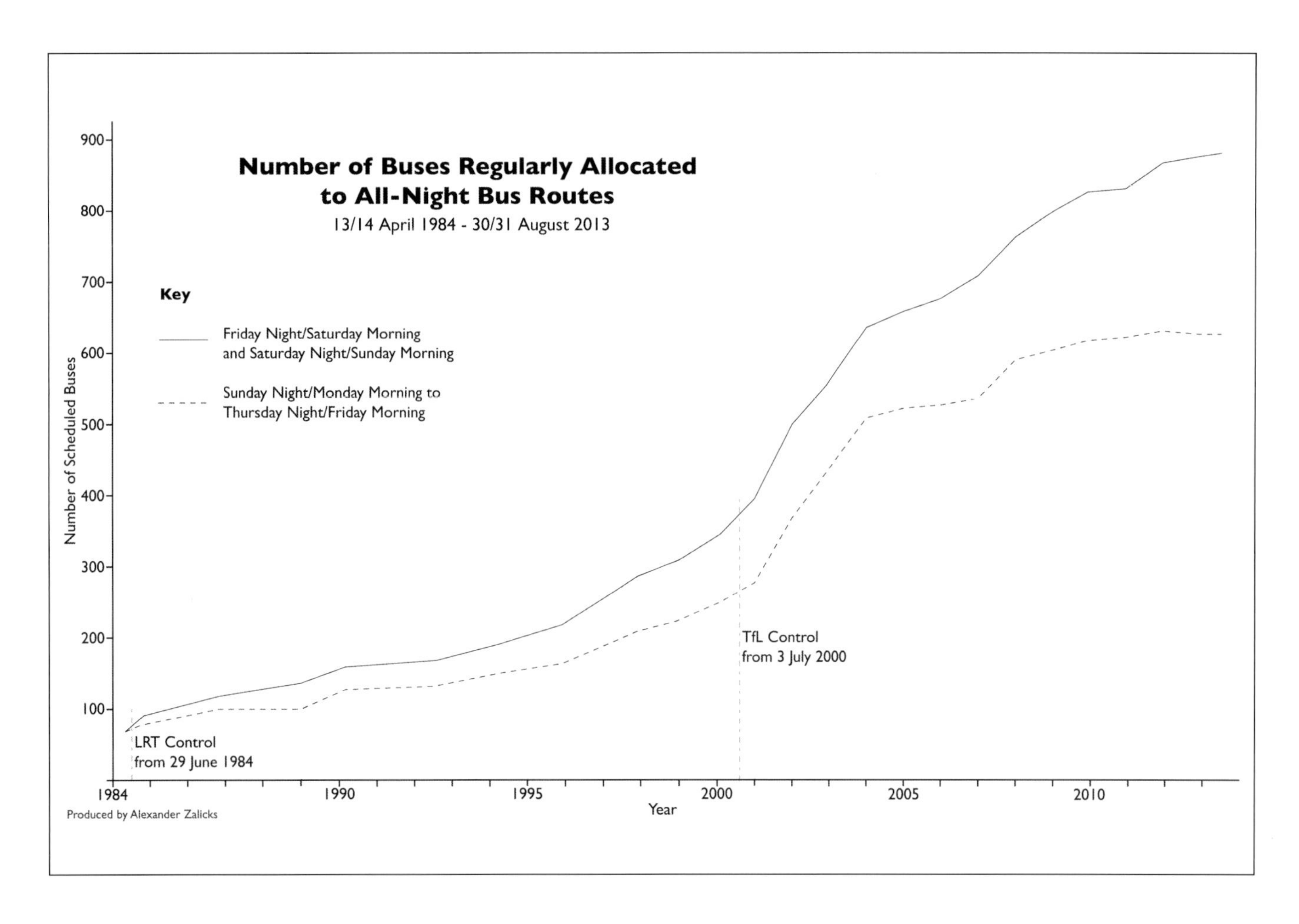

CREW RELIEF-BREAK JOURNEYS WITHIN CENTRAL LONDON

The principle of extending selected journeys on all-night bus routes in service within central London for the purpose of reaching a crew relief-break point with canteen facilities had been established by London Transport from 1/2 July 1964 (see Volume One, Chapter 7) and expanded from 5/6 March 1976 (see Volume One, Chapter 8). The number of all-night bus routes with such journeys increased substantially during the first eight years of London Regional Transport control, between 1984 and 1992.

As a result of the closure of long-established canteen facilities at Liverpool Street (August 1985) and also at Waterloo (July 1987), Victoria garage's canteen became the focal point for such journeys, which reached their zenith from 17/18 July 1992 when 32 all-night bus routes had crew relief-break, or occasional, journeys to Victoria. 26 of these routes operated journeys between Trafalgar Square and Victoria via Whitehall and Victoria Street – a route corridor which, at that time, was provided with regular services by a further nine Nighters. Another five routes ran crew relief-break journeys to Victoria from Marble Arch and/or Hyde Park Corner, whilst inbound N87 crew relief-break journeys bifurcated from their line of route at Stockwell to reach Victoria via Vauxhall. Following the closure of Victoria garage, after service on 16 July 1993, expediency saw canteen facilities replaced by a former Portsmouth Corporation Leyland Atlantean bus AN 1 (VTP 258L), equipped as a rest room for night bus drivers, with seats, tables, a microwave and a fridge, which was parked overnight on the forecourt of Victoria Bus Station. In due course AN 1 was replaced by similarly equipped London Central Leyland Titan T 875.

Restructuring and expansion of the all-night bus route network in 1994 and 1995 was accompanied by a change in policy towards scheduling crew relief-break points away from central London such that the number of routes with crew relief-break journeys in service to Victoria had declined to just ten by 27/28 November 1995. Numbers continued to dwindle and the final two such routes, London Central-operated N21 and N81, ran their last Victoria crew relief-break journeys on 27/28 June 2002.

REDUCING NIGHT TIME TRAFFIC CONGESTION

Night time traffic congestion in the West End, attributable in part to the growth of the all-night bus route network since 13/14 April 1984 but also very much a result of private car and taxi usage, has remained a persistent problem, which can be particularly acute at weekends. As long ago as 3/4 August 1984, congestion caused by Nighters banking up for stand space at stop V outside Canada House, on the western side of Trafalgar Square, was partially alleviated by re-routeing all Victoria-bound crew relief-break journeys to stop B in Pall Mall East. Further alterations to stopping places and re-routeings, to reduce the incidence of buses running loops around the Square, followed over the years but any gains achieved were offset by greater numbers of buses accessing the Square, due to service frequency increases and the need to build dwell times of up to five minutes into schedules, to allow sufficient passenger boarding time at Trafalgar Square.

The continued use of Trafalgar Square as the focal point for all central London-serving Nighters, a recommendation of the Oxford Report to which London Regional Transport had adhered, became questionable on practical grounds. The first breaks came between 1996 and 1999 when four all-night routes – N8, N14, N19 and N38 – were diverted at Piccadilly Circus to avoid Trafalgar Square and re-routed to align them with daytime routes of equivalent number. A fifth route, N253, was truncated away from Trafalgar Square to terminate at Tottenham Court Road Station. A further five routes – N9, N23, N44, N77 and N155 – which had terminated at Trafalgar Square continued to serve the Square but were projected to terminate at Aldwych, where stand space was more plentiful. These routes joined N6 which had earlier been extended to terminate at Aldwych on 28/29 January 1994, following Aldwych's previous use as the terminus for routes N1 and N5 between 27/28 October 1989 and 16/17 July 1992. A portent of changing route patterns for some central London-serving Nighters came with the introduction of Acton Green route N94, on 22/23 July 1999, which terminated short of Trafalgar Square at Piccadilly Circus.

Arriva London North's MCW Metrobus M 1308 was photographed outside the National Gallery in Trafalgar Square on Saturday morning 26 June 1999 on the N73's original routeing. The central London routeing of the N73 was aligned with that of daytime route 73 from 28/29 April 2000 so that buses on both routes travelled between Victoria and Oxford Circus via Hyde Park Corner, Marble Arch and Oxford Street. *Philip Wallis*

The biggest shake-up of all for central London-serving Nighters came on 28/29 April 2000 when nine services were re-routed away from Trafalgar Square. This move not only aligned most of those routes – N1, N25, N35, N68, N73, N98, N134, N171 and N207 – more closely with numerically equivalent daytime bus routes as 'part of an ongoing move towards a 24-hour bus network' but also improved service reliability, as buses on those routes became less impeded by West End traffic congestion. It also increased the importance of night bus hubs peripheral to the West End, such as Oxford Circus, but more especially the vicinity of Tottenham Court Road Station where seven Nighters now terminated and a further 14 routes called.

The reversion to two-way traffic flows on roads in the vicinity of Trafalgar Square, from 1 September 2002, affected many Nighters for which the Square still remained a focal point. Pedestrianisation of the Square's northern carriageway, outside the National Gallery, undoubtedly benefited the tourist industry but, when combined with the reversal of traffic flow direction along the Square's western perimeter outside Canada House, deprived the all-night bus route network of its two principal bus stands at the Square, each of which was capable of accommodating several buses simultaneously. The revised road system forced equivalent volumes of traffic, previously carried around or past the Square on a minimum two-carriageway width gyratory system, on to single lane carriageways freshly encumbered with a multitude of traffic lights. It was akin to trying to get the proverbial quart into a pint pot and traffic congestion worsened. Routeing and bus stops were altered for most Nighters. Cockspur Street and the easternmost section of Strand, between Trafalgar Square and Charing Cross Station, bore eastbound Nighters for the first time since 26 April 1926, when introduction of the Square's gyratory traffic flow had caused the re-routeing of eastbound journeys on then-extant LGOC routes 91 (Willesden – Liverpool Street Station) and 94 (Cricklewood – Liverpool Street Station) via Pall Mall East, the north side of Trafalgar Square and Duncannon Street. Two contemporary routes, N2 and N381, were truncated to terminate at Whitehall, Horse Guards, short of Trafalgar Square.

Most recently, from 20/21 February 2009, four routes – N21, N47, N89 and N343 – were revised to have their first pick-up point in Duncannon Street in order to reduce congestion for eastbound Nighters loading in Strand, opposite Charing Cross Station.

The southern side of Trafalgar Square was used by buses on layover such as Metroline's Plaxton-bodied bodied Dennis Trident TPL 277 seen there on Sunday morning 30 June 2002. Since 1 September 2002 buses on layover have mostly stood in streets to the east of Whitehall, such as Great Scotland Yard or Whitehall Place, as well as in Northumberland Avenue. *Philip Wallis*

Nearly-new Wrightbus-bodied Volvo B7TL WVL 4 was seen using the wide four lane carriageway on the northern perimeter of Trafalgar Square on 30 June 2002. This entire section of road outside the National Gallery was closed to vehicular traffic from 1 September 2002 and transformed into a pedestrian-only area. *Philip Wallis*

UNDERGROUND PARALLELS

The core period of all night bus route operation is between the hours of 00.30 and 05.30, which broadly coincides with the weekday closure time of the London Underground.

A strong emphasis was placed on the Underground parallels of routes N1 and N5 when they were launched on 27/28 October 1989. Branded in LRT publicity and timetables as *Northern Line Night Bus N1 and N5,* the two London Northern-operated services served, or stopped near to, all Northern Line Underground stations between Charing Cross and High Barnet (N1) or Edgware (N5). Contemporary bus blind displays carried *Northern Line* route branding, although this was discontinued in later years. TfL continued to emphasise the Northern Line connection on bus stop panel timetable displays up until those posted at stops from 4 February 2005 (N20 – renumbered from N1 on 23/24 June 1995) and 25 July 2008 (N5).

When route N21 was re-routed away from North Finchley, to operate instead between Trafalgar Square and Cockfosters Station, from 17/18 July 1992, its service ran more or less in parallel with the Piccadilly Line between Piccadilly Circus and Cockfosters Station. The N21 was branded as *Piccadilly Line Night Bus N21* in contemporary publicity and timetables, and bus blind displays also gained *Piccadilly Line* branding. The branded association between a Nighter and the Piccadilly Line ended from 23/24 June 1995 when the N21 was withdrawn and largely replaced by a re-routed N91.

In more recent years a number of Nighters have gained later departure times on Sunday mornings, applied to both their inbound and outbound timetables, to fill the void in service until London Underground starts running at around 07.30 on that day of the week.

Table F Last Departure Times from central London of all-Night Bus Routes with Parallel Service to London Underground Lines at 30/31 August 2013

Route Number	Termini	Underground Line	Last Departure	
			Weekdays	Sunday
N5	Trafalgar Square – Edgware Station	Northern	05.40	07.10*
N9	Aldwych – Heathrow Airport Terminal 5	Piccadilly	05.30	06.50
N20	Trafalgar Square – Barnet Church	Northern	05.35	07.05*
N91	Trafalgar Square – Cockfosters Station	Piccadilly	05.20	06.40
N97	Trafalgar Square – Hammersmith	Piccadilly	05.15	06.35
N98	Holborn – Stanmore Station	Jubilee	05.55	07.15

Key: * Route N20 gained a temporary extended 12 minute frequency service between Euston and Barnet Church between 23 October 2011 and 4 November 2012 to cover closure of the High Barnet branch of the Northern Line for engineering work. Route N5 gained a similar frequency Sunday morning service between Euston and Edgware from 25 November 2012 to cover closure of the Northern Line's Edgware branch for similar purpose. The N5's 09.10 departure from Euston Bus Station, with 10.00 arrival at Edgware Bus Station, represented the latest-ever scheduled all-night bus route journey to have operated in London. The N5's Sunday morning replacement service was expected to cease operation during September 2013.

The link between route N21 and the Piccadilly Line was clearly evident on the intermediate-points blind display of Finchley Garage's MCW Metrobus M 691 seen on layover in Pall Mall East during 1992. *JGS Smith*

NON-RADIAL AND SUBURBAN NIGHTERS

Historically, most of London's all-night bus routes had linked outlying areas with the centre of the metropolis. Principal exceptions had comprised the services between Catford and Vauxhall on route 185 and between New Cross Garage and Woolwich on route N82.

Innovatory route N31 became the first non-radial all-night bus route to serve inner London districts exclusively when introduced on Saturday night/Sunday morning 11/12 November 1989. Branded *Night Arrow*, the N31 built upon the success of daytime *Gold Arrow* routes 28 (Golders Green – Wandsworth) and 31 (Camden Town – Chelsea), which had been introduced by London Buses' subsidiary company Centrewest on 4 March and 15 April 1989 respectively. Conventional double-deck buses, mainly Routemasters, on both of those routes had been replaced by MA-type 28-seat midibuses at a much higher frequency. The N31 used MA-types, too, on its Friday and Saturday night service which linked Camden Town with Earls Court and Fulham. The N31 was expanded to operate nightly from 17/18 July 1992.

A description of route N253 as an inner London Nighter must be qualified by pointing out that, in its original form upon introduction on 3/4 September 1993, its two termini were on the fringes of central London, at Aldgate and Euston Station. The Euston end was extended to Trafalgar Square from 25/26 November 1994 but subsequently cut back to Tottenham Court Road Station from 29/30 May 1998. The N253's route describes an arc across a great tract of inner east and north east London serving Whitechapel, Hackney, Clapton, Stamford Hill, Manor House, Finsbury Park, Holloway and Camden Town. In a similar vein, the N35 is an inner London Nighter with a tail end service into central London. Originally operated by London Central, and introduced on 25/26 April 1997, the N35's route describes an arc across south London from Clapham Junction via Clapham Common, Brixton, Loughborough Junction and Camberwell Green before entering central London at Elephant & Castle and continuing to run in parallel with long established daytime route 35 as far as Great Eastern Street in Shoreditch whence, in its original form, the N35 continued to Trafalgar Square until it was re-routed to Tottenham Court Road Station from 28/29 April 2000.

London General-operated route N37 formed an element of LRT's first 24-hour bus service to operate between common termini when introduced on 25/26 April 1997. The N37 and daytime 37 both operated between Peckham and Putney Station. The daytime 37 had a long established origin, which dated back to LGOC days on 30 March 1912, and it is likely that the established traffic on the daytime 37 encouraged LRT to pioneer 24-hour service operation along its route corridor in conjunction with the N37.

London Regional Transport oversaw the introduction of one further inner London and two suburban Nighters in the time remaining to it. Inner London route N28 (Camden Town – Wandsworth), operated by Centrewest, was introduced on 28/29 May 1999 and complemented route N31, with a co-ordinated timetable on both routes between Camden Town and Kensington High Street. The N31 was restructured from the same date to operate between Camden Town and Clapham Junction. London United-operated route N72 linked East Acton with Roehampton via Hammersmith, upon its introduction from 3/4 September 1999, and became the third contemporary single-deck bus operated Nighter, with an allocation of three Dennis Darts. Lengthy Metroline-operated route N140 (Harrow Weald – Heathrow Airport) formed a 24-hour service with existing daytime route 140 upon its introduction from 31 March/1 April 2000.

Since Transport for London assumed powers, from 3 July 2000, the number of purely suburban Nighters has increased dramatically to comprise 33 such routes at 30/31 August 2013. More recently, certain suburban routes have replaced outer London sections of central London serving Nighters, such as when new route (N)33, introduced on 29/30 January 2010, replaced route N10's link between Hammersmith and Richmond and when new route N64 replaced the N159's service between Thornton Heath Pond and New Addington from 27/28 August 2010, albeit that, in both those instances, partially different intermediate routeings were followed.

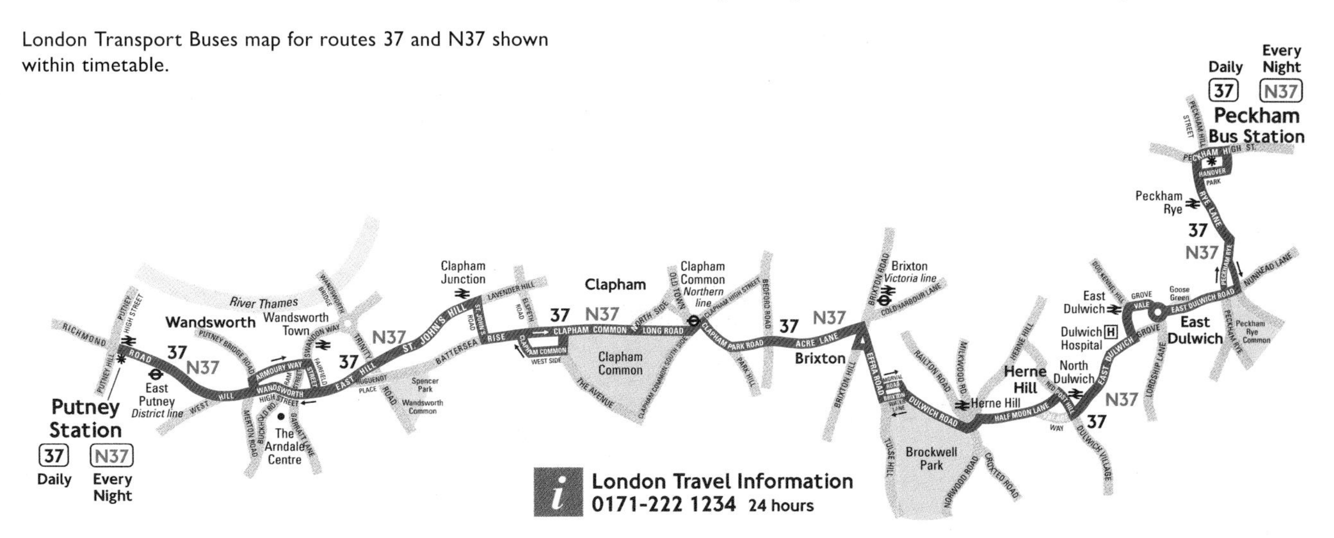

London Transport Buses map for routes 37 and N37 shown within timetable.

Central London shuttle services first operated on New Year's Eve 1989 when London Northern's Leyland Titan T 474 was photographed in Aldwych. *Roy Waterhouse*

London Northern's MCW Metrobus M 921 headed up a line of Night Buses as it loaded passengers for route N100 in Aldwych on New Year's Day 1993. *Roy Waterhouse*

NEW YEAR'S EVE

The celebration on New Year's Eve on a massive scale is a comparatively recent phenomenon in England. Traditionally, such celebrations as there were in central London took place around the Eros Statue in Piccadilly Circus and which, whilst boisterous enough to necessitate the temporary boarding up of that memorial, caused little other disruption in the vicinity. 1 January 1975 was the first time that New Year's Day was declared a Bank Holiday across the whole of the United Kingdom and so, with many people absolved from possible concerns about having to get up for work the next morning, the scale of New Year's Eve revelries increased appreciably and their focus in London switched to Trafalgar Square. Based upon their experience in 1975, the authorities decided, on safety grounds, to close Trafalgar Square to vehicular traffic until 02.30 on New Year's Day 1976. As a result all-night bus routes which served Trafalgar Square were subject to curtailment or re-routeing. Routes N83, N92 and N93 were curtailed at Aldwych, routes N84, N90, N95 and N98 at Cambridge Circus and route N97 at Haymarket. Routes 11, N68, N85, N86, N87 and N88 were diverted via Arundel Street, Temple Place and Victoria Embankment, with the N85 and N86 terminating at Horse Guards Avenue. Routes N91 and N94 were diverted via New Oxford Street and High Holborn. This pattern was repeated for several years.

Free travel on New Year's Eve for passengers using London Transport's bus and Underground train services was initiated on New Year's Eve 31 December 1979 through sponsorship from FIAT (UK). Since then, London Regional Transport and Transport for London have continued to offer free travel on New Year's Eve by attracting sponsorship over the years from a variety of sources, including drinks companies and banks. Free travel has expanded to include the Docklands Light Railway, along with Croydon's trams and, since New Year's Eve 2001, has been offered between 23.45 on New Year's Eve and 04.30 on New Year's Day.

As a result of increased passenger demand for the Nighters, following the expansion of the network from 13/14 April 1984, London Regional Transport re-focussed New Year's Eve route curtailments and re-routeings to Aldwych in respect of most Nighters from 31 December 1984/1 January 1985 although other termini, such as Victoria and Oxford Circus, were also used. By New Year's Eve 31 December 1988/1 January 1989, the scale of operations had become such that three central London shuttle services were introduced to help move crowds away from the celebrations to night bus terminal points and railway stations. Thereafter central London shuttle services operated annually up to and including 31 December 2003/1 January 2004, after which their usefulness was negated by the introduction of a 24-hour New Year's Eve service on the Underground system from 31 December 2004/1 January 2005. (A 24-hour Underground service had also operated on Millennium Eve 31 December 1999/1 January 2000.) The threat of disruption to Underground services on New Year's Eve 2005, due to industrial action, led to a hastily arranged central London shuttle bus service. Further details of central London New Year's Eve shuttle bus services follow in Table G.

Metrobus's East Lancs-bodied Volvo Olympian 842 was photographed in Victoria's Wilton Road working Millennium Eve route 2000 between Vauxhall and Marble Arch. *Graham Saunders courtesy Peter Larking*

Table G: New Year's Eve
Central London Shuttle Bus Services

Date	Routes
31.12 88 – 1.1.89	**Special Service. Clockwise Circular.** Aldwych – Waterloo – Victoria – Hyde Park Corner – Knightsbridge (double run) – Marble Arch – Oxford Street – Holborn – Aldwych. **Special Service. Anticlockwise Circular.** Reverse of clockwise circular route but omitted double run to Knightsbridge. **Operators: London General** (M-type from Victoria garage) and **London Northern** (T-type from Chalk Farm garage and M-type from Holloway garage). **Special Service. Non-stop.** Aldwych – Tower Gateway, Docklands Light Railway Station. **Operator: East London** (T-type from Bow garage).
31.12.89 – 1.1.90	**Special Service.** Aldwych – Holborn – Oxford Circus – Marble Arch – Knightsbridge (double run) – Hyde Park Corner – Victoria. **Opeator: London Northern** (T-type from Chalk Farm garage). **Special Service. Non Stop.** Aldwych – Victoria. **Operator: London United** (M-type from Fulwell garage). **Special Service. Non-stop.** Aldwych – Tower Gateway, Docklands Light Railway Station. **Operator: East London** (T-type from Bow garage).
31.12.90 – 1.1.91	**Central London Link.** Aldwych – Holborn – Oxford Circus – Marble Arch – Hyde Park Corner – Knightsbridge (double run) – Victoria. **Operator: London Northern** (T-type from Chalk Farm garage). **Victoria Express. Non-stop.** Aldwych – Victoria. **Operator: London United** (M-type from Fulwell garage).
31.12.91 – 1.1.92	**Central London Link.** Routeing as 1990/1991. **Operator: London Northern.** Allocation: 6 T-type from Chalk Farm garage.
31.12.92 – 1.1.93	**Route N 100.** Routeing as Central London Link 1990/1991. **Operator: London Northern** (M and T-types from Chalk Farm and Holloway garages).
31.12.93 – 1.1.94	**Route N 100.** Exact routeing unconfirmed. Buses photographed in Aldwych and Lower Regent Street with destination blind displays: 'N100 Oxford Circus Piccadilly Victoria Aldwych'. **Operator: London Central.** Allocation: 7 T-type from Camberwell garage.
31.12.94 – 1.1.95	**Route N100.** Aldwych – Holborn – Oxford Circus – Piccadilly Circus – Hyde Park Corner – Victoria. **Operator: London Central.** Allocation: 8 T-type from Bexleyheath garage. NV-types from New Cross garage also observed in service.
31.12.95 – 1.1.96	**Route N100.** Exact routeing unconfirmed. **Operator: London Central (**T, L and NV-types from Bexleyheath and New Cross garages).

31.12.96 – 1.1.97	**Route N 100.** Aldwych – Waterloo – Victoria – Hyde Park Corner – Piccadilly Circus – Regent Street (southern end). **Operator:** London Central (from Bexleyheath garage).
31.12.97 – 1.1.98	**Route N 100.** Aldwych – Waterloo – Victoria – Hyde Park Corner – Piccadilly Circus – Pall Mall. **Operator: Capital Citybus.**
31.12.98 – 1.1.99	**Route N 100.** Routeing as 1997/1998. **Operator: First Capital.**
31.12.99 – 1.1.00	**Millennium Eve** **Route 2000.** Marble Arch – Hyde Park Corner – Victoria – Vauxhall. Observed all bus stops normally served by daytime route 2 in both directions of travel. **Scheduled frequency:** 16.30 – 22.00 5 minutes 22.00 – 23.50 10 minutes 23.50 – 03.00 4 minutes 03.00 – 05.30 10 minutes **Operator:** Metrobus using Olympians. **Note** After 23.30 hours it proved impossible to operate route 2000 due to crowds so buses were re-routed via Chelsea Bridge to Vauxhall. Buses then worked *ad hoc* extra journeys to Brixton, Camberwell, Clapham Common and Wandsworth until 03.30. Most buses then returned to Metrobus' depot, working as extras on routes N2 or N36. Four buses returned to resume route 2000 until 05.30
31.12.00 – 1.1.01	**Route 2001A.** Marble Arch – Hyde Park Corner – Victoria – Vauxhall – Camberwell. **Route 2001B.** Aldwych – Holborn – Euston. **Route 2001C.** Euston – Marylebone Road – Edgware Road – Marble Arch. **Operator: Blue Triangle**. Allocation: 38 buses, with some duties on route 2001A sub-contracted to Frank Thorpe & Sons (Metrobuses) and to Sullivan Buses (using Metrobuses and Leyland Titans), and some duties on route 2001C sub-contracted to Metroline Travel (Dennis Tridents).
31.12.01 – 1.1.02	**RouteA.** Aldwych – Victoria – Hyde Park Corner – Marble Arch. **Operator: Metrobus**. Allocation: 16 buses. **Route B.** Aldwych – Holborn – Euston – Warren Street – Marble Arch – Hyde Park Corner – Victoria. **Operator: Blue Triangle.** Allocation: 23 buses.
31.12.02 – 1.1.03	**Route A.** Routeing as 2001/2002. **Operator: Metrobus** (using Volvo Olympians and Dennis Tridents). **Route B.** Routeing as 2001/2002. **Operator: Blue Triangle** (using Leyland Titans and Dennis Tridents).
31.12.03 – 1.1.04	**Route A**. Routeing as 2001/2002. **Operator: Metrobus.** Allocation: 28 buses. **Route B.** Routeing as 2001/2002. **Operator: Stagecoach** (using Dennis Tridents plus one Dennis Dart).
31.12.05 – 1.1.06	**Un-numbered route.** Aldwych – Holborn – Oxford Circus – Marble Arch – Hyde Park Corner – Victoria. **Operator: Sullivan Buses.** Allocation: 17 buses.

The scale of New Year's Eve celebrations in London has necessitated supplementation of bus allocation to the Nighters which has led to some memorable and unusual vehicle appearances at times, particularly so up to the mid-1990s. New Year's Eve 31 December 1988/1 January 1989 saw the debut operation of route N19 between Victoria or Trafalgar Square and Clapham Junction on that night only, prior to the subsequent introduction of the regular, nightly N19 (Finsbury Park – Clapham Junction) service from 27/28 October 1989.

Millennium Eve 2000 attracted vast crowds with buses progressively withdrawn from the West End, City, Greenwich and North Greenwich areas from 16.00 on 31 December 1999, prior to a traffic limitation zone coming into force at 17.00. The largest cordon zone up to the date of writing was created, with central London-serving Nighters truncated to terminate at Aldgate, Bermondsey Station, Hyde Park Corner, Lambeth North, Liverpool Street, London Bridge Station, Oxford Circus, Tottenham Court Road Station, Vauxhall and Victoria, according to route.

On New Year's Eve 31 December 2002/1 January 2003 four daytime bus routes, 161, 422, 472 and 486, which served the entertainment venue of the Dome at North Greenwich, each operated a 30-minute frequency all-night service. This operation was the precursor for much more extensive operation of an all-night bus service over selected daytime bus routes on New Year's Eve night which, from 31 December 2004/1 January 2005, was expanded to include 41 such routes across London, as well as the Croydon Tramlink service between Wimbledon, Croydon and New Addington or Beckenham Junction. This practice has been perpetuated on successive New Years' Eves, with some variations to routes worked, with such services typically running at 20 or 30-minute frequencies although some operate every 15 minutes. Routes have been chosen because of heavy expected demand or because they connect with National Rail, Underground or tram services.

Route 217 (Turnpike Lane Station – Waltham Cross) was one of 41 daytime bus routes which gained an all-night service for New Year's Eve 2005. Metroline's Plaxton-bodied TransBus Trident TP 438 was seen at Turnpike Lane Station working the 217's 20 minute frequency night-time service on 1 January 2005. Provenance is given to the night-time authenticity of this image by the fact that the bus station's clock, visible on the original photograph, read 02.40. *Philip Wallis*

NOTTING HILL CARNIVAL

The Notting Hill Carnival, founded in 1966 as a local pageant and fair, has developed over the years into a full-blooded Caribbean carnival, held annually on August Bank Holiday. Buses have always played a vital role in transporting people to and from the Carnival. In both 1986 and 1987, the Red Stripe Beer Company sponsored free travel on all-night bus routes in the Carnival area on the Bank Holiday Monday night. This applied to existing routes N18 and N89 as well as the N50 which gained an additional special service to West Norwood for the night. Additionally three Nighters – N12, N36, N73 – made their debut some years in advance of the introduction of a regular nightly service over those routes.

Table H
Notting Hill Carnival
Special Operation of Routes N12, N36, N50, N73
Bank Holiday Monday nights/Tuesday mornings 25/26 August 1986 and 31 August/1 September 1987 only

Notes: Routes operated northbound or southbound only with buses returning 'dead'. Special destination blind displays were made, although it was reported that N36 buses did not display them on at least 25/26 August 1986. Regular nightly services were introduced on route N12 from 27/28 October 1989, route N36 from 8/9 October 1993, route N73 from 22/23 September 1989. Although no special all-night bus routes have operated from the Notting Hill Carnival since 1987, the Nighters have continued to provide an important service for carnival goers, with extra bus allocations and route diversions to avoid processional routes.

N12	**Shepherd's Bush – Dulwich, Plough** via Bayswater Road, Marble Arch, Oxford Street, Trafalgar Square, Westminster, Elephant & Castle, Camberwell Green, Peckham.	Peckham Shepherd's Bush	T M
N36	**Harrow Road, Prince of Wales – Lewisham** via Paddington, Marble Arch, Victoria, Vauxhall, Camberwell Green, Peckham.	Catford	T
N50	**Harrow Road, Prince of Wales – West Norwood** via Paddington, Marble Arch, Oxford Street, Trafalgar Square, Westminster, Victoria, Vauxhall, Stockwell, Brixton, Tulse Hill.	Norwood	M
N73	**Shepherd's Bush – Tottenham Garage** via Bayswater Road, Marble Arch, Oxford Street, Tottenham Court Road Station, Euston, King's Cross, Islington, Stoke Newington.	Wood Green	M

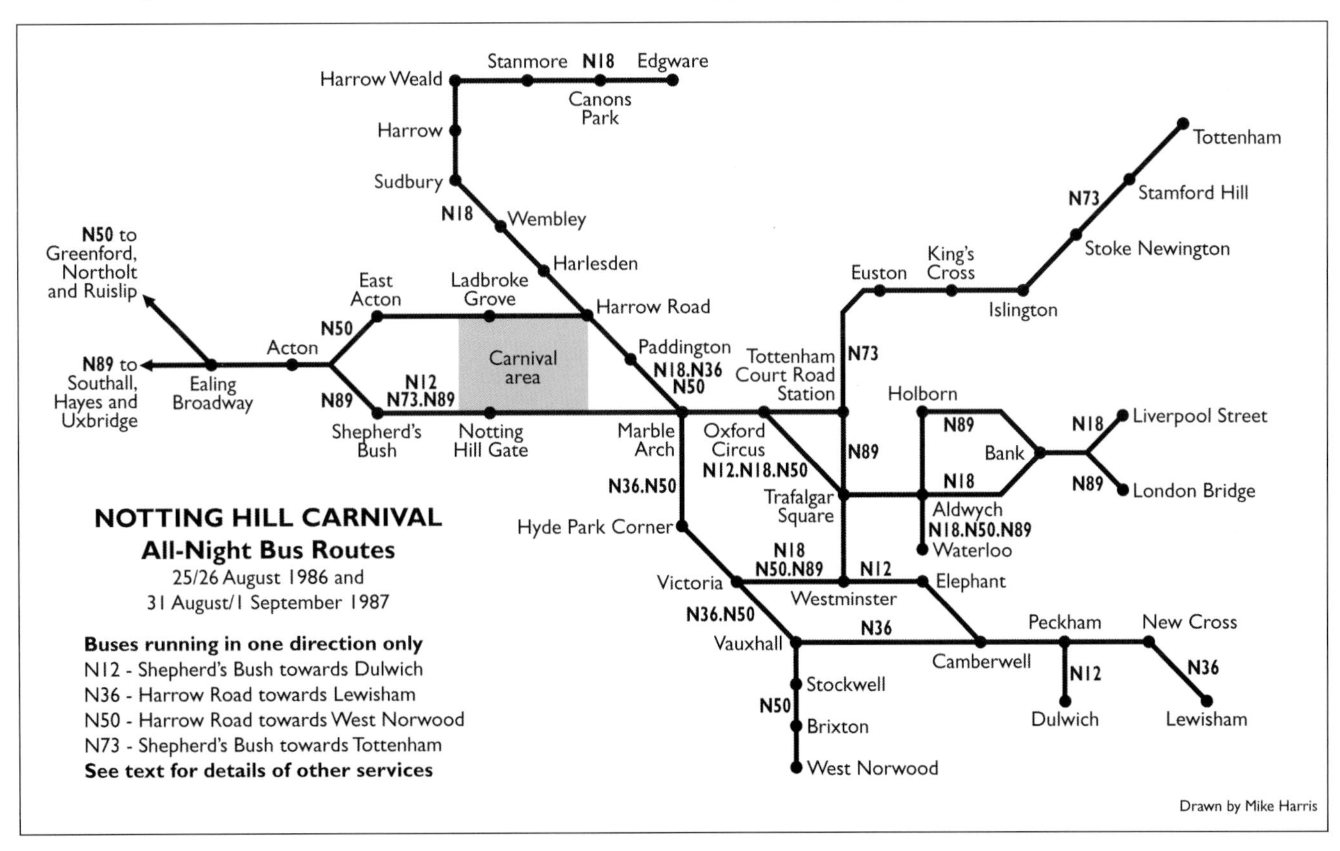

VEHICLE TRENDS 1984–1997

The expansion of the all-night bus route network, from 13/14 April 1984, saw the majority of routes at that time operated by either MCW Metrobuses or Leyland Titans. DM/DMS-type Fleetlines were allocated to routes N2, N11, N78, N87 and N92 whilst the N96 remained the only single-deck bus Nighter with LS-type Leyland Nationals. Surprisingly, in view of the modernisation theme associated with the network's expansion, route N93 gained an official RML-type Routemaster allocation (it had previously been crew-operated DMS-type) and remained one of only four Nighters to have retained crew operation with driver and conductor. Other such routes comprised the N29 (Metrobus) and Inter-Station Route (Titan) along with the Special Night Journeys on route 9, which retained RM-type Routemaster operation. Starting in March 1984, trials had been put in hand to evaluate the next generation of double-deck buses for London service. The vehicles comprised H-type Hestair Dennis Dominators, L-type Leyland Olympians, M-type MCW Metrobuses Mk 2 and V-type Volvo Ailsas which were based at Stockwell garage at various times and which buses, in addition to use on daytime services, were regularly deployed on route N87 until August 1986, although that route's official allocation remained D-type Fleetline throughout the trial period.

Regular Routemaster operation of N-prefixed all-night bus routes ceased from 26/27 October 1984 when a route extension to the N93 was combined with its conversion to one-person operated Metrobus. This ended almost 25 years of continuous Routemaster operation across the former 2xx and N-prefixed Nighters which had started with route 284 on 10/11 November 1959. The Routemaster maintained a tenuous presence on the all-night bus route network for nearly another three years until the withdrawal of the remaining Saturday night Liverpool Street Station – Mortlake Special Night Journey on route 9 after operation on 18/19 September 1987. Crew-operation of route N29 ceased from 1/2 February 1985 with that route's conversion to one-person operation whilst, as detailed earlier, the Inter-Station Route last operated on 21/22 April 1985.

MCW Metrobuses and Leyland Titans dominated vehicle allocations across the Nighters for a lengthy period between 1984 and 1996. Fleetline usage experienced an early initial decline when routes N2, N11, N78 and N92 were converted to Metrobus operation during 1984. However, the fortune of that vehicle-type on the Nighters was revived as a result of the re-allocation of routes N68 and N88 to Fleetline-operating Sutton garage in 1987. That garage ran Fleetlines on those routes for around four years until a progressive vehicle-type change to Metrobus was completed by 13/14 December 1991, which date marked the Fleetline's demise from the all-night bus route network. Route N87, another bulwark of Fleetline service from Stockwell garage, had earlier been converted to Metrobus-operation from 1/2 February 1991. Daimler/Leyland Fleetline usage across the Nighters had spanned almost 21 years since the entry into service of 'Londoner' DMS 1 on route 220's Special Night Journey on 1/2 January

Route N93 (Fulwell or Victoria – Hampstead Heath) was operated by both a Leyland Titan from Chalk Farm garage and MCW Metrobuses from Holloway and Shepherd's Bush or Stamford Brook garages between 25/26 September 1987 and 20/21 September 1990. Chalk Farm garage's Leyland Titan T 386 was photographed in Euston Road opposite St Pancras Station on Sunday morning 11 October 1987. *Roy Waterhouse*

1971. Leyland Nationals, and with them single-deck bus operation on the Nighters at that time, succumbed to Leyland Titan operation on route N96 from 5/6 June 1987.

London's first production Leyland Olympians entered service from Plumstead garage on daytime routes from 22 March 1986 and that garage's allocation to route N77 became the first Nighter to gain an Olympian allocation from 20/21 June 1986. New Cross was the second garage to put out Olympians on to the Nighters, with the conversion of Dartford route N72 by 10/11 July 1987. The pace of all-night route conversions to Olympian-type operation was slow, which was a function of smaller batch orders for new buses placed by LRT, and it was well over two years before the next Olympians on the Nighters were allocated to newly-introduced routes N53 from Plumstead garage and N62 from New Cross garage from 27/28 October 1989. That same year also saw the return of single-deck bus operation on the Nighters with MA-type Mercedes-Benz 811D midibuses allocated to innovative route N31 (Camden Town – Fulham Broadway) upon its introduction from 11/12 November 1989. The N31 was subsequently converted to Wright-bodied Dennis Dart DW-type from 15/16 June 1991.

The 1990s witnessed comparatively brief time-span allocations to the Nighters for two marques of double-deck bus new to London service. London Northern deployed Alexander-bodied Scania N113s on varying dates between 1992 and 1997 on routes N1, N5, N21, N91 and N92, sometimes in mixed allocations with Metrobuses, whilst East London, subsequently Stagecoach East London, allocated Northern Counties-bodied Scania N113s to routes N8, N15, N50 and N76 at various periods from 1992 onwards. London Central's DAF DB250/Optare Spectras based at Camberwell garage were allocated, at various times between 26/27 March 1993 and 6/7 November 1997, to routes N3, N35, N79 and N176.

Second-hand ex London Regional Transport Leyland Titans were the vehicles of choice selected by London Coaches when it assumed operation of daytime route 52 and complementary all-night route N52, which between them provided a new 24-hour service between Victoria Station and Willesden, Roundwood Park from 3/4 December 1993. Another newcomer of that period, London Suburban Bus, chose new Leyland Olympians on its assumption of the LRT contract for routes 6 and N6, which gave a 24-hour service between Aldwych and Kensal Rise Station, from 28/29 January 1994, although its fleet did contain some ex LRT Leyland Titans too, which could sometimes be encountered on the N6.

Earlier commentary has alluded to the slow take-up of Nighter allocations by Leyland Olympians but the pace quickened between 1995 and 1997 when hosts of what by-then had transmuted into Volvo Olympians flooded into service, displacing not only Optare Spectras from the Nighters but also reducing the number of Titans and denting Metrobus allocations, although this latter vehicle-type continued to retain a significant presence on the Nighters, particularly with Centrewest, Arriva London North, London General, London United and London Northern.

London Transport Buses final order for Leyland Olympians comprised a batch of 40 Alexander RH-bodied models which all entered service from Leaside Buses' Stamford Hill garage during 1992. L 333 (the only one of the batch with an out of sequence registration number as delivered) was photographed outside the National Gallery in Trafalgar Square shortly after entering service. *JGS Smith*

VEHICLE TRENDS 1998–2013

The first low-floor buses to be allocated to London's Nighters entered service from 1/2 May 1998 in the form of DM-type Marshall-bodied Dennis Darts which superseded step-floor DW-type Darts on route N31. The N31, which had remained London's sole single-deck bus operated Nighter for 9½ years since its introduction on 11/12 November 1989, was complemented from 28/29 May 1999 by the introduction of DM-type operated route N28, which shared a co-ordinated timetable with route N31 over a lengthy common section of routeing between Camden Town and Kensington High Street.

London United-operated route N72 (East Acton – Roehampton) became LRT's third single-deck bus operated Nighter upon its introduction from 3/4 September 1999. The N72's initial, but temporary, allocation of step-floor DR-type Dennis Darts was superseded by DPS-type low-floor Darts during December 1999. Shepherd's Bus garage, which operated the N72, also started to deploy DP and DPS-types on routes N11 (Liverpool Street Station – Shepherd's Bush Green) and N94 (Piccadilly Circus – Acton Green) from mid-December 1999, although these two routes' official allocations remained double-deck Metrobus. London United's practice of substituting single-deck buses on route N11, at least, persisted after the route's official vehicle-type was changed to low–floor Volvo B7TL VA-type double deckers in March 2000. Indeed, DP/DPS-type Darts appear to have been frequently substituted for VA-types on route N11 for at least the next 19 months. The author encountered DPS 5 at Strand, Charing Cross station, loading passengers for an outbound route N11 journey in the early morning hours of Sunday 28 October 2001. The capacity of this single-deck bus was quite unable to absorb the large queue of potential passengers, many of whom were left behind. This deployment by London United of Dennis Dart SLFs on route N11 (and earlier on route N94), would had to have ceased by 27/28 June 2003, when the LBSL contract for route N11 was awarded to London General.

The distinction of inaugurating low-floor double-deck bus operation on the Nighters fell to Stagecoach East London when Alexander-bodied Dennis Tridents replaced Leyland Titans as Barking garage's allocation for route N15 from 12/13 April 1999. For a fleeting period of just one month, that operator's Bow garage allocated Dennis Tridents to its weekend nights allocation on route N25 but this brief second-ever allocation of low-floor double deckers on the Nighters ended when Stagecoach East London lost the contract for the N25 (and daytime 25) from 25/26 June 1999. However the change of contract heralded in London's second operator of low-floor double-deck buses on the Nighters when First Capital, the successful bidder, deployed TN-type Plaxton President-bodied Dennis Tridents on the N25. Problems soon emerged for these short 9.9 metre Tridents, with their 59-seat capacity proving to be inadequate for weekend nights peak demand on the N25, which forced First Capital to supplement that route's weekend nights allocation with step-floor 77-seat Dennis Arrows for about one year until the TN-types could be replaced by 69-seat TAL-type Tridents. First Capital also assumed operation of route N1 from 25/26 June 1999 with official conversion to low-floor operation with TN-types but, pending delivery of enough Tridents, older Metrobuses helped out for a couple of months. First Centrewest started a progressive conversion on 9/10 July 1999 of route N18 from M-type Metrobus to TN-type Trident in respect of that route's allocation from Westbourne Park garage, with that garage's allocations to routes N23 and N139 also switching to Tridents in the same month. Metroline-London Northern became London's fourth operator to adopt the use of low-floor double-deckers on the Nighters with the conversion of route N43 from M-type Metrobus to TP-type Plaxton President-bodied Dennis Tridents from 23/24 July 1999, followed by routes N13 and N134 from 8/9 October 1999. The fifth operator to go low-floor double-deck on the Nighters was Arriva London North with an official type change to Alexander or Plaxton-bodied DAF DB250LF DLA or DLP-types on route N279 from 15/16 October 1999, although examples had entered service earlier, such as DLA 116 which had worked the N279's very last Upshire journey the preceding night.

The first reported example of low-floor Volvo B7TLs in service on the Nighters occurred on the night of 31 January/1 February 2000 when London Central started a progressive conversion of route N159's allocation from Camberwell garage from NV-type Olympian to AVL-type, which was quickly followed by the conversion of that garage's allocation on route N12 to AVL-type, from 4/5 February 2000. On the same night, Peckham garage converted partial allocations on routes N36 and N84 to AVL-type, which worked inter-mixed with step-floor AV-type Volvo Olympians. These type changes at London Central meant the end of regular Leyland Titan allocation to the Nighters, which had spanned almost 20 years since the first T-type Titans had been introduced from Romford garage on route N98 from 16/17 May 1980. However the three 'emergency stand-by' Leyland Titans, based at Camberwell garage, continued to give back-up to any central London-serving all-night bus route of any operator for over a further two years until they were stood down after 23/24 May 2002 without replacement.

Increasingly new LBSL bus route contracts specified low-floor buses from inception, such as when Connex Bus replaced incumbent operator London Central on the N3 (and daytime 3) from 4/5 February 2000 with the use of TA-type Alexander-bodied Dennis Tridents or when Metroline inaugurated an all-night service over route N140 (Harrow Weald – Heathrow Airport) from 31 March/1 April 2000 with the use of similar-type buses. In other instances, step-floor buses were used for part of the contract term as, for example, when London General inaugurated route N22 (Piccadilly Circus – Richmond) from 24/25 November 2000 with NV-type Olympians which were superseded exactly two years later by WVL-type low-floor Wright-bodied Volvo B7TLs.

Single-deck bus operation on the Nighters expanded between 1/2 September 2000 and 31 January/1 February 2003 with the introduction of seven routes – N101, N106, N108, N214, N236, N274 and N285 – initially worked by a mixture of step-floor and low-floor saloons, according to route. Although the ubiquitous Dennis Dart dominated allocations some variety was added by Stagecoach East London's use of SLW-type Scania N113CRLs on the N101, whilst East Thames initially deployed Optare Excels on the N108.

By 28/29 April 2001, just two years after Stagecoach East London had inaugurated the use of low-floor double-deck buses on the Nighters, 37 all-night bus routes were worked entirely by low-floor buses, another 13 routes shared mixed step-floor and low-floor bus allocations whilst a further 20 routes remained operated by step-floor buses. The rapid advance of low-floor buses had eroded the Metrobus presence on the Nighters which, by July 2001, had become confined to a partial allocation on Arriva London North's N29, a partial allocation on Metroline's N16 as well as forming the entire allocation for Metroline's N98. Progressive conversion of these three routes to entire low-floor operation was completed during October 2001, thereby eliminating Metrobuses from the all-night bus route network. The M-type Metrobus had given stalwart service spanning 22½ years on the Nighters since the introduction of M 1-3 to Cricklewood route N94 by 9/10 February 1979.

Following the demise of the Metrobus, scheduled step-floor double-deck operation across the Nighters was confined to Leyland or Volvo Olympians as well as Dennis Arrows, which vehicle type had made its debut on the Nighters following the award of contracts for routes N20 and N50 to First Capital in 1998. The Dennis Arrow's period on the Nighters spanned just five years until displaced when First Capital lost the contracts for the N20 and N50 to Metroline London Northern and Stagecoach East London respectively during the summer of 2003. That same summer saw the end of the only instance of sustained use of step-floor Dennis Darts on a TfL-initiated Nighter when Metroline London Northern route N214 was converted to low-floor DLS/DMS-type Dennis Dart SLF operation, following three years of operation by step-floor DNL-type Dennis Darts.

Transport for London's ambition to achieve complete low-floor bus operation across its entire bus network by the end of 2005 sealed the fate of remaining Olympian-type operations. Casual substitution of step-floor buses on LBSL bus routes contracted for low-floor bus operation became precluded by TfL's non-compliant vehicles edict, effective from 24 July 2004, and which threatened operators with disallowance of contract payments for journeys on such routes worked by 'low-floor wheelchair-accessible vehicles . . . without a working ramp, or any high-floor bus being used where not permitted'. The end for step-floor buses on the Nighters came on 8/9 October 2004 with London Central's loss of the contract for route N381 (Peckham – Whitehall, Horse Guards). The N381 had been the last Nighter to have retained a step-floor bus allocation, which officially comprised three NV-type Volvo Olympians, although in practice London Central had habitually mixed NV-types with low-floor AVL or PVL-types on the route since at least 18/19 July 2000. The new operator of the N381, Travel London, used low-floor V-type Volvo B7TLs. Leyland or Volvo Olympian operation on the Nighters had spanned over 18 years, since the introduction of Olympians to route N77 from 20/21 June 1986.

A new type of bus made its debut on the Nighters from 14/15 March 2003, in the form of Mercedes-Benz Citaro articulated low-floor single-deckers introduced by Stagecoach Selkent onto route N453 (and daytime 453). Dubbed bendy buses, articulated Citaros also took up operation of all-night (and complementary daytime) services on routes (N)12 (London Central), (N)25 (Stagecoach East London) and (N)149 (Arriva London North) in 2004, whilst Arriva London North's route N29 became the fifth bendy bus-operated Nighter, from 13/14 January 2006.

Sovereign London's Alexander-bodied Volvo Olympian VA 16 was photographed at Charing Cross Station on Sunday morning 18 July 2004 when this step-floor bus had been substituted for a low-floor bus on route N13 just a few nights before TfL's non-compliant vehicle edict came into force from 24 July. *Philip Wallis*

The number of single-deck bus-operated routes increased significantly upon completion of the bendy bus conversion programme. From 13/14 January 2006, 11 Nighters became operated by single-deck buses. These comprised routes (N)72, (N)108, (N)214, (N)236, (N)274 and (N)285, all of which were operated by fixed chassis single deckers, and bendy bus-operated routes (N)12, (N)25, N29, (N)149 and (N)453. The number of single-deck bus-operated Nighters reached its peak of 12 such routes with the introduction of route (N)33 from 29/30 January 2010, initially operated by London Sovereign from the former NCP Challenger garage in Twickenham, using Dennis Dart SLFs. Completion of the programme to convert bendy bus routes back to double-deck operation (or to introduce permanent double-deck bus operation to the route in the case of (N)453) during 2011, along with the withdrawal of route (N)274 after 23/24 June 2011 and route (N)236 after 4/5 October 2012, reduced the number of single-deck bus operated Nighters to just five such routes at 30/31 August 2013. These comprised routes (N)33, (N)72, (N)108, (N)214 and (N)285, four of which are night-time elements of 24-hour service routes that operate in outer London, whilst daytime 214 and (N)214 combine to provide a 24-hour service between Liverpool Street and Highgate Village. Four of these routes were operated by AD Dart Enviro 200s and the (N)108 by DWL-type Volvo Merits at 30/31 August 2013.

Liverpool Street Station to Highgate Village route N214 had been introduced on 1/2 September 2000 and was operated for over 2½ years by step-floor DNL-type Dennis Darts. A progressive vehicle-type change to DLS and DMS-type Dennis Dart SLFs was completed by September 2003. Holloway garage's Plaxton Pointer-bodied Dennis Dart SLF DLS 3 was seen in Liverpool Street Bus Station in the early hours of Saturday morning 1 November 2003. *Philip Wallis*

The first recorded use of a hybrid-powered bus on the Nighters occurred during March 2010 when Metroline sometimes substituted a TEH-type AD Trident Enviro 400H for a diesel-powered Trident on route (N)139. Route (N)94 became London's first Nighter to gain an official hybrid-powered bus allocation, with ADH-type AD Trident Enviro 400Hs, from 4/5 November 2010. Since then the number of night-time routes with a full or partial hybrid-bus allocation has rapidly increased to 24 at 30/31 August 2013.

75% of TfL's 116 contracted all-night bus routes remained operated exclusively by diesel-engine double-deck buses at 30/31 August 2013. Alexander Dennis Trident or E40D Enviro400s and Volvo B9TLs formed numerically high allocations to such routes. London United remained a stronghold of Scania operation with its OmniCity models deployed on six night-time routes whilst another four such routes were Scania-operated by Metrobus, Metroline and Stagecoach East London. Arriva deployed Wrightbus DB300 Gemini Integrals on some of its night routes. Dominant vehicle-types of former years have declined although Stagecoach continued to allocate Tridents to five of its night-time routes as did London United to two routes. Volvo B7TLs were represented in night-time allocations from the fleets of London Central, London General, Metroline and Tower Transit. Arriva's once numerous DAF DB250LFs have disappeared from night-time allocations but a fair presence of DLA-types at Brixton garage means that they are likely to be substituted on that garage's night-time routes for a while longer.

The increasing use of hybrid-powered buses on Night Bus routes is exemplified by Stagecoach East London's Alexander Dennis E400H 12138 from Bow garage which was photographed in Strand opposite Charing Cross Station early on Friday morning 30 March 2012. *Philip Wallis*

Route 24 (Pimlico – Hampstead Heath) became the first London Buses route to become fully operated by New Bus for London hybrid-powered LT-types from 22 June 2013. Holloway garage running number 833 indicated that Metroline's LT 30 was allocated to the night-time element of this 24-hour service when photographed at Tottenham Court Road Station in the early hours of Wednesday morning 10 July 2013. *Philip Wallis*

ROUTE NUMBERING SINCE 1984

Immediately prior to the network expansion from 13/14 April 1984, the majority of all-night bus routes had been numbered in a numerically-descending series from route number N99. This system had been introduced by London Transport on 11/12 October 1960 (see Volume One, Chapter 6), who had adapted it from the London General Omnibus Company's comparable numerically-descending series from route number 299, introduced on 3 October 1934 (see Volume One, Chapter 4). Exceptions were route numbers N29 and N68, originated to achieve numerical affinity with daytime bus route numbers, the all-night service or Special Night Journeys on routes 9, 11, 109, 177, 185, 220 and 221, which displayed the same route numbers as daytime services, and the un-numbered Inter-Station Route.

Upon expansion of the network from 13/14 April 1984, London Transport Executive's policy moved towards designating every all-night bus route with an N-prefixed route number. New routes introduced from that date were partially numbered in continuance of the numerically-descending series from N99, *viz* N79, N78, N77, N76, N74 (although N75 was omitted), and partially to indicate affinity with a daytime bus service with some common section of routeing, *viz* N2, N11, N13, N14, N18 and N27, although route number N21 only bore affinity with the last two digits of daytime route 221. Former all-night routes which had borne daytime route numbers were mostly incorporated into new N-prefixed all-night route. Exceptions were the Special Night Journeys on routes 9 and 220 which, along with the un-numbered Inter-Station Route, were left alone. This was probably in anticipation of their imminent demise, which happened during the London Regional Transport era when the Special Night Journeys on route 220 were withdrawn after operation on 16/17 May 1985, having been subsumed by route N88's extension beyond Wandsworth from 26/27 April 1985, on which same night the Inter-Station Route had been incorporated into new routes N50/N51. This left just the Special Night Journeys on route 9 as the sole non N-prefixed route number element of the all-night bus route network. The withdrawal of the last surviving Saturday night route 9 SNJ, after operation on 18/19 September 1987, might have been expected to have extinguished non-N-prefixed route numbers from the network at that time. Rather surprisingly, just one week later, a new dedicated all-night bus service to Waltham Abbey and Upshire, introduced from 25/26 September 1987, and which partially replaced a route N90 journey, displayed daytime route numbers 279 or 279A without an N-prefix. This continued until 30/31 January 1992, after which the withdrawal of the all-night element of routes 279/279A finally eliminated non-N-prefixed route numbers from London Regional Transport's all-night bus route operations.

Route N14 (Liverpool Street/Farringdon Street – Roehampton), introduced from 13/14 April 1984, shared a common section of routeing between Piccadilly Circus and Putney with established daytime route 14 (Hornsey Rise – Putney). The N14 was projected beyond Roehampton to Kingston from 26/27 April 1985 and was further revised from 10/11 July 1987 such that most journeys operated between Trafalgar Square and Kingston. Putney garage's MCW Metrobus M 1433 was seen on layover in Pall Mall East before taking up service from Cockspur Street on one of the hourly frequency journeys to Kingston on Sunday morning 11 December 1988.
Roy Waterhouse

London Regional Transport maintained two parallel N-prefixed route numbering sequences until the summer of 1995. One sequence continued to extend the original London Transport numerically-descending series from N99, whilst the other matched N-prefixed all-night bus route numbers with daytime bus route numbers. During this period, two further sub-series of route numbers were developed. The first of these was a numerically-ascending series from route number N50 which started on 26/27 April 1985, following the incorporation of the Inter-Station Route and separate Railair Link into routes N50, N51 and N56. The second sub-series started when two new all-night routes from Aldwych to High Barnet and to Edgware were introduced on 27/28 October 1989 numbered N1 and N5 respectively, which route numbers bore no relationship to any daytime service. There may have been an intention, at that time, to build up a route number series starting from N1, comprising both services with a unique all-night routeing, such as N1 and N5, and all-night routes with a numerical affinity to sections of daytime services, which contemporaneously comprised routes N2, N3, N6, N8, N11, N12, N13, N14, N18 and N19.

It is not possible to categorise with certainty some route numbers in the N5x and N6x ranges, since they could have fitted into more than one sequence. An example is provided by route number N54 (East Croydon Station – Banstead), which was introduced on 20/21 June 1986 and possibly fitted into the numerically-ascending series from N50. However, the N54 and daytime 54 (Woolwich – Croydon (Mondays–Fridays) or West Croydon (Saturdays and Sundays) did share a short common section of routeing at East and West Croydon so there might have been an intention of numerical affinity between N54 and daytime 54. Other route numbers from the LRT era which are difficult to categorise comprise N51 (second-time use of that route number for a Trafalgar Square-Woolwich service, introduced on 8/9 October 1993, which just met up in Woolwich with daytime route 51 from Orpington), N61 (Trafalgar Square – Sidcup Station), also introduced on 8/9 October 1993, which shared a short common section of routeing with daytime 61 (Bromley North – Eltham) in New Eltham and N62 (Victoria – Orpington), introduced on 27/28 October 1989, with its route number seemingly selected to give all-night bus routes along the Camberwell Green to Eltham via New Cross corridor route numbers ending with the digit '2', *viz* N62, N72, N82.

Route number N66 was the last-ever route number to be issued in the numerically-descending sequence from N99. This route number was issued on 30/31 October 1993 to designate the obscure single journey unidirectional service, which ran on Friday, Saturday and Sunday nights only, between Cricklewood Broadway and Edgware Station via Harlesden. Route number N65 introduced slightly earlier, on 17/18 July 1992, for a new night-time service between Archway Station and Kingston, bore numerical affinity with daytime Ealing Broadway to Chessington route 65, with which route the N65 shared a common section of routeing between Richmond and Kingston.

During much of 1993 Holloway garage deployed its Red Express X43-liveried Alexander RH-bodied Scania N113DRBs to its Night Bus allocations, presumably to achieve greater utilisation of these newish buses otherwise restricted to two peak hour X43 return trips on Mondays to Fridays by virtue of their dedicated livery. The result sent a mixed message to passengers as exemplified by S 17 seen outside the National Gallery in Trafalgar Square promoting route X43 as well as route N1's association with the Underground's Northern Line. *JGS Smith*

On occasions, dormant route numbers in the London Transport-originated numerically-descending sequence from N99 were re-issued. The most prolific was route number N99 itself, which first fell out of use following withdrawal of the Chingford Station to Victoria & Albert Docks all-night route after operating on 31 October/1 November 1985. N99 was revived for the Friday and Saturday nights-only service between Romford and Cranham, introduced on 8/9 August 1986. Following a two-month hiatus in operation, in early 1987, route number N99 continued in use when Ensignbus took up the service on 27/28 March 1987 under LRT contract and later extended it to start at Chadwell Heath, from 8/9 January 1988. That version of the N99 ran for the last time on 12/13 September 1991 but within less than one year route number N99 had entered its third incarnation, on 17/18 July 1992, when it was allocated to a newly introduced service between Trafalgar Square and Queensbury Station. Route number N81, which had previously been used by the infrequent Saturday night/ Sunday morning-only service between Streatham and Victoria, until its last night of operation on 22/23 October 1983, was brought back into use again upon the introduction of the London Central-operated route N81 between Trafalgar Square and Crayford, with projections onwards to Gravesend and Gillingham, introduced on 8/9 October 1993. That same night saw the revival of dormant route number N84, last used by the Victoria to Becontree Heath night service until its withdrawal after operating on 12/13 April 1984. This time around N84 was used to designate a new all-night bus service between Trafalgar Square and Nunhead.

Route number NX1 was uniquely issued to identify the quasi-commercial Medway Night Express route to Gillingham, introduced on 19/20 October 1990.

N100 became the first three digit N-prefixed route number when it was issued to designate the formerly un-numbered New Year's Eve-only Central London Link on 31 December 1992/1 January 1993 and it continued in such annual usage up to 31 December 1998/1 January 1999. The first regular Nighter to bear a three digit route number was the N253 (Aldgate Bus Station – Euston Bus Station), upon its introduction on 3/4 September 1993.

London Regional Transport dismantled much of the former-London Transport all-night bus route numbering sequence, descending from route number N99, during the summer of 1995 to '. . . make the service even easier Night Bus Routes, where possible, have been based on the corresponding Day Routes, using the same numbers prefixed by an 'N'. In practice, almost-complete elimination of the London Transport-inspired route numbers spanned eleven years, having already started in 1991 and ending in 2002, during the TfL era.

The first Nighter to be re-numbered was historically significant route N94, which had originated as the LGOC's first motor bus-operated all-night bus route 94 (Cricklewood – Liverpool Street Station) introduced on 14/15 July 1913. Re-numbering of the N94, which shared a lengthy common section of routeing with daytime route 16 between Cricklewood and Marble Arch, to N16 on 18/19 January 1991 was as much a by-product of eliminating confusion for passengers using new daytime Acton Green route 94, which shared common routeing with the N94 between Trafalgar Square and Marble Arch, as it was of aligning route numbers 16 and N16.

Edgware garage's MCW Metrobus M 696 displayed recently adopted route number N 16 as it paused in Cockspur Street in the early hours of Sunday morning 3 March 1991. *Roy Waterhouse*

Table J
All-Night Bus Route Re-Numbering 18/19 January 1991 – 28/29 June 2002

Original Route Number	New Route Number	Date of Change
N1	N20	23/24 June 1995
N21	N91*	23/24 June 1995
N50	N23	21/22 May 1993
N59	N139	28/29 January 1994
N68	N77	18/19 August 1995
N70	N381	8/9 October 1999
N77	N1	28/29 July 1995
N81	N89	28/29 June 2002
N83	N243	24/25 November 1995
N84	N343	2/3 February 2001
{N86	{N71	{8/9 October 1993
{N71	{N171	{26/27 April 1996
N87	N155	18/19 August 1995
N88	N44	18/19 August 1995
N89	N207	11/12 October 1996
N90	N279	26/27 April 1996
N92	N43	23/24 June 1995
N94	N16	18/19 January 1991
N95	N15	14/15 July 1995
N96	N38	14/15 July 1995
N98	N25	14/15 July 1995
N99	N98	18/19 August 1995
{N78 {N109	{N109 {N159	{11/12 March 1994 {17/18 September 1999

* Route N21 (Cockfosters) largely absorbed into an extension of extant route N91.
Note: London Regional Transport and Transport for London regarded all original routes as having been withdrawn and replaced by new route contracts, mostly with elements of revised routeing.

As may be seen from Table J, the main thrust of route re-numbering was phased in on Friday nights, 23 June 1995 for north London, 14 July for north east London, 28 July for south east London and 18 August 1995 for south west London. The complete programme also involved some new route introductions, route extensions, frequency increases over busy sections of routes and, in some instances, better, faster and more direct links to and from central London were created. This network growth was partially offset by withdrawals over some sections of route, such as that of the N14 between Roehampton and Chessington from 18/19 August 1995, or the N95's section between Becontree Heath and Dagenham, which was not replaced by the N15 from 14/15 July 1995. Historically, the most significant loss was that of route N87's all-night service between Streatham and Tooting Broadway, from 18/19 August 1995, since that link had formed the southern loop of London County Council Tramways' cyclical all-night tram service to and from Victoria Embankment via Brixton and via Clapham as introduced on 17/18 July 1928, later numbered route 1 by the LPTB and which subsequently had been incorporated into LT's all-night bus route 287/N87. Other withdrawals reflected LRT's retreat from 'out-county' services, such as the N68 and N88 journeys to Banstead in Surrey, which last operated on 17/18 August 1995, and the N96's projection to Loughton and Debden in Essex, which last ran on 13/14 July 1995.

The all-night bus route re-numbering programme created one further route number anomaly in that route number N20, which had superseded N1 to designate the High Barnet Station service when it was projected to Barnet Church from 23/24 June 1995, so that N1 could be re-allocated to the Plumstead service from 28/29 July 1995, bore no relationship whatsoever to daytime bus route 20, which, at that time, operated between Walthamstow Central and Debden. Sub-series route numbers N50/N51, originally used to designate outbound and inbound journeys respectively on the King's Cross – Ladbroke Grove service when it started on 26/27 April 1985, and which later fell into disuse, were revived for new routes N50 (Oxford Circus – Ilford Broadway), introduced on 14/15 July 1995, and N51 (Trafalgar Square – Woolwich), introduced on 8/9 October 1993.

When Transport for London assumed powers, from 3 July 2000, it inherited from London Regional Transport an all-night bus route network across which all routes were numbered with an N-prefix with, in most instances, the route number indicating a shared common section of routeing with a correspondingly numbered daytime service. The few exceptions comprised route numbers N5, N20, N50, N81, N84 and N97, which bore no relationship to daytime bus routes of equivalent number. As detailed in Table J, Transport for London oversaw the penultimate and final re-numbering of routes from the London Transport-originated sequence of all-night bus route numbers descending from N99 when route number N84 became N343 on 2/3 February 2001 and N81 became N89 on 28/29 June 2002. This left just route number N97 (Trafalgar Square – Hammersmith) as the sole all-night bus route to have retained numerical continuity from the London Transport original sequence descending from N99.

When TfL had taken control nine all-night bus routes – N6, N12, N24, N37, N72, N94, N134, N139 and N140 – shared absolutely identical routeing between termini with daytime bus routes of equivalent number. The rapid expansion of the all-night bus route network in the first three years or so of TfL control – between 3 July 2000 and 29/30 August 2003 – saw the introduction of 42 new all-night bus routes, out of which total 30 routes, at their dates of introduction, formed 'seamless' 24-hour services between common termini with daytime bus routes. The remaining twelve new night routes shared common sections of routeing with daytime services of equivalent number. All these new routes were designated with an N-prefixed route number but hints of an ambivalent attitude within TfL to the continued blanket use of the 'N' route number prefix on 24-hour service corridors could be detected in some publicity material, such as that for new routes 148/N148 (Shepherd's Bush – Camberwell Green), introduced on 4/5 October 2002, for which the cover of the slimline timetable simply referred to 'New Route 148 – A Major New 24 Hour Bus service for Central London', although the timetable and map inside did differentiate between daytime 148 and all-night N148.

Route N96 had been projected beyond Chingford to give a nightly hourly frequency service to Loughton and Debden from 27/28 October 1989. London Forest's Leyland Titan T 303 was photographed loading passengers outside the National Gallery in Trafalgar Square for an Essex-bound journey on 1 January 1990. *Roy Waterhouse*

TfL announced that it was going to discontinue use of the N-prefix from three all-night bus routes – N108, N119 and N176 – from 14/15 November 2003 'as an experiment', to facilitate which the Penge terminus of the daytime 176 and (N)176 was standardised at the Pawleyne Arms. The experiment seemed to be something of a *fait accompli* following the announcement of a roll-out programme for dropping the N-prefix from almost all other 24-hour service routes during the first four months of 2004, as detailed in Table K. It should be noted that use of the N-prefixed route number identification was retained for internal use within TfL and contractor operators and that the daytime and all-night schedules of 24-hour routes continued to be compiled separately, as is still the case at the date of writing this book. Separate garage running number sequences (when used by contractor operators) continue to differentiate between daytime and all-night bus allocations.

Table K
24-hour Service Roll-Out – Loss of 'N' Route Number Prefix

Date	**Route Numbers**
14/15 November 2003	108, 119, 176
23/24 January 2004	12, 65, 72, 94, 148, 285
19/20 March 2004	27, 53, 75, 250, 264, 274, 453
26/27 March 2004	6, 58, 277
2/3 April 2004	14, 37, 85, 88, 93, 345
16/17 April 2004	23, 83, 105, 140, 214, 236, 266, 271, 341
23/24 April 2004	24, 134, 139, 149, 189, 242
30 April/1 May 2004	69, 369

Notes to Table K:
Note 1: Post 30 April/1 May 2004 the all-night elements of just two 24-hour services retained N-prefixed route numbers. These comprised:

Route N41 (Tottenham Hale Station – Archway Station). N-prefix presumably retained in anticipation of that route's future extension beyond Archway to Trafalgar Square, which became effective from 4/5 February 2005.

Route N101 (Wanstead Station – North Woolwich, Free Ferry). N-prefix presumably retained in anticipation of that route's imminent withdrawal which, after deferments, occurred following last night of operation on 16/17 September 2004.

Note 2: If TfL had maintained a consistent policy by continuing to identify with an N-prefixed route number all those all-night bus routes which followed a unique routeing then the all-night elements of 24-hour service routes 75 (Lewisham –Croydon) , as re-routed from 29/30 August 2003, and 250 (Brixton – Croydon), both of which followed different routeings from their numerically associated daytime services in Croydon in order to serve East Croydon Station at night only should have retained N-prefixed route numbers. The all-night element of route 75 was withdrawn after operation on 17/18 May 2007 whilst, at 30/31 August 2013, route (N)250 continued to follow a different night-time routeing in Croydon from the daytime 250.

Note 3: A further route numbering anomaly was created from 27/28 July 2007 when the night-time element of newly introduced 24-hour route 188 (Russell Square – North Greenwich Station) was excluded from Canada Water Bus Station as served by the daytime element of the 188. No route numbering differentiation between the daytime and night-time 188 was made upon the route's introduction and this anomalous route numbering practice continued at 30/31 August 2013.

Daytime route 134 and night-time N134 had formed a 24-hour service between common termini at Tottenham Court Road Station and North Finchley since 28/29 April 2000 when the N134 had been withdrawn from Trafalgar Square. Holloway garage running number 854 indicated that Metroline's Alexander President-bodied Volvo B7TL VPL 633 was one of ten buses allocated to the 12 minute weekend nights frequency of the (N)134 when photographed at Tottenham Court Road Station in the early hours of Saturday morning 2 April 2005. *Philip Wallis*

A certain *esprit de corps* exists within the ranks of all-night bus drivers and the loss of the distinguishing N-route number prefix from bus blind displays caused resentment amongst some drivers. It was not unusual to see N-prefixed route numbers still displayed by buses working the all-night elements of 24-hour services for at least a couple of years following the official discontinuance of the N-prefix, although this was dependent upon the retention of buses with appropriate blind displays at garages.

The long-established practice of night buses treating all bus stops as 'request' stops ended in November 2008, when TfL abolished the distinction between 'compulsory' and 'request' bus stops across its network. TfL's research had shown that passengers no longer generally distinguished between these two categories of bus stop. All bus stops are now served in the same manner, both in daytime and night-time; if intending passengers are waiting at a bus stop, they should not have to signal the driver to stop. Whereas, passengers onboard a bus are required to ring the bell to notify the driver of their intention to alight at the next bus stop. TfL believed that this essentially formalised what had evolved in practice.

Following the abolition of the N-route number prefix across 24-hour service corridors, all such future route introductions have simply displayed the same route number as the daytime service. The first all-night route to have been introduced without an N-prefix during the TfL era occurred when an all-night element was added to extant daytime route 390 (Marble Arch – Archway Station), to transform it into a 24-hour service, from 3/4 September 2004. Since then, most new all-night bus route introductions have created 24-hour service corridors, with both the daytime and all-night elements displaying identical route numbers. The first-ever addition of an 'N' route number prefix to a previously non-prefixed 24-hour route occurred from 30/31 August 2013 when the night-time element (only) of 24-hour route 205 (Paddington – Bow) was extended beyond Bow to Leyton and re-numbered N205.

Other all-night bus routes have, in general, retained an N-route number prefix, with the route number usually indicating numerical affinity with a daytime bus route which shares some common section of routeing. Between 2004 and 30/31 August 2013 only seven all-night bus routes have been introduced which bear an N-route number prefix – N64, N86, N109 (which absorbed elements of N159), N113, N136 (which absorbed elements of N36), N550 (which absorbed elements of N50) and N551. Over the same period six further Nighters lost their N-route number prefixes, due to either re-routeing or shortening to allow their incorporation into 24-hour service corridors. Those routes comprised N10 from 29/30 January 2010, N25 from 25/26 June 2004, N43 from 4/5 February 2005, N52 from 7/8 December 2012, N213 from 3/4 July 2009 and N243 from 2/3 September 2005.

Transport for London broke with previously-established all-night bus route numbering convention when the all-night element (only) of extant 24-hour route 65 (Ealing Broadway – Kingston) was extended a significant distance beyond Kingston to Chessington, from 3/4 July 2009 and continued to use route number 65 without an N-route number prefix.

Route numbers N550 and N551, introduced on 29/30 August 2008, started a new sequence of all-night bus route numbers. Since both routes follow unique night-time routeings it is possible that these route numbers may be precursors for a new route numbering sequence which may come to encompass, through re-numbering, route numbers N5, N20 and N97, whose routeings have no relationship or numerical affinity to daytime services, as well as any future new, similarly-qualified route introductions.

For the record, the following potential N-prefixed route numbers, derived from the London Transport Exective's numerically-descending sequence from N99, have never been issued by London Transport (Executive or Board), London Regional Transport or Transport for London up until 30/31 August 2013 – N4, N32, N33, N34, N39, N40, N42, N45, N46, N48, N49, N57 – although (N)33 and (N)57 did come into use during the TfL era.

The Route Number That Never Was: The night-time element of route 220 had been introduced on 21/22 October 2005 when it formed a 24-hour service between Willesden Junction Station and Wandsworth with pre-existing daytime route 220. The night-time element has never been designated with an 'N' route number prefix but clearly at least one N220 blind had been made up as displayed by Shepherd's Bush garage's Alexander ALX400-bodied TransBus Trident TLA 17 when photographed at Garratt Lane, Wandsworth in the early hours of Sunday morning 20 January 2008. The other two Tridents allocated to the route on that night displayed plain 220 route numbers. *Philip Wallis*

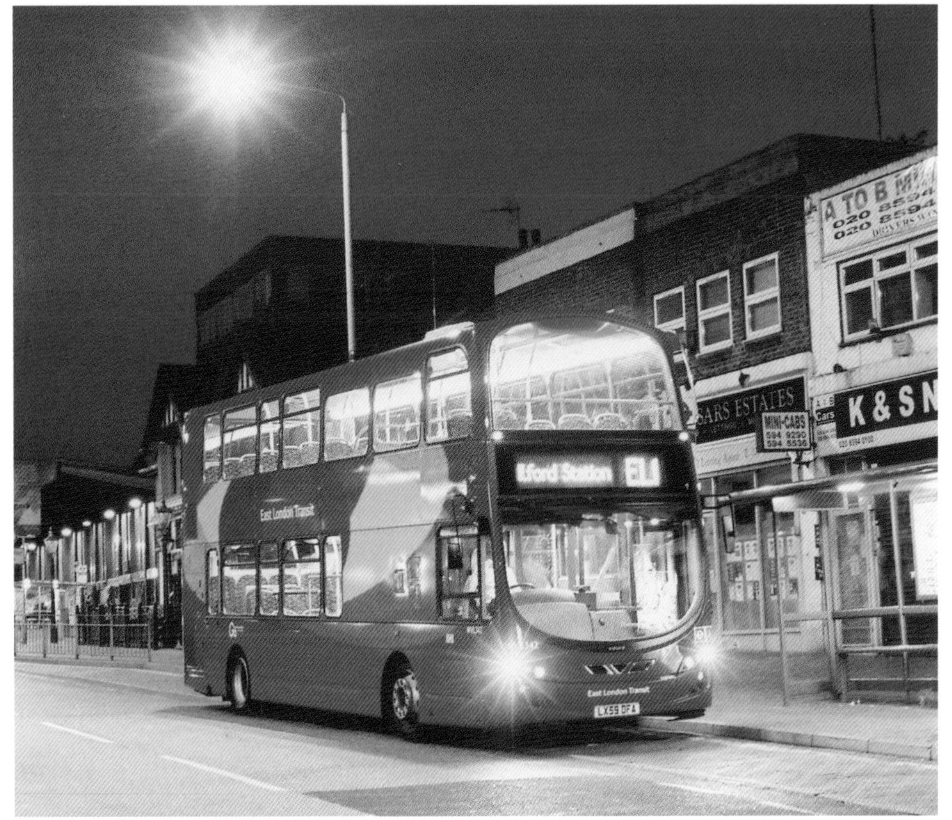

Transport for London has expanded the density of the capital's Night Bus network and much increased the number of 24-hour routes. The (N)344 was introduced from 10/11 November 2006 when it formed a 24-hour service with pre-existing daytime route 344. It provided the first ever night-time bus link between Vauxhall and Elephant & Castle as well as the first modern-time night bus service across Southwark Bridge. Travel London's Dennis Trident 9819, displaying night-time Battersea garage running number 77 in its windscreen, was photographed at Clapham Junction, Meyrick Arms early on Sunday morning 30 September 2007. *Philip Wallis*

Go-Ahead Blue Triangle's Wrightbus-bodied Volvo B9TL WVL 342 carried garage code and running number BE 122 which indicated that it was one of two buses from Rainham garage allocated to the night-time element of 24-hour East London Transit route EL1 when photographed near Barking Station early on Tuesday morning 20 July 2010. *Philip Wallis*

CHAPTER 3
SERVICE FREQUENCIES

Route N18 had developed from a modest three return journeys service upon its introduction from 13/14 April 1984 to give an hourly Sunday to Thursday night and 30 minute Friday and Saturday night service between central London and Harrow with five journeys further projected to Stanmore and three to Watford Junction Station from 27/28 October 1989. Westbourne Park garage's MCW Metrobus M 1051 was photographed in Cockspur Street. *Mike Harris*

London Transport Executive

London Transport applied nominal nightly hourly clock face headways to the majority of all-night bus routes upon the expansion of the network from 13/14 April 1984. In practice a number of such routes, including the N2, N11, N13, N79, N83, N92, N93 and Inter-Station Route had two-hour gaps in service at some stage in the night in order to allow for crew relief-breaks – route N95 had a 90 minute interval in service for similar purpose. Certain other routes had journeys foreshortened in order to provide for crew relief-break time. For example, route N29 (Trafalgar Square – Enfield Town) had hourly departures from Trafalgar Square between 00.20 and 06.20 but the 02.20 and 03.20 journeys terminated at Wood Green Station where the buses then went out of service so that crews could take their relief-breaks at Wood Green garage. The respective buses then re-entered service to form 03.43 and 04.43 departures from Wood Green Station to Trafalgar Square (the last departure at 06.20 from Trafalgar Square also went out of service at Wood Green).

Two routes had nightly nominal 30 minute frequencies. These comprised routes N78 (Victoria Station – South Croydon via Brixton) and N87 (Trafalgar Square – Streatham Garage via Clapham). These two routes replaced much of the pre-13/14 April 1984 route N87's 'figure of eight' loop working between Trafalgar Square and Tooting Broadway via Brixton and Clapham, which had worked to a 24 minute frequency in both directions around its loop.

Other new route introductions had wider headways or irregular schedules. New route N18 (Liverpool Street Station –Sudbury) comprised three nightly journeys of which only one reached Liverpool Street Station and two travelled out to Sudbury. The N18's timetable was co-ordinated with a much modified timetable over pre-existing route N91 (Liverpool Street Station – Willesden Garage) to give an hourly headway between Aldwych and Craven Park. Route N21 (Trafalgar Square – North Finchley) operated three nightly return journeys, one of which was truncated to run between Holborn Circus and North Finchley. Route N27 (Liverpool Street Station – Richmond) was given a nightly two hourly frequency which was co-ordinated with that of pre-existing route N97 (Liverpool Street Station – Heathrow Airport) to give a 30 minute headway over a lengthy common section of routeing between Liverpool Street Station and Kew Bridge Station.

Circuitous pre-existing route N80 continued to operate four nightly journeys between Potters Bar Garage and Finchley Garage to slightly modified timings to allow for its re-routeing via Oakwood Station from 13/14 April 1984. Route N99 (Chingford Station – Victoria & Albert Docks) maintained its pre-13/14 April 1984 timetable which comprised two journeys to Chingford Station (except on early Sunday mornings when one journey turned short at Chingford Mount) along with a once nightly bifurcation between Plaistow and Canning Town and short workings between Plaistow and Victoria & Albert Docks. Extant Special Night Journeys on route 9 between central London and Mortlake (one on Monday to Friday nights, two on Saturday nights) and 220 (one outbound journey from Willesden Junction to Tooting with return journey to Shepherd's Bush except Saturday nights) remained unchanged.

The N87 had always been one of London's highest frequency Night Bus routes with origins in all-night tram routes. Since 27/28 October 1989 it had operated a 30 minute Sunday to Thursday night and 15 minute Friday and Saturday night service between Trafalgar Square and Tooting Broadway with hourly projections onwards to both Streatham and Surbiton. M 257 was photographed outside Canada House in Trafalgar Square on Sunday morning 3 March 1991 just as Stockwell garage's allocation to the route was being changed to MCW Metrobus after around eight years of Fleetline operation. *Roy Waterhouse*

A notable feature of the expanded network's design was the co-ordination of timetables to give enhanced frequencies between points served by two or more all-night bus routes, albeit often with different intermediate routeings. Co-ordination between routes N18/N91 and N27/N97 has already been detailed. Routes N68 and N88 were co-ordinated to give a 30 minute headway between Trafalgar Square and Wandsworth. Routes N74 and N85 combined to form a 30 minute headway between Trafalgar Square and Bromley Road, Downham Way. The timetables of routes N29 and N90 were co-ordinated to give a 30 minute headway between Trafalgar Square and Manor House Station, further supplemented by occasional N21 journeys. Routes N76 and N98 offered passengers a combined 30 minute frequency service between Trafalgar Square and Stratford. Liverpool Street Station terminating routes N11, N14, N27 and N97 shared co-ordinated timetables which gave a 15 minute frequency service out to Fulham Broadway for much of the night. The highest co-ordinated service frequency of 10 minutes was achieved between Trafalgar Square and New Cross Gate by a combination of routes N74, N77, N85 and N86.

London Transport only introduced one further new all-night bus route following the network's expansion from 13/14 April 1984. This occurred on Sunday night/ Monday morning 13/14 May 1984 when the Railair Link, under contract to British Rail, first operated. Its service comprised one nightly outbound departure from Euston Station which ran non-stop to Victoria Station and thence non-stop to Heathrow Airport, Terminal 3. The return journey from Heathrow operated non-stop to Euston Station. The final journey comprised a non-stop run from Euston to Victoria Station.

London Regional Transport

By the time London Regional Transport assumed powers from 29 June 1984 increased passenger demand for all-night bus travel at weekends had manifested itself. Unscheduled duplicate buses were hastily brought into use to supplement the scheduled service by offering additional capacity to meet surges in demand. Unscheduled duplicate buses were recorded as having been in use on Friday and Saturday nights on routes N2, N29 and N90 by July 1984. Their use became extended to routes N89 and N97 from 26/27 October 1984 and to routes N13, N78 and N82 by 9/10 August 1985. At various dates during 1985 such unscheduled duplicate bus allocations were incorporated into enhanced route timetables whilst certain other routes also gained increased Friday and Saturday night bus allocations. A tipping point in meeting increased weekend nights passenger demand was reached when schedules effective from 1/2 November 1985 required an allocation of 106 buses on Friday and Saturday nights which was 27% higher than the Sunday to Thursday nights allocation of 86 buses. By or from this date routes N2, N13, N89, N90, and N94 worked to 30 minute frequencies on Friday and Saturday nights over sections of their routes – Heathrow Airport route N97 had earlier gained a nightly 30 minute frequency between Liverpool Street Station and Brentford when it absorbed much of withdrawn Richmond route N27's service from 26/27 April 1985.

Some new routes introduced between 1984 and 1988 maintained nightly hourly clock face frequencies. Such routes comprised the N50/N51 which, as detailed in Chapter 2, absorbed the Inter Station Route from 26/27 April 1985, the N47 (Victoria Station – Bromley South Station) introduced on 1/2 November 1985 and which replaced elements of withdrawn route N74, the N59 over its section of route between Trafalgar Square and Watford Junction Station when introduced from 20/21 June 1986, and the N8 which in its original form, upon introduction from 12/13 August 1988, operated between Queensbury Station and Bow Church. Route N72 (Victoria Station –Dartford) was introduced from1/2 November 1985 with a two hourly frequency which was co-ordinated with two hourly route N82 (then running out to Thamesmead) to give an hourly headway between Trafalgar Square and Shooters Hill.

Despite the immediacy of the Oxford Report, with one of its main tenets emphasising the importance of regular clock face headways to passengers, London Regional Transport introduced five irregular frequency all-night bus routes during its first 3¼ years of existence.

Route N60, introduced on 26/27 October 1984, operated four nightly round trips from and back to Clapham Common Station over a unidirectional 'figure of eight' route via Streatham and West Croydon. The N60 replaced former privately-operated staff bus journeys and also helped with the transfer of Streatham garage crews to Clapham garage for the duration of the closure of Streatham garage for re-building work. The N60 was withdrawn after operating on 5/6 February 1987 upon the completion of such work. Route N56, introduced from 26/27 April 1985, has been described in Chapter 2 under the account of the Inter-Station Route.

Irregular frequency route N54 was introduced on 20/21 June 1986 at the request of the London Borough of Sutton. The N54 operated between East Croydon Station and Banstead Village via Roundshaw, Wallington and Sutton. Its nightly schedule offered four departures from East Croydon Station, with some journeys terminating at Sutton, and two departures from Banstead Village. The contemporary timetable advertised connections on certain journeys at Sutton with London-bound N68 or N88 journeys. Route N54 last operated on Thursday night/Friday morning 21/22 May 1987. It was replaced from the following night by bifurcated projections of route N88 between Sutton and East Croydon (four journeys nightly) and between Sutton and Banstead (two journeys nightly).

Sutton garage's Leyland Fleetline D 2616 was seen in Banstead Village on Thursday morning 26 June 1986. *Mike Harris*

Romford North Street garage's Leyland Titan T 570 was seen at Cranham's Moor Lane terminus early on Saturday morning 9 August 1986 during the inaugural night of route N99's operation. *Paul Davis*

Route N99 (second-time use of this route number) was London Regional Transport's first Friday and Saturday nights-only Nighter when introduced on 8/9 August 1986 and worked from Romford North Street garage with an allocation of one T-type Leyland Titan. The N99 operated between Romford Market to Cranham with more or less hourly outbound departures between 01.07 and 05.03 although the 02.12 journey only ran as far as Upminster Station. All outbound journeys offered connection at Romford Station with route N98 buses arriving from central London. Route N99 last operated in this form on the night of 31 January/1 February 1987 after which the service was suspended. Operation of route N99 resumed on 27/28 March 1987 under an LRT contract awarded to Ensignbus. The N99 continued to operate between Romford Market and Cranham on Friday and Saturday nights only but as a reduced outbound-only service with departures from Romford Market at 23.46. 00.16 and 01.01. Connections were no longer afforded with N98 journeys from central London since the first such bus did not arrive at Romford Station until 01.59. Route N99 was back-projected to start from Chadwell Heath, Wangey Road from 8/9 January 1988. It remained a unidirectional service with departures to Cranham via Romford timed at 23.36, 00.06 and 00.52 on Friday and Saturday nights. The N99, by then operated by Ensign Citybus, was withdrawn after operation on 7/8 September 1991.

A dedicated nightly all-night service and allocation of one M-type MCW Metrobus from Ponders End (Enfield) garage was added to extant daytime Monday to Saturday route 279 (Smithfield – Waltham Cross) and Sunday route 279A (Liverpool Street Station – Waltham Cross) from Friday night/Saturday morning 25/26 September 1987. The core all-night service over routes 279/279A comprised four irregularly-timed journeys between Ponders End Garage and Upshire via Waltham Cross and Waltham Abbey but some journeys originated from or continued to Liverpool Street Station, Smithfield or Islington on certain nights of the week. The all-night service on the 279/279A absorbed the single nightly inbound route N90 journey which had double-run between Waltham Cross and Waltham Abbey. Operation of an all-night service on routes 279/279A continued until 30/31 January 1992 after which it was withdrawn without replacement although the frequency of route N90 was enhanced from the following night with an increased allocation of one bus nightly from Ponders End garage.

The trend towards increased frequencies on Friday and Saturday nights continued during 1986 and 1987 when enhanced weekend-night frequencies were applied to sections of routes N18, N29, N68, N92, N93, N95 and N96. The Trafalgar Square – Clapham Common leg of route N87 became the first section of an LRT Nighter to gain a 15 minute frequency on Friday and Saturday nights from 24/25 October 1986. The Trafalgar Square – Hammersmith section of route N97 was similarly enhanced from 25/26 September 1987. By 20/21 November 1987 the Friday and Saturday nights allocation of 130 buses to all-night routes was 35% higher than the Sunday to Thursday nights allocation of 96 buses. This scale of proportionate differential between weekend and Sunday to Thursday night allocations would be maintained over successive years.

New route introductions since the all-night bus route network's expansion on 13/14 April 1984 had been on a piecemeal basis, often just one route at a time. The first major expansion of the network since that date occurred in autumn 1989 when twelve new routes were introduced whilst a number of extant routes were modified or projected to new destinations.

Regular operation over route N73 was introduced on 22/23 September 1989 with a nightly hourly frequency service between Trafalgar Square and Walthamstow Central Station, two journeys of which originated from Victoria Station.

Ten further all-night bus routes were introduced on Friday night/Saturday morning 27/28 October 1989, seven of which had nightly hourly frequencies over their core sections of route. These seven comprised routes N1 (Aldwych – High Barnet Station), N3 (Marble Arch – Beckenham Junction Station, which replaced the Trafalgar Square – West Dulwich section of N59), N5 (Aldwych – Edgware Station) and N53 (Trafalgar Square – Erith) – these four routes also had crew relief-break journeys in service to and from Victoria Station – along with cross-London routes N6 (Walthamstow Central Station – Willesden Garage, which replaced the Oxford Circus – Willesden Garage section of N79), N12 (Dulwich – Shepherd's Bush Green) and N19 (Finsbury Park Stn – Clapham Junc).

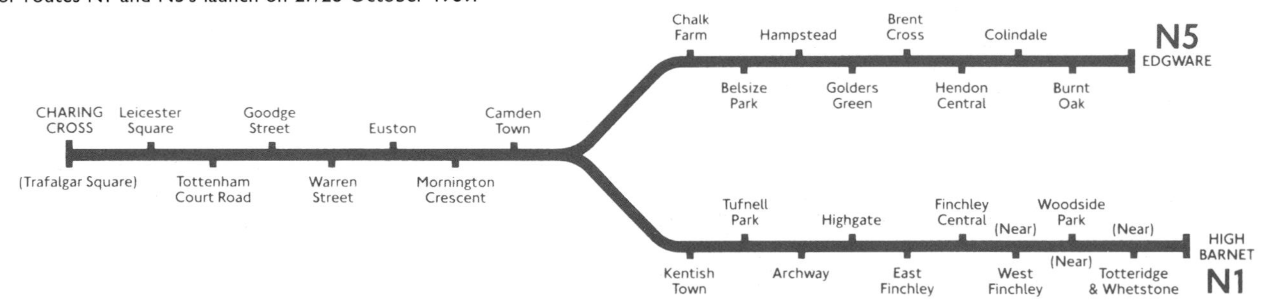

Diagrammatic Underground-style map included in publicity material for routes N1 and N5's launch on 27/28 October 1989.

Orpington became linked into LRT's all-night bus route network for the first time with the introduction of three nightly journeys on new route N62 from Victoria Station via Sidcup as well as by the hourly bifurcated projection of extant route N47 beyond Bromley South Station via either Petts Wood or Farnborough.

New route N69 comprised four nightly journeys between Trafalgar Square and Norwood Junction (two of which originated from Victoria Station). The N69's timetable was co-ordinated with that of the N78 (with which it shared a joint allocation from Brixton garage and which had earlier, from 22/23 May 1987, been projected to form a marathon 1½ hour journey time route between Victoria Station and New Addington via Croydon, Purley and Sanderstead) to give an approximate 20 minute headway between Trafalgar Square and Streatham Common.

New route N70 operated to an hourly frequency on Friday and Saturday nights only. The N70 ran in parallel with route N47 (except for the N70's routeing via Rotherhithe) and timetables of both routes were co-ordinated to give a 30 minute headway over the N70's entire route length between Trafalgar Square and Bromley South Station via Lewisham on weekend nights.

Significant route changes from 27/28 October 1989 included the formation of an Isle of Dogs loop on route N8 (irregular headway), the bolstering of route N77's service to give a nightly hourly frequency to Thamesmead, partially in replacement of route N82 which was much reduced to become a Friday and Saturday nights only service between Trafalgar Square and either Welling Corner (two journeys) or Woolwich Arsenal Station (two journeys) and the nightly hourly projection of route N87 beyond Raynes Park Station to give the first all-night bus service to New Malden, Tolworth, Hook and Surbiton. Frequency gains included a 15 minute Friday and Saturday night headway over the Trafalgar Square – Crystal Palace section of route N2 and a nightly 30 minute headway between Trafalgar Square and Edgware Station on the N94.

In its original form upon introduction from 11/12 November 1989 innovatory single-deck bus-operated route N31 (Camden Town – Fulham Broadway) ran every 30 minutes for just three hours on Friday and Saturday nights with buses in service at any point along the route only between 23.41 and 02.41. The N31 was expanded from 17/18 July 1992 to run later journeys on Friday and Saturday nights. Operation on Sunday to Thursday nights was also introduced from this date to a 90-minute frequency (worked by one bus).

Route N47 became jointly operated by London Central from New Cross and Peckham garages and by Selkent from Catford garage upon its projection to Orpington from 27/28 October 1989. The latter garage's Leyland Titan T 728 was photographed outside Canada House in Trafalgar Square loading passengers on the inaugural night of the N47's service to Orpington. *Roy Waterhouse*

1990 witnessed the introduction of three further LRT-sponsored all-night bus routes, two of which crossed the Greater London boundary to reach destinations in Kent and Surrey.

Route N67 first operated on 5/6 January 1990 and linked central London with Staines in Surrey. The N67 operated on Friday and Saturday nights only with hourly departures from Trafalgar Square at 24.00, 01.00, 02.00 and 03.00. The inbound service comprised garage journeys from both Hounslow and Shepherd's Bush (routes N67/N97 shared a co-ordinated timetable and bus allocations) and three departures from Staines at 01.35, 03.35 and 04.35 – this latter journey went out of service at Shepherd's Bush Garage. The N67 was extended from 17/18 July 1992 to operate beyond Staines to Egham (five outbound and three inbound journeys on Friday and Saturday nights) and also expanded to give a service on Sunday to Thursday nights between central London and Lower Feltham (four journeys). Route N67 last operated on 24/25 February 1994 after which its service was partially replaced by a bifurcated projection of route N97 to Sunbury Cross.

Route N9 (first-time use of this route number) was introduced from 9/10 February 1990. The N9's service of two nightly return journeys was complementary to and co-ordinated with established route N29 between Trafalgar Square and Palmers Green, Triangle. The N9 then followed the line of daytime route 121 via Aldermans Hill, Southgate Station, Chase Road, Oakwood Station, Enfield Road, Slades Hill and Windmill Hill to reach its terminus at Enfield Town, Cecil Road. A seperate nightly N9 journey departed from Palmers Green at 05.00 and travelled via Edmonton and Lower Edmonton to Ponders End Garage where, to meet requests for an early morning connection from the Waltham Cross area to Enfield Town, it connected with the 05.16 route 279 bus from Upshire. This N9 journey then continued via Enfield Town, Oakwood and Southgate to Wood Green Station where it made connections with a N29 bus to Victoria Station and a N83 bus to Trafalgar Square via Tottenham, before terminating at Turnpike Lane Station at 05.42. The bus then formed a return N9 departure at 05.50 which operated back to Ponders End Garage via Southgate, Oakwood and Enfield Town. The Friday and Saturday nights service on the N9 was enhanced from 31 January/1 February 1992 when an additional bus allocation allowed three return central London journeys on those nights of the week and additional outbound journeys were projected beyond Enfield Town to Ponders End Garage. Route N9 last operated on 24/25 June 1993 and its bus allocation from Palmers Green Garage was switched to route N29 giving an enhanced service on that route from the following night.

Quasi-commercial route NX1 was London Regional Transport's most ambitious night-time bus route to operate beyond the Greater London boundary. The NX1's Friday and Saturday nights service was introduced from 19/20 October 1990 and operated by London Central with a coach-seated double-deck Leyland Olympian. It linked central London with the Medway Towns in Kent. Two outbound departures were timed to depart from Trafalgar Square at 01.00 and 03.50 and took 90 minutes to reach the route's Gillingham terminus. The NX1 operated limited-stop between Trafalgar Square and Dartford and then observed all authorised bus stops via Greenhithe, Swanscombe, Northfleet, Gravesend, Chalk, Higham, Strood, Rochester and Chatham to Gillingham. The two corresponding return journeys departed from Gillingham at 02.35 and 05.25 but followed the outbound routeing only as far as Strood after which the Olympian hurried back to London non-stop along the A2 trunk road apart from one intermediate stop at Bexley, Black Prince (off the A2). The earlier of the return journeys then continued non-stop to Trafalgar Square whilst the later journey ran non-stop to New Cross Gate. The first outbound journey was back-projected to start from Victoria Station, Bus Station at 00.50 from 25/26 January 1991. Scheduling of lengthy route NX1 seemed particularly tight with only five minute layover periods at the Gillingham end and a ten minute layover at Trafalgar Square which would need to have incorporated boarding time. Route NX1 last operated on Saturday night/ Sunday morning 2/3 October 1993 after which much of its service was absorbed into new route N81 from the following weekend.

London United's MCW Metrobus M 1172 was photographed on arrival in Staines Bus Station in the early hours of Sunday morning 14 January 1990. *Roy Waterhouse*

Five new all-night bus routes were introduced in 1992. Two of these routes, the N26 (Victoria Station – Walthamstow Central Station) and third-time use of route number N99 (Trafalgar Square – Queensbury Station) were both introduced from 17/18 July and conformed to the then mainly prevailing nightly hourly frequency.

The core service of new Friday and Saturday nights-only route N65 (first-time use of this route number), also introduced on 17/18 July 1992, operated hourly between Trafalgar Square and Kingston. The N65 was a joint operation between London Northern and London United with each operator providing one bus. London Northern's allocation came from Holloway garage with that bus entering service from Archway Station at 00.35 and working through to Kingston via Trafalgar Square Its final journey of the night comprised a 06.26 departure from Kingston back to Archway Station with arrival at 07.40. Route N65's timetable was co-ordinated with that of route N92, also jointly operated by London United and London Northern, with a core service which operated hourly on a nightly basis between North Finchley and Kingston although through journeys operated in a northbound direction only (Kingston to North Finchley) since southbound journeys formed onward connections at Trafalgar Square with buses to Kingston. Buses which had arrived from North Finchley then continued in service to Victoria Station via Whitehall where they went out of service for drivers' relief-break purpose. Joint operation of route N92 was dissolved from 26/27 March 1993 when London Northern assumed responsibility for the entire operation of that route. Thus much of south-west London's all-night bus routes became operated by buses based at garages in north London (Holloway) or Hertfordshire (Potters Bar). London United's allocation for Friday and Saturday nights route N65 was changed to Hounslow Garage from that same date. This led to the 04.00 N65 departure from Trafalgar Square operating a garage journey in service beyond Kingston (05.01) to Hounslow (05.30) over the route of daytime 111. Route N65 last operated on 19/20 February 1994 and the Trafalgar Square to Kingston section of route N92 was withdrawn after operation on 24/25 February 1994. Much of their routeing was replaced from Friday night/Saturday morning 25/26 February 1994 by new 30 minute frequency London United-operated route N9 (second-time use of this route number) from Trafalgar Square to Kingston.

What were arguably London's two oddest-ever all-night bus routes were introduced on 30/31 October 1992, both operated by Metroline.

Route N17 comprised a single outbound-only journey which departed at 02.25 on Saturday and Sunday mornings from Trafalgar Square bound for the north-western suburbs. The N17 ran in parallel with established route N18 as far as Harrow, after which it was routed via South Harrow, Rayners Lane Station and North Harrow to reach Pinner. The N17 continued beyond Pinner only 'if passengers are already on board' via Northwood and South Oxhey (in Hertfordshire) to terminate at Harrow Weald. A contemporary report indicated that for the first few weeks of the N17's operation drivers were instructed to follow the route's leg beyond Pinner, irrespective of whether any passengers were aboard the bus, in order 'to learn the route'.

Harrow Weald garage's MCW Metrobus M 968 was photographed loading homeward-bound New Year's revellers in Aldwych during the early hours Saturday morning 1 January 1994. *Mike Harris*

It would seem from publicity material that LRT hoped new route N66 would attract the custom of patrons of Ashton's night-club in Cricklewood and the 'Mean Fiddler' music venue in Harlesden. Route N66's service comprised one unidirectional journey early on Saturday, Sunday and Monday mornings which departed from Cricklewood Broadway, Ashton's at 02.25. The N66 bus then travelled via Willesden, Harlesden, Wembley, Preston Road, Kingsbury and Queensbury before terminating at Edgware Station at 03.07.

Neither route prospered, the N17 was withdrawn after operating on Sunday morning 23 January 1994 whilst the N66, because it had a Monday morning service, last ran in the early hours of 24 January 1994. The demise of routes N17 and N66 marked the end of the individual irregular frequency all-night bus route in London, although some outer sections of routes continued to have infrequent services. Particular examples included the inbound Isle of Dogs loop of route N8 (three journeys nightly, although the outbound frequency was hourly), the Banstead bifurcations of routes N68 (one journey nightly) and N88 (two journeys nightly) and the Ruislip leg of route N89 (two journeys nightly). In addition, there remained a host of Victoria-bound crew relief-break journeys in service, described in Chapter Two, as well as garage journeys in service on several routes.

Frequency increases had continued to reflect the burgeoning demand for Friday and Saturday night travel, such as when route N89's section of route between Trafalgar Square and Shepherd's Bush and route N29's section from Trafalgar Square to Wood Green both gained 15 min frequencies from 5/6 February and 25/26 June 1993 respectively.

Nine new all-night bus routes were introduced over the autumn and winter of 1993/1994. Three of these routes – N36 (Trafalgar Square – Grove Park Station), N84 (core service Trafalgar Square – Nunhead with two journeys to/from Oxford Circus) and N134 (Trafalgar Square – North Finchley) – had nightly hourly frequencies whilst a further three – N9 (Trafalgar Square – Kingston), N52 (Victoria Station – Willesden, Roundwood Park) and N253 (Aldgate – Euston) ran every thirty minutes nightly. A further pair of new routes N51 (Trafalgar Square – Woolwich) and N61 (Trafalgar Square – Sidcup) each operated every two hours and comprised the last Friday and Saturday nights-only routes to be introduced by LRT. New route N81 replaced both route N72's service to Dartford – and shaved 25 minutes off the journey time from central London because of its more direct routeing via Old Kent Road – as well as the Medway Towns service of route NX1. The N81 gave Gravesend in Kent a nightly service from central London for the first time – two journeys on Sunday to Thursday nights and four journeys on Friday and Saturday nights – although the onward service to Gillingham comprised one return journey early on Saturday and Sunday mornings.

That section of route N8 between Marble Arch and Queensbury was replaced by new route N99 from 17/18 July 1992 and the N8 was re-routed to terminate at Victoria Station. One week later Bow garage's Leyland Titan T 103 was seen at its new terminus early on Saturday morning 25 July 1992. The intermediate points blind displayed carried no reference to the N8's Isle of Dogs routeing which continued to operate until 13/14 July 1995 after which it was replaced by new route N50 from the following night. *Roy Waterhouse*

Demand for all-night bus travel had grown to the extent that by the issue of the November 1995 Night Bus Guide (effective from 24/25 November) twenty one routes had nightly 30 minute (or greater) frequencies over part or all of their route lengths whilst a further nine routes (including the Trafalgar Square – Eltham section of Foots Cray/Sidcup route N21 introduced on 28/29 July 1995) had their frequencies increased to 30 minutes on Friday and Saturday nights. Seventeen routes operated to hourly frequencies nightly (including new Oxford Circus to Ilford route N50 introduced on 14/15 July 1995) whilst route N70 (by this date a unidirectional circular service from Trafalgar Square via Surrey Quays and Peckham) ran hourly on Friday and Saturday nights only. The highest individual route frequency of 10 minutes on Friday and Saturday nights was achieved over the Trafalgar Square to Tooting Broadway section of Sutton route N155. 15 minute frequencies were applied over the Trafalgar Square to Craven Park section of route N18 (Friday and Saturday nights), the Trafalgar Square to Wood Green section of route N29 (Friday and Saturday nights), the Trafalgar Square to Shepherd's Bush section of route N89 (nightly), the Trafalgar Square to Hounslow section of route N97 (Friday and Saturday nights) and the Aldwych to Streatham section of route N109 (nightly). New LRT-contracted all-night bus routes introduced in 1996 and 1997 operated with hourly frequencies. These comprised route N176 (Oxford Circus – Penge), introduced on 26/27 April 1996 and which had its frequency increased to 30 minutes nightly from 13/14 November 1998, along with routes N35 (Trafalgar Square – Clapham Junction) and N37 (Peckham – Putney), both introduced from 25/26 April 1997. The N35's timetable was notable for its skew towards outbound journeys with four departures from Trafalgar Square at 01.05, 02.05, 03.05 and 04.05 but only three inbound departures from Clapham Junction at 01.06, 02.06 and 03.06 – this was because the first daytime route 35 bus set off from Clapham Junction at 04.10 bound for Shoreditch.

In 1999 London Regional Transport's policy moved closer towards the adoption of 30 minute frequencies on new all-night bus routes. This frequency was applied to routes N68 (Trafalgar Square – Purley), N94 (Piccadilly Circus – Acton Green), N72 (East Acton – Roehampton), and N24 (Pimlico-Hampstead Heath) introduced in that year. New route N28 (Camden Town – Wandsworth), introduced from 28/29 May, ran hourly on Sunday to Thursday nights and every 30 minutes on Friday and Saturday nights.

Metroline's TransBus President-bodied Volvo B7TL VP 329 was seen at Tottenham Court Road Station in the early hours of Saturday morning 7 June 2003. Route N24 had formed a 24-hour service with long-established daytime route 24 since its introduction on 26/27 November 1999 which was recognised in route numbering terms when N24 buses officially discontinued display of the 'N' route number prefix from 23/24 April 2004. The lorry in the background is evidence of the extensive street cleaning and rubbish collection activities carried out at night in central London. *Philip Wallis*

The year 1999 also witnessed the near-demise of 'out-county' routes which crossed the Greater London boundary into neighbouring counties. This type of route had been in decline since 1994 when route N18's service to Watford Junction had been cut after operation on 27/28 January. Further retractions of 'out-county' routes into Essex, Kent, Hertfordshire and Surrey had followed in 1995 and 1996 after which route N81's Friday and Saturday nights hourly service to Gravesend, with one return journey further projected to Gillingham, and route N279's nightly 30 minute frequency service to Waltham Cross (in Hertfordshire), with one nightly return journey further projected to Upshire (in Essex), remained the sole survivors of this route category. Kent journeys on route N81 last operated on 17/18 July 1999 after which the N81 was revised to become an hourly frequency service between central London and Bexleyheath from 23/24 July (London Central introduced commercially-operated routes N80/N82 into Kent from this same date – see Chapter 8). Route N279's Upshire journey last ran on 14/15 October 1999 but its service to Waltham Cross was retained, thereafter giving the N279 a unique status as the only 'out-county' London all-night bus route.

Route N70 (by then operating between Trafalgar Square and Norwood Junction) had been the last surviving LRT-contracted Friday and Saturday nights-only Nighter until its hourly frequency service operated form the last time on Saturday night/Sunday morning 2/3 October 1999. Much of the N70's service was incorporated into nightly 30 minute frequency route N381 (Trafalgar Square – Peckham) from 8/9 October.

The final new LRT-contracted all-night bus route N140 (Harrow Weald – Heathrow Airport) was introduced on 31 March/1 April 2000 with a 30 minute frequency service.

The continued growth in demand for the Nighters had led to repeated frequency increases on many routes. Examples of higher frequency routes at the end of London Regional Transport's control (2 July 2000) included:

N25: Oxford Circus – Ilford (30 minutes (Su-Th), 10 minutes (Fr-Sa) – Hainault (1 hour) or Harold Hill (1 hour). Allocation: 6 buses (Su-Th), 16 buses (Fr-Sa).

N29: Trafalgar Square – Wood Green (20 minutes (Su-Th), 8 minutes (Fr-Sa) – Enfield Town (20 minutes (Su-Th), 15 minutes (Fr-Sa) – Ponders End Garage (20/40 minutes (Su-Th), 30/45 minutes (Fr-Sa). Allocation: 8 buses (Su-Th), 17 buses (Fr-Sa).

N155: Aldwych – Colliers Wood (15 minutes (Su-Th), 10 minutes (Fr-Sa) – Sutton (30 minutes nightly). Allocation: 9 buses nightly.

N207: Holborn – Ealing (20 minutes (Su-Th), 10 minutes (Fr-Sa) – Hayes By-Pass (20 minutes nightly) – Uxbridge (1 hour nightly). Allocation: 10 buses (Su-Th), 15 buses (Fr-Sa).

Fifteen other routes had 15 minute frequencies over sections of their routeing, mainly on Friday and Saturday nights.

Enfield Garage's TransBus President-bodied DAF DB250LF DLP 87 was photographed at Tottenham Court Road Station in the early hours of Sunday morning 11 June 2006. This outbound bus stop has since been relocated about 300 yards further north along Tottenham Court Road. *Philip Wallis*

Transport for London

When Transport for London assumed control from 3 July 2000 fourteen all-night bus routes, along with the outer bifurcated sections of a further four such routes and the Hayes By-Pass to Uxbridge section of route N207 operated to hourly frequencies. Route N149 (Victoria Station – Edmonton Green), TfL's first new all-night bus route, also operated hourly when introduced on 18/19 August 2000. Most of these routes were upgraded to 30 minute frequencies between 2001 and 2003 and the bifurcated sections of two routes were withdrawn. This left just three routes (N28, N31, N37), the outer bifurcated sections of two routes (N8, N25) and the Hayes By-Pass – Uxbridge leg of the N207 with hourly frequencies.

London's surviving bifurcated all-night bus routes operated for the last time on Thursday night/Friday morning 24/25 June 2004. These comprised route N8 (Victoria Station – Newbury Park Station or Woodford Wells) and route N25 (Oxford Circus – Hainault or Harold Hill). The N8's hourly service to Woodford Wells was replaced by the projection of a 30 minute frequency service on route N55 from Oxford Circus from the following night whilst the N8's hourly section of route between Gants Hill and Newbury Park Station was abandoned. Route N8 itself was partially re-routed to give a 30 minute frequency service to Hainault, replacing much of the N25's bifurcated routeing to that destination. Route N25 was re-numbered (N)25, truncated to operate as a nightly 15 minute frequency service between Oxford Circus and Ilford and converted to operation by Mercedes-Benz Citaro bendy-buses. Route N25's hourly service to Harold Hill was replaced by new 30 minute frequency route N86 (second-time use of this route number) from Stratford.

Frequency of the Hayes By-Pass to Uxbridge section of route N207 was increased to 30 minutes from 8/9 April 2005. Route (N)37's frequency was increased to 30 minutes from 20/21 April 2007 coincident with that routes extension to form a Peckham to Putney Heath, Green Man service.

Routes N28 (Camden Town – Wandsworth) and N31 (Camden Town – Clapham Junction) have retained hourly frequencies on Sunday to Thursday nights, the only LBSL-contracted all-night bus routes with such frequencies at 30/31 August 2013. The pair of routes share a lengthy common section of routeing and co-ordinated timetables to give a 30 minute headway between Camden Town and Kensington High Street so that the N28's section of route beyond Kensington High Street to Wandsworth and the N31's to Clapham Junction remain the only true sections of all-night bus route to be served just once an hour on Sunday to Thursday nights. Both the N28 and N31 have 30 minute frequencies on Friday and Saturday nights.

Transport for London has adopted the 30 minute frequency as standard on almost all its new all-night and night-time element of 24-hour route introductions since route N214 (Liverpool Street – Highgate Village) was introduced on 1/2 September 2000. A few routes have been introduced with higher frequencies. Route N453 (Marylebone – Deptford Broadway) and (N)159 (Paddington Basin – Streatham) both had nightly 20 minute frequencies upon their introductions from 14/15 February 2003 and 27/28 August 2010 respectively whilst routes (N)36 (New Cross – Queens Park Station) and N136 (Oxford Circus – Chislehurst) both had 20 minute Friday and Saturday night frequencies upon their introduction from 8/9 February 2008 (each route ran every 30 minutes on Sunday to Thursday nights).

TfL's period of control has been characterised by growth of the all-night and night-time element of the 24-hour bus route network. This expansion has come through a combination of new route introductions and frequency increases on established routes, particularly along trunk routes from central London on Friday and Saturday nights. Suburban routes have generally retained nightly 30 minute frequencies.

Frequency reductions have indeed been rare but have happened occasionally, sometimes caused by an increase in

The copper covered barrel-vaulted roof structure of Newbury Park Bus Station, now a 'listed' building of architectural merit, was the setting for Bow garage's TransBus ALX400 Trident 17543s photographed there in the early hours of Sunday morning 25 April 2004. *Philip Wallis*

other services over particular route corridors – route N16 was reduced from 15 to 20 minutes nightly from 7/8 November 2003, route N2 from 15 to 20 minutes on Friday and Saturday nights from 1/2 April 2005, route (N)214 from 15 to 20 minutes on Sunday to Thursday nights from 19/20 August 2005, route N97 from 15 to 20 minutes on Sunday to Thursday nights and from 8/9 to 10 minutes on Friday and Saturday nights from 11/12 November 2005 and route N13 from 15 to 30 minutes on Sunday to Thursday nights and from 10 to 15 minutes on Friday and Saturday nights from 29/30 June 2012.

Examples of higher frequency all-night and night-time element of 24-hour bus routes at 30/31 August 2013 included:

(N)25: Oxford Circus – Ilford (8 minutes (Su-Th), 6 minutes (Fr-Sa). Allocation: 19 buses (Su-Th), 29 buses (Fr-Sa).

N29: Trafalgar Square – Wood Green (7½ minutes (Su-Th), 3/4 minutes (Fr-Sa) – Enfield Town (7½ minutes (Su-Th), 10 minutes (Fr-Sa). Allocation: 23 buses (Su-Th), 37 buses (Fr-Sa). Note: Route N29's Friday and Saturday night frequency of 18 buses per hour is higher than the Monday to Friday peak hour frequency of 15 buses per hour on daytime route 29 (Trafalgar Square – Wood Green).

N38: Victoria Station – Piccadilly Circus (12 minutes nightly) – Walthamstow Central Station (12 minutes (Su-Th), 6 minutes (Fr-Sa). Allocation: 15 buses (Su-Th), 26 buses (Fr-Sa).

N155: Aldwych – Morden (15 minutes (Su-Th), 8 minutes (Fr-Sa). Allocation: 11 buses (Su-Th), 20 buses (Fr-Sa).

N207: Holborn – Hayes By-Pass (15 minutes (Su-Th), 7½ minutes (Fr-Sa) – Uxbridge (30 minutes nightly). Allocation: 10 buses (Su-Th), 21 buses (Fr-Sa).

Fourteen other central-London serving Nighters had 10 or 12 minute frequencies over sections or all of their routes on Friday and Saturday nights, often matched with a 15 minute (but sometimes 20 or 30 minute) frequency on Sunday to Thursday nights.

London's highest frequency and highest allocation Night Bus route N29 has been predominantly operated by hybrid-powered buses since July 2013. Wood Green garage's Wrightbus Eclipse Gemini 2-bodied Volvo B5LH HV 102 was photographed at Tottenham Court Road Station in the early hours of Wednesday morning 10 July 2013.
Philip Wallis

Crew Shift Patterns

Crew shift patterns were influenced for many years by one of the terms negotiated between the London Passenger Transport Board and the Trades Unions to settle the May 1937 strike by Central Bus crews. This was an agreement not to extend joint compilation of service schedules on Central Buses which meant that bus crews could not be made to work on more than one route during a shift. This arrangement was particularly attractive to crews on comparatively short-duty period all-night bus routes. Night bus crews worked a six night week with every Saturday night off duty when most all-night bus routes did not operate. Crews generally worked either a straight six hour shift without meal break or a full shift with a minimum 40 minute meal break. Some crews worked the same shift all the time. This arrangement created a high wage cost for all-night rosters and taken together with no crew cover on Saturday nights may have acted as an inhibitory factor in the development of all-night bus services for many years to come.

A five day (or night) working week was implemented from late 1966 as part of the settlement of an industrial dispute on London Transport's Central Buses earlier that year. Friday and Saturday nights became the two rest nights but, by local arrangement, night bus crews worked Friday nights as overtime. One effect was to make night bus crews some of the highest paid staff on the fleet and the job became even more sought after as some shifts only involved about 5½ hours work per night.

Changes to the long established pattern of crew duty compilation on all-night bus routes were influenced by the adoption of near-universal Saturday night/Sunday morning operation across the Nighters from 29/30 October 1983 after which services ran on all seven nights of the week, the network's expansion from 13/14 April 1984 and the spread of one-person operation. The major restructuring of day bus routes in central London, particularly so between 1989 and 1992, resulted in later last journeys on daytime routes and a shorter operating period for all-night bus routes. These factors combined with London Regional Transport's preparations for privatisation and route tendering in the late 1980s and led to changes in crew scheduling and union agreements. Most significantly, joint compilation of route schedules was no longer proscribed.

Scheduling practice at 30/31 August 2013 varies across different operating companies. Some duties are scheduled such that the driver might work part of a shift on a daytime route (late evening/early morning) and part on an all-night route. For example, a driver working a shift from, say, 21.30 to 05.30 might spend the first two to three hours on a day route and the remaining four to five hours on a night route. Some companies and garages continue to have dedicated night crews who only work night duties.

CHAPTER 4
THE APRIL 1984 PROGRAMME: EXTANT ROUTES

New routes and route changes on the Night Bus network increased enormously from and after 13/14 April 1984. This chapter lists the night routes already in place at 13/14 April 1984 and changes to those routes up to 30/31 August 2013.

Inter-Station Route
13/14 April 1984: Operated Sa-Su: **Waterloo Station – Waterloo Station** via Victoria Station, Paddington Station, Euston Station, St Pancras Station, King's Cross Station, St Pancras Station again, Euston Station. Allocation: New Cross Garage 1 T (crew-operated).
21/22 April 1985: Last night of operation. Elements of Inter-Station Route incorporated into N50/N51/N56 from 26/27 April 1985.

Route 9 (Special Night Journeys)
13/14 April 1984: Special Night Journeys (1 M-Fr, 2 Sa) on daytime route 9. Operated: **Liverpool Street Station/Mansion House Station – Mortlake, Avondale Road** via Ludgate Circus, Aldwych, Trafalgar Square, Piccadilly Circus, Hyde Park Corner, Kensington, Hammersmith, Barnes. Allocation: Stamford Brook Garage 1 RM (M-Fr), 2 RM (Sa).
26/27 October 1994: Route 9's SNJs co-ordinated with timetable for route N93 in order to maintain an even headway Ludgate Circus – Hammersmith.
26/27 April 1985: M-Fr and earlier of the Sa SNJs absorbed into the timetable of N93 upon that route's extension Hammersmith – Fulwell. 1 Sa SNJ continued to operate: Liverpool Street – Ludgate Circus (01.32) – Trafalgar Square (01.38) – Mortlake, Avondale Road (02.14). Allocation: Stamford Brook Garage 1 RM (Sa).
18/19 September 1987: Last night of operation.

Route N29
13/14 April 1984: Operated: **Trafalgar Square – Enfield Town, Little Park Gardens** via Piccadilly Circus, Shaftesbury Avenue, Tottenham Court Road (outbound), Gower Street (inbound), Camden Town, Holloway, Finsbury Park, Manor House, Turnpike Lane Station, Wood Green, Palmers Green, Winchmore Hill. Allocation: Wood Green Garage 2 M (crew-operated) nightly. By July 1984: Additional bus allocated Fr-Sa as unscheduled duplicate.
1/2 February 1985: Converted to one-person operation. Frequency increased to 1 hr nightly with additional buses Fr-Sa 'in accordance with demand'. Allocation: Wood Green Garage 3 M (Su-Th), 4 M (Fr-Sa). Fr-Sa allocation increased to 5 M and frequency to 30 min by March 1987, with very substantial subsequent frequency increases transforming the service to every 3½ minutes between Trafalgar Square and Wood Green on Friday and Saturday nights by 2011 – more frequent than many daytime routes.
1 April 1989: **Leaside Buses** commenced trading.
9/10 February 1990: One early am jny projected Trafalgar Square – Victoria Station via Whitehall. Allocation unchanged. Now operated: **Victoria Station, Bus Station – Enfield Town, Little Park Gardens**.
25/26 June 1993: Certain jnys projected Enfield Town – Ponders End, Bus Garage. Now operated: **Victoria Station, Bus Station – Ponders End, Bus Garage.** 1 daily am inbound jny operated Edmonton Green (05.18) via Ponders End and Enfield to Victoria (06.24). Allocation: Palmers Green Garage 1 M (Su-Th), 2 M (Fr-Sa), Wood Green Garage 3 M (Su-Th), 5 M (Fr-Sa).
29 September 1994: Operated by **Cowie Leaside**.
31May/1 June 1996: Allocation: Wood Green Garage 4 M (Su-Th), 7 M (Fr-Sa).

Opposite Three Hestair Dennis Dominators were included in the evaluation trials conducted from Stockwell Garage between March 1984 and August 1986 to determine London's next generation of double-deck buses. H 1 was photographed along Clapham Road whilst working an inbound N87 journey on Sunday morning 15 June 1986. *Mike Harris*

Below The vicinity of Tottenham Court Road Station forms an important hub for central London-serving Night Bus routes. Arriva London North's Wrightbus-bodied Volvo B7TL VLW 22 was seen heading up a line of Night Buses outside the Centrepoint building on Saturday morning 19 February 2005. Use of this particular bus stop has since been discontinued. *Philip Wallis*

25/26 April 1997: Section of route Victoria – Trafalgar Square withdrawn. Early am jny ex Edmonton Green withdrawn. Re-routed Trafalgar Square – Cambridge Circus via Charing Cross Road. Regular service to Ponders End established. Now operated: **Trafalgar Square – Ponders End, Bus Garage.** Allocation: Wood Green Garage 9 M (Su-Th), 14 M (Fr-Sa).

2 April 1998: Operated by **Arriva London North**.

19/20 May 2000: Allocation: Wood Green Garage 8 M (Su-Th), 17 M (Fr-Sa). By November 2000 allocation included low-floor DLA-type DAF DB250LF.

27/28 April 2001: Allocation: Wood Green Garage 15 M/DLA (Su-Th), 24 M/DLA (Fr-Sa).

October 2001: Completion of conversion to low-floor bus at Wood Green Garage 15 DLA/DLP (Su-Th), 24 DLA/DLP (Fr-Sa).

January 2002: Allocation now DLA/DLP/VLW-types.

13/14 January 2006: Converted to articulated single-deck low-floor Mercedes-Benz Citaro bendy bus. Section of route Enfield Town – Ponders End withdrawn. Now operated: **Trafalgar Square – Enfield Town, Little Park Gardens** via Charing Cross Road, Tottenham Court Road (outbound), Gower Street (inbound), Camden Town, Holloway, Finsbury Park, Manor House, Turnpike Lane Station, Wood Green, Palmers Green, Winchmore Hill. Allocation: Edmonton Garage 15 MA (Su-Th), 24 MA (Fr-Sa).

27 August 2010: Arriva acquired by Deutsche Bahn.

25/26 November 2011: Re-converted to double-deck bus operation. Re-allocated to Wood Green Garage 23 DW/VLW (Su-Th), 37 DW/VLW (Fr/Sa).

c. February 2012: Allocation from Wood Green Garage now mixed T-type AD E40D – AD Enviro 400 and DW-type Wrightbus Gemini 2DL integral.

By 8/9 July 2013: Predominantly operated by Volvo B5LH hybrid (started April 2013). Allocation: Wood Green Garage 23 HV/DW (Su-Th), 37 HV/DW (Fr-Sa).

Routes N68 (via Wandsworth), N77 (Tolworth), N87 (Kingston)

13/14 April 1984: **N68** converted to one-person operation. Ludgate Circus – Farringdon Street bifurcation withdrawn. Now operated: **Liverpool Street Station – Wandsworth, Wandsworth Plain** via Bank, Ludgate Circus, Aldwych, Trafalgar Square, Whitehall, Millbank, Lambeth Bridge, Vauxhall, Wandsworth Road, Clapham Junction. Allocation: Wandsworth Garage 1 M nightly.

26/27 April 1985: Projected Wandsworth – Sutton. Now operated: **Liverpool Street Station – Sutton Station** via Bank, Ludgate Circus, Aldwych, Trafalgar Square, Whitehall, Millbank, Lambeth Bridge, Vauxhall, Wandsworth Road, Clapham Junction, Wandsworth, Wimbledon Park, Wimbledon, South Wimbledon, Morden, St Helier. Wandsworth Garage jnys. Allocation: Wandsworth Garage 2 M (Su-Th), 2 M + 1 M (joint N88) (Fr-Sa).

9/10 August 1985: Section of route Liverpool Street – Ludgate Circus withdrawn. Now operated: **Ludgate Circus – Sutton Station**. Wandsworth Garage jnys. Allocation unchanged.

10/11 July 1987: Projected Ludgate Circus – Farringdon Street. Bifurcation to Sutton Garage introduced. Wandsworth Garage jnys withdrawn. Now operated: **Farringdon Street, Stonecutter Street – Sutton Station *or* Sutton Garage.** Jnys to Wandsworth Plain, 1 jny from Clapham Junction, Meyrick Arms. Vehicle-type change to Fleetline. Joint allocation with N88 (Fr-Sa) dissolved. Re-allocated to Sutton Garage 2 D (Su-Th), 3 D (Fr-Sa).

31 Oct/1 Nov 1987: One nightly dep only Banstead via Belmont to Sutton and thence line of route to Trafalgar Square introduced. Now

operated: **Farringdon Street, Stonecutter Street – Sutton Station *or* Sutton Garage *or* Banstead, Victoria.** Allocation unchanged. Note: Positioning jny for Banstead dep worked Sutton – Banstead as Surrey County Council tendered route 522.

1 April 1989: **London General** commenced trading.

4/5 March 1990: Su jny Sutton, Marshalls Road – Banstead, Victoria introduced. M-Sa positioning jny Sutton – Banstead continued to operate as Surrey County Council route 522.

By 13/14 Dec 1991: Completion of progressive vehicle-type change to Metrobus at Sutton Garage 2 M (Su-Th), 3 M (Fr-Sa).

By June 1993: Joint allocation N68/N88 reinstated at Sutton Garage 5 M (Su-Th), 6 M (Fr-Sa).

1/2 September 1993: Surrey County Council M-Sa positioning jny Sutton – Banstead re-numbered 520. Su night positioning jny continued to operate as N68.

2 November 1994: London General acquired by management/ employee buy-out.

18/19 August 1995: **Re-numbered N77.** Sections of route Farringdon Street – Trafalgar Square, Wimbledon – Sutton *or* Banstead, Wandsworth Plain and Clapham Junction jnys withdrawn. Projected Wimbledon – Tolworth. Re-routed via Vauxhall Bridge. Now operated: **Trafalgar Square – Tolworth, Ewell Road** via Whitehall, Millbank, Vauxhall Bridge, Vauxhall, Wandsworth Road, Clapham Junction, Wandsworth, Wimbledon Park, Wimbledon, Raynes Park, New Malden, Norbiton, Kingston, Surbiton. Joint allocation N68/N88 dissolved. Re-allocated to Stockwell Garage 4 M nightly.

26/27 April 1996: Projected Trafalgar Square – Aldwych. Now operated: **Aldwych – Tolworth, Ewell Road**. Allocation: Stockwell Garage 5 M nightly.

24 May 1996: Operated by Go-Ahead group t/a **London General**.

28/29 November 1997: Stockwell Garage 5 M (Su-Th), 7 M (Fr-Sa). 11/12 December 1998 increased to 6 M (Su-Th), 10 M (Fr-Sa).

c. June 2000: Vehicle-type change to low-floor Volvo B7TL at Stockwell Garage 6 PVL (Su-Th), 10 PVL (Fr-Sa). By June 2002 allocation PVL/WVL-types, c. May 2003 allocation all WVL-type.

2/3 June 2006: **Re-numbered N87.** Section of route Kingston – Tolworth withdrawn (replaced by (N)281). Now operated: **Aldwych – Kingston, Fairfield Bus Station**. Allocation: Stockwell Garage 11 WVL (Su-Th), 19 WVL (Fr-Sa).

By 8/9 July 2013: Allocation: Stockwell Garage 11 WVL/E (Su-Th), 19 WVL/E (Fr-Sa).

Opposite Arriva London North's articulated Mercedes-Benz Citaro bendy bus MA 155 was photographed at route N29's outbound pick-up bus stop on Trafalgar Square's eastern perimeter on Sunday morning 11 June 2006. *Philip Wallis*

Below DMS 2448 was seen loading passengers outside Canada House in Trafalgar Square during the early morning hours of Sunday 11 October 1987 for a route N68 journey which would terminate at the Leyland Fleetline's home garage. *Roy Waterhouse*

Victoria Garage's MCW Metrobus M 865 was seen loading passengers outside Canada House having been pressed into service at around 03.30 on New Year's Day 1990 to supplement Sutton Garage's normal allocation of Fleetlines to route N68. The hand-written paper destination display in the windscreen being studied by a passenger read 'Sutton & Trafalgar Square'. *Roy Waterhouse*

Go-Ahead London General's Wrightbus-bodied Volvo B7TL WVL 113 was seen loading passengers at Charing Cross Station for a Tolworth-bound N77 journey on 18 July 2004. Identical bus-type WVL 137 was seen at the same spot on 11 June 2006, shortly after route N77 had been re-numbered N87, on a short-working journey to Raynes Park Station.
Both Philip Wallis

Route N80
13/14 April 1984: **N80** re-routed to serve Oakwood Station. Continued to operate: **Potters Bar Bus Garage – Potters Bar Bus Garage.** Operated along four linked-loop sections of route via South Mimms, Barnet, Station Road, New Barnet Station, Oakwood Station, Southgate Station, Osidge Lane, Whetstone, Friern Barnet, North Finchley (Tally Ho Corner), then double-run to Finchley Bus Garage, then Whetstone, Longmore Avenue, New Barnet Station, Meadway, Barnet, Hadley Highstone. Allocation: Potters Bar Garage 1 M nightly.

26/27 April 1985: Restructured to form a bidirectional route. Now operated: **Potters Bar Bus Garage – North Finchley, Tally Ho Corner** via *either* South Mimms *or* Hadley Highstone, then Barnet, New Barnet Station, Oakwood Station, Southgate Station, Osidge Lane, Whetstone. Allocation unchanged.

19/20 June 1986: Last night of operation. Note: Replaced by projection of N92.

Route N82
13/14 April 1984: **N82** converted to one-person operation. Projected New Cross Gate – Kensal Rise. Now operated: **Kensal Rise Station – Woolwich Arsenal Station** via West Kilburn, Warwick Avenue Station, Edgware Road, Marble Arch, Oxford Circus, Piccadilly Circus, Trafalgar Square, Aldwych, Ludgate Circus, Blackfriars Bridge, Elephant & Castle, Walworth Road, Camberwell Green, Peckham, New Cross, Lewisham, Lee Green, Eltham, Shooters Hill. Allocation: New Cross Garage 4 T (Su-Th), 5 T (Fr-Sa).

26/27 October 1984: Section of route Kensal Rise – Trafalgar Square withdrawn (replaced by re-routeing of N79). Projected Trafalgar Square – Victoria, Woolwich – Thamesmead via Plumstead, Abbey Wood. Now operated: **Victoria Bus Station – Thamesmead, Bentham Road.** Allocation: New Cross Garage 4 T (Su-Th), 5 T (Fr-Sa). By 9/10 August 1985 an unscheduled duplicate had been added to the Fr-Sa allocation.

26/27 April 1985: Re-routed Lewisham – Lee Green via Blackheath Village.

1/2 November 1985: Allocation: New Cross Garage 2 T (Su-Th), 3 T (Fr-Sa)

1 April 1989: **London Central** commenced trading.

27/28 October 1989: Revised to operate Fr-Sa only. Sections of route Victoria – Trafalgar Square, Woolwich – Thamesmead withdrawn. Re-routed Trafalgar Square – Elephant & Castle, Lewisham – Lee Green. Bifurcation Shooters Hill – Welling introduced. Now operated: **Trafalgar Square – Woolwich Arsenal Station *or* Welling, Nags Head** via Whitehall, Westminster Bridge, Elephant & Castle, Walworth Road, Camberwell Green, Peckham, New Cross, Lewisham, Lee Green, Eltham, Shooters Hill to *either* Woolwich *or* Welling. Allocation: New Cross Garage 2 T (Fr-Sa). Woolwich – Thamesmead section of N82 replaced by enhanced service on route N77. Lewisham – Blackheath section of N82 replaced by new route N53. Elements of nightly N82 service Trafalgar Square – Eltham incorporated into new route N62. Co-ordinated timetable Trafalgar Square – Eltham with N62/N72 and onwards to Welling with N72.

2/3 October 1993: Last night of operation. Camberwell – Lewisham section of N82 replaced by new route N36, Lewisham – Eltham section by new routes N51/N61 and onwards to Woolwich by N51.

London Central's Leyland Titan T 1062 was photographed outside Canada House in Trafalgar Square in the early hours of Saturday morning 2 October 1993 during the penultimate night of route N 82's operation. The N82 had been reduced to run just two journeys to Welling and two journeys to Woolwich on Friday and Saturday nights only from 27/28 October 1989. *Malc McDonald*

Routes N83 (Wood Green), N243, (N)243

13/14 April 1984: **N83** converted to one-person operation. Projected Trafalgar Square – Victoria, Tottenham – Wood Green. Jny to Liverpool Street Station withdrawn. Now operated: **Victoria, Wilton Road (dep) *or* Garage (arr) – Wood Green Station** via Buckingham Palace Road (inbound only), Victoria Street, Whitehall, Trafalgar Square, Aldwych, Ludgate Circus, Farringdon Street, Clerkenwell Green, Old Street, Shoreditch, Dalston Junction, Stoke Newington, Stamford Hill, Tottenham. Allocation: Stamford Hill Garage 1 M nightly, Tottenham Garage 1 M nightly.

27/28 October 1984: Victoria terminus now Bus Station.

26/27 April 1985: Re-routed Old Street Station – Shoreditch via Moorgate and Liverpool Street Station.

1 April 1989: **Leaside Buses** commenced trading.

20/21 July 1990: Unscheduled duplicate introduced nightly. Allocation: Stamford Hill Garage 1 M + 1 M (joint N73) nightly, Tottenham Garage 1 M nightly.

By September 1992: Vehicle-type change to Leyland Olympian at Stamford Hill Garage 1 L (Su-Th), 1 L + 1 L (joint N73) (Fr-Sa), Tottenham Garage 1 M nightly.

By April 1994: Joint allocation with N73 dissolved, now: Stamford Hill Garage 1 L nightly, Tottenham Garage 1 M nightly.

29 September 1994: Operated by **Cowie Leaside**.

12/13 May 1995: Re-allocated to Tottenham Garage 2 M (Su-Th), 3 M (Fr-Sa).

24/25 November 1995: **Re-numbered N243.** Allocation: Tottenham Garage 3 M nightly.

2 April 1998: Operated by **Arriva London North**.

18/19 August 2000: Re-routed Aldwych – Clerkenwell Green via Holborn Station, Old Street Station – Shoreditch via Old Street. Continued to operate: **Victoria Bus Station – Wood Green Station.** Vehicle-type change to low-floor DAF DB250 LF at Tottenham Garage 2 DLA nightly. Note: New route N149 provided a replacement link along the Tottenham/Shoreditch axis to Liverpool Street Station and Fleet Street areas formerly served by N243. New route N214 replaced Old Street Station – Liverpool Street Station section of N243 from 1/2 September 2000.

2/3 November 2001: Section of route Victoria – Trafalgar Square withdrawn. Now operated: **Trafalgar Square – Wood Green Station**. Allocation unchanged.

c. May 2003: Vehicle-type change at Tottenham Garage to Volvo B7TL 2 VLW nightly.

24/25 October 2003 increased to 4 VLW nightly, 26/27 November 2004 increased to 5 VLW nightly.

2/3 September 2005: **Re-numbered (N)243.** Section of route Trafalgar Square – Aldwych withdrawn. Projected Aldwych – Waterloo. Now operated: **Waterloo Station – Wood Green Station** via Waterloo Bridge, Aldwych, Holborn Station, Clerkenwell Green, Old Street, Shoreditch, Dalston Junction, Stoke Newington, Stamford Hill, Tottenham. Allocation: Tottenham Garage 4 VLW nightly.

18/19 April 2008: Re-allocated to Wood Green Garage 4 VLW (Su-Th), 5 VLW (Fr-Sa).

27 August 2010: Arriva acquired by Deutsche Bahn. By 27/28 May 2011 allocation 4 DLA/VLW (Su-Th), 5 DLA/VLW (Fr-Sa).

25/26 November 2011: Re-allocated to Tottenham Garage 5 VLA nightly. By 29/30 June 2012 allocation mixed DLA/VLA/HV types.

c. February 2013: Allocation: Tottenham Garage 5 DW/HV nightly.

Tottenham Garage's MCW Metrobus M 1309 was seen in Trafalgar Square shortly before forming the 05.38 route N83 departure to Wood Green Station on Saturday morning 11 July 1987. At this time the N83 had a nominal nightly hourly frequency with a two hour gap in service in the middle of the night to facilitate crew relief-breaks for Tottenham garage's bus at Victoria garage and for Stamford Hill garage's bus at Wood Green garage. The use of upper case lettering on the intermediate blind display was unusual by this date. *Eamonn Kentell*

Above Arriva London North's Wrightbus-bodied Volvo B7TL VLW 134 was photographed at Charing Cross Station loading passengers for the then-30 minute frequency route N243 on Sunday morning 18 July 2004. *Philip Wallis*

Below Peckham garage's Leyland Titan T 1021 was seen outside Canada House in Trafalgar Square prior to departing on hourly frequency Grove Park route N85 on Sunday morning 11 December 1988. *Roy Waterhouse*

Route N85 (Grove Park)

13/14 April 1984: **N85** projected Trafalgar Square – Victoria. Re-routed outbound Trafalgar Square – Blackfriars Bridge. Now operated: **Victoria, Wilton Road (dep) *or* Vauxhall Bridge Road (arr) – Grove Park Station** via Victoria Street, Whitehall, Trafalgar Square, Aldwych, Ludgate Circus, Blackfriars Bridge, Elephant & Castle, Old Kent Road, New Cross, Lewisham, Catford, Bromley Road, Downham Way. Allocation: Peckham Garage 3 T nightly.

26/27 October 1984: Victoria terminus now Bus Station.

1/2 November 1985: Allocation: Peckham Garage 5 T (Su-Fr – joint N85/N86), 3 T (Sa).

1 April 1989: **London Central** commenced trading.

27/28 October 1989: Joint allocation N85/N86 dissolved, now: Peckham Garage 1 T + 1 T (joint N12) nightly.

7/8 October 1993: Last night of operation. Section of route Elephant & Castle – New Cross replaced by new route N81, section New Cross Gate – Grove Park replaced by new route N36. Note: The withdrawal of route N85 broke the long-established pattern of all-night service between Downham, Catford, New Cross and Blackfriars via Old Kent Road, the origins of which dated back almost one hundred years to the introduction of LCC Tramways New Cross Gate – Blackfriars Road via Old Kent Road all-night horse-tram route on 12/13 February 1899.

Routes N85 and N86 shared a joint allocation from Peckham garage on Sunday to Friday nights but each route had its own allocation on Saturday nights/Sunday mornings. T 695 was seen outside Canada House in Trafalgar Square in the early hours of Sunday morning 11 December 1988 on the one night of the week when the N86's hourly service to Crystal Palace was enhanced by additional short-working journeys between Trafalgar Square and New Cross Gate. *Roy Waterhouse*

Routes N86 (via Brockley Rise), N71, N171

13/14 April 1984: **N86** projected Trafalgar Square – Victoria, Brockley Rise – Crystal Palace. Re-routed outbound Trafalgar Square – Blackfriars Bridge. Now operated: **Victoria, Wilton Road (dep) *or* Vauxhall Bridge Road (arr) – Crystal Palace Parade** via Victoria Street, Whitehall, Trafalgar Square, Aldwych, Ludgate Circus, Blackfriars Bridge, Elephant & Castle, Walworth Road, Camberwell Green, Peckham, New Cross Gate, Brockley Rise, Forest Hill, Sydenham. Allocation: Peckham Garage 2 T nightly.

26/27 October 1984: Victoria terminus now Bus Station.

1/2 November 1985: Projected Crystal Palace – Penge. Now operated: **Victoria Bus Station – Penge, Crooked Billet.** Allocation: Peckham Garage 5 T (Su-Fr – joint N85/N86), 3T (Sa).

20/21 June 1986: Unidirectional terminal-loop routeing introduced from Sydenham via Penge, Anerley, Crystal Palace. Now operated: **Victoria Station, Bus Station – Crystal Palace.**

1 April 1989: **London Central** commenced trading.

27/28 October 1989: Joint allocation N85/N86 dissolved. Allocation: Peckham Garage 2 T + 1 T (joint N47) nightly.

8/9 October 1993: **Re-numbered N71** Allocation: Peckham Garage (joint N12/N36/N84) 6 T (Su-Th), 7 T (Fr-Sa).

18 October 1994: Operated by Go-Ahead group t/a **London Central**. By c. June 1995: Peckham Garage allocation (joint N12/N36/N84) 6 T/AV (Su-Th), 7 T/AV (Fr-Sa) and by 13/14 October 1995 (joint N12/N36/N84) 9 T/AV (Su-Th), 13 T/AV (Fr-Sa).

26/27 April 1996: **Re-numbered N171.** Sections of route Victoria – Trafalgar Square, Brockley Rise – Crystal Palace withdrawn. Re-routed Aldwych – Elephant & Castle. Projected Brockley Rise – Hither Green Station. Now operated: **Trafalgar Square – Hither Green Station** via Aldwych, Waterloo Bridge, Elephant & Castle, Walworth Road, Camberwell Green, Peckham, New Cross Gate, Brockley Rise, Catford. Allocation: New Cross Garage 2 T/L nightly. Note: Replaced Brockley – Hither Green Station section of N79. New Cross Gate – Anerley section of N71 replaced by projection of route N70 (Fr-Sa), supplemented nightly Forest Hill – Penge by new N176.

c. July 1996: Vehicle-type change to Volvo Olympian at New Cross Garage 2 NV nightly.

28/29 April 2000: Section of route Trafalgar Square – Aldwych withdrawn. Projected Aldwych via Kingsway to Tottenham Court Road Station. Now operated: **Tottenham Court Road Station – Hither Green Station.** Allocation unchanged.

27/28 April 2001: Vehicle-type change to low-floor Volvo B7TL at New Cross Garage 2 PVL nightly. 27/28 July 2001 increased to 4 PVL nightly.

28/29 April 2006: Section of route Catford – Hither Green Station withdrawn. Projected Catford – Catford Bus Garage. Now operated: **Tottenham Court Road Station – Catford Bus Garage.** Allocation unchanged.

29/30 April 2011: Section of route Catford – Catford Bus Garage withdrawn. Projected Catford – Hither Green Station. Now operated:**Tottenham Court Road Station – Hither Green Station.** Allocation: New Cross Garage 4 WVL nightly.

By 27/28 July 2013: Allocation: New Cross Garage 4 E/WVL nightly.

Peckham garage's Leyland Titan T 981 was loading outside Canada House in Trafalgar Square for the 05.04 N71 journey to Crystal Palace on Saturday morning 11 June 1994. *JGS Smith*

London Central's Plaxton President-bodied Volvo B7TL PVL 244 had paused at Holborn Station bus stop in Kingsway during the early hours of Tuesday morning 6 December 2005 on 30-minute frequency route N171. *Philip Wallis*

Routes N87 (via Tooting), N155

13/14 April 1984: **N87** converted to one-person operation. Section of route Trafalgar Square – Streatham via Blackfriars, Brixton withdrawn, along with garage jnys Brixton – Clapham Common via Acre Lane. Service from Tooting direction projected beyond Streatham, St Leonard's Church to Streatham Bus Garage. Bifurcation Stockwell – Victoria introduced. Now operated: **Trafalgar Square *or* Victoria, Vauxhall Bridge Road (dep) *or* Wilton Road (arr) – Streatham Bus Garage** via Whitehall, Westminster Bridge, Kennington, Stockwell, Clapham Common, Balham, Tooting Broadway, Southcroft Road *or* via Vauxhall (from/to Victoria only). Allocation: Stockwell Garage 3 DMS nightly. Note: Kennington – Streatham section of N87 replaced by new route N78, with onward service to/from central London via Waterloo.

26/27 October 1984: Section of route Streatham, St Leonard's Church – Bus Garage withdrawn. Now operated: **Trafalgar Square *or* Victoria, Vauxhall Bridge Road (dep) *or* Wilton Road (arr) – Streatham, St Leonard's Church**. Allocation: Stockwell Garage 3 D nightly.

Period March 1984 – 30 August 1986: Evaluation Hestair-Dennis Dominator, Leyland Olympian, MCW Metrobus Mark 2 and Volvo Ailsa buses were allocated to Stockwell Garage at varying dates during this period. These buses were regularly deployed on route N87, although the official allocation remained 3 D-type Fleetlines.

26/27 April 1985: Allocation: Stockwell Garage 3 D (Su-Fr), 4 D (Sa). Fr night allocation increased to 4 D from 1/2 November 1985.

24/25 October 1986: Bifurcation Tooting Broadway – Raynes Park via Colliers Wood, Merton, South Wimbledon, Wimbledon introduced. Victoria jnys revised to operate inbound only. Now operated: **Trafalgar Square *or* Victoria, Wilton Road (arr only) – Streatham, St Leonard's Church *or* Raynes Park, Raynes Park Hotel** Allocation: Stockwell Garage 4 D (Su-Th), 5 D (Fr-Sa).

1 April 1989: **London General** commenced trading.

27/28 October 1989: Projected Raynes Park – Surbiton via New Malden, Tolworth, Hook. Now operated: **Trafalgar Square *or* Victoria, Wilton Road (arr only) – Streatham, St Leonard's Church *or* Surbiton Station** Allocation: Stockwell Garage 5 D (Su-Th), 7 D (Fr-Sa).

c. March 1991: Vehicle-type change to Metrobus at Stockwell Garage 5 M (Su-Th), 7 M (Fr-Sa).

26/27 April 1991: Section of route New Malden – Surbiton withdrawn. Projected New Malden – Hampton Court. Now operated: **Trafalgar Square *or* Victoria, Wilton Road (arr only) – Streatham, St Leonard's Church *or* Hampton Court Station** via Whitehall, Westminster Bridge, Kennington *or* Vauxhall (to Victoria only), Stockwell, Clapham Common, Balham, Tooting Broadway then *either* Southcroft Road to Streatham *or* Colliers Wood, Merton, South Wimbledon, Wimbledon, Raynes Park, New Malden, Norbiton, Kingston to Hampton Court. Allocation: Stockwell Garage 5 M (Su-Th), 7 M (Fr-Sa). Note: Alternative all-night bus facility for Surbiton, Tolworth and Hook provided by projection of N14 beyond Kingston.

2 November 1994: London General acquired by management/employee buy-out.

London General's Leyland Fleetline DMS 2287 was seen loading passengers on the western side of Trafalgar Square on 27/28 October 1989 – the first night of the N87's extended service to Surbiton. At this time five nightly N87 departures left Trafalgar Square for Surbiton at hourly intervals between 24.00 and 04.00. *Roy Waterhouse*

Stockwell garage's DMS 2498 was loading passengers at Aldwych during the early hours of New Year's Day 1990. This view was taken towards the close of the Fleetline era on route N87. *Roy Waterhouse*

Sutton garage had put out MCW Metrobus M 355 to supplement Stockwell garage's allocation to route N87 on New Year's Eve 1993. An improvised route number display is in use in this view taken at Aldwych in the early hours of 1 January 1993. *Roy Waterhouse*

18/19 August 1995: **Re-numbered N155.** Stockwell – Victoria, Tooting Broadway – Streatham, South Wimbledon – Hampton Court sections withdrawn. Projected South Wimbledon – Sutton. Now operated: **Trafalgar Square – Sutton Station** via Whitehall, Westminster Bridge, Kennington, Stockwell, Clapham Common, Balham, Tooting Broadway, Colliers Wood, Merton, South Wimbledon, Morden, St Helier, Sutton Green. Allocation: Stockwell Garage 2 M (Fr-Sa), Sutton Garage 5 M (Su-Th), 7 M (Fr-Sa). Note: Wimbledon – Kingston section of N87 replaced by route N77. The withdrawal of Tooting Broadway – Streatham via Southcroft Road section of N87 severed a long established all-night link which dated back to 17/18 July 1928 when LCC Tramways had joined the Tooting – Victoria Embankment and Brixton – Victoria Embankment all-night tram routes to form a loop-working via Southcroft Road.

24 May 1996: Operated by Go-Ahead group t/a **London General**.

28/29 June 1996: Re-routed Lambeth North – Kennington via Elephant & Castle and Kennington Park Road. Allocation unchanged.

11/12 July 1997: Revised terminus in Sutton. Now operated: **Trafalgar Square – Sutton, Sutton Court Road.** Vehicle-type changed to Volvo Olympian at Sutton Garage 7 NV (Su-Th), 8 NV (Fr-Sa), Stockwell Garage 2 M (Fr-Sa).

28/29 May 1999: Projected Trafalgar Square – Aldwych. Revised terminus in Sutton. Now operated: **Aldwych – Sutton Station.** Allocation: Sutton Garage 9 NV nightly.

16/17 June 2000: Allocation: Stockwell Garage 1 PVL (Fr-Sa), Sutton Garage 9 NV nightly.

c. September 2002: Completion of progressive type change at Sutton Garage to low-floor Volvo B7TL (started July 2002) 9 EVL nightly, Stockwell Garage 1 PVL (Fr-Sa).

12/13 December 2003: Section of route Morden – Sutton withdrawn. Now operated: **Aldwych – Morden Station.** Allocation: Stockwell Garage 1 PVL (Fr-Sa), Sutton Garage 9 EVL (Su-Th), 15 EVL (Fr-Sa). Note: Morden – Sutton section of N155 not replaced with an all-night service. St Helier – Sutton axis benefited from the re-routeing of N44.

29/30 April 2005: Stockwell Garage allocation (Fr-Sa) withdrawn. Sutton Garage allocation unchanged and increased to 9 EVL (Su-Th), 18 EVL (Fr-Sa) from 5/6 December 2008.

c. March 2009: Vehicle-type change to AD Trident/Optare Olympus at Sutton Garage 9 DOE (Su-Th), 18 DOE (Fr-Sa).

10/11 December 2010: Additional nightly allocation introduced from Merton Garage to work two outbound Aldwych – Morden jnys. Allocation: Merton Garage 2 PVL nightly, Sutton Garage 9 DOE (Su-Th), 18 DOE (Fr-Sa). By 29/30 March 2012 Merton Garage allocation was 2 WVL/E nightly, Sutton Garage allocation unchanged.

Sutton garage's step-floor Northern Counties Palatine-bodied Volvo Olympian NV 118 swept up from Whitehall and into Trafalgar Square at 05.23 on Sunday morning 30 June 2002, shortly before the N155 was converted to low-floor bus operation. *Philip Wallis*

Go-Ahead London General's Optare Olympus-bodied AD Trident DOE 39 was seen loading at Charing Cross Station early on Sunday morning 25 April 2010. The weekend night frequency of route N155 is eight minutes and reduces to fifteen minutes on Sunday to Thursday nights. *Philip Wallis*

Routes N88 (via Wandsworth), N44

13/14 April 1984: **N88** converted to one-person operation. Ludgate Circus – Farringdon Street bifurcation withdrawn. Now operated: **Liverpool Street Station – Wandsworth, Wandsworth Plain** via Bank, Ludgate Circus, Aldwych, Trafalgar Square, Whitehall, Westminster Bridge, Vauxhall, Nine Elms Lane, Battersea. Allocation: Wandsworth Garage 1 M nightly.

26/27 April 1985: Projected Wandsworth – Sutton via Earlsfield, Tooting, Mitcham, St Helier, Sutton Green. Now operated: **Liverpool Street Station – Sutton Station.** Allocation: Wandsworth Garage 2 M nightly + 1 M (joint N68 (Fr-Sa).

9/10 August 1985: Section of route Liverpool Street – Ludgate Circus withdrawn. Now operated: **Ludgate Circus – Sutton Station**. Allocation unchanged.

22/23 May 1987: Bifurcations Sutton – East Croydon, Sutton – Banstead introduced. Now operated: **Ludgate Circus – Sutton Garage *or* East Croydon Station *or* Banstead** via Aldwych, Trafalgar Square, Whitehall, Westminster Bridge, Vauxhall, Nine Elms Lane, Battersea, Wandsworth, Earlsfield, Tooting, Mitcham, St Helier, Sutton Green, Sutton thence *either* to Sutton Garage *or* via Belmont to Banstead *or* via Sutton Green, St Helier, Carshalton, Wallington, Roundshaw, West Croydon to East Croydon. Allocation: Sutton Garage 1 D nightly, Wandsworth Garage 2 M nightly + 1 M (joint N68 (Fr-Sa). Note: Bifurcations to Banstead and East Croydon replaced N54.

10/11 July 1987: Projected Ludgate Circus – Farringdon Street. Now operated: **Farringdon Street, Stonecutter Street – Sutton Garage *or* East Croydon Station *or* Banstead.** Joint allocation N68/N88 dissolved. Allocation: Sutton Garage 3 D nightly.

1 April 1989: **London General** commenced trading.

By 13/14 Dec 1991: Completion of vehicle-type change to Metrobus at Sutton Garage 3 M nightly.

By June 1993: Joint allocation N68/N88 reinstated at Sutton Garage 5 M (Su-Th), 6 M (Fr-Sa).

2 November 1994: London General acquired by management/employee buy-out.

18/19 August 1995: **Re-numbered N44.** Sections of route Farringdon Street – Trafalgar Square, St Helier – Sutton, Sutton – Banstead and Wallington – East Croydon withdrawn. Re-routed at Wallington to Sutton via Stanley Park Road, Carshalton. Now operated: **Trafalgar Square – Sutton Station**. Re-allocated to Stockwell Garage 3 M nightly. Note: St Helier – Sutton section of N88 replaced by projection of N155. Sutton – Banstead abandoned.

26/27 April 1996: Projected Trafalgar Square – Aldwych. Now operated: **Aldwych – Sutton Station**. Allocation: Stockwell Garage 4 M nightly.

24 May 1996: Operated by Go-Ahead group t/a **London General**.

28/29 May 1999: Re-allocated to Sutton Garage 4 NV nightly.

16/17 June 2000: Re-allocated to Stockwell Garage 4 PVL nightly. By 29/30 June 2002 was 4 PVL/WVL-types.

12/13 December 2003: Re-routed St Helier – Sutton via Rose Hill. Allocation: Stockwell Garage 6 WVL (Su-Th), 9 WVL (Fr-Sa). Note: Replacement all-night bus service between Sutton, Carshalton, Wallington (and onwards to Croydon) provided by N213.

10/11 November 2006: Re-routed Westminster – Battersea Park Station. Now operated: **Aldwych – Sutton Station** via Trafalgar Square Whitehall, Victoria, Ebury Bridge Road, Chelsea Bridge, Battersea, Wandsworth, Earlsfield, Tooting, Mitcham, St Helier, Rose Hill, Sutton Green. Allocation unchanged. Note: Lambeth Palace – Battersea Park Station (and onwards to Battersea) section of N44 replaced by new route (N)344.

By 8/9 July 2013: Allocation: Stockwell Garage 6 WVL/E (Su-Th), 9 WVL/E (Fr-Sa).

Sutton garage's Leyland Fleetline DMS 2518 was seen in Whitehall during the night of 1/2 December 1987. Four nightly N88 journeys ran from central London to East Croydon via Sutton over the period between 22/23 May 1987 and 17/18 August 1995.
Malc McDonald

Victoria garage's MCW Metrobus M 863 was supplementing route N88's Fleetlines from Sutton garage by helping to move crowds away from London's New Year's Eve celebrations when photographed in Aldwych early on 1 January 1990.
Roy Waterhouse

London General's TransBus President-bodied Dennis Trident PDL 41 was seen at Charing Cross Station at 04.45 on Wednesday morning 11 June 2003 working that night's last outbound departure on the-then hourly frequency route N44. *Philip Wallis*

Stockwell garage's Wrightbus-bodied Volvo B7TL WVL 10 was photographed in Garratt Lane, Wandsworth in the early hours of Sunday morning 20 January 2008. Route N44 has operated between Aldwych and Sutton Station to a 30 minute frequency on Sunday to Thursday nights and to a 20 minute frequency on weekend nights since 12/13 December 2003. *Philip Wallis*

Route N89 (via Shepherd's Bush), N207

13/14 April 1984: Bifurcation Southall – Uxbridge introduced on extant route **N89.** Re-routed Monument – Holborn Viaduct, Holborn – Tottenham Court Road Station, Marble Arch – Lancaster Gate. Now operated: **Liverpool Street Station – Southall, Brent Road *or* Uxbridge Station** via Bank, Monument then double-run to London Bridge Station then Cannon Street, New Change, Holborn Circus, Holborn Station, Aldwych, Trafalgar Square, Charing Cross Road, Tottenham Court Road Station, Oxford Circus, Marble Arch, Notting Hill Gate, Shepherd's Bush, Acton Vale, Acton, Ealing Common, Ealing, Hanwell, Southall, Town Hall then *either* to Southall, Brent Road *or* via Hayes, Hillingdon Hill to Uxbridge. Inbound jnys did not double-run to London Bridge Station, instead *either* terminating at London Bridge Station *or* running from Cannon Street via Bank to Liverpool Street Station. One outbound jny from Liverpool Street Station also ran via Bank to line of route in Cannon Street. Allocation: Hanwell Garage 4 M nightly

26/27 October 1984: Fr-Sa unscheduled duplicate introduced from Hanwell Garage 4 M (Su-Th), 5 M (Fr-Sa).

1/2 February 1985: Unscheduled duplicate absorbed into timetable. Outbound jny Liverpool Street direct to Cannon Street revised to double-run via London Bridge Station. Re-allocated to Southall Garage 4 M (Su-Th), 5 M (Fr-Sa).

9/10 August 1985: Section of route Liverpool Street – Monument withdrawn. Bifurcation Waterloo – Aldwych via Waterloo Bridge introduced. Now operated: **London Bridge Station *or* Waterloo Station – Southall, Brent Road *or* Uxbridge Station.** Allocation: Southall Garage 4 M (Su-Th), 7 M (Fr-Sa).

8/9 August 1986: Reduction in eastbound jnys beyond Trafalgar Square. Re-allocated to Hanwell Garage 4 M (Su-Th), 7 M (Fr-Sa).

10/11 July 1987: Waterloo – Aldwych bifurcation withdrawn. Bifurcation Victoria – Trafalgar Square via Whitehall introduced. Southall, Brent Road served Fr-Sa only. Now operated: **London Bridge Station *or* Victoria, Bus Station – Southall, Brent Road *or* Uxbridge Station**. Allocation unchanged.

1 April 1989: **Centrewest** commenced trading.

5/6 May 1989: Sunday 04.35 jny Trafalgar Square – Southall, Brent Road projected via Cranford to Heathrow Airport North (05.42). 05.48 return jny via Cranford and Southall to Hanwell Broadway (06.09). Now operated: **London Bridge Station *or* Victoria Bus Station – Heathrow Airport North *or* Uxbridge Station**. Allocation: Hanwell Garage 4 M (Su-Th), 7 M (Fr-Sa).

5/6 February 1993: Early Sunday am jny to Heathrow Airport North projected to Uxbridge via double-run to Heathrow Airport Central Bus Station then Harmondsworth, West Drayton, Yiewsley, Cowley. Now operated: **London Bridge Station *or* Victoria Bus Station – Uxbridge Station.** Re-allocated to Uxbridge Garage 4 M (Su-Th), 8 M (Fr-Sa).

21/22 May 1993: Bifurcation Ealing – Ruislip via Scotch Common, Greenford, Yeading, Northolt, South Ruislip introduced. Now operated: **London Bridge Station *or* Victoria Bus Station – Ruislip Station *or* Uxbridge Station.** Allocation: Alperton Garage 3 M nightly, Uxbridge Garage 5 M (Su-Th), 8 M (Fr-Sa). Note: Ruislip bifurcation replaced that section of N50.

2 September 1994: Centrewest acquired by management/employee buy-out.

7/8 October 1995: Last operation of early Sunday am jny routed Southall – Uxbridge via Heathrow Airport. From 14/15 October 1995 this jny re-routed to follow standard routeing Southall – Uxbridge via Hayes.

Shepherd's Bush garage had sent MCW Metrobus M 1240 to help move the crowds away from Aldwych on New Year's Eve 1990. *Roy Waterhouse*

The southern end of Regent Street, beyond Piccadilly Circus, was used as a marshalling point for Night Bus routes on New Year's Eve 1994. Centrewest's MCW Metrobus M 496 was photographed there loading for an N89 journey to Ruislip Station. *Mike Harris*

Centrewest seemed to use anything with seats to supplement route N89's service on New Year's Eve 1995. 28-seat Wright-bodied Renault 50 RW 23 was seen in Oxford Street (*middle*) and 29-seat Wright-bodied Dennis Dart DW 168 was photographed at the Centrepoint building near Tottenham Court Road Station (*bottom*). Centrewest also hired in Routemasters RM 1571 and 1959 from Routemaster Travel Ltd for use on the N89 on this night. *Both Mike Harris*

11/12 October 1996: **Re-numbered N207.** Bifurcations London Bridge – Trafalgar Square, Ealing – Ruislip withdrawn. Now operated: **Victoria Bus Station – Uxbridge Station** via Victoria Street, Whitehall, Trafalgar Square, Charing Cross Road, Tottenham Court Road Station, Oxford Circus, Marble Arch, Notting Hill Gate, Shepherd's Bush, Acton Vale, Acton, Ealing Common, Ealing, Hanwell, Southall, Hayes, Hillingdon Hill. Allocation: Alperton Garage 3 M nightly, Uxbridge Garage 5 M (Su-Th), 9 M (Fr-Sa). Note: Ealing – Northolt Station section of N89 replaced by projection of N23. Northolt – Ruislip section abandoned in respect of all-night service.

By December 1996: Vehicle-type change at Uxbridge Garage to Volvo Olympian 5 V (Su-Th), 9 V (Fr-Sa), Alperton Garage 3 M nightly.

26 March 1997: Operated by **First Bus**, re-titled **First Group** December 1997, **First London** March 2001.

By October 1998: Allocation: Alperton Garage 3 M/LN nightly, Uxbridge Garage 5 V (Su-Th), 9 V (Fr-Sa). From 31 March/1 April 1999 Alperton Garage allocation became 3 VN nightly, Uxbridge Garage unchanged.

12/13 November 1999: Section of route Victoria – Trafalgar Square withdrawn. Now operated: **Trafalgar Square – Uxbridge Station**. Allocation: Acton Garage 5 M (Su-Th), 9 M (Fr-Sa), Uxbridge Garage 5 V (Su-Th), 6 V (Fr-Sa).

c. February 2000: Vehicle-type conversion at Uxbridge Garage to low-floor Dennis Trident 5 TNL (Su-Th), 6 TNL (Fr-Sa), Acton Garage 5 M (Su-Th), 9 M (Fr-Sa).

28/29 April 2000: Section of route Trafalgar Square – Tottenham Court Road Station withdrawn. Projected Tottenham Court Road Station – Holborn via New Oxford Street. Now operated: **Holborn, Red Lion Square – Uxbridge Station.** Allocation unchanged.

By 28/29 July 2000: Allocation: Acton Garage 5 TNL (Su-Th), 9 TNL (Fr-Sa), Uxbridge Garage 5 TNL (Su-Th), 6 TNL (Fr-Sa). By 19/20 June 2004 both garages often substituted TN-types.

8/9 April 2005: Allocation: Acton Garage 8 TNL (Su-Th), 12 TNL (Fr-Sa), Uxbridge Garage 5 TNL (Su-Th), 9 TNL (Fr-Sa). Note: TN-types habitually substituted.

15/16 March 2008: Partially re-allocated to Hayes Garage 8 TNL (Su-Th), 12 TNL (Fr-Sa), Uxbridge Garage 5 TNL (Su-Th), 9 TNL (Fr-Sa). Note. TN-types habitually substituted.

15/16 January 2010: Holborn terminus now New Oxford Street jct Bury Place (pick-up), Bloomsbury Square (set-down).

10/11 December 2011: Entire allocation now from Hayes Garage 10 SN/VN (Su-Th), 21 SN/VN (Fr-Sa).

21/22 June 2013: Operated by **Metroline West** SN/VW-types.

By 30/31 August 2013: Allocation now all SN-type.

Top First London's 10.5 metre Plaxton President-bodied Dennis Trident TNL 32893 was seen at route N207's Uxbridge Station pick-up bus stop in Bakers Road early on Sunday morning 19 September 2004. Uxbridge N207 journeys operated hourly at this time whilst a 20-minute frequency applied between Holborn and Hayes By-Pass with the N207 further enhanced to give a 10-minute service between Holborn and Ealing on Friday and Saturday nights. *Philip Wallis*

Centre First London's TN 33194 represented the shorter 9.9 metre Tridents often to be encountered on route N207. This view in New Oxford Street dates from the early hours of Sunday morning 25 April 2010. The N207's frequency had been increased from 8/9 April 2005 to give a 15 minute Sunday to Thursday night and 10 minute weekend nights frequency between Holborn and Hayes By-Pass with a nightly 30-minute service beyond the By-Pass to Uxbridge. *Philip Wallis*

Right Crossrail construction works have caused disruption and necessitated diversions to many daytime and night-time bus routes across central London. Eastbound buses along Oxford Street were subjected to a particularly long period of diversion between 14 February 2011 and 5 May 2012 caused by work at Bond Street Station. Eastbound route N207 buses were diverted between Marble Arch and Oxford Circus via Gloucester Place, Marylebone Road and Portland Place for the duration. First London's Scania OmniCity SN 36062 was seen at Baker Street Station bus stop in Marylebone Road at around 04.00 on Friday morning 24 February 2012. *Philip Wallis*

Routes N90, N279

13/14 April 1984: **N90** converted to one-person operation. Victoria – Pimlico section of route withdrawn (replaced by N92). Projected Waltham Cross – Hammond Street. Now operated: **Victoria, Wilton Road (dep) *or* Garage (arr) – Hammond Street, Smiths Lane** via Buckingham Palace Road (inbound only), Victoria Street, Whitehall, Trafalgar Square, Charing Cross Road, Tottenham Court Road (outbound), Gower Street (inbound), Euston Station, Euston Road, King's Cross, Camden Town, Holloway, Finsbury Park, Manor House, Stamford Hill, Tottenham, Upper Edmonton, Lower Edmonton, Ponders End, Enfield Highway, Waltham Cross, Cheshunt, Flamstead End. One inbound jny double-ran Waltham Cross – Waltham Abbey. Allocation: Edmonton Garage 2 M nightly, Enfield Garage 2 M nightly.

By July 1984: Unscheduled duplicate introduced Fr-Sa. Allocation: Edmonton Garage 2 M nightly, Enfield Garage 2 M (Su-Th), 3 M (Fr-Sa).

26/27 October 1984: Victoria terminus now Bus Station.

By 9/10 August 1985: Allocation: Edmonton Garage 2 M (Su-Th), 3 M (Fr-Sa), Enfield Garage 2 M (Su-Th), 3 M (Fr-Sa).

31 Jan/1 Feb 1986: Allocation: Enfield Garage 4 M (Su-Th), 6 M (Fr-Sa).

25/26 September 1987: Inbound double-run Waltham Cross – Waltham Abbey withdrawn (absorbed into new all-night service routes 279/279A). Fr-Sa allocation increased for reliability; now Enfield Garage 4 M (Su-Th), 7 M (Fr-Sa).

1 April 1989: **Leaside Buses** commenced trading.

31 Jan/1 Feb 1992: Enhanced service to partially compensate for the withdrawal of all-night element of 279/279A. Allocation: Enfield Garage 5 M (Su-Th), 8 M (Fr-Sa).

29 September 1994: Operated by **Cowie Leaside**.

26/27 April 1996: **Re-numbered N279.** Section of route Waltham Cross – Hammond Street withdrawn. Projected Waltham Cross – Upshire via Waltham Abbey. Re-routed direct between Seven Sisters Bridge and South Tottenham. Re-routed at Ponders End direct via Hertford Road and no longer deviated via Enfield Bus Garage as had route N90. Now operated: **Victoria Bus Station – Upshire, Princesfield Road.** All-night service Waltham Cross – Hammond Street abandoned.

2 April 1998: Operated by **Arriva London North**.

15/16 October 1999: Section of route Waltham Cross – Upshire withdrawn. Now operated: **Victoria Bus Station – Waltham Cross, Bus Station**. Vehicle-type change to low-floor DAF DB250LF at Enfield Garage 8 DLA/DLP (Su-Th), 12 DLA/DLP (Fr-Sa). All-night service Waltham Cross – Upshire abandoned.

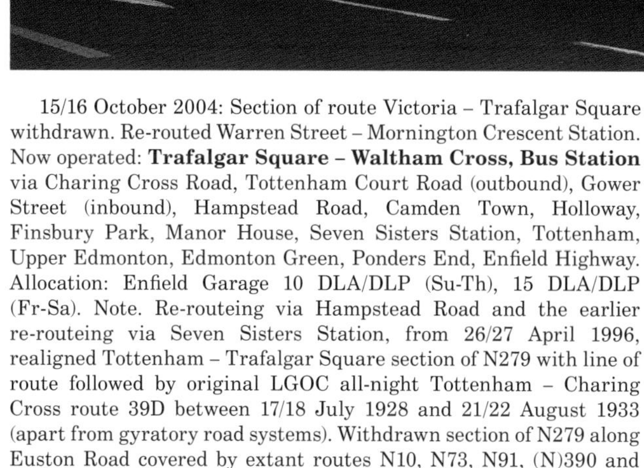

15/16 October 2004: Section of route Victoria – Trafalgar Square withdrawn. Re-routed Warren Street – Mornington Crescent Station. Now operated: **Trafalgar Square – Waltham Cross, Bus Station** via Charing Cross Road, Tottenham Court Road (outbound), Gower Street (inbound), Hampstead Road, Camden Town, Holloway, Finsbury Park, Manor House, Seven Sisters Station, Tottenham, Upper Edmonton, Edmonton Green, Ponders End, Enfield Highway. Allocation: Enfield Garage 10 DLA/DLP (Su-Th), 15 DLA/DLP (Fr-Sa). Note. Re-routeing via Hampstead Road and the earlier re-routeing via Seven Sisters Station, from 26/27 April 1996, realigned Tottenham – Trafalgar Square section of N279 with line of route followed by original LGOC all-night Tottenham – Charing Cross route 39D between 17/18 July 1928 and 21/22 August 1933 (apart from gyratory road systems). Withdrawn section of N279 along Euston Road covered by extant routes N10, N73, N91, (N)390 and withdrawn section along Pancras Road by extant route (N)214.

27 August 2010: Arriva acquired by Deutsche Bahn.

c. February 2012: Allocation from Enfield Garage now included T-type AD E40D – AD Enviro400 10 DLA/T (Su-Th), 15 DLA/T (Fr-Sa). By 29/30 June 2012: Allocation all T-type.

Above Enfield garage's MCW Metrobus M 703 was photographed in Charing Cross Road on the night of 3/4 February 1988 working one of then-three nightly route N90 journeys which terminated at Hammond Street in Hertfordshire. *Malc McDonald*

Left Arriva London North's TransBus President-bodied DAF DB250 LF DLP 98 paused at the Centrepoint bus stop near Tottenham Court Road Station in the early morning hours of Saturday 19 February 2005. Trafalgar Square to Waltham Cross route N279 has had a 20 minute Sunday to Thursday night and 12 minute Friday and Saturday night frequency over its entire route length since 15/16 October 2004. *Philip Wallis*

Route N91 (Willesden)

13/14 April 1984: **N91** converted to one-person operation. Operated: **Liverpool Street Station – Willesden Garage** via Bank, Ludgate Circus, Aldwych, Trafalgar Square, Piccadilly Circus, Oxford Circus, Marble Arch, Paddington Station, Westbourne Park, Ladbroke Grove, Harlesden. Allocation: Willesden Garage 1 M nightly. Note: Co-ordinated timetable Aldwych – Harlesden/Craven Park with new route N18. Due to an industrial dispute at Willesden Garage did not operate east of Marble Arch until 18/19 April 1984.

25/26 October 1984: Last night of operation. Absorbed into N18.

Routes N92, N43, (N)43

13/14 April 1984: **N92** converted to one-person operation. Projected Trafalgar Square – Pimlico (replaced N90), Archway Station – Muswell Hill. Now operated: **Pimlico, Grosvenor Road – Muswell Hill Broadway** via Lupus Street, Belgrave Road, Wilton Road (outbound), Buckingham Palace Road (inbound), Victoria, Whitehall, Trafalgar Square, Aldwych, Holborn Station, Rosebery Avenue, Islington, Highbury Corner, Archway, Crouch End. Allocation: Holloway Garage 2 DMS nightly. Mid-May 1984: 2 M nightly.

26/27 October 1984: Section of route Pimlico – Trafalgar Square withdrawn (replaced by N2). Now operated: **Trafalgar Square – Muswell Hill Broadway.** Allocation unchanged.

20/21 June 1986: Section of route Archway – Muswell Hill withdrawn. Projected Archway – Potters Bar via East Finchley, North Finchley, Whetstone, Osidge, Southgate, Oakwood, New Barnet Station, Barnet, South Mimms. Now operated: **Trafalgar Square – Potters Bar Garage.** One inbound jny operated Potters Bar – Barnet via Hadley Highstone. One Sa inbound jny operated Potters Bar – Southgate Station via Cockfosters Station. Allocation: Holloway Garage 2 M nightly, Potters Bar Garage 1 M nightly. Note: North Finchley – Potters Bar section of N92 replaced N80.

25/26 September 1987: Projected Trafalgar Square – Victoria via Whitehall. Jnys via Hadley Highstone and via Cockfosters Station withdrawn. Now operated: **Victoria Bus Station – Potters Bar Garage**. Allocation: Holloway Garage 1 M + 1 M (joint N93), Potters Bar Garage 1 M nightly.

1 April 1989: **London Northern** commenced trading.

16/17 June 1989: 06.19 Victoria dep projected Archway – Highgate Village via Highgate Hill. Now operated: **Victoria Bus Station – Highgate Village, North Road *or* Potters Bar Garage**.

17/18 July 1992: Section of route Whetstone – Barnet Hill withdrawn. Bifurcation Trafalgar Square – Kingston introduced. Now operated: **Kingston, Fairfield Bus Station *or* Victoria Bus Station – Highgate Village, North Road *or* Potters Bar Garage** via Teddington, Fulwell, Twickenham, Richmond, Mortlake, Barnes, Barnes Common, Putney Bridge, Hammersmith, Olympia, Kensington High Street, Knightsbridge, Hyde Park Corner, Piccadilly Circus, Trafalgar Square, then *either* via Whitehall (to/from Victoria only) *or* Aldwych, Holborn Station, Rosebery Avenue, Islington, Highbury Corner, Holloway, Archway, then *either* Highgate Hill to Highgate Village *or* East Finchley, North Finchley, Whetstone, Barnet, South Mimms to Potters Bar. 1 jny deviated Hyde Park Corner – Victoria via Grosvenor Place. Joint allocation with N93 dissolved. Jointly operated by **London Northern** Holloway Garage 3 M (Su-Th), 4 M (Fr-Sa), Potters Bar Garage 1 S nightly and **London United** Shepherds Bush Garage 1 M (Su-Th). Note: Elements of route N92's service in Southgate and Oakwood areas replaced by re-routeing of N21. Co-ordinated timetable Fr-Sa with N65 Trafalgar Square – Kingston (intermediate routeing differences).

26/27 March 1993: Joint operation dissolved. Now operated by **London Northern**. Allocation: Holloway Garage 4 S nightly, Potters Bar Garage 1 S nightly. 3/4 December 1993: Allocation: Holloway Garage 4 M nightly, Potters Bar Garage 1 S nightly.

25/26 February 1994: Sections of route Kingston – Trafalgar Square, Archway – Highgate Village, North Finchley – Potters Bar and Victoria jny via Grosvenor Place withdrawn. Re-routed Trafalgar Square – Holborn via Charing Cross Road, New Oxford Street. Now operated: **Victoria Bus Station – North Finchley, Tally Ho Corner.** Allocation: Holloway Garage 2 M nightly. Note: Kingston – Trafalgar Square section of N92 largely replaced by new route N9. Section of N92 via Aldwych and Kingsway replaced by new route N91. North Finchley – Potters Bar section of N92 abandoned.

26 October 1994: Operated by **MTL London Northern**.

Potters Bar garage's MCW Metrobus M 634 was seen on layover in Pall Mall East prior to forming the 05.31 route N92 departure from Trafalgar Square back to its home garage on Saturday morning 11 July 1987 with a journey time of 1 hour 19 minutes. *Eamonn Kentell*

During much of 1993 London Northern's Holloway garage often deployed Red Express X43-liveried Alexander-bodied Scania N113s on its all-night route allocations, presumably to achieve greater utilisation of these modern buses otherwise restricted to Monday to Friday peak-hour use by their dedicated livery. S 18 was photographed in full early morning summer sunshine in Islington High Street at 06.37 on Thursday 3 June 1993 working the sole nightly N92 journey to Highgate Village. *Mike Harris*

23/24 June 1995: **Re-numbered N43.** Sections of route Victoria – Trafalgar Square, Archway – North Finchley withdrawn. Now operated: **Trafalgar Square – Archway Station**. Allocation: Holloway Garage 1 M nightly. Note: Archway – North Finchley section of N92 compensated for by enhanced frequency on N20. N92's routeing via High Road, East Finchley abandoned.

11/12 October 1996: Projected Fr-Sa Archway – Muswell Hill via Highgate Station. Now operated: **Trafalgar Square – Muswell Hill Broadway.** Allocation: Holloway Garage 1 M (Su-Th), 2 M (Fr-Sa).

30/31 January 1998: Projected to Friern Barnet. Now operated: **Trafalgar Square – Friern Barnet, Woodhouse Road.** Allocation: Holloway Garage 2 M nightly.

17 August 1998: Operated by **Metroline London Northern**.

23/24 July 1999: Vehicle-type change to low-floor Dennis Trident at Holloway Garage 4 TP nightly.

18 February 2000: Metroline acquired by DelGro group.

By 2/3 February 2001: Allocation 4 TP/VPL-types, by 29/30 June 2002 4 TP/TPL/VPL-types. 12/13 March 2004: Friern Barnet terminus now Library.

1 January 2005: Re-assigned to **Metroline Travel.**

4/5 February 2005: **Re-numbered (N)43.** Section of route Trafalgar Square – Islington withdrawn. Projected Islington – London Bridge Station. Now operated: **London Bridge Station – Friern Barnet, Library** via Monument, Bank, Moorgate, Old Street Station, City Road, Islington, Highbury Corner, Holloway, Archway, Highgate Station, Muswell Hill. Allocation: Holloway Garage 4 VPL nightly. Note: Trafalgar Square – Islington section of N43 replaced by projection of N41. The N41 also supplemented the (N)43's service Islington – Archway.

6/7 November 2009: Allocation: Holloway Garage 4 VPL (Su-Th), 6 VPL (Fr-Sa), c. April 2012 now 4 VPL/VW (Su-Th), 6 VPL/VW (Fr-Sa), 29/30 June 2012 now all VW-type.

Holloway garage's TransBus Trident TP 353 was seen in New Oxford Street in the early hours of Saturday morning 29 January 2005, just one week before route N43 would lose its 'N'-prefix and be substantially re-routed to form the night-time element of 24-hour route 43 between London Bridge Station and Friern Barnet. *Philip Wallis*

Route N93 (Hampstead Heath)

13/14 April 1984: Crew-operated route **N93** continued unaltered, apart from timing changes. Operated: **Victoria Station, Wilton Road (dep) *or* Garage (arr) – Hampstead Heath, South End Green** via Buckingham Palace Road (inbound only), Victoria Street, Whitehall, Trafalgar Square, Aldwych, Ludgate Circus, Farringdon Street, Farringdon Road, King's Cross, Euston, Camden Town, Kentish Town, Malden Road. Garage jnys Camden Town – Tufnell Park. Allocation: Holloway Garage 1 RML nightly.

26/27 October 1984: Converted to one-person operation. Bifurcation Trafalgar Square – Hammersmith introduced. Re-routed from Camden Town to form a unidirectional loop working to/from Hampstead Heath. Victoria terminus now Bus Station. Now operated: **Hammersmith Broadway *or* Victoria Bus Station – Hampstead Heath, South End Green** via Olympia, Kensington High Street, Knightsbridge, Hyde Park Corner, Piccadilly Circus *or* Whitehall (to/from Victoria only), then Trafalgar Square, Aldwych, Ludgate Circus, Farringdon Street, Farringdon Road, King's Cross, Euston, Camden Town, thence loop via Chalk Farm, Belsize Park to Hampstead Heath. Return via Malden Road to line of route at Camden Town. Garage jnys Camden Town – Tufnell Park. Allocation: Holloway Garage 2 M nightly.

26/27 April 1985: Projected Hammersmith – Fulwell via Castelnau, Barnes, Mortlake, Richmond, Twickenham. Now operated: **Fulwell Garage *or* Victoria Bus Station – Hampstead Heath, South End Green.** Garage jnys Camden Town – Tufnell Park, Hammersmith – Stamford Brook Garage. Allocation: Holloway Garage 2 M nightly, Stamford Brook Garage 1 M nightly.

By July 1986: Allocation: Holloway Garage 2 M nightly, Stamford Brook Garage 1 M (Su-Th), 2 M (Fr-Sa).

9/10 August 1986: Additional allocation from Ash Grove Garage on this night only to operate 10 min frequency unidirectional N93 shuttle service King's Cross – Trafalgar Square for persons returning from Knebworth Festival to King's Cross station by train.

By January 1987: Allocation: Holloway Garage 2 M (Su-Fr), 3 M (Sa), Stamford Brook Garage 1 M (Su-Th), 2 M (Fr-Sa).

25/26 September 1987: Allocation: Chalk Farm Garage 1 T nightly, Holloway Garage 1 M (Su-Th), 3 M (Fr-Sa) + 1M (joint N92) nightly, Stamford Brook Garage 1 M nightly

1 April 1989: **London Northern** and **London United** commenced trading.

5/6 January 1990: Allocation: London Northern: Chalk Farm Garage 1 T nightly, Holloway Garage 1 M (Su-Th), 3 M (Fr-Sa) + 1M (joint N92) nightly. London United: Shepherds Bush Garage 1 M nightly.

21/22 September 1990: Allocation: London Northern: Holloway Garage 2 M (Su-Th), 4 M (Fr-Sa) + 1M (joint N92) nightly. London United: Shepherds Bush Garage 1 M nightly.

17/18 July 1992: Joint operation dissolved. Now operated by **London Northern**. Section of route Fulwell – Trafalgar Square withdrawn. Re-routed Camden Town – Hampstead Heath to form a bidirectional service. Now operated: **Victoria Bus Station – Hampstead Heath, South End Green** via Whitehall, Trafalgar Square, Aldwych, Ludgate Circus, Farringdon Street, Farringdon Road, King's Cross, Euston, Camden Town, Malden Road. Garage jnys Archway – Camden Town. Allocation: Holloway Garage 1 M nightly. Note: Fulwell – Trafalgar Square section of N93 replaced by projection of N92.

26 October 1994: Operated by **MTL London Northern**.

22/23 June 1995: Last night of operation. Camden Town – Hampstead Heath section of N93 replaced by N2. Note: The withdrawal of route N93 ended nearly 100 years of all-night service between Hampstead Heath, Camden Town, King's Cross and the newspaper printing area around Holborn and Fleet Street which had originated with the North Metropolitan Tramway Company's Hampstead Heath – Holborn all-night horse tram route, started by 13/14 January 1899. The tram service was subsequently maintained by LCC Tramways and LPTB until converted to trolleybus operation on 9/10 July 1938 (numbered 513/613 from 18/19 June 1946) and converted by LTE to bus operation, as N93, on 31 January/1 February 1961 when the service was extended to Charing Cross.

The first night of one-person operation on route N93 was recorded in this view of Holloway garage's MCW Metrobus M 1059 at Hampstead Heath, South End Green taken early on Saturday morning 27 October 1984. *Paul Davis*

Routes N94 (Cricklewood), N16

13/14 April 1984: **N94** converted to one-person operation. Projected Cricklewood – Edgware. Now operated: **Liverpool Street Station – Edgware Station** via Bank, Ludgate Circus, Aldwych, Trafalgar Square, Piccadilly Circus, Oxford Circus, Marble Arch, Edgware Road, Kilburn, Cricklewood, Staples Corner, West Hendon, Colindale, Burnt Oak. Jnys to Kilburn Park Station. Allocation: Cricklewood Garage 3 M nightly. Note: Due to an industrial dispute at Cricklewood Garage did not work east of Marble Arch until 18/19 April 1984.

9/10 August 1985: Bifurcated projection Waterloo – Aldwych introduced. Now operated: **Liverpool Street Station *or* Waterloo Station – Edgware Station**. Allocation: Cricklewood Garage 4 M (Su-Th), 5 M (Fr-Sa).

10/11 July 1987: Bifurcation Trafalgar Square – Victoria via Whitehall introduced. Now operated: **Liverpool Street Station *or* Waterloo Station *or* Victoria Bus Station – Edgware Station.** Allocation: Cricklewood Garage 4 M nightly.

By November 1987 timetable: Waterloo bifurcation withdrawn. Now operated: **Liverpool Street Station *or* Victoria Bus Station – Edgware Station**. Allocation: Cricklewood Garage 4 M (Su-Th), 5 M (Fr-Sa).

1 April 1989: **Metroline** commenced trading

18/19 January 1991: **Re-numbered N16.** Re-allocated to Edgware Garage 4 M (Su-Th), 5 M (Fr-Sa).

5/6 March 1993: Re-allocated to Cricklewood Garage 4 M (Su-Th), 5 M (Fr-Sa).

28/29 January 1994: Liverpool Street – Trafalgar Square bifurcation and Kilburn Park Station jnys withdrawn. Now operated: **Victoria Bus Station – Edgware Station** via Whitehall, Trafalgar Square, Piccadilly Circus, Oxford Circus, Marble Arch, Edgware Road, Kilburn, Cricklewood, Staples Corner, West Hendon, Colindale, Burnt Oak. Re-allocated to Edgware Garage 4 M nightly.

7 October 1994: Metroline acquired by management/employee buy-out.

17/18 November 1995: Allocation: Edgware Garage 4 M (Su-Th), 7 M (Fr-Sa).

18 February 2000: Metroline acquired by DelGro group.

2/3 February 2001: Allocation: Cricklewood Garage (low-floor Dennis Trident) 3 TAL (Su-Th), 6 TAL (Fr-Sa), Edgware Garage 4 M (Su-Th), 5 M (Fr-Sa).

c. October 2001: Completion of vehicle-type change at Edgware Garage to low-floor Volvo B7TL 4 VPL (Su-Th), 5 VPL (Fr-Sa), Cricklewood Garage 3 TAL (Su-Th), 6 TAL (Fr-Sa).

11/12 October 2002: Re-routed Victoria – Marble Arch via Hyde Park Corner. Continued to operate: **Victoria Bus Station – Edgware Station.** Allocation: Edgware Garage 7 VPL (Su-Th),8 VPL (Fr-Sa).

7/8 February 2003: Victoria pick-up now Wilton Road. 22/23 April 2003: Victoria set-down now Terminus Place.

7/8 November 2003: Allocation: Edgware Garage 5 VPL (Su-Th), 6 VPL (Fr-Sa).

4/5 February 2005: Allocation: Edgware Garage 5 VPL (Su-Th), 6 VPL (Fr-Sa). Harrow Weald Garage 1 VP (Fr-Sa). By 26/27 April 2008: Allocation: Edgware Garage 5 VPL/TE (Su-Th), 6 VPL/TE (Fr-Sa), Harrow Weald Garage 1 VP (Fr-Sa).

16/17 November 2011: Victoria set-down now Bus Station.

29/30 June 2012: Re-allocated to Cricklewood Garage and predominantly operated by AD Enviro400H hybrid 6 TE/TEH (Su-Th), 5 TE/TEH (Fr-Sa), Harrow Weald Garage 1 VP (Fr-Sa). Cricklewood Garage all TEH-type by 30/31 August 2013.

Top MCW Metrobus M 1218 was seen on layover at Victoria Bus Station in the early hours of Sunday morning 24 September 1989. At this time four nightly Victoria-terminating route N94 journeys facilitated relief-breaks for the drivers of Cricklewood garage's four buses allocated to the route. *Roy Waterhouse*

Above Passengers board Edgware garage's MCW Metrobus M 387 in busy Kilburn High Road in the early hours of Sunday morning 3 March 1991, shortly after route N94 had been re-numbered N16. *Roy Waterhouse*

Routes N95, N15

13/14 April 1984: **N95** projected Becontree Heath – Dagenham. Re-routed Bank – Aldgate East. Now operated: **Victoria, Wilton Road (dep) *or* Garage (arr) – Dagenham, Kent Avenue** via Buckingham Palace Road (inbound only), Victoria Street, Whitehall, Trafalgar Square, Piccadilly Circus, Shaftesbury Avenue, New Oxford Street, Holborn Circus, Bank, Moorgate and Liverpool Street (outbound), Bishopsgate (inbound), Shoreditch, Commercial Street, Aldgate East, Commercial Road, Limehouse, Poplar, Canning Town, Plaistow, Upton Park, East Ham, Barking, Longbridge Road, Becontree Heath, Dagenham Heathway. Allocation: Barking Garage 3 T nightly. Note: Absorbed elements of N84.

26/27 October 1984: Re-routed Bishopsgate – Aldgate East via Houndsditch (outbound), Bevis Marks (inbound), Aldgate. Victoria terminus now Bus Station.

20/21 November 1987: Allocation: Barking Garage 3 T (Su-Th), 4 T (Fr-Sa).

1 April 1989: **East London** commenced trading.

9/10 March 1992: Diverted via Liverpool Street Bus Station.

6 September 1994: Operated by: **Stagecoach East London**.

14/15 July 1995: **Re-numbered N15.** Sections of route Victoria – Aldgate, Becontree Heath – Dagenham withdrawn. Projected Aldgate – Marble Arch with one inbound jny only (Fr-Sa) continuing to Paddington. Now operated: **Paddington – Becontree Heath, Bus Station** via Marble Arch, Oxford Circus, Piccadilly Circus, Trafalgar Square, Aldwych, Ludgate Circus, Bank, Leadenhall Street, Aldgate, Commercial Road, Limehouse, Poplar, Canning Town, Plaistow, Upton Park, East Ham, Barking, Longbridge Road. Re-allocated to Upton Park Garage 5 S nightly.

21/22 August 1998: Fr-Sa inbound Paddington jny withdrawn. Projected Becontree Heath – Romford Market via Rush Green, Romford Station. Now operated: **Marble Arch – Romford Market**. Re-allocated to Barking Garage 6 T nightly.

12/13 April 1999: Vehicle-type change to low-floor Dennis Trident at Barking Garage 6 TA nightly.

3/4 December 1999: Allocation: Barking Garage 5 TA (Su-Th), 9 TA (Fr-Sa).

23/24 March 2001: Projected Marble Arch – Paddington. Re-routed Mansion House Station – Aldgate via Cannon Street, Tower Hill. Now operated: **Paddington Station, Eastbourne Terrace – Romford Market, St Edward's Way.** Allocation: Barking Garage 8 TA (Su-Th), 13 TA (Fr-Sa).

29/30 August 2003: Allocation: Barking Garage 7 TA (Su-Th), 10 TA (Fr-Sa), Bow Garage 7 TA (Su-Th), 9 TA (Fr-Sa).

31 March/1 Apr 2006: Re-routed Monument Station – Tower Hill via Eastcheap.

30 August 2006: Operated by Macquarie Bank Ltd t/a East London Bus Group. Fleetname: **East London.**

12/13 October 2007: Projected Paddington via Bishop's Bridge and Harrow Road gyratory to Paddington Basin. Now operated: **Paddington Basin, North Wharf Road – Romford Market, St Edward's Way**. Allocation unchanged.

27/28 November 2009: Allocation: Barking Garage 7 TA (Su-Th), 10 TA (Fr-Sa), West Ham Garage 7 TA (Su-Th), 9 TA (Fr-Sa).

27/28 August 2010: Section of route Paddington Basin – Regent Street, Conduit Street withdrawn and replaced by new route (N)159. Now operated: **Regent Street, Conduit Street – Romford Market, St Edward's Way**. Allocation: Barking Garage 6 TA (Su-Th), 8 TA (Fr-Sa), West Ham Garage 6 TA (Su-Th), 8 TA (Fr-Sa).

14 October 2010: Operated by Stagecoach Bus Holdings Ltd t/a **East London.**

2/3 March 2012: West Ham Garage allocation transferred to Bow Garage, vehicle-type change to AD E40H – AD Enviro400H hybrid 6 TEH (Su-Th), 8 TEH (Fr-Sa), Barking Garage 6 TA (Su-Th), 8 TA (Fr-Sa).

30/31 March 2012: Allocation: Barking Garage 6 TA (Su-Th), 10 TA (Fr-Sa), Bow Garage 7 TEH (Su-Th), 8 TEH (Fr-Sa). 13/14 July 2012: Allocation: Barking Garage 6 TA (Su-Th), 14 TA (Fr-Sa), Bow Garage 7 TEH (Su-Th), 8 TEH (Fr-Sa).

27/28 July – 12/13 August and 29/30 August – 9/10 September 2012: Su-Th frequency increased to 10 min (to match Fr-Sa) for duration of Olympic and Paralympic Games. Allocation temporarily increased: Barking Garage 10 TA (Su-Th), 14 TA (Fr-Sa), Bow Garage 8 TEH nightly.

By 8/9 July 2013: Allocation: Barking Garage 6 TE (Su-Th), 14 TE (Fr-Sa), Bow Garage 7 TEH (Su-Th), 8 TEH (Fr-Sa).

Stagecoach East London's Alexander ALX400-bodied Dennis Trident 17361 was seen loading passengers at Charing Cross Station just as dawn was breaking on Sunday morning 18 July 2004. Stagecoach's London buses usually display garage running numbers in their front windscreens and the number 307 indicated that 17361 was one of ten Tridents then allocated from Barking garage to route N15 on Friday and Saturday nights. Bow garage also allocated nine Tridents to the N15 on those nights of the week. *Philip Wallis*

Leyton garage's Leyland National LS 84 was seen at bus stop C outside the National Gallery in Trafalgar Square loading passengers for the 04.55 route N96 departure to Chingford Mount on Friday morning 1 June 1984. A timetable revision from 26/27 October 1984 would eliminate short-working N96 journeys to Chingford Mount. *Malcolm Papes*

Routes N96, N38

13/14 April 1984: Sections of extant route **N96** to Waterloo Road terminus and Leyton – Chingford Mount via Highams Park Station withdrawn. Projected Waterloo Road – Trafalgar Square, Leyton – Chingford Station. Now operated: **Trafalgar Square – Chingford Station** via Whitehall, Westminster Bridge, York Road, Waterloo Bridge, Aldwych, Ludgate Circus, Farringdon Street, Farringdon Road, King's Cross, Islington, Essex Road, Dalston, Hackney, Clapton, Lea Bridge Road, Leyton, Walthamstow, Chingford Mount, Chingford Hatch. Jnys to/from Leyton Green. Allocation: Leyton Garage 2 LS nightly.

26/27 April 1985: Re-routed Chingford Mount – Chingford Station via The Ridgeway.

2/3 August 1985: Allocation: Leyton Garage 3 LS nightly.

1/2 November 1985: Revised to terminate at Waterloo. Re-routed Trafalgar Square – Aldwych. Now operated: **Waterloo Station, York Road – Chingford Station** via Westminster Bridge, Whitehall, Trafalgar Square, Aldwych, Ludgate Circus, Farringdon Street, Farringdon Road, King's Cross, Islington, Essex Road, Dalston, Hackney, Clapton, Lea Bridge Road, Leyton, Walthamstow, Chingford Mount, The Ridgeway. Jnys to/from Leyton Green. Allocation unchanged.

By March 1987 timetable: Allocation: Leyton Garage 3 LS (Su-Th), 5 LS (Fr-Sa).

5/6 June 1987: Vehicle-type change to Leyland Titan at Leyton Garage 3 T (Su-Th), 5 T (Fr-Sa).

10/11 July 1987: Bifurcation Trafalgar Square – Victoria via Whitehall, Victoria Street introduced. Now operated: **Victoria Bus Station *or* Waterloo, York Road – Chingford Station.** Jnys to/from Leyton Green. Allocation unchanged.

By November 1987: 02.59 departure ex Victoria introduced which operated to Waterloo, York Road and thence line of route to Chingford Station (this bus had previously run 'dead' between Victoria and Waterloo after driver's relief-break).

1 April 1989: **London Forest** commenced trading.

27/28 October 1989: Bifurcations Victoria – Trafalgar Square, Waterloo – Trafalgar Square withdrawn. Re-routed Trafalgar Square – Mount Pleasant and via Leyton Green. Bifurcation Chingford – Debden introduced along with further bifurcation to Loughton Station. Now operated: **Trafalgar Square – Chingford Station *or* Loughton Station *or* Debden Station** via Piccadilly Circus, Shaftesbury Avenue, New Oxford Street, Holborn, Rosebery Avenue, Mount Pleasant, King's Cross, Islington, Essex Road, Dalston, Hackney, Clapton, Lea Bridge Road, Leyton Green, Walthamstow, Chingford Mount The Ridgeway then *either* Station Road to Chingford Station *or* Whitehall Road, Woodford Wells to Loughton then *either* to Loughton Station *or* Church Hill to Debden Station. Allocation: Leyton Garage 5T nightly.

14/15 September 1990: Bifurcations to both Chingford Station and Loughton Station withdrawn. Re-routed Chingford – Woodford Wells via Chingford Hatch, Woodford Green. Now operated: **Trafalgar Square – Debden Station.** Allocation: Leyton Garage 7 T (Su-Th), 8 T (Fr-Sa).

22/23 November 1991: LRT contract awarded to **East London**. Allocation unchanged.

6 September 1994: Operated by **Stagecoach East London**.

London Forest's Leyland Titan T 670 was photographed in Pall Mall East on Sunday morning 29 October 1989, the second night of route N96's extension beyond Chingford out to Loughton and Debden in Essex. Passengers appear to be boarding the bus although the N96's official first pick-up point was just along the road at bus stop C outside the National Gallery. At this time five nightly N96 journeys were scheduled to work through to Debden with departures from Trafalgar Square at hourly intervals between 23.36 and 03.36. Fleet Street has been blanked out on the re-routed N96's intermediate blind display. *Roy Waterhouse*

Arriva London North's Wrightbus-bodied Volvo B7TL VLW 89 was seen in Grosvenor Gardens, Victoria loading passengers for an outbound N38 journey in the early hours of Sunday morning 27 April 2008 with Stamford Hill garage running number 151 displayed in the windscreen. *Philip Wallis*

14/15 July 1995: **Re-numbered N38.** Section of route Chingford – Debden Station withdrawn. Projected Chingford – Chingford Station. Bifurcation Chingford Mount – Chingford Hatch introduced. Now operated: **Trafalgar Square – Chingford Station *or* Chingford Hatch** via Piccadilly Circus, Shaftesbury Avenue, New Oxford Street, Holborn, Rosebery Avenue, Mount Pleasant, King's Cross, Islington, Essex Road, Dalston, Hackney, Clapton, Lea Bridge Road, Leyton Green, Walthamstow, Chingford Mount then *either* The Ridgeway to Chingford Station *or* New Road to Chingford Hatch. Allocation: Leyton Garage 5 T nightly. Note: Chingford – Debden Station section of N96 largely abandoned in respect of all-night bus services although Woodford Green – Woodford Wells axis benefited from projection of N8 whilst Chingford Hatch continued to be served by N38 from a different direction.

By 11/12 January 1997: Allocation from Leyton Garage increased for reliability to 6 T/S nightly.

18/19 July 1997: LRT contract awarded to **Cowie Leaside.** Section of route Trafalgar Square – Piccadilly Circus withdrawn. Projected Piccadilly Circus – Victoria via Hyde Park Corner. Re-routed Mount Pleasant – Islington via Rosebery Avenue and away from Leyton Green. Now operated: **Victoria Bus Station – Chingford Station *or* Chingford Hatch.** Allocation: Clapton Garage 7 L (Su-Th), 12 L (Fr-Sa).

2 April 1998: Operated by **Arriva London North**.

29/30 September 2000: Allocation: Clapton Garage 7 L (Su-Th), 14 L (Fr-Sa).

27/28 April 2001: Sections of route northwards beyond Walthamstow Central withdrawn. Now operated: **Victoria Bus Station – Walthamstow Central Station**. Allocation: Clapton Garage 8 L (Su-Th), 13 L (Fr-Sa). Note: Walthamstow Central – Chingford Station section of N38 replaced by projection of N26.

c. April 2003: Completion of conversion to low-floor DAF DB250LF (started 19/20 July 2002) at Clapton Garage 10 DLA (Su-Th), 18 DLA (Fr-Sa). 28/29 October 2005: Allocation now 11 DLA (Su-Th), 18 DLA (Fr-Sa).

31 March/1 April 2006: Re-allocated to Stamford Hill Garage 11 DLA (Su-Th), 18 DLA (Fr-Sa). By 26/27 April 2008 mixed DLA/VLW-types.

13/14 November 2009: Re-allocated to Clapton Garage. Vehicle-type change to Wright/DB 300 integral and AD Trident Enviro400 15 DW/T (Su-Th), 26 DW/T (Fr-Sa). Subsequently all DW-type.

27 August 2010: Arriva acquired by Deutsche Bahn.

Route N38 was re-allocated to Clapton garage from 13/14 November 2009 coincident with the conversion of daytime route 38 (Victoria – Clapton Pond) from Mercedes-Benz Citaro bendy bus to double-deck operation so that buses for both the 38 and N38 worked out of the same garage. Previously Ash Grove garage had housed Citaros for the daytime 38 whilst Stamford Hill garage had provided the N38's double-deck allocation. The new generation of double deckers used on both the 38 and N38 is represented by Arriva London North's Wrightbus Gemini 2DL integral DW 262 seen in New Oxford Street on Sunday morning 25 April 2010. *Philip Wallis*

Route N97

13/14 April 1984: **N97** reduced in frequency. Bifurcation Ludgate Circus – Farringdon Street, Stonecutter Street withdrawn. Now operated: **Liverpool Street Station – Heathrow Airport, Terminal 2 *or* Central Bus Station** via Bank, Ludgate Circus, Aldwych, Trafalgar Square, Piccadilly Circus, Hyde Park Corner, Knightsbridge, South Kensington, Cromwell Road, Earls Court, Fulham Broadway, Hammersmith, Turnham Green, Chiswick, Kew Bridge Station, Brentford, Isleworth, Hounslow, Bath Road, Harlington Corner. Allocation: Stamford Brook Garage 5 M nightly.

26/27 October 1984: Unscheduled duplicate introduced Fr-Sa, allocation 5 M (Su-Th), 6 M (Fr-Sa).

26/27 April 1985: Re-routed Earls Court – Fulham Cross via West Brompton and Lillie Road. Allocation: Stamford Brook Garage 7 M nightly.

c. July 1985: Unscheduled duplicate reintroduced Fr-Sa, allocation 7 M (Su-Th), 8 M (Fr-Sa).

10/11 July 1987: Bifurcation Victoria – Trafalgar Square via Whitehall introduced. Now operated: **Liverpool Street Station *or* Victoria Bus Station – Heathrow Airport, Terminal 2 *or* Central Bus Station**. Allocation: Stamford Brook Garage 7 M nightly.

25/26 September 1987: Level of service Liverpool Street – Trafalgar Square drastically reduced. Allocation: Stamford Brook Garage 6 M (Su-Th), 9 M (Fr-Sa).

22/23 April 1988: Allocation: Shepherd's Bush Garage 1 M (Fr-Sa), Stamford Brook Garage 6 M (Su-Th), 9 M (Fr-Sa).

1 April 1989: **London United** commenced trading.

5/6 January 1990: Allocation (joint N67): Hounslow Garage 3 M (Su-Th), 6 M (Fr-Sa), Shepherd's Bush Garage 3 M (Su-Th), 6 M (Fr-Sa).

17/18 July 1992: Section of route Liverpool Street – Trafalgar Square withdrawn. Heathrow journeys standardised to terminate at Central Bus Station. Now operated: **Victoria Bus Station – Heathrow Airport, Central Bus Station**. Allocation (joint N67): Hounslow Garage 3 M (Su-Th), 5 M (Fr-Sa), Shepherd's Bush Garage 3 M (Su-Th), 5 M (Fr-Sa).

26/27 March 1993: Allocation (joint N67): Hounslow Garage 3 M (Su-Th), 5 M (Fr-Sa), Stamford Brook Garage 3 L (Su-Th), 5 L (Fr-Sa).

25/26 February 1994: Section of route Victoria – Trafalgar Square withdrawn. Bifurcation Hounslow – Sunbury introduced. Now operated: **Trafalgar Square – Heathrow Airport, Central Bus Station *or* Sunbury Village, Three Fishes** via Piccadilly Circus, Hyde Park Corner, Knightsbridge, South Kensington, Cromwell Road, Earls Court, West Brompton, Lillie Road, Hammersmith, Turnham Green, Chiswick, Kew Bridge Station, Brentford, Isleworth, Hounslow then *either* Bath Road, Harlington Corner to Heathrow Airport *or* Feltham, Lower Feltham, Sunbury Cross to Sunbury Village. Allocation: Hounslow Garage 5 M (Su-Th), 8 M (Fr-Sa). Note: Replaced Hounslow – Sunbury Cross section of N67.

5 November 1994: London United acquired by management/ employee buy-out.

17/18 November 1995: Allocation: Hounslow Garage 5 M (Su-Th), 14 M (Fr-Sa).

30/31 August 1996: Hounslow – Sunbury Village bifurcation withdrawn. Now operated: **Trafalgar Square – Heathrow Airport, Central Bus Station**. Allocation unchanged. Note. Hounslow – Sunbury Village section of N97 abandoned in respect of all-night bus service.

July 1997: Operated by Transdev group t/a **London United**.

5/6 March 1999: Allocation: Hounslow Garage 5 M (Su-Th), 13 M (Fr-Sa), Shepherd's Bush Garage 1 M (Fr-Sa). By 25/26 June 1999: Hounslow Garage's allocation mixed M-type Metrobus and L-type Leyland Olympian. 3/4 September 1999: Hounslow Garage's allocation reverted to all M-type.

By 21/22 January 2000: Allocation: Hounslow Garage 7 M (Su-Th), 13 M (Fr-Sa), Shepherd's Bush Garage 1 M (Fr-Sa).

c. May 2000: Start of progressive conversion to low-floor Volvo B7TL, when completed allocation became: Hounslow Garage 7 VA/VP (Su-Th), 13 VA/VP (Fr-Sa), Shepherd's Bush Garage 1 VA (Fr-Sa).

30/31 March 2001: Allocation: Hounslow Garage 8 VA/VP (Su-Th), 18 VA/VP (Fr-Sa), Shepherd's Bush Garage 2 VA (Fr-Sa).

28/29 September 2001: Section of route Hammersmith – Heathrow Airport withdrawn (replaced by projection of route N9). Now operated: **Trafalgar Square – Hammersmith Broadway.** Allocation: Hounslow Garage 7 VA/VP (Su-Th), 10 VA/VP (Fr-SA), Shepherd's Bush Garage 3 VA (Fr-Sa).

22/23 February 2002: Hammersmith terminus now Bus Station.

27/28 June 2003: Allocation: Hounslow Garage 2 VA/VP (Su-Th), 3 VA/VP (Fr), 4 VA/VP (Sa), Shepherd's Bush Garage 4 VA (Su-Th), 7 VA (Fr-Sa).

23/24 January 2004: Entire allocation now from Shepherd's Bush Garage 6 VA (Su-Th), 10 VA (Fr-Sa).

3/4 September 2004: Hounslow Garage allocation re-introduced: 6 VA/VP (Su-Th), 8 VA/VP (Fr), 9 VA/VP (Sa), Shepherd's Bush Garage 2 VA (Fr-Sa).

11/12 November 2005: Frequency reduced. Allocation: Shepherd's Bush Garage 4 VA (Su-Th), 9 VA (Fr-Sa).

4 April 2006: **Transdev** corporate logo adopted.

By 23/24 April 2010: Allocation now mixed Volvo B7TL and Scania OmniCity from Shepherd's Bush Garage 4 VA/SP (Su-Th), 9 VA/SP (Fr-Sa).

3 March 2011: Operated by RATP DEV UK Ltd t/a **London United**.

By 8/9 July 2013: Allocation: Shepherd's Bush Garage 4 SP (Su-Th), 9 SP (Fr-Sa).

London United's Plaxton President-bodied Volvo B7TL VP 117 had reached journey's end in Trafalgar Square and, having set-down any passengers in Pall Mall East, was making its way around the Square to the N97's pick-up point in Cockspur Street on Sunday morning 30 June 2002. Note that outbound points beyond Hammersmith had been blanked out on the truncated N97's intermediate blind display. *Philip Wallis*

Routes N98 (Romford), N25, (N)25

13/14 April 1984: Romford Market – Romford Station section of route **N98** withdrawn. Projected Romford Market – Harold Hill. Now operated: **Victoria, Wilton Road (dep) *or* Garage (arr) – Harold Hill, Gooshays Drive** via Buckingham Palace Road (inbound only), Victoria Street, Whitehall, Trafalgar Square, Piccadilly Circus, Shaftesbury Avenue, New Oxford Street, Holborn Station, Holborn Circus, Bank, King William Street, Monument, Fenchurch Street, Aldgate, Whitechapel, Stepney Green, Mile End, Bow, Stratford, Forest Gate, Manor Park, Ilford, Seven Kings, Chadwell Heath, Romford Market, Gallows Corner, Straight Road, Hilldene Avenue. Allocation: Romford North Street Garage 4 T nightly.

26/27 October 1984: Victoria terminus now Bus Station. 26/27 April 1985: Re-routed in Romford to serve Romford Station. Allocation unchanged.

1/2 November 1985: Allocation: Romford North Street Garage 4 T (Su-Th), 5 T (Fr-Sa).

1 April 1989: **East London** commenced trading.

6 September 1994: Operated by **Stagecoach East London**.

14/15 July 1995: **Re-numbered N25.** Section of route Victoria – Trafalgar Square withdrawn. Re-routed Trafalgar Square – Cambridge Circus, Bank – Aldgate. Bifurcation Ilford – Romford via Barkingside introduced. Now operated: **Trafalgar Square – Harold Hill, Gooshays Drive *or* Romford Station** via Charing Cross Road, New Oxford Street, Holborn Station, Holborn Circus, Bank, Cornhill, Leadenhall Street, Aldgate, Whitechapel, Stepney Green, Mile End Bow, Stratford, Forest Gate, Manor Park, Ilford then *either* via Seven Kings, Chadwell Heath, Romford Station, Romford Market, Gallows Corner, Straight Road, Hilldene Avenue to Harold Hill, Gooshays Drive *or* via Gants Hill, Barkingside, Hainault, Collier Row to terminate at Romford Station. Allocation: Romford North Street Garage 6 T nightly.

18/19 July 1997: Allocation: Bow Garage 4 T/VN (Fr-Sa), Romford North Street Garage 7 T nightly. 3/4 August 1997: Bow Garage allocation now included VA/VN-type Volvo Olympians.

21/22 May 1999: Vehicle-type change at Bow Garage to low-floor Dennis Trident 4 TA (Fr-Sa), Romford North Street 7 T nightly.

25/26 June 1999: LRT contract awarded to **First Group**, re-titled **First London** March 2001. Barkingside – Romford Station via Hainault section of bifurcation withdrawn. Re-routed Trafalgar Square – Tottenham Court Road Station via Piccadilly Circus, Regent Street, Oxford Circus. Now operated: **Trafalgar Square – Harold Hill, Gooshays Drive *or* Barkingside, Fullwell Cross.** Allocation: Low-floor Dennis Trident from Dagenham Dock Garage 6 TN (Su-Th), 11 TN (Fr-Sa).

c. August 1999: Due to passenger capacity problems with 59-seat TN-type Tridents, 77-seat step-floor AE-type Dennis Arrows were partially substituted at weekends. Allocation: Dagenham Dock Garage 6 TN (Su-Th), 11 TN/AE (Fr-Sa).

19/20 November 1999: Allocation: Dagenham Dock Garage 6 TN (Su-Th), 16 TN/AE (Fr-Sa).

28/29 April 2000: Section of route Trafalgar Square – Oxford Circus withdrawn. Barkingside bifurcation projected to Hainault. Now operated: **Oxford Circus – Harold Hill, Gooshays Drive *or* Hainault, The Lowe**. Allocation: Dagenham Dock Garage 6 TN/TAL (Su-Th), 16 TN/TAL/AE (Fr-Sa).

c. June 2000: Completion of conversion to 69-seat Dennis Tridents at Dagenham Dock Garage 6 TAL (Su-Th), 16 TAL (Fr-Sa).

17/18 August 2001: Allocation: Dagenham Dock Garage 10 TAL/TNL (Su-Th), 16 TAL/TNL (Fr-Sa).

22/23 March 2002: Re-allocated to Rainham Garage, no numerical or vehicle-type changes.

22/23 November 2002: Allocation: Rainham Garage 11 TAL/TNL (Su-Th), 16 TAL/TNL (Fr-Sa).

25/26 June 2004: **Re-numbered (N)25.** LBSL contract awarded to **Stagecoach East London.** Converted to single-deck articulated Mercedes-Benz Citaro bendy bus operation. Bifurcated sections of route Ilford – Harold Hill, Ilford – Hainault withdrawn. Now operated: **Oxford Circus – Ilford, Hainault Street** via New Oxford Street, Holborn, Holborn Circus, Bank, Cornhill, Leadenhall Street, Aldgate, Whitechapel, Stepney Green, Mile End, Bow, Stratford, Forest Gate, Manor Park. Allocation: Waterden Road Garage 9 MA (Su-Th), 10 MA (Fr-Sa). Note: Ilford – Harold Hill section of N25 replaced by new route N86, which also supplemented the N25's service to Stratford. Gants Hill – Hainault section of N25 replaced by projection of N8. Withdrawn section of N25 Ilford – Gants Hill via Cranbrook Road left without an all-night service until the introduction of route (N)128 from 5/6 October 2007.

Thornton Heath garage's Leyland Fleetline DMS 2307 had been loaned to supplement route N98's service when seen in Aldwych in the early hours of New Year's Day 1989. *Roy Waterhouse*

30 August 2006: Operated by Macquarie Bank Ltd t/a East London Bus Group. Fleetname: **East London**.

30 Nov/1 Dec 2006: Allocation: Waterden Road Garage 9 MA (Su-Th), 12 MA (Fr-Sa). Increased 29/30 June 2007 to 13 MA (Su-Th), 15 MA (Fr-Sa).

28/29 December 2007: Re-allocated to Rainham Garage, no numerical or vehicle-type changes. 17/18 May 2008: Re-allocated to West Ham Garage, no numerical or vehicle-type changes.

14 October 2010: Operated by Stagecoach Bus Holdings Ltd t/a **East London.**

24/25 June 2011: LBSL contract awarded to **First London**. Re-converted to double-deck bus operation using Volvo B9TLs from Lea Interchange Garage 19 VN (Su-Th), 29 VN (Fr-Sa).

27/28 July – 12/13 August and 29/30 August – 9/10 September 2012: Su-Th frequency increased to 6 min (to match Fr-Sa frequency) for duration of Olympic and Paralympic Games. Allocation temporarily increased to 29 VN nightly from Lea Interchange Garage.

21/22 June 2013: Operated by **Tower Transit**.

Route N99 (Victoria & Albert Docks)

13/14 April 1984: **N99** continued to operate to an unchanged timetable. **Chingford Station – Victoria & Albert Docks** via The Ridgeway, Chingford Mount, Walthamstow, Leyton, Leytonstone, Stratford, Plaistow, Prince Regent Lane. Bifurcation Plaistow – Canning Town via Hermit Road. Allocation: West Ham 1 T nightly.

31 Oct/1 Nov 1985: Last night of operation.

Route 220 (Special Night Journey)

13/14 April 1984: Special Night Journey (Su-Fr) on daytime route **220** continued to operate to an unchanged timetable. **Harlesden, Willesden Junction – Tooting, Mitre** via Harlesden, College Park, Scrubs Lane, White City, Shepherd's Bush, Hammersmith, Fulham Palace Road, Putney Bridge, Putney, Wandsworth, Earlsfield. Allocation: Shepherd's Bush Garage 1 M (Su-Fr).

16/17 May 1985: Last night of operation. Note: The extension of N88 beyond Wandsworth via Earlsfield and Tooting to Sutton from 26/27 April 1985 contributed to the demise of 220's SNJ.

East London's T 1 was seen on layover in Vauxhall Bridge Road early on Saturday morning 20 October 1990. The Leyland Titan would then have taken up service from Victoria Bus Station on its 1 hour 27 minute journey along the full length of route N98 to Harold Hill. This bus has subsequently been preserved. *Roy Waterhouse*

First London's Plaxton President-bodied Dennis Trident TN 33061 was photographed in Oxford Street early on Sunday morning 20 June 2004 just five nights before route N25's Hainault bifurcation was withdrawn. *Philip Wallis*

East London's articulated Mercedes-Benz Citaro 23031 had paused in Romford Road, Manor Park at around 03.00 on Sunday morning 29 June 2008. Running number 704 displayed in the bendy bus's windscreen indicated that it was one of fifteen Citraos from West Ham garage allocated to the 10-minute frequency weekend nights service on the (N)25. *Philip Wallis*

CHAPTER 5
THE APRIL 1984 PROGRAMME: NEW ROUTES

Having set down passengers in Pall Mall East, First London's Plaxton President-bodied Dennis Trident TN 960 was rounding the north side of Trafalgar Square to take a lay-over on the Square's south side before commencing its return N18 journey from Cockspur Street on Sunday morning 30 June 2002. *Philip Wallis*

Round London Sightseeing Tour-liveried Leyland Fleetline DM 2645 was the single bus allocated to hourly frequency West Norwood route N2 on Sunday night/Monday morning 29/30 April 1984 when it was photographed outside Victoria garage. *Paul Davis*

This chapter lists the new routes introduced on 13/14 April 1984 and the changes to those routes up to 30/31 August 2013.

Route N2

13/14 April 1984: Introduced. Operated: **Trafalgar Square – West Norwood Station** via Whitehall, Victoria, Vauxhall, Stockwell, Brixton, Tulse Hill. Allocation: Victoria Garage 1 DMS nightly.

12/13 July 1984: Fr-Sa unscheduled duplicate introduced. Start of progressive vehicle-type change to Metrobus, initially using M-types from daytime Round London Sightseeing Tour, at Victoria Garage 1 M (Su-Th), 2 M (Fr-Sa).

26/27 October 1984: Projected Trafalgar Square – Friern Barnet, West Norwood – Crystal Palace. Victoria – Pimlico bifurcation introduced. Now operated : **Friern Barnet – Pimlico, Grosvenor Road *or* Crystal Palace, Parade** via Muswell Hill, Crouch End, Hornsey Rise, Archway, Kentish Town, Camden Town, Tottenham Court Road, Piccadilly Circus, Trafalgar Square, Whitehall, Victoria, then *either* via Belgrave Road to Pimlico *or* via Vauxhall Bridge Road, Vauxhall, Stockwell, Brixton, Tulse Hill, West Norwood to Crystal Palace. Allocation: Holloway Garage 1 M nightly, Victoria Garage 2 M nightly.

26/27 April 1985: All journeys routed via Belgrave Road. By 9/10 August 1985: Allocation: Holloway Garage 1 M nightly, Victoria Garage 2 M (Su-Th), 3 M (Fr-Sa).

1/2 November 1985: Allocation: Holloway Garage 1 M (Su-Th), 2 M (Fr-Sa), Victoria Garage 2 M (Su-Th), 4 M (Fr-Sa). By July 1986: Allocation: Holloway Garage 2 M nightly, Victoria Garage 2 M (Su-Th), 4 M (Fr-Sa).

25/26 September 1987: Allocation: Holloway Garage 2 M nightly, Muswell Hill Garage 2 M (Su-Th), 3 M (Fr-Sa), Victoria Garage 1 M (Fr-Sa).

c. November 1988: Muswell Hill Garage allocation now mixed M/T-types.

1 April 1989: **London General** (Victoria Garage)**, London Northern** (Holloway/Muswell Hill Garages) commenced trading.

27/28 October 1989: Joint operation dissolved. Now operated by **London Northern** from Muswell Hill Garage 4 T (Su-Th), 7 T (Fr-Sa).

20/21 July 1990: Re-allocated upon closure of Muswell Hill Garage. Jnys to Finchley Garage introduced. Allocation: Finchley Garage 4 T (Su-Th), 5 T (Fr-Sa), Holloway Garage 2 M (Fr-Sa). 5/6 August 1990: Mixed M/T-type at Finchley Garage.

17/18 July 1992: Projected Friern Barnet – North Finchley (only garage jnys previously). Now operated: **North Finchley – Pimlico, Grosvenor Road *or* Crystal Palace, Parade.** Allocation: Finchley Garage 4 M/T (Su-Th), 5 M/T (Fr-Sa), Holloway Garage 3 M (Fr-Sa).

Muswell Hill garage's Leyland Titan T 1008 was seen at Victoria Bus Station early on Saturday morning 5 November 1988. At this time the N2's southbound service between Muswell Hill and Crystal Palace operated hourly but some northbound journeys formed a connecting service at Victoria to allow for drivers' relief-breaks. Additional journeys operated between Archway and Crystal Palace on weekend nights whilst the Pimlico bifurcation was served by two journeys nightly. *Roy Waterhouse*

27/28 November 1992: Now M-type at Finchley Garage.

3/4 December 1993: Re-allocated upon closure of Finchley Garage to Holloway Garage 4 M (Su-Th), 8 M (Fr-Sa).

26 October 1994: Operated by **MTL London Northern**.

23/24 June 1995: Sections of route North Finchley – Camden Town and Pimlico bifurcation withdrawn. Projected Camden Town – Hampstead Heath. Re-routed Cambridge Circus – Trafalgar Square. Now operated: **Hampstead Heath, South End Green – Crystal Palace, Parade** via Chalk Farm, Camden Town, Tottenham Court Road, Charing Cross Road, Trafalgar Square, Whitehall, Victoria, Vauxhall, Stockwell, Brixton, Tulse Hill, West Norwood. Allocation: Holloway Garage 3 M (Su-Th), 6 M (Fr-Sa). Note: Camden Town – Hampstead Heath section of N2 replaced that section of N93. North Finchley – Archway section of N2 replaced by enhanced frequency on N134 (partially-different intermediate routeing). Alternative service to Crouch End provided by extension of N91. Pimlico remained without an all-night bus service until the introduction of N24 on 26/27 November 1999.

17 August 1998: Operated by **Metroline London Northern.**

26/27 November 1999: Section of route Hampstead Heath – Trafalgar Square withdrawn. Re-routed Victoria – Vauxhall. Now operated: **Trafalgar Square – Crystal Palace, Parade** via Whitehall, Victoria, Vauxhall Bridge Road, Vauxhall, Stockwell, Brixton, Tulse Hill, West Norwood. Allocation: Holloway Garage 4 M (Su-Th), 6 M (Fr-Sa). Note: Hampstead Heath – Trafalgar Square section of N2 replaced by new route N24.

31 March/1 April 2000: LRT contract awarded to **Arriva London South**. Allocation: Norwood Garage 4L (Su-Th), 7 L (Fr-Sa).

31 August/ 1 September 2001 : Vehicle-type change to low-floor DAF DB250LF at Norwood Garage 4 DLA (Su-Th), 7 DLA (Fr-Sa).

1 September 2002: Truncated to terminate at Whitehall, Horse Guards. Now operated: **Whitehall, Horse Guards – Crystal Palace, Parade.** Allocation unchanged.

c. September 2003: Vehicle-type change to low-floor Volvo B7TL at Norwood Garage 4 VLA (Su-Th), 7 VLA (Fr-Sa).

1/2 April 2005: Fr-Sa frequency reduced. Allocation: Norwood Garage 4 VLA (Su-Th), 6 VLA (Fr), 5 VLA (Sa). 19/20 March 2009: Allocation: Norwood Garage 4 VLA (Su-Th), 5 VLA (Fr-Sa).

27 August 2010: Arriva acquired by Deutsche Bahn.

By 23/24 February 2012: Vehicle-type change to AD Trident Enviro400 at Norwood Garage 4 T (Su-Th), 5 T (Fr-Sa).

Holloway garage's MCW Metrobus M 1078 was seen loading passengers outside Canada House in Trafalgar Square for a southbound N2 journey on the night of 4/5 February 1995. *Malc McDonald*

Arriva London South's TransBus ALX400 bodied- Volvo B7TL VLA 23 was photographed at Terminus Place, Victoria on Thursday morning 22 June 2006. Route N2 has had a 30-minute Sunday to Thursday and 20-minute Friday and Saturday night frequency service between Whitehall and Crystal Palace since 1/2 April 2005. *Philip Wallis*

Victoria garage's London Transport Sightseeing Tour-liveried MCW Metrobus M 1045 was seen outside Canada House, Trafalgar Square in the early hours of Saturday morning 15 June 1985 working one of four nightly N11 journeys to Acton. *Malc McDonald*

Below Ash Grove garage's T 99 was drafted in to help out with London General's operation of route N11 on New Year's Eve 1989. This Leyland Titan was seen in Aldwych displaying an intermediate blind display for daytime route 6 (Kensal Rise – Hackney Wick) adapted to display route number N11 although only the last four intermediate points listed were on the N11's routeing. *Roy Waterhouse*

Route N11

13/14 April 1984: All-night service on route 11 **re-numbered N11**. Projected Hammersmith, Brook Green Hotel – Shepherd's Bush Green. Re-routed Trafalgar Square – Victoria. Now operated: **Liverpool Street Station – Shepherd's Bush Green** via Bank, Ludgate Circus, Aldwych, Trafalgar Square, Piccadilly Circus, Hyde Park Corner, Victoria, Sloane Square, Chelsea, Fulham Broadway, Hammersmith. Allocation: Victoria Garage 2 DMS nightly.

12/13 July 1984: Start of progressive vehicle-type change to Metrobus, initially using M-types from Round London Sightseeing Tour, at Victoria Garage 2 M nightly.

26/27 April 1985: Projected Liverpool Street Station – Hackney via Bethnal Green, Cambridge Heath, Shepherd's Bush Green – Acton. Now operated: **Hackney, Town Hall – Acton, Gunnersbury Lane.** Allocation: Victoria Garage 3 M nightly.

1/2 November 1985: Bifurcation Waterloo – Aldwych introduced. Projected Hackney, Town Hall – Hackney Wick. Now operated: **Hackney Wick, Eastway *or* Waterloo Station – Acton, Gunnersbury Lane** (set-down)**, High Street/King Street** (pick-up). 05.51 dep from Hackney Wick operated between Trafalgar Square and Victoria via Whitehall. Allocation unchanged.

18/19 April 1986: 05.51 dep from Hackney Wick revised to follow normal line of route.

8/9 August 1986: Sections of route Shepherd's Bush Green – Acton and Waterloo bifurcation withdrawn. Projected Shepherd's Bush Green – Turnham Green via Acton Green. Now operated: **Hackney Wick, Eastway – Turnham Green, Church**. Allocation: Victoria Garage 3 M nightly.

1 April 1989: **London General** commenced trading.

27/28 October 1989: Section of route Hackney Wick – Trafalgar Square withdrawn (replaced by new route N6). Now operated: **Trafalgar Square – Turnham Green, Church**. Operated jointly by **London General** Victoria Garage 1 M nightly and **London United** Shepherd's Bush Garage 1 M nightly.

27/28 April 1990: Allocation: London General: Victoria Garage 1M nightly. London United: Hounslow Garage 1 M nightly. Shepherd's Bush Garage 1 M nightly.

26/27 March 1993: Allocation: London General: Victoria Garage 1 M nightly. London United: Hounslow Garage 2 M nightly.

16/17 July 1993: London General re-allocated to Stockwell Garage. No numerical/vehicle-type change.

25/26 February 1994: Joint operation London General/London United dissolved. LRT contract awarded to **London United.** Section of route Shepherd's Bush Green – Turnham Green withdrawn. Projected Trafalgar Square – Liverpool Street. Re-routed Trafalgar Square – Victoria. Now operated: **Liverpool Street, Bus Station – Shepherd's Bush Green** via Bank, Ludgate Circus, Aldwych, Trafalgar Square, Whitehall, Victoria, Sloane Square, Chelsea, Fulham, Hammersmith. Allocation: Stamford Brook 2 L nightly.

5 November 1994: London United acquired by management/ employee buy-out.

30/31 August 1996: Allocation: Stamford Brook Garage 2 M nightly.

8/9 November 1996: Re-allocated to Hounslow Garage 2 M nightly (joint route N9).

July 1997: Operated by Transdev group t/a **London United.**

By 16/17 October 1998: Joint allocation with N9 dissolved. Allocation: Hounslow Garage 2 M (Su-Th), 3 M (Fr-Sa).

5/6 March 1999: Re-allocated to Shepherd's Bush Garage 4 M nightly.

23/24 July 1999: 1 bus now jointly with N94 (Su-Th).

16/17 December 1999: DP 87, single-deck low-floor Dennis Dart SLF, noted on N11.

c. March 2000: Official vehicle-type change to low-floor double-deck VA-type Volvo B7TL but in practice single-deck DP-type Dennis Dart SLFs were regularly deployed on the N11. Allocation: Shepherd's Bush Garage 4 DP/ VA (1 joint N94 (Su-Th) nightly.

30/31 March 2001: Section of route Hammersmith – Shepherd's Bush Green withdrawn (covered by extant N72). Projected Hammersmith – Wembley Central Station. Now operated: **Liverpool Street Bus Station – Wembley Central Station** via Bank, Ludgate Circus, Aldwych, Trafalgar Square, Whitehall, Victoria, Sloane Square, Chelsea, Fulham, Hammersmith, Turnham Green, Acton, Northfields, West Ealing, Perivale, Alperton. Joint allocation N94 dissolved, now: Stamford Brook Garage 8 VA nightly.

27/28 October 2001: Single-deck low-floor Dennis Dart SLF DPS 5 noted by author in service on route N11.

27/28 June 2003: LBSL contract awarded to **London General**. Allocation: Stockwell Garage 7 WVL nightly.

6/7 June 2008: Section of route West Ealing – Wembley Central Station withdrawn. Projected to Ealing Broadway. Now operated: **Liverpool Street Bus Station – Ealing Broadway Station.** Allocation unchanged. Note: Scotch Common – Wembley Central Station section of N11 replaced by new route (N)297.

By 27/28 July 2013: Allocation: Stockwell Garage 7 E/WVL nightly.

Route N11 was scheduled with a nightly 30-minute frequency service between Liverpool Street and Wembley Central at the time this view WVL 123 was taken at Charing Cross Station on Sunday morning 18 July 2004. The Volvo B7TL was on a short-working journey to Ealing, Scotch Common which had probably been curtailed for operational reasons. *Philip Wallis*

Route N13

13/14 April 1984: Introduced. Operated: **Trafalgar Square – North Finchley, Tally Ho Corner** via Piccadilly Circus, Oxford Circus, Gloucester Place (outbound), Baker Street (inbound), St Johns Wood, Swiss Cottage, Golders Green, Finchley. Allocation: Finchley Garage 2 M nightly.

26/27 October 1984: Projected North Finchley – Barnet via Whetstone. Now operated: **Trafalgar Square – Barnet Church**. Allocation unchanged.

By 9/10 August 1985: Unscheduled duplicate introduced Fr-Sa from Finchley Garage 2 M (Su-Th), 3 M (Fr-Sa). 1/2 November 1985: Allocation: Finchley Garage 2 M (Su-Th), 4 M (Fr-Sa).

1 April 1989: **London Northern** commenced trading.

27/28 October 1989: Allocation: Finchley Garage 3 M (Su-Th), 4 M (Fr-Sa). 5/6 August 1990: Allocation now M/T-types.

16/17 July 1992: Projected Trafalgar Square – Victoria via Whitehall, Victoria Street. Now operated: **Victoria Bus Station – Barnet Church**. Allocation: Finchley Garage 3 M (Su-Th), 4 M (Fr-Sa) + 1 M (joint N21) nightly.

3/4 December 1993: Re-allocated to Potters Bar Garage. Jnys Potters Bar Garage – Barnet Church introduced. Now operated: **Victoria Bus Station – Potters Bar Garage** via Whitehall, Trafalgar Square, Piccadilly Circus, Oxford Circus, Gloucester Place (outbound), Baker Street (inbound), St Johns Wood, Swiss Cottage, Golders Green, Finchley, North Finchley, Whetstone, Barnet, Hadley Highstone. Joint allocation with N21 dissolved, now: Potters Bar Garage 3 S nightly.

26 October 1994: Operated by **MTL London Northern**.

23/24 June 1995: Sections of route Victoria – Trafalgar Square, North Finchley – Potters Bar withdrawn. Now operated: **Trafalgar Square – North Finchley, Tally Ho Corner.** Allocation: Holloway Garage 3 M nightly.

17 August 1998: Operated by **Metroline London Northern**.

By 8/9 October 1999: Vehicle-type change to low-floor TP-type Dennis Trident at Holloway Garage 3 TP nightly.

18 February 2000: Metroline group acquired by DelGro group.

By 2/3 February 2001: Vehicle-type change to low-floor Volvo B7TL at Holloway Garage 3 VPL nightly.

31 Aug/1 Sept 2001: LBSL contract awarded to **Sovereign London** (Blazefield group). Projected Trafalgar Square – Aldwych. Now operated: **Aldwych – North Finchley, Tally Ho Corner.** Vehicle-type change to DAF DB250LF. Allocation: Edgware Garage 6 DLO (Su-Th), 9 DLO (Fr-Sa). Note: Due to a misunderstanding, Sovereign London did not start operation of N13 until 1/2 September 2001. All three of London Central's 'emergency cover' Leyland Titans were mustered to provide an hourly service over route N13 on the night of 31 August/1 September 2001.

3 November 2002: Operated by Transdev group t/a **Sovereign London**.

20/21 June 2003: Allocation: 7 buses (Su-Th), 9 buses (Fr-Sa) from Edgware Garage. At around this time DLO-types were displaced by VA-type Volvo Olympians and VLP-type Volvo B7TLs transferred from associated Transdev company London United.

4 April 2006: Transdev corporate logo adopted.

September 2004: Fleet name **London Sovereign.**

13/14 August 2005: North Finchley terminus now Bus Station.

21/22 October 2005: Vehicle-type change to Scania N94UD OmniDekka at Edgware Garage 7 SLE (Su-Th), 9 SLE (Fr-Sa). 24/25 February 2006: Allocation: Edgware Garage 9 SLE (Su-Th), 11 SLE (Fr-Sa). 29/30 August 2008: Allocation: Edgware Garage 11 SLE (Su-Th), 14 SLE (Fr-Sa).

3 March 2011: With the split of Trandev's operations, London Sovereign remained under Veolia-Transdev group ownership.

29/30 June 2012: Allocation reduced upon introduction of new route N113, now: Edgware Garage 6 SLE (Su-Th), 10 SLE (Fr-Sa).

30/31 August 2013: Vehicle-type change to Volvo B5LH hybrid at Edgware garage 6 VH (Su-Th), 10 VH (Fr-Sa) – progressive conversion started 10/11 August 2013.

Top London Northern's MCW Metrobus M 623 was photographed at route N13's Barnet Church terminus on Saturday morning 1 August 1992. *Roy Waterhouse*

Centre Sovereign London's Plaxton President Volvo B7TL VLP 23 was seen in Baker Street on Sunday morning 11 April 2004. *Philip Wallis*

Bottom London Sovereign's East Lancs-bodied Scania OmniDekka SLE 23 paused for long enough at the traffic lights between Cockspur Street and the south side of Trafalgar Square to allow this nearside view to be taken on Sunday morning 11 June 2006. *Philip Wallis*

Routes N14, (N)14

13/14 April 1984: Introduced. Operated: **Liverpool Street Station *or* Farringdon Street, Stonecutter Street – Roehampton, Danebury Avenue** via Bank (to/from Liverpool Street only), Ludgate Circus, Aldwych, Trafalgar Square, Piccadilly Circus, Hyde Park Corner, South Kensington, Fulham, Putney, Upper Richmond Road, Dover House Road, Roehampton Lane. Jnys to/from Putney High Street, Chelverton Road and Putney Bridge Station. Allocation: Putney Garage 3 M nightly.

26/27 April 1985: Sections of route Roehampton Lane, Earl Spencer – Danebury Avenue and Farringdon Street bifurcation withdrawn. Projected Roehampton – Kingston Station via Kingston Vale, Norbiton. Bifurcation to Victoria (outbound via Whitehall, inbound from Hyde Park Corner) introduced. Now operated: **Liverpool Street Station *or* Victoria Bus Station – Kingston Station.** Allocation unchanged.

By 9/10 August 1985: Inbound jnys to Liverpool Street re-routed at Aldwych to Waterloo Station. This was for crew relief-break purposes, after which buses re-entered service from Liverpool Street Station. Now operated: **Liverpool Street Station (outbound) *or* Waterloo Station (inbound) *or* Victoria Bus Station – Kingston Station.** Allocation unchanged.

1/2 November 1985: Re-routed Upper Richmond Road – Roehampton via Roehampton Lane. Allocation: Putney Garage 3 M (Su-Fr), 4 M (Sa).

10/11 July 1987: Bifurcation to Waterloo Station withdrawn; such jnys resumed former line of route Aldwych – Liverpool Street. Outbound bifurcation Victoria – Trafalgar Square via Whitehall withdrawn. In Putney, certain jnys now terminated at Oxford Road, in addition to High Street, Chelverton Road and Putney Bridge Station. Now operated: **Liverpool Street Station *or* Victoria Bus Station (inbound) – Kingston Station**. Allocation: Putney Garage 3 M (Su-Th), 4 M (Fr-Sa).

22/23 November 1987: Kingston terminus now Fairfield Bus Station.

1 April 1989: **London General** commenced trading.

26/27 April 1991: Sections of route Liverpool Street Station – Trafalgar Square and inbound bifurcation Hyde Park Corner – Victoria withdrawn. Projected Kingston – Chessington. Bifurcation Victoria – Trafalgar Square via Whitehall introduced. Jnys to Oxford Road, Putney withdrawn. Jny (Fr-Sa) to/from Putney Heath, Green Man introduced. Operated: **Victoria Bus Station *or* Trafalgar Square – Chessington, World of Adventures** via Whitehall to Trafalgar Square (from/to Victoria only), Piccadilly Circus, Hyde Park Corner, South Kensington, Fulham, Putney, Barnes Common, Roehampton, Kingston Vale, Norbiton, Kingston, Surbiton, Tolworth, Hook. Allocation: Putney Garage 3 M (Su-Th), 5 M (Fr-Sa).

2 November 1994: London General acquired by management/ employee buy-out.

18/19 August 1995: Sections of route Roehampton – Chessington, bifurcation Victoria – Trafalgar Square and all short working Putney area jnys withdrawn. Projected Trafalgar Square – Tottenham Court Road Station. Re-routed Upper Richmond Road – Roehampton, Earl Spencer. Now operated: **Tottenham Court Road Station – Roehampton, Earl Spencer** via Charing Cross Road, Trafalgar Square, Piccadilly Circus, Hyde Park Corner, South Kensington, Fulham, Putney, Upper Richmond Road, Dover House Road. Allocation: Putney Garage 2 M (Su-Th), 4 M (Fr-Sa). Note: Kingston – Tolworth section of N14 replaced by projection of route N77.

24 May 1996: Operated by Go-Ahead group t/a **London General**.

By 11/12 January 1997: Putney Garage 3 M (Su-Th), 6 M (Fr-Sa).

12/13 September 1997: Section of route in Putney via Upper Richmond Road and Dover House Road withdrawn. Projected Putney Station – Roehampton, Danebury Avenue via Putney Hill, Putney Heath. Re-routed Tottenham Court Road Station – Piccadilly Circus via Shaftesbury Avenue. Now operated: **Tottenham Court Road Station – Roehampton, Danebury Avenue.** Allocation: Putney Garage 6 M (Su-Th), 7 M (Fr-Sa).

c. February 1998: Completion of vehicle-type change to Volvo Olympian at Putney Garage 6 NV (Su-Th), 7 NV (Fr-Sa).

Putney garage's MCW Metrobus M 1206 was photographed at Trafalgar Square's Cockspur Street bus stands on Saturday morning 8 June 1991. The recently extended N14 operated three nightly outbound journeys to Chessington with a further two journeys on Friday and Saturday nights. The inbound service from Chessington comprised two nightly journeys to central London along with a further two such journeys on Friday and Saturday nights as well as a short-working journey from Chessington to Putney Bridge Station. *Roy Waterhouse*

London General's Northern Counties Palatine I-bodied Volvo Olympian NV 105 was seen at Hyde Park Corner on Friday morning 5 July 2002 towards the end of step-floor bus operation on route N14. *Philip Wallis*

16/17 March 2001: Jointly operated by **London General** Putney Garage 4 NV (Su-Th), 5 NV (Fr-Sa), and **London Central** Camberwell Garage 4 AVL (Su-Th), 5 AVL (Fr-Sa).

28/29 September 2001: Joint operation dissolved. Now operated by **London General** from Putney Garage 8 NV (Su-Th), 10 NV (Fr-Sa).

26/27 June 2002: Start of progressive vehicle-type change to low-floor Volvo B7TL at Putney Garage 8 NV/WVL (Su-Th), 10 NV/WVL (Fr-Sa).

22/23 November 2002: Section of route Putney Heath – Roehampton withdrawn. Now operated: **Tottenham Court Road Station – Putney Heath, Green Man.** Allocation: Putney Garage 7 WVL (Su-Th), 13 WVL (Fr-Sa). Note: Replacement service to Roehampton, Danebury Avenue provided by new route N74.

2/3 April 2004: **Re-numbered (N)14.**

12/13 January 2007: Projected Tottenham Court Road Station – Warren Street Station. Now operated: **Warren Street Station – Putney Heath, Green Man** via Gower Street (outbound), Tottenham Court Road (inbound), Shaftesbury Avenue, Piccadilly Circus, Hyde Park Corner, South Kensington, Fulham, Putney, Putney Hill. Allocation unchanged.

Putney garage's Wrightbus-bodied Volvo B7TL WVL 46 was seen pulling out of the bus stand at route N14's Putney Heath, Green Man terminus on Sunday morning 28 March 2004. Daytime route 14 and night-time route N14 had formed a 24-hour service between Tottenham Court Road Station and Putney Heath since 22/23 November 2002 which was recognised in route numbering terms just six nights after this view when the N14 dropped the use of its 'N' route number prefix. *Philip Wallis*

Route N18

13/14 April 1984: Introduced. Operated: **Liverpool Street Station – Sudbury, Swan** via Bank, Ludgate Circus, Aldwych, Trafalgar Square, Piccadilly Circus, Oxford Circus, Marble Arch, Paddington Station, Westbourne Park, Ladbroke Grove, Harrow Road, Harlesden, Craven Park, Stonebridge Park, Wembley. Willesden Garage jny. Allocation: Willesden Garage 1 M nightly. Note: Due to an industrial dispute at Willesden Garage route N18 did not operate east of Marble Arch until 18/19 April 1984.

26/27 October 1984: Absorbed route N91. Allocation: Willesden Garage 2 M nightly.

26/27 April 1985: Projected Sudbury – Edgware Station via Harrow, Harrow Weald, Stanmore, Canons Park Station. Now operated: **Liverpool Street Station – Edgware Station.** Allocation: Willesden Garage 2 M nightly, Harrow Weald Garage 1 M nightly.

By 9/10 August 1985: Inbound jnys to Liverpool Street Station re-routed at Aldwych to Waterloo Station, for crew relief-break purposes, after which buses re-entered service from Liverpool Street Station or Ludgate Circus. Now operated: **Liverpool Street Station (outbound) *or* Waterloo Station (inbound) – Edgware Station.** Allocation: Willesden Garage 2 M nightly, Harrow Weald Garage 1 M (Su-Th), 2 M (Fr-Sa).

20/21 June 1986: Re-routed Paddington Station – Harrow Road via Royal Oak. Outbound jnys from Waterloo Station introduced. Now operated: **Liverpool Street Station (outbound) *or* Waterloo Station – Edgware Station.** Allocation: Harrow Weald Garage 1 M (Su-Th), 2 M (Fr-Sa), Westbourne Park Garage 1 M (Fr-Sa), Willesden Garage 2 M nightly.

10/11 July 1987: Sections of route Liverpool Street Station – Aldwych, Waterloo Station – Aldwych withdrawn. Bifurcation Trafalgar Square – Victoria via Whitehall introduced. Now operated: **Aldwych *or* Victoria Bus Station – Edgware Station**. Allocation unchanged.

25/26 September 1987: Section of route Aldwych – Trafalgar Square withdrawn. Bifurcation Stanmore – Watford Junction Station introduced. Now operated: **Victoria Bus Station – Watford Junction Station *or* Edgware Station** via Whitehall, Trafalgar Square, Piccadilly Circus, Oxford Circus, Marble Arch, Paddington Station, Royal Oak Station, Harrow Road, Harlesden, Craven Park, Stonebridge Park, Wembley, Sudbury, Harrow, Harrow Weald, Stanmore Station, then *either* Bushey Heath, Bushey, Watford to Watford Junction Station *or* Canons Park Station to Edgware Station. Willesden Garage jnys. Allocation: Edgware Garage 1 M (Su-Th), 2 M (Fr-Sa), Willesden Garage 2 M (Su-Th), 3 M (Fr-Sa). Note: Replaced Stanmore Station – Watford Junction Station section of N59. The 25½ mile N18 became LRT's then-longest bus route.

1 April 1989: **Metroline** commenced trading.

27/28 October 1989: Bifurcation Stanmore Station – Edgware Station withdrawn. Joint operation **Centrewest** Westbourne Park Garage 1 M nightly and **Metroline** Willesden Garage 2 M (Su-Th), 4 M (Fr-Sa) introduced. Now operated: **Victoria Bus Station – Watford Junction Station**.

28/29 January 1994: Joint operation dissolved. LRT contract awarded to **Centrewest**. Sections of route Victoria – Trafalgar Square, Harrow Weald – Watford Junction Station and Willesden Garage jnys withdrawn. Now operated: **Trafalgar Square – Harrow Weald.** Allocation: Alperton Garage 1 M (Su-Fr), Westbourne Park Garage 5 M (Su-Th), 9 M (Fr-Sa). Note: Harrow Weald – Watford Junction section of N18 abandoned by LRT. Contemporary LRT publicity advised passengers of the British Rail Euston – Watford Junction night train service. London Central subsequently introduced a commercial all-night bus service to the Watford area from 25/26 October 1996 (see Chapter 8).

2 September 1994: Centrewest acquired by management/employee buy-out.

26 March 1997: Centrewest acquired by **First Bus,** re-titled **First Group** December 1997, **First London** March 2001.

21/22 August 1998: Re-routed Oxford Circus – Paddington via Portland Place, Marylebone Road, Old Marylebone Road (outbound), Chapel Street (inbound). Allocation: Alperton Garage 1 M (Su-Fr), Westbourne Park Garage 8 M (Su-Th), 12 M (Fr-Sa).

9/10 July 1999: Introduction of low-floor Dennis Tridents at Westbourne Park Garage 8 TN (Su-Th), 12 TN (Fr-Sa), Alperton Garage 1 VN (Su-Th).

19/20 November 1999: Fr-Sa 'extras' introduced, operated by **London Traveller** using Metrobuses. Such 'extras' last ran on New Year's Eve 2000.

2/3 February 2001: Re-routed westbound direct from Marylebone Road to Harrow Road. Re-routed eastbound from Harrow Road via Edgware Road to line of route at Chapel Street. Allocation: Alperton Garage 5 VN (Su-Th), 7 VN (Fr-Sa), Westbourne Park Garage 2 TN (Su-Th), 11 TN (Fr-Sa).

13/14 September 2002: Allocation: Westbourne Park Garage 13 TN (Su-Th), 18 TN (Fr-Sa).

14/15 November 2003: Su-Th allocation now 12 TN. c. January 2004: Allocation now TN/TNA-types. By June 2006: Allocation now TN/TNA/VNW/VNL-types.

22/23 June 2007: Re-allocated to Alperton Garage 12 VNW (Su-Th), 18 VNW (Fr-Sa).

9/10 January 2009: Re-routed eastbound direct from Harrow Road to Marylebone Road (as westbound routeing). By 8/9 May 2010: Allocation now VN/VNW-types.

13/14 November 2010: Re-allocated to Willesden Junction Garage 10 VN (Su-Th), 15 VN (Fr-Sa).

21/22 June 2013: Operated by **Metroline West** VW-type.

Willesden garage's M 1003 had attracted a good number of passengers as it loaded in Regent Street early on Saturday morning 15 June 1985. The MCW Metrobus was working one of three nightly outbound N18 journeys from Liverpool Street Station to Edgware Station – passengers would have needed good eyesight to discern the ultimate destination which appears to have been squeezed onto a pre-existing blind display. *Malc McDonald*

Route N21 (via Wood Green)
13/14 April 1984: Extant Special Night Journeys on route 221 **re-numbered N21.** Projected Holborn Circus – Trafalgar Square. Now operated: **Trafalgar Square – North Finchley, Tally Ho Corner** via Piccadilly Circus, Shaftesbury Avenue, New Oxford Street, High Holborn, Holborn Circus, Farringdon Road, King's Cross, Caledonian Road, Holloway, Finsbury Park, Manor House, Turnpike Lane Station, Wood Green, Bounds Green, Friern Barnet. Allocation: Finchley Garage 1 M nightly, from 26/27 April 1985 increased to 2 M nightly.

1 April 1989: **London Northern** commenced trading.

20/21 July 1990: Allocation: Finchley Garage 2 M/T-types.

17/18 July 1992: Section of route New Southgate Station – North Finchley withdrawn. Projected Trafalgar Square – Victoria, New Southgate Station – Cockfosters Station. Re-routed Holborn Station – King's Cross. Now operated: **Victoria Bus Station – Cockfosters Station** via Whitehall, Trafalgar Square, Piccadilly Circus, Shaftesbury Avenue, New Oxford Street, Russell Square, Euston Station, King's Cross, Caledonian Road, Holloway, Finsbury Park, Manor House, Turnpike Lane Station, Wood Green, Bounds Green, New Southgate Station, Southgate, Oakwood. Two inbound early morning jnys maintained original routeing King's Cross – Holborn Station via Farringdon Road, Holborn Circus. Garage jnys New Southgate – North Finchley. Allocation: Finchley Garage 2 M/T nightly + 1 M/T (joint N13). Note: Replaced route N92 in Southgate and Oakwood areas.

27/28 November 1992: Allocation now M-type.

3/4 December 1993: Sections of route Victoria – Trafalgar Square and North Finchley garage jnys withdrawn. The two inbound jnys via Farringdon Road re-routed to operate as main service via Euston Station. Projected Cockfosters Station – Potters Bar Garage. Now operated: **Trafalgar Square – Potters Bar Garage** via Piccadilly Circus, Shaftesbury Avenue, New Oxford Street, Russell Square, Euston Station, King's Cross, Caledonian Road, Holloway, Finsbury Park, Manor House, Turnpike Lane Station, Wood Green, Bounds Green, New Southgate Station, Southgate, Oakwood, Cockfosters Station. Allocation: Potters Bar Garage 2 S (Su-Th), 3 S (Fr-Sa).

Finchley garage's Leyland Titan T 607 was seen at bus stop C outside the National Gallery in Trafalgar Square early on Saturday morning 8 June 1991. Route N21 had provided a nightly hourly frequency service between Trafalgar Square and North Finchley since 26/27 April 1985. *Roy Waterhouse*

Below The prestigious Waldorf Hotel in Aldwych provided the backdrop for Potters Bar garage's MCW Metrobus M 957 as it loaded passengers for an outbound N21 journey which would terminate at its home garage in the early hours of New Year's Day 1995. *Mike Harris*

26 October 1994: Operated by **MTL London Northern**.

22/23 June 1995: Last night of operation. Note: Largely replaced by projection of route N91 to Potters Bar Garage. Holloway – Turnpike Lane Station section of N21 already served by route N29.

Route N27 (Richmond)
13/14 April 1984: Introduced. Operated: **Liverpool Street Station – Richmond Bus Station** via Bank, Ludgate Circus, Aldwych, Trafalgar Square, Piccadilly Circus, Hyde Park Corner, Knightsbridge, South Kensington, Cromwell Road, Earls Court, Fulham Broadway, Hammersmith, Turnham Green, Chiswick, Kew Bridge. Allocation: Stamford Brook Garage 2 M nightly.

25/26 April 1985: Last night of operation. Note: Frequency over common section of N97 increased as a compensatory measure. Richmond served by extension to N93.

Route N74 (Bromley North)
13/14 April 1984: Introduced. Operated: **Victoria, Wilton Road (dep) *or* Vauxhall Bridge Road (arr) – Bromley North Station** via Victoria Street, Whitehall, Trafalgar Square, Aldwych, Ludgate Circus, Blackfriars Bridge, Elephant & Castle, Old Kent Road, New Cross, Lewisham, Catford, Bromley Road. Allocation: Peckham Garage 2 T nightly.

26/27 October 1984: Victoria terminus now Bus Station.

31 Oct/1 Nov 1985: Last night of operation. Note: Lewisham – Bromley section of N74 replaced by route N47.

Route N76 (via Leytonstone)
13/14 April 1984: Introduced. Operated: **Victoria, Wilton Road (dep) *or* Garage (arr) – Leytonstone, Green Man** via Buckingham Palace Road (inbound), Victoria Street, Whitehall, Trafalgar Square, Piccadilly Circus, Shaftesbury Avenue, New Oxford Street, Holborn Circus, Bank, Liverpool Street (outbound), Bishopsgate (inbound), Houndsditch (outbound), Bevis Marks (inbound), Aldgate, Whitechapel, Stepney Green, Mile End, Bow, Stratford, Maryland. Jnys West Ham Garage – Stratford. Allocation: West Ham Garage 2 T nightly.

26/27 October 1984: Projected Leytonstone – Wanstead Station. Victoria terminus now Bus Station. Now operated: **Victoria Bus Station – Wanstead Station.** Allocation unchanged.

8/9 August 1986: Projected Wanstead Station – Hainault via Snaresbrook, South Woodford, Gants Hill, Barkingside. Jnys Plaistow – Stratford and West Ham Garage – Stratford. Now operated **Victoria Bus Station – Hainault, The Lowe.** Allocation: West Ham Garage 3 T nightly.

1 April 1989: **East London** commenced trading.

20/21 April 1990: Sections of route Victoria – Trafalgar Square and Plaistow garage jnys withdrawn. Now operated: **Trafalgar Square – Hainault, The Lowe**. Allocation: West Ham Garage 3 T (Su-Th), 5T (Fr-Sa).

9/10 May 1992: Diverted to serve Liverpool Street Bus Station.

9/10 October 1992: Re-allocated to Upton Park Garage 3 T (Su-Th), 5 T (Fr-Sa). West Ham Garage jnys withdrawn. By 26/27 March 1993: Allocation: Upton Park Garage 3 T/S (Su-Th), 5 T/S (Fr-Sa).

6 September 1994: Operated by **Stagecoach East London**.

4/5 November 1994: Allocation: Upton Park Garage 3 S (Su-Th), 5 S (Fr-Sa).

13/14 July 1995: Last night of operation. Note: Bow – South Woodford section of N76 replaced by N8, which also served Gants Hill. Gants Hill – Hainault section of N76 replaced by N25.

Routes N77 (Thamesmead), N1 (Thamesmead)
13-14 April 1984: Introduced. **Numbered N77.** Operated: **Victoria, Wilton Road (dep) *or* Vauxhall Bridge Road (arr) – Thamesmead, Bentham Road** via Victoria Street, Whitehall, Trafalgar Square, Aldgate, Ludgate Circus, Blackfriars Bridge, Elephant & Castle, Old Kent Road, New Cross, Deptford, Greenwich, Charlton, Woolwich, Plumstead, Abbey Wood. Allocation: New Cross Garage 2 T nightly. Note: Absorbed elements of Saturday night/ Sunday morning service on route 177.

26/27 October 1984: Victoria terminus now Bus Station.

2/3 August 1985: Enhanced service Monday – Saturday mornings to replace early morning jnys on daytime route 177. Allocation: New Cross Garage 3 T (Su-Fr), 2 T (Sa).

1/2 November 1985: Allocation: New Cross Garage 3 T nightly.

20/21 June 1986: Largely re-allocated to Plumstead Garage 3 L (M-Sa), 2 L (Su), New Cross Garage 1 T (Su).

1 April 1989: **London Central** (New Cross Garage) and **Selkent** (Plumstead Garage) commenced trading. Allocation unchanged.

27/28 October 1989: Allocation: London Central: New Cross Garage 1 T + 1 T (joint N53) nightly, Selkent: Plumstead Garage 2 L + 2 L (joint N53) nightly.

23/24 November 1990: Plumstead Garage allocation now L/T-types.

Paul Davis recorded the first-ever Night Bus journey to reach Hainault with the arrival of West Ham garage's Leyland Titan T 429 there at 01.36 on Saturday morning 9 August 1986. *Paul Davis*

Plumstead garage's Eastern Coach Works-bodied Leyland Olympian L 123 was photographed outside Canada House in Trafalgar Square prior to setting off on the 05.17 N77 journey to Thamesmead on Sunday morning 11 July 1987. This bus was fitted with the experimental Autocheck automated fare collection system which was trialled in south east London but abandoned in April 1989. *Eamonn Kentell*

28/29 April 1991: Allocation (joint N47/N53): London Central (New Cross Garage) 2 T/L nightly, Selkent (Plumstead Garage) 5 T/L (Su-Th), 4 T/L (Fr-Sa).

8/9 October 1993: Allocation (joint N53): London Central (New Cross Garage) 1 T/L (Su-Th), 2 T/L (Fr-Sa), Selkent (Plumstead Garage) + 5 T/L (Su-Th), 4 T/L (Fr-Sa).

6 September 1994: Plumstead Garage operated by **Stagecoach Selkent**.

18 October 1994: London Central (New Cross Garage) operated by Go-Ahead group t/a **London Central**.

28/29 July 1995: **Re-numbered N1.** LRT contract awarded to **London Central**. Section of route Plumstead – Thamesmead withdrawn. Re-routed Aldwych – Deptford. Now operated: **Victoria Bus Station – Plumstead Garage** via Whitehall, Trafalgar Square, Aldwych, Waterloo Bridge, Elephant & Castle, Bricklayers Arms, Bermondsey, Surrey Quays, Pepys Estate, Deptford, Greenwich, Charlton, Woolwich. Allocation: New Cross Garage (joint N21/N81) 8 T (Su-Th), 11 T (Fr-Sa). Note: Replaced Trafalgar Square – Deptford section of N51/N61. Plumstead – Thamesmead section of N77 replaced by bifurcation of N53.

c. June 1996: Allocation now T/NV-types.

16/17 May 1997: Joint allocation N21/N81 dissolved. Allocation: Bexleyheath Garage 2 T (Fr-Sa), New Cross Garage 3 NV (Su-Th), 2 NV (Fr-Sa).

7/8 November 1997: Joint allocation reinstated: Bexleyheath Garage (joint N21/N81) 2 NV (Su-Th), 4 NV (Fr-Sa), New Cross Garage (joint N81) 4 NV (Fr-Su), 5 NV (M-Th).

13/14 November 1998: LRT contract awarded to **First Group**, re-titled **First London** March 2001. Section of route Victoria – Trafalgar Square withdrawn. Now operated: **Trafalgar Square – Plumstead Station**. Allocation: Northumberland Park Garage 4 M nightly.

c. September 1999: Vehicle-type change to low-floor Dennis Trident completed (started 24/25 June 1999) at Northumberland Park Garage 4 TN nightly.

7/8 January 2000: Projected Plumstead – Thamesmead via Abbey Wood, Crossway. Re-routed in Deptford via Creek Road. Now operated: **Trafalgar Square – Thamesmead, Bentham Road.** Allocation: Dagenham Dock Garage 6 TN nightly.

28/29 April 2000: Section of route Trafalgar Square – Aldwych withdrawn. Projected Aldwych – Tottenham Court Road Station via Kingsway. Now operated: **Tottenham Court Road Station, New Oxford Street – Thamesmead, Bentham Road.**

30 Nov/1 Dec 2001: Re-allocated to Hackney Wick Garage 6 TN nightly.

14/15 October 2005: LBSL contract awarded to **East Thames Buses**. Allocation: Belvedere Garage 6 VWL (Su-Th), 9 VWL (Fr-Sa).

2/3 October 2009: East Thames Buses acquired by Go-Ahead group. Operation re-assigned to **London General**. Allocation unchanged.

30 April/1 May 2010: Partially re-allocated: Belvedere Garage 3 VWL (Su-Th), 5 VWL (Fr-Sa), Mandela Way East Garage 3 VWL (Su-Th), 4 VWL (Fr-Sa). Mandela Way East E-type by 27/28 July 2013.

First London's Plaxton President-bodied Dennis Trident TNL 33017 was photographed at Holborn Station bus stop in Kingsway in the early hours of New Year's Day 2005. At this time route N1 operated a nightly 30-minute frequency between Tottenham Court Road station and Thamesmead but its Friday and Saturday night frequency would be increased to 20 minutes upon the award of route N1's LBSL contract to East Thames Buses from 14/15 October 2005. *Philip Wallis*

Routes N78, N109, N159, N109

13/14 April 1984: Introduced. **Numbered N78.** Operated: **Victoria, Wilton Road (dep)** ***or*** **Vauxhall Bridge Road (arr) – South Croydon, Swan & Sugar Loaf** via Whitehall, Trafalgar Square, Aldwych, Waterloo Bridge, Elephant & Castle, Kennington, Brixton, Streatham Hill, Streatham, Norbury, Thornton Heath Pond, West Croydon Station, East Croydon Station. Allocation: Brixton Garage 3 DMS nightly, Thornton Heath Garage 1 DMS nightly. Note: N78 absorbed Brixton leg of N87 as well as the limited all-night service on route 109. Most outbound journeys connected at Kennington, Oval with N87 to Clapham.

26/27 October 1984: Victoria terminus now Bus Station. Allocation: Brixton Garage 4 DMS nightly. Note: Timetable now detailed connections at Kennington, Oval with outbound N87 jnys to Clapham and inbound N87 jnys to Trafalgar Square via Westminster.

11/12 December 1984: Completion of vehicle-type change (started November 1984) to Metrobus at Brixton Garage 4 M nightly.

By 9/10 August 1985: Unscheduled duplicate introduced Fr-Sa. Allocation: Brixton Garage 4 M (Su-Th), 5 M (Fr-Sa). 1/2 November 1985: Fr-Sa duplicate jnys incorporated into timetable.

22/23 May 1987: Projected South Croydon – New Addington. Bifurcation introduced Streatham Common – Thornton Heath. Now operated: **Victoria Bus Station – New Addington, Homestead Way** via Whitehall, Trafalgar Square, Aldwych, Waterloo Bridge, Elephant & Castle, Kennington, Brixton, Streatham Hill, Streatham, Streatham Common then *either* via Norbury *or* via Streatham Vale, Pollards Hill to London Road, then Thornton Heath Pond, West Croydon Station, East Croydon Station, South Croydon, Purley, Sanderstead, Selsdon, Addington, Lodge Lane. Allocation: Brixton Garage 5 M (Su-Th), 6 M (Fr-Sa). Note: Restored an all-night bus service to Streatham Vale and Pollards Hill, previously served by route N60 until 5/6 February 1987.

1 April 1989: **South London** commenced trading.

27/28 October 1989: Timetable changes in conjunction with the introduction of N69. Allocation: Brixton Garage (joint N69) 7 M nightly: Note: Connections at Kennington, Oval with N87 no longer detailed in timetable.

20/21 July 1990: Re-allocated to Thornton Heath Garage (joint N69) 7 L nightly.

11/12 March 1994: **Re-numbered N109.** LRT contract awarded to **London Central**. Sections of route Victoria – Trafalgar Square, Purley – Gravel Hill and bifurcation via Streatham Vale withdrawn. Revised to terminate at Aldwych. Re-routed Trafalgar Square – Elephant & Castle. Projected Purley – Coulsdon and bifurcation East Croydon – New Addington introduced. Now operated: **Aldwych – New Addington, Homestead Way** ***or*** **Coulsdon, Red Lion** via Trafalgar Square, Whitehall, Westminster Bridge, Elephant & Castle, Kennington, Brixton, Streatham Hill, Streatham, Streatham Common, Norbury, Thornton Heath Pond, West Croydon Station, East Croydon Station then *either* Shirley Park, Gravel Hill, Addington, Lodge Lane to New Addington *or* South Croydon, Purley to Coulsdon. Joint allocation with N69 dissolved, now: Camberwell Garage 9 T nightly. Note: Streatham Vale did not regain an all-night bus service until the re-routeing of N133 from 31 August/1 September 2007. Selsdon – Gravel Hill regained an all-night bus service with the introduction of N64 from 27/28 August 2010. Purley – Selsdon section of N78 not replaced with an all-night bus service.

18 October 1994: Operated by Go-Ahead t/a **London Central**.

By 10/11 October 1997: Allocation: Camberwell Garage 9 T (Su-Th), 10 T (Fr-Sa). By June 1998: Vehicle-type change to Volvo Olympian at Camberwell Garage 9 NV (Su-Th), 10 NV (Fr-Sa).

17/18 September 1999: **Re-numbered N159.** Section of route Aldwych – Trafalgar Square withdrawn. Projected Trafalgar Square – Marble Arch via Piccadilly Circus, Oxford Circus. Re-routed Westminster Bridge Road – Kennington via Kennington Road. Now operated: **Marble Arch – New Addington, Homestead Way** ***or*** **Coulsdon, Red Lion.** Allocation: Camberwell Garage 10 NV (Su-Th), 11 NV (Fr-Sa).

Brixton garage's Leyland Fleetline DMS 2462 was parked at Victoria bus garage early on Saturday morning 27 October 1984. At this time most journeys of nightly 30-minute frequency route N78 operated between Trafalgar Square and South Croydon but four nightly journeys were projected in service beyond Trafalgar Square to and from Victoria via Whitehall to facilitate drivers' relief breaks at Victoria garage. *Paul Davis*

The prospective passengers seem to be asking the driver of Brixton garage's M 1092 about the N78's routeing as the MCW Metrobus paused at East Croydon Station in the early hours of Tuesday 2 June 1987. Having taken about one hour to reach East Croydon from central London this bus still had over half-an-hour's journey time ahead of it before reaching New Addington terminus after following the N78's circuitous onward routeing via Purley and Sanderstead. *Malc McDonald*

South London's Thornton Heath garage-based Leyland Olympian L 183 was seen at Brixton Police Station bus stop during the early hours of Saturday morning 20 October 1990. *Roy Waterhouse*

31 Jan/1 Feb 2000: Start of progressive vehicle-type change to low-floor Volvo B7TL at Camberwell Garage 10 NV/AVL (Su-Th), 11 NV/AVL (Fr-Sa).

28/29 April 2000: Bifurcation East Croydon Station – Coulsdon withdrawn (replaced by projection of N68). Now operated: **Marble Arch – New Addington, Homestead Way.** Allocation: Camberwell Garage 10 AVL (Su-Th), 12 AVL (Fr-Sa).

16/17 March 2001: LBSL contract awarded to **Arriva London South**. Re-routed in New Addington off Lodge Lane via Fieldway, Headley Drive, Goldcrest Way and King Henry's Drive to Homestead Way. Allocation: Thornton Heath Garage 12 L/DLA nightly.

c. February 2003: Fully converted to low-floor DAF DB250 LF at Thornton Heath Garage 12 DLA nightly.

26/27 November 2004: Allocation: Thornton Heath Garage 16 DLA nightly.

31 March/1 April 2006: Allocation: South Croydon Garage 3 DW (Sa-Th), 4 DW (Fr), Thornton Heath Garage 13 DLA (Su-Th), 14 DLA (Fr), 15 DLA (Sa).

27 August 2010: Arriva acquired by Deutsche Bahn.

27/28 August 2010: **Re-numbered N109.** Sections of route Marble Arch – Oxford Circus, Croydon, Wellesley Road – New Addington withdrawn. Projected to Croydon, Park Street. Now operated: **Oxford Circus – Croydon, Park Street.** Allocation: Thornton Heath Garage 8 DLA/T (Su-Th), 9 DLA/T (Fr-Sa). Note: Marble Arch – Oxford Circus section of N159 covered by new (N)159 (and many other extant Nighters). Croydon – New Addington section of N159 replaced by N64 (partially different intermediate routeing). Shirley – Addington Park section of N159 not replaced with an all-night bus service.

30/31 March 2012: Re-allocated to Brixton Garage 8 DLA/DW (Su-Th), 9 DLA/DW (Fr-Sa). All DW by 30/31 August 2013.

Above Arriva London South's TransBus ALX400-bodied DAF DLA 343 was seen at Streatham Station taking up service on route N159 at 22.34 on Saturday evening 25 June 2005. At the time this was the earliest Night Bus to enter service across Transport for London's network. *Philip Wallis*

Left Arriva London South's Alexander Dennis Trident Enviro400 T 138 was photographed at Whitehall during the early hours of Friday morning 30 March 2012 on the last night of Thornton Heath garage's operation of nightly 20-minute frequency route N109. *Philip Wallis*

Route N79

13/14 April 1984: Introduced. Operated: **Archway Station – Lewisham Bus Station *or* Catford Garage** via Holloway, Highbury Corner, Islington, Rosebery Avenue, Holborn LT Station, Aldwych, Trafalgar Square, Whitehall, Victoria, Vauxhall, Kennington, Camberwell Green, East Dulwich, Dulwich, Forest Hill, Catford. Allocation: Walworth Garage 3 T nightly. Note: Replaced Victoria – Lewisham all-night service on route 185.

26/27 October 1984: Section of route Archway – Trafalgar Square withdrawn. Projected Trafalgar Square – Willesden Garage. Now operated: **Willesden Garage – Lewisham Bus Station *or* Catford Garage** via Kensal Rise, West Kilburn, Warwick Avenue Station, Edgware Road, Marble Arch, Oxford Circus, Piccadilly Circus, Trafalgar Square, Whitehall, Victoria, Vauxhall, Kennington, Camberwell Green, East Dulwich, Dulwich, Forest Hill, Catford. Allocation unchanged. Note: Replaced Kensal Rise Station – Trafalgar Square section of N82.

1/2 November 1985: Re-allocated to Camberwell Garage 3 T (Su-Th), 4 T (Fr-Sa).

By 30/31 January 1989: Fr-Sa unscheduled duplicate introduced from Willesden Garage 1 M.

1 April 1989: **London Central** (Camberwell Garage) and **Metroline** (Willesden Garage) commenced trading.

27/28 October 1989: Joint operation dissolved. Now operated by **London Central**. Sections of route Willesden Garage – Oxford Circus, Catford – Lewisham and Catford – Catford Garage withdrawn. Projected Catford – Hither Green Station. Now operated: **Oxford Circus – Hither Green Station.** Allocation: Camberwell Garage 2 T nightly. Note: Willesden Garage – Oxford Circus section of N79 replaced by new route N6. Catford – Lewisham and Catford – Catford Garage sections of N79 covered by N47, N70 and N85.

By 26/27 March 1993: Vehicle-type change to Optare Spectra at Camberwell Garage 2 SP nightly.

18 October 1994: Operated by Go-Ahead t/a **London Central**.

25/26 November 1994: Allocation: Camberwell Garage 2 SP + 1 SP (joint N3) nightly.

25/26 April 1996: Last night of operation. Note: Camberwell Green – Forest Hill section of N79 replaced by new route N176. Brockley Road – Hither Green Station section of N79 replaced by route N171.

Routes introduced later in 1984

Railair Link

13/14 May 1984: Introduced. Operated: **Outbound: Euston Station, Bus Station *non-stop* to Victoria Bus Station *non-stop* to Heathrow Airport, Terminal 3, Inbound: Heathrow Airport, Terminal 3 *non-stop* to Euston Station.** Allocation: Ash Grove Garage 1 T nightly. Note: Operated by London Transport Executive under contract to British Rail. Timed to connect with 00.15 Birmingham – Euston train. Also connected at Victoria Station with British Rail trains to Gatwick Airport. Designated as route number 556 in *Allocation of Scheduled Buses*, route number not displayed.

26/27 October 1984: Revised to also serve Waterloo Station. The newly commissioned 'emergency cover' M-type allocated to Victoria Garage from this date included route number 556 blind display.

25/26 April 1985: Last night of operation. Note: Elements of Railair Link incorporated into new route N56.

Route N60

26/27 October 1984: Introduced. Operated: **Clapham Common Station – Clapham Common Station.** Unidirectional 'figure of eight' service via Acre Lane, Brixton, Streatham Hill, Streatham, Streatham Common, Streatham Vale, Pollards Hill, Thornton Heath Pond, West Croydon Station, Whitehorse Road, Thornton Heath High Street, Green Lane, Streatham Common, Streatham, Streatham Hill, Poynders Road. Allocation: Clapham Garage 1 M nightly.

5/6 February 1987: Last night of operation.

Camberwell garage's Leyland Titan T 949 was seen at Victoria Bus Station during the early hours of Saturday morning 28 October 1989 during the first night of re-routed hourly frequency route N79's operation between Oxford Circus and Hither Green Station. *Roy Waterhouse*

After completing a return trip from Euston Station to Heathrow Airport the Railair Link bus made a further journey from Euston to Victoria Station. Ash Grove garage's Leyland Titan T 399, bedecked in an overall advertising display for ASDA stores, was photographed on its early morning arrival at Victoria Station Bus Station on Sunday 5 August 1984. *Mike Harris*

MCW Metrobus M 1066 was photographed inside Clapham garage immediately prior to taking up service on the first-ever route N60 journey at 00.03 on Saturday morning 27 October 1984. *Paul Davis*

CHAPTER 6
ROUTES INTRODUCED 1985 TO 1999

Second-time use of route number N50 occurred from 14/15 July 1995 with the introduction of an Oxford Circus to Ilford Broadway route operated by Stagecoach East London. LRT's contract for the N50 was awarded to First Capital from 21/22 August 1998 when its service was revised to operate between Trafalgar Square and East Beckton. Northumberland Park garage's Northern Counties-bodied Volvo Olympian 220 was photographed at the N50's Trafalgar Square pick-up bus stop in Duncannon Street on Wednesday morning 19 July 2000. *Mike Wiffen*

This chapter lists new routes introduced between 1985 and 1999 and the subsequent changes to those routes up to 30/31 August 2013.

Routes introduced 1985

Routes N50 (Ladbroke Grove), N23, (N)23

26/27 April 1985: Introduced. **Numbered N50.** Unidirectional service westbound only. **King's Cross Station – Ladbroke Grove, Eagle** via Euston Station, Holborn LT Station, Aldwych, Waterloo Station (arrive via Taxi Road, depart via York Road), Westminster Bridge, Victoria Embankment, Trafalgar Square, Whitehall, Victoria Street, Victoria Station, Hyde Park Corner, Marble Arch, Paddington Station, Westbourne Grove. Jny Ladbroke Grove Station – Shepherd's Bush, Wells Road. Allocation (joint N51): New Cross Garage 1 T nightly, Shepherd's Bush Garage 1 M nightly. Note: Corresponding eastbound service numbered N51. N50/N51 absorbed elements of Inter-Station Route.

1/2 November 1985: Projected Ladbroke Grove – Greenford. Re-routed Waterloo,York Road – Marble Arch. Garage jny withdrawn. Now operated: **King's Cross Station – Greenford, Red Lion** via Euston Station, Holborn LT Station, Aldwych, Waterloo Station, Lambeth Bridge, Horseferry Road, Victoria Street, Victoria Station, Whitehall, Trafalgar Square, Piccadilly Circus, Oxford Circus, Marble Arch, Paddington Station, Westbourne Grove, Ladbroke Grove, Wormwood Scrubs, East Acton, Acton, Ealing Broadway. Allocation: Ash Grove Garage 1 M (joint N51/N56) nightly, New Cross Garage 1 T (joint N51) nightly, Shepherd's Bush Garage 1 M (joint N51) nightly.

20/21 June 1986: Formed bidirectional service with absorption of N51. Section of route King's Cross – Trafalgar Square withdrawn. Bifurcated termini introduced at Victoria and Waterloo stations. Projected Greenford – Ruislip. Now operated: **Victoria Bus Station *or* Waterloo Station – Ruislip Station** via *either* Victoria Street, Whitehall (Victoria jnys) *or* Aldwych (Waterloo jnys) then Trafalgar Square, Piccadilly Circus, Oxford Circus, Marble Arch, Paddington Station, Westbourne Grove, Ladbroke Grove, Wormwood Scrubs, East Acton, Acton, Ealing Broadway, Greenford, Yeading, Northolt, Eastcote Lane. Jnys to Ladbroke Grove, Eagle. Jny Shepherd's Bush Green – Ladbroke Grove Station. Allocation: Ash Grove Garage 1 M (joint N56) nightly, Shepherd's Bush Garage 1 M nightly, Westbourne Park Garage 1 M nightly.

25/26 August 1986, 31 Aug/1 Sept 1987: Supplementary service operated on these nights only on occasion of the Notting Hill Carnival: **Harrow Road, Prince of Wales – West Norwood** (see Chapter 2).

By November 1986: Ash Grove Garage allocation 1 T-type.

10/11 July 1987: Section of route Waterloo Station – Trafalgar Square withdrawn. Most jnys now originated from/terminated at Trafalgar Square, with only one nightly dep from Victoria. Two inbound jnys operated Marble Arch – Victoria via Hyde Park Corner. Allocation unchanged.

25/26 September 1987: Allocation: Ash Grove Garage 1 T (joint N56) nightly, Shepherd's Bush Garage 2 M nightly.

1 April 1989: **London Forest** (Ash Grove Garage) and **London United** (Shepherd's Bush Garage) commenced trading.

27/28 October 1989: Jointly operated by **Centrewest** (Westbourne Park Garage 1 M nightly) and **London United** (Shepherd's Bush Garage 1 M + 1 M (joint N56) nightly.

26/27 March 1993: Joint operation dissolved. LRT contract awarded to **Centrewest** from Westbourne Park Garage 2 M + 1 M (joint N56) nightly.

Shepherd's Bush garage's MCW Metrobus M 1363 was seen loading passengers at bus stop W on the south side of Trafalgar Square for one of two nightly N50 journeys to Ruislip Station early on Sunday morning 11 October 1987. *Roy Waterhouse*

21/22 May 1993: **Re-numbered N23.** Sections of route Ealing Broadway – Ruislip and Marble Arch – Victoria withdrawn. Bifurcation Trafalgar Square – Aldwych introduced. Jny to Ladbroke Grove, Sainsbury's. Now operated: **Aldwych *or* Victoria Bus Station – Ealing Broadway Station.** Joint allocation with N56 dissolved, now: Westbourne Park Garage 2 M nightly. Note: Ealing Broadway – Ruislip section of route replaced by bifurcation of route N89.

23/24 July 1993: Projected Aldwych – Liverpool Street Station via Ludgate Circus, Bank. Now operated: **Liverpool Street Station *or* Victoria Bus Station – Ealing Broadway Station.** Allocation unchanged.

2 September 1994: Centrewest acquired by management/employee buy-out.

11/12 October 1996: Victoria – Trafalgar Square bifurcation and jny to Ladbroke Grove, Sainsbury's withdrawn. Projected Ealing Broadway – Northolt Station via Greenford, Yeading. Now operated: **Liverpool Street Station – Northolt Station.** Allocation: Westbourne Park Garage 4 M nightly. Note: Replaced Ealing Broadway – Northolt section of route N89's Ruislip bifurcation.

26 March 1997: Operated by **First Bus**, re-titled **First Group** December 1997, **First London** March 2001.

21/22 August 1998: Section of route Liverpool Street – Aldwych withdrawn. Now operated: **Aldwych – Northolt Station.** Allocation: Westbourne Park Garage 4 M (Su-Th), 8 M (Fr-Sa).

July 1999: Progressive vehicle-type change to low-floor Dennis Trident at Westbourne Park Garage 4 TN (Su-Th), 8 TN (Fr-Sa).

13/14 September 2002: Re-allocated to Alperton Garage 7 TN nightly, vehicle-type change to 7 VTL nightly c. October 2002.

29/30 August 2003: Section of route Ladbroke Grove – Northolt Station withdrawn (replaced by new route N7). Projected Ladbroke Grove – Westbourne Park Station and Aldwych – Liverpool Street Station. Now operated: **Liverpool Street Station – Westbourne Park Station** via Bank, Ludgate Circus, Aldwych, Trafalgar Square, Piccadilly Circus, Oxford Circus, Marble Arch, Paddington Station, Westbourne Grove, Ladbroke Grove, Kensal Road. Re-allocated to Westbourne Park Garage 5 TN nightly, vehicle-type change to 5 TNA nightly c. January 2004.

16/17 April 2004: **Re-numbered (N)23.**

12/13 November 2010: Allocation: Westbourne Park Garage 4 TNA nightly.

18/19 May 2012: Vehicle-type change to AD E40H Enviro400H hybrid from Westbourne Park Garage 4 DNH nightly.

21/22 June 2013: Operated by **Tower Transit**.

First London's TransBus Trident ALX400 TNA 33365 was seen in Oxford Street early on Sunday morning 20 June 2004 whilst working nightly 30-minute frequency route (N)23. This picture provides an example of a Night Bus continuing to display an 'N'-prefixed route number after a route had officially discontinued the use of such a prefix, since route N23 had been re-numbered (N)23 about two months earlier on 16/17 April 2004. *Philip Wallis*

Shepherd's Bush garage's MCW Metrobus M 895 clearly emphasised route N51's continuity from London Transport's Inter Station Service when it paused at Victoria Station Bus Station in June 1985. *David Bowker*

Route N51 (Ladbroke Grove)
26/27 April 1985: Introduced. Unidirectional service eastbound only. **Ladbroke Grove, Eagle – King's Cross Station** via Westbourne Grove, Paddington Station, Marble Arch, Hyde Park Corner, Victoria Station, Victoria Street, Whitehall, Trafalgar Square, Victoria Embankment, Westminster Bridge, Waterloo Station (arrive via Taxi Road, depart via Tenison Way), Aldwych, Holborn LT Station, Euston Station. Jny Shepherd's Bush, Wells Road – Ladbroke Grove Station. Allocation (joint N50): New Cross Garage 1 T nightly, Shepherd's Bush Garages 1 M nightly. Note. Corresponding westbound service numbered N50. N50/N51 absorbed elements of the Inter-Station Route.

1/2 November 1985: Projected to start from Greenford. Re-routed Victoria Street – Aldwych. Now operated: **Greenford, Red Lion – King's Cross Station** via Ealing Broadway, Acton, East Acton, Wormwood Scrubs, Ladbroke Grove, Westbourne Grove, Paddington Station, Marble Arch, Hyde Park Corner, Victoria Station, Victoria Street, Horseferry Road, Lambeth Bridge, Waterloo Station (approach via Taxi Road, depart via York Road), Westminster Bridge, Victoria Embankment, Trafalgar Square, Aldwych, Holborn LT Station, Euston Station. Allocation: Ash Grove Garage 1 M (joint N50/N56) nightly, New Cross Garage 1 T (joint N50) nightly, Shepherd's Bush Garage 1 M (joint N50) nightly.

19/20 June 1986: Last night of operation. Absorbed into N50.

The intermediate blind display on Shepherd's Bush garage's MCW Metrobus M 896 had been expanded to reflect the westward extension beyond Ladbroke Grove of route N51 from 1/2 November 1985 when this view was taken at Euston Bus Station early on Saturday morning 19 April 1986. *Malc McDonald*

Ash Grove garage's Leyland Titan T 61 was seen at Trafalgar Square's bus stop B in Pall Mall East at 05.17 on Friday morning 23 June 1989 during the period when route N56 otherwise operated non-stop between Waterloo and Victoria stations. *Malcolm Papes*

London General's Victoria garage-based emergency stand-by MCW Metrobus M 1354 had been called in to substitute for an absent London Central T-type Leyland Titan when seen loading passengers for route N47 on the western side of Trafalgar Square early on Sunday morning 29 October 1989. The emergency stand-by bus was equipped with route number displays for all London's Night Bus routes. *Roy Waterhouse*

Route N56

26/27 April 1985: Introduced. Operated: **King's Cross Station – Heathrow Airport** via Euston Station, Holborn LT Station, Aldwych, Waterloo Station (arrive via Taxi Road, depart via York Road), Westminster Bridge, Victoria Embankment, Trafalgar Square, Whitehall, Victoria Street, Victoria Station, Hyde Park Corner then **non-stop** to Heathrow Airport (Terminals 1, 2 and 3). Return jny from Heathrow Airport **non-stop** to King's Cross Station (Su-Fr) *or* **non-stop** to Victoria Station (Sa). Allocation: Ash Grove Garage 1M nightly. Note: Absorbed elements of Railair Link.

1/2 November 1985: Service re-cast. Now operated: **Paddington Station – Heathrow Airport** via Chapel Street, Marylebone Road, Euston Road, Euston Station, King's Cross Station, then **non-stop** to Waterloo Station (arrive via Taxi Road, depart via York Road), Lambeth Bridge, Horseferry Road, Victoria Street, Victoria Station, Hyde Park Corner then **non-stop** to Heathrow Airport (Terminals 1, 2 and 3). Return jny operated from Heathrow Airport **non-stop** to Paddington Station then as outbound jny to King's Cross Station. Allocation (joint N50/N51 until 19/20 June 1986, N50 from 20/21 June 1986): Ash Grove Garage 1 M nightly.

3/4 October 1986: Revised routeing and pick-up points in central and west London. Now operated: **Paddington Station – Heathrow Airport** via Chapel Street, Marylebone Road, Euston Road, Euston Station, King's Cross Station, Russell Square, Holborn LT Station, Aldwych, Waterloo Station (York Road) then **non-stop** to Trafalgar Square then **non-stop** to Victoria Station, Hyde Park Corner, Cromwell Road (Forum Hotel), Cromwell Road (junction Earls Court Road) then **non-stop** to Heathrow Airport (Terminals 1, 2 and 3). Return jny operated from Heathrow Airport **non-stop** to Paddington Station then as outbound jny to King's Cross Station. Allocation: Ash Grove Garage (joint N50) 1 M nightly.

By November 1986: Ash Grove Garage allocation now 1 T-type.

1 April 1989: **London Forest** commenced trading.

27/28 October 1989: Operation reassigned to **London United** at Shepherd's Bush Garage 1 M (joint N50) nightly. Non-stop conditions within central London rescinded so that buses now observed all stops (on request) between Waterloo and Victoria stations. Non-stop conditions remained in force Cromwell Road (junction Earls Court Road) – Heathrow Airport and Heathrow Airport – Paddington Station.

26/27 March 1993: Operation reassigned to **Centrewest** at Westbourne Park Garage 1 M (joint N50) nightly.

20/21 May 1993: Last night of operation.

Route N47

1/2 November 1985: Introduced. Operated: **Victoria Station, Bus Station – Bromley South Station** via Victoria Street, Whitehall, Trafalgar Square, Aldwych, Ludgate Circus, Cannon Street, London Bridge, Jamaica Road, Rotherhithe, Surrey Docks, Deptford, Lewisham, Catford, Bromley Road. Jnys Peckham Garage – Deptford Broadway, Surrey Docks Station – Peckham Garage. Allocation: Peckham Garage 2 T nightly. Note: Replaced Lewisham – Bromley section of N74.

1 April 1989: **London Central** commenced trading.

27/28 October 1989: Bifurcations Bromley South Station – Orpington via Bromley Common then *either* Locks Bottom, Farnborough, Green Street Green (five journeys) *or* Petts Wood (two journeys) introduced. Peckham garage jnys withdrawn. Now operated: **Victoria Bus Station – Orpington, Goodmead Road.** Joint operation introduced between **London Central** New Cross Garage 2 T nightly, Peckham Garage 1 T (joint N86) nightly and **Selkent** Catford Garage 1 T nightly.

26/27 April 1991: Allocation: London Central: New Cross Garage 4 T/L* (Su-Th), 2T/L (Fr-Sa), Peckham Garage 1 T (joint N86 Fr-Sa), Selkent: Catford Garage 1 T nightly. * One bus joint N77 (Su-Th).

8/9 October 1993: Projected Orpington – St Mary Cray Station. Now operated: **Victoria Bus Station – St Mary Cray Station.** Joint allocations N77/N86 dissolved, now London Central: New Cross Garage 2 T/L (Su-Th), 1 T/L (Fr-Sa), Selkent: Catford Garage 1 T (Su-Th), 2 T (Fr-Sa).

6 September 1994: Catford Garaage operated by **Stagecoach Selkent**.

18 October 1994: New Cross Garage operated by Go-Ahead group t/a **London Central**.

By 16/17 October 1998: London Central allocation had become NV-type Volvo Olympian.

By 25/26 June 1999: Allocation now all Volvo Olympian: London Central: New Cross Garage 2 NV (Su-Th), 1 NV (Fr-Sa), Stagecoach Selkent: Catford Garage 1 VN (Su-Th), 2 VN (Fr-Sa).

26/27 May 2000: Bifurcation via Farnborough withdrawn. All Orpington jnys now routed via Petts Wood. Allocation unchanged.

19/20 January 2001: LBSL contract awarded to **Stagecoach Selkent**. Section of route Victoria – Trafalgar Square withdrawn. Now operated: **Trafalgar Square – St Mary Cray Station** via Aldwych, Ludgate Circus, Cannon Street, London Bridge, Jamaica Road, Rotherhithe, Surrey Quays, Deptford, Lewisham, Catford, Bromley Road, Bromley, Bromley Common, Petts Wood. Allocation: Catford Garage 6 VN nightly. Note: The award of route N47's contract to Stagecoach Selkent dissolved the last instance of joint operation of an LBSL-contracted all-night bus route.

c. October 2002: Completion of progressive vehicle-type change to low-floor Dennis Trident at Catford Garage 6 TAS nightly.

30 August 2006: Operated by Macquarie Bank t/a East London Bus Group. Fleetname: **Selkent**.

31 Aug/1 Sept 2007: Allocation: Catford Garage 6 TA/TAS (Su-Th), 10 TA/TAS (Fr-Sa).

20/21 February 2009: Trafalgar Square pick-up point now Duncannon Street.

14 October 2010: Operated by Stagecoach Bus Holdings Ltd t/a **Selkent**. Continued operation by TA-type. Mixed TA/TE-types by 30/31 August 2013.

London Central's New Cross garage-based Leyland Titan T 1056 was photographed at Victoria Station Bus Station on Sunday morning 29 October 1989 loading passengers for the 01.06 departure on route N47's newly-extended service to Orpington. *Roy Waterhouse*

Stagecoach Selkent's shorter 9.9 metre length TransBus Trident ALX400 17578s was photographed in Lewisham High Street during the early hours of Friday morning 24 March 2006 working an inbound journey on then-30 minute frequency route N47. *Philip Wallis*

Route N72 (via Welling)
1/2 November 1985: Introduced. Operated: **Victoria Bus Station – Dartford, Market Street** via Victoria Street, Whitehall, Trafalgar Square, Aldwych, Ludgate Circus, Blackfriars Bridge, Elephant & Castle, Walworth Road, Camberwell Green, Peckham, New Cross, Lewisham, Blackheath, Lee Green, Eltham, Shooters Hill, Welling, Bexleyheath, Crayford. Allocation: New Cross Garage 2 T nightly.

By 10/11 July 1987: Allocation: New Cross Garage 2 L nightly. Dartford terminus now Dartford Station.

1 April 1989: **London Central** commenced trading.

27/28 October 1989: Dartford terminus now Market Street. Re-routed Lewisham – Lee Green via Lee High Road. Allocation unchanged.

8/9 October 1993: Section of route Welling Corner – Dartford withdrawn (replaced by new route N81). Now operated: **Victoria Station – Welling Corner.** Allocation: New Cross Garage 1 L nightly.

18 October 1994: Operated by Go-Ahead group t/a **London Central**.

27/28 July 1995: Last night of operation. Lewisham – Eltham section of N72 replaced by N21. Shooters Hill – Welling section of N72 already covered by N81.

Routes introduced 1986

Route N54
20/21 June 1986: Introduced. Operated: **East Croydon Station – Banstead, Victoria** via West Croydon Station, Roundshaw, Wallington, Carshalton, St Helier, Sutton, Belmont. Allocation: Sutton Garage 1 D nightly.

21/22 May 1987: Last night of operation. Note: Replaced by projections of N88.

Routes N59, N139, (N)139
20/21 June 1986: Introduced. **Numbered N59.** Operated: **Victoria Bus Station, – Watford Junction Station** via Victoria Street, Whitehall, Trafalgar Square, Piccadilly Circus, Oxford Circus, Gloucester Place (outbound), Baker Street (inbound), Lisson Grove, Abbey Road, West Hampstead, Hendon Way, Hendon Central Station, Watford Way, Mill Hill Circus, Mill Hill Broadway Station, Hale Lane, Edgware Station, Canons Park Station, Stanmore Broadway, Bushey Heath, Bushey, Watford Town Centre. Allocation: Edgware Garage 2 M nightly, Hendon Garage 1 M nightly.

27/28 February 1987: Re-routed off Hendon Way via Childs Hill, Finchley Road, Golders Green (Clock Tower), Golders Green Road, Hodford Road, The Vale to re-join Hendon Way.

5/6 June 1987: Allocation: Edgware Garage 2 M nightly, Muswell Hill Garage 1 M nightly.

25/26 September 1987: Section of route Stanmore Broadway – Watford Junction Station withdrawn (replaced by projection of N18). Bifurcation Trafalgar Square – West Dulwich introduced. Re-routed Golders Green – Mill Hill Broadway. Now operated: **West Dulwich, South Croxted Road *or* Victoria Bus Station – Stanmore Station** via *either* West Dulwich, Herne Hill, Brixton, Kennington, Kennington Road, Lambeth Bridge, Millbank *or* Victoria Street (Victoria Station jnys) then Whitehall, Trafalgar Square, Piccadilly Circus, Oxford Circus, Gloucester Place (outbound), Baker Street (inbound), Lisson Grove, Abbey Road, West Hampstead, Childs Hill, Finchley Road, Golders Green, Hendon (The Quadrant), Holders Hill Road, Mill Hill East Station, Pursley Road, Mill Hill Broadway Station, Hale Lane, Edgware Station, Canons Park Station. Jnys Westbourne Park Station – West Hampstead via Kilburn. Allocation: Westbourne Park Garage 3 M nightly.

20/21 November 1987: Re-routed via Hendon Central Station.

1 April 1989: **Centrewest** commenced trading.

27/28 October 1989: LRT contract awarded to **Metroline**. Sections of route West Dulwich – Trafalgar Square, Edgware – Stanmore Station and Westbourne Park garage jnys withdrawn.

Top Victoria garage's emergency stand-by MCW Metrobus M 946 was photographed outside Canada House in Trafalgar Square substituting for an absent New Cross garage Leyland Titan to work this well patronised N72 journey from central London to Dartford in Kent early on Saturday morning 20 September 1986. *Malc McDonald*

Centre Sutton garage's Leyland Fleetline DMS 2320 was waiting at East Croydon Station for the departure time of the 04.40 N54 journey to Banstead towards the end of that route's existence in May 1987. *David Bowker*

Bottom Westbourne Park garage's MCW Metrobus M 892 was photographed at bus stop W on the southern side of Trafalgar Square in the early hours of Sunday morning 4 October 1987 loading passengers for one of route N59's four nightly journeys to Stanmore Station. *Roy Waterhouse*

Re-routed in Hendon. Now operated: **Victoria Bus Station – Edgware Station.** Allocation: Edgware Garage 2 M nightly. Note: Trafalgar Square – West Dulwich section of N59 replaced by new route N3. Hendon Central Station served by new route N5. Edgware Station – Stanmore Station section of N59 abandoned.

By September 1992: Allocation: Edgware Garage 2 M (Su-Fr), 3 M (Sa). Re-allocated to Cricklewood Garage 2 M (Su-Fr), 3 M (Sa) from 5/6 March 1993.

28/29 January 1994: **Re-numbered N139.** LRT contract awarded to **Centrewest**. Sections of route Victoria – Trafalgar Square, West Hampstead – Edgware Station withdrawn. Now operated: **Trafalgar Square – West Hampstead, West End Green** via Piccadilly Circus, Oxford Circus, Gloucester Place (outbound), Baker Street (inbound), Lisson Grove, Abbey Road. Allocation: Alperton Garage (joint N99) 1 M (M-Sa), Westbourne Park Garage 1 M nightly. Note: Section of N59 north of West Hampstead not replaced by all-night service although route N13 already served Finchley Road into Golders Green and N5 served Golders Green – Hendon with an onward link to Edgware. Mill Hill routeing of N59 abandoned. A latter-day all-night bus link Hendon – Edgware Station via Watford Way and Mill Hill Circus was created with the introduction of route N113 from 29/30 June 2012.

2 September 1994: Centrewest acquired by management/employee buy-out.

By 11/12 January 1997: Joint allocation dissolved, now: Alperton Garage 1 M (M-Sa), Westbourne Park Garage 1 M nightly.

26 March 1997: Operated by **First Bus**, re-titled **First Group** December 1997, **First London** March 2001.

July 1999: Allocation: Alperton Garage 1 M (M-Sa), Westbourne Park Garage 1 TN nightly, Alperton Garage allocation changed to 1 VN (M-Sa) by 25/26 September 1999.

2/3 February 2001: LBSL contract awarded to **Metroline London Northern**. Allocation: Holloway Garage 2 VPL (Su-Th), 3 VPL (Fr-Sa).

31 Jan/1 Feb 2003: Reassigned to **Metroline Travel**. Projected Trafalgar Square – Waterloo Station via Aldwych (inbound), Waterloo Bridge. Now operated: **Waterloo Station, Concert Hall Approach** (pick-up), **York Road** (set-down) – **West Hampstead, West End Green.** Allocation: Cricklewood Garage 3 TP/TAL (Su-Th), 4 TP/TAL (Fr-Sa). Waterloo pick-up became Tenison Way from 14/15 November 2003.

23/24 April 2004: **Re-numbered (N)139.**

18/19 June 2004: Waterloo set-down now Mepham Street and became Waterloo Road from 23/24 October 2009.

March 2010: TEH-type AD Trident-Enviro 400Hs noted in service on (N)139, the first recorded use of hybrid-design buses on all-night service. Allocation: Cricklewood Garage 3 TP/TAL/TEH (Su-Th), 4 TP/TAL/TEH (Fr-Sa).

14/15 November 2010: Allocation: Cricklewood Garage 3 TE/TEH (Su-Th), 4 TE/TEH (Fr-Sa), became entirely TEH-type Enviro 400H hybrid c. November 2011.

29/30 June 2012: Right-hand turn introduced from Strand into Lancaster Place and Waterloo Bridge. Inbound jnys no longer served Aldwych.

Centrewest's MCW Metrobus M 885 was seen loading passengers in Cockspur Street for an outbound journey on then-hourly frequency route N139 in the early hours of Sunday morning 5 February 1995. *Malc McDonald*

Route N99 (Cranham)

8/9 August 1986: Introduced. Operated: **Romford Market, St Edward's Way – Cranham, Moor Lane** via Romford Station, Hornchurch, Upminster, Upminster Park Estate. Jnys Romford North Street Garage with allocation 1 T (Fr-Sa). Note: Most outbound jnys connected at Romford Station with N98 buses from central London.

31 Jan/1 Feb 1987: Last night of operation, then suspended.

27/28 March 1987: Reinstated. LRT contract awarded to **Ensignbus**. Revised to operate as a unidirectional route: **Romford, St Edward's Way – Cranham, Moor Lane.** Allocation: Purfleet Garage buses off daytime routes 62/62A.

8/9 January 1988: Back-projected to start at Chadwell Heath. Now operated: **Chadwell Heath, Wangey Road – Cranham, Moor Lane** via Romford Market, Romford Station, Hornchurch, Upminster, Upminster Park Estate. Allocation: Purfleet Garage buses off daytime routes 62/62A.

1/2 December 1989: Re-allocated to Dagenham Dock Garage.

21 July 1990: Operation of Ensignbus LRT and commercial routes from Dagenham Dock Garage transferred within the Ensign group to **Frontrunner Buses South East Ltd,** in anticipation of the sale of the business to Whitehall Investments Inc, USA. In the event, the proposed sale did not proceed. 29 December 1990: Ensignbus sold to Hong Kong-based CNT Group. New fleetname: **Ensign Citybus**.

7/8 September 1991: Last night of operation. Note: Later compensatory jnys added to Ensign Citybus-operated LRT daytime route 248.

Routes introduced 1987

Routes 279, 279A

25/26 September 1987: All-night service added to extant daytime routes 279/279A. Operated: **Ponders End Garage – Upshire, Princesfield Road** via Waltham Cross, Waltham Abbey. Certain jnys originated from or continued to Islington, Liverpool Street Station and Smithfield. Allocation: Enfield (Ponders End) Garage 1 M nightly. Note: Absorbed nightly inbound N90 jny via Waltham Abbey.

1 April 1989: **Leaside Buses** commenced trading.

30/31 January 1992: Last night of operation. Note: Compensatory increase to N90's frequency.

Romford North Street garage's Leyland Titan T 564 was photographed at route N99's outbound Romford Station bus stop Y in South Street at 01.07 on Sunday morning 31 August 1986.
Malc McDonald

Route introduced 1988

Route N8

12/13 August 1988: Introduced. Operated: **Queensbury Station – Bow Church** via Kingsbury, Neasden, Willesden, Kilburn, Maida Vale, Edgware Road, Marble Arch, Oxford Circus, Piccadilly Circus, Trafalgar Square, Charing Cross Road, New Oxford Street, Holborn, Bank, Bishopsgate, Bethnal Green, Old Ford. Allocation: Bow Garage 3 T (Su-Th), 4 T (Fr-Sa).

1 April 1989: **East London** commenced trading.

27/28 October 1989: Projected beyond Bow Church to form a circular routeing via Blackwall Tunnel Northern Approach, Poplar, Isle of Dogs, Limehouse, Mile End and back to Bow Church. Re-routed off Bishopsgate to serve Liverpool Street Station. Now operated: **Queensbury Station – Bow Church – Isle of Dogs loop – Bow Church**. Allocation: Bow Garage 4 T (Su-Th), 5 T (Fr-Sa).

20/21 April 1990: Isle of Dogs jnys re-routed away from Blackwall Tunnel Northern Approach to travel Bow Church – Poplar via Campbell Road, Violet Road, Morris Road, Chrisp Street. Re-routed directly via Bishopsgate (no longer served Liverpool Street).

9/10 May 1992: Inbound jnys re-routed to serve Liverpool Street Bus Station.

17/18 July 1992: Section of route Marble Arch – Queensbury Station withdrawn (replaced by new route N99). Projected Marble Arch – Victoria via Hyde Park Corner. Now operated: **Victoria Station – Bow Church – Isle of Dogs loop – Bow Church.** Allocation: Bow Garage 3 T (Su-Th), 4 T (Fr-Sa). By 11/12 October 1992: Allocation: Bow Garage 3 T/S (Su-Th), 4 T/S (Fr-Sa).

6 September 1994: Operated by **Stagecoach East London**.

4/5 November 1994: Allocation: Bow Garage 3 T (Su-Th), 4 T (Fr-Sa).

14/15 July 1995: Sections of route Victoria – Trafalgar Square and around Isle of Dogs loop to/from Bow withdrawn. Projected Bow – Wanstead with bifurcations to Woodford Wells or Newbury Park Station. Now operated: **Trafalgar Square – Woodford Wells, Horse and Well *or* Newbury Park Station** via Charing Cross Road, New Oxford Street, Holborn, Bank, Liverpool Street Bus Station (inbound only), Bethnal Green, Old Ford, Bow, Stratford, Leytonstone, Wanstead Station then *either* Snaresbrook, South Woodford to Woodford Wells *or* Redbridge, Gants Hill to Newbury Park Station. Allocation: Bow Garage 6 T nightly. Note: Replaced Bow – South Woodford section of N76 and its service to Gants Hill as well as element of N96's service to Woodford Green. Isle of Dogs section of N8 replaced by new route N50.

11/12 October 1996: Re-routed at Bow Bridge directly to High Street, Stratford (no longer served Bow Street and Bromley High Street).

3/4 August 1997: Allocation now all Volvo Olympian (conversion started 6/7 December 1996) at Bow Garage 6 VA/VN nightly.

25/26 June 1999: Section of route New Oxford Street – Trafalgar Square withdrawn. Projected New Oxford Street – Victoria Station via Oxford Circus, Regent Street, Piccadilly Circus, Hyde Park Corner. Now operated: **Victoria Station, Bus Station – Woodford Wells or Newbury Park Station.** Allocation: Bow Garage 6 VA nightly.

28/29 April 2000: Re-routed Piccadilly – Oxford Circus via Berkeley Square, Oxford Street. Inbound jnys no longer served Liverpool Street Bus Station. Allocation: Bow Garage 6 VA (Su-Th), 10 VA (Fr-Sa), increased to 8 VA (Su-Th), 12 VA (Fr-Sa) from 27/28 April 2001.

22/23 April 2003: Victoria set-down now Terminus Place, pick-up now Victoria Street.

Roy Waterhouse travelled on the inaugural route N8 journey from Bow Church to Queensbury Station and so was able to take this photograph of Bow garage's Leyland Titan T 340 in Cheapside at 23.50 on Friday night 12 August 1988. Note the branding on the Titan's front panels for daytime route 25 which was also worked by Bow garage. *Roy Waterhouse*

By 29/30 August 2003: Completion of progressive vehicle-type change to low-floor Trident at Bow Garage (started April 2003) 8 TA/TAS (Su-Th), 12 TA/TAS (Fr-Sa).

19/20 September 2003: Victoria pick-up now Wilton Road.

25/26 June 2004: Bifurcation Wanstead – Woodford Wells withdrawn and Gants Hill – Newbury Park Station section of bifurcation withdrawn. Projected Gants Hill – Hainault. Now operated: **Victoria Station, Wilton Road (dep) *or* Terminus Place (arr) – Hainault, The Lowe** via Hyde Park Corner, Piccadilly, Berkeley Square, Oxford Circus, New Oxford Street, Holborn, Bank, Bishopsgate, Bethnal Green, Old Ford, Bow, Stratford, Leytonstone, Wanstead, Redbridge, Gants Hill, Barkingside. Allocation: Bow Garage 7 TA (Su-Th), 14 TA (Fr-Sa). Note: Replaced Gants Hill – Hainault bifurcation of N25. Wanstead – Woodford Wells section of N8 replaced by projection of N55. Gants Hill – Newbury Park Station section of N8 not replaced with an all-night service.

30 August 2006: Operated by Macquarie Bank Ltd t/a East London Bus Group. Fleetname: **East London**.

20/21 April 2007: Allocation: Bow Garage 10 TA (Su-Th), 14 TA (Fr-Sa).

26/27 June 2009: Victoria – Oxford Circus section of route withdrawn. Now operated: **Oxford Circus – Hainault, The Lowe.** Allocation: Bow Garage 11 TA (Su-Th), 17 TA (Fr-Sa). Note: Victoria – Oxford Circus section of N8 replaced by projection of route (N)C2 (different routeing in vicinity of Oxford Circus).

14 October 2010: Operated by Stagecoach Bus Holdings Ltd t/a **East London**.

22/23 July 2011: Allocation: Bow Garage 10 TA (Su-Th), 23 TA (Fr-Sa), increased to 11 TA on Su-Th from 13/14 July 2012.

27/28 July – 12/13 August and 29/30 August – 9/10 September 2012: Oxford Circus – Wanstead frequency increased to 7½ min nightly for duration of Olympic and Paralympic Games. Bow Garage allocation temporarily increased to 25 TA (Su-Th), 26 TA (Fr-Sa).

By 30/31 August 2013: Allocation: Bow Garage 11 TA/SC (Su-Th), 23 TA/SC (Fr-Sa).

Top Stagecoach East London's Northern Counties Palatine I bodied Volvo Olympian VN 35 was seen on lay-over on the south side of Trafalgar Square on Friday morning 27 June 1997. At this time route N8 operated a 30 minute frequency service between Trafalgar Square and Wanstead whence the route formed a bifurcation to give an onward hourly service to both Newbury Park Station and to Woodford Wells. *Mike Wiffen*

Centre Stagecoach East London's Alexander RL-bodied Volvo Olympian VA 135 was seen at bus stop C outside the National Gallery in Trafalgar Square working an end of the night short-working N8 journey to Bow Church on Friday morning 3 July 1998. *Mike Wiffen*

Bottom East London's TransBus Trident ALX400 18216 was photographed at Grosvenor Gardens, Victoria in the early hours of Sunday morning 27 April 2008. At this time route N8 operated a nightly 20 minute frequency service between Victoria and Hainault with an enhanced 10 minute frequency service between Victoria and Wanstead on Friday and Saturday nights. *Philip Wallis*

Routes introduced 1989

Route N73

25/26 August 1986, 31 Aug/1 Sept 1987: Operated these nights only on occasion of the Notting Hill Carnival: **Shepherd's Bush – Tottenham Garage** (see Chapter 2).

22/23 September 1989: Regular service introduced. Operated: **Victoria Station – Walthamstow Central Station** via Whitehall, Trafalgar Square, Piccadilly Circus, Oxford Circus, Tottenham Court Road (outbound), Gower St (inbound), Euston Station, King's Cross Station, Islington, Essex Road, Newington Green, Stoke Newington, Stamford Hill, Tottenham, Tottenham Hale, Forest Road, Hoe Street. Operator: **Leaside Buses**. Allocation: Tottenham Garage 2 M nightly.

20/21 July 1990: Unscheduled duplicate introduced from Stamford Hill Garage 1 M (joint N83) nightly, Tottenham Garage 2 M nightly.

By September 1992: Vehicle-type changed to Leyland Olympian at Stamford Hill Garage (joint N83) 1 L (Su-Th), 2 L (Fr-Sa), Tottenham Garage 2 M nightly.

By April 1994: Joint allocation with N83 dissolved, now: Tottenham Garage 2 M (Su-Th), 4 M (Fr-Sa).

29 September 1994: Operated by **Cowie Leaside**.

26/27 April 1996: Allocation: Tottenham Garage 5 M nightly, Fr-Sa allocation increased to 9 M from 27/28 March 1998.

2 April 1998: Operated by **Arriva London North**.

28/29 April 2000: Re-routed Victoria – Oxford Circus via Hyde Park Corner, Marble Arch. Continued to operate: **Victoria Station – Walthamstow Central Station.** Allocation unchanged.

By June 2001: Converted to low-floor DAF DB250LF (started c. November 2000) from Tottenham Garage 5 DLA (Su-Th), 9 DLA (Fr-Sa).

c. May 2003: Vehicle-type change to Volvo B7TL at Tottenham Garage 5 VLW (Su-Th), 9 VLW (Fr-Sa), Fr-Sa allocation increased to 10 VLW from 3/4 September 2004.

By 26/27 April 2008: Allocation: Tottenham Garage 5 DLA/VLW (Su-Th), 10 DLA/VLW (Fr-Sa).

27 August 2010: Arriva acquired by Deutsche Bahn.

2/3 September 2011: Re-allocated to Stamford Hill Garage. Vehicle-type change to mixed Wrightbus Gemini and Volvo B5LH hybrid 7 DW/HV (Su-Th), 13 DW/HV (Fr-Sa).

27/28 July – 12/13 August and 29/30 August – 9/10 September 2012: Frequency increased to 10 min nightly for duration of Olympic and Paralympic Games. Stamford Hill Garage allocation temporarily increased to 20 DW/HV nightly.

c. January 2013: Allocation entirely HV-type Volvo B5LH hybrid.

Top The second night of regular operation of route N73 was recorded in this view of Leaside Buses MCW Metrobus M 1406 loading passengers at Tottenham Court Road Station for an outbound journey on the-then hourly frequency route early on Sunday morning 24 September 1989. *Roy Waterhouse*

Centre Tottenham garage's Wrightbus-bodied Volvo B7TL VLW 184 was seen at Grosvenor Gardens, Victoria early on Sunday morning 27 April 2008. Route N73 had operated a 30 minute Sunday to Thursday night and 15 minute Friday and Saturday night frequency service between Victoria and Walthamstow Central since 3/4 September 2004. *Philip Wallis*

Bottom Route N73's Friday and Saturday night frequency was increased to 12 minutes over its entire route length from 2/3 September 2011 although the route's Sunday to Thursday night frequency was retained at 30 minutes. The N73 was partially converted to hybrid-powered bus operation from the same date with full conversion being achieved in early 2013. Stamford Hill garage's Wrightbus-bodied Volvo B5LH HV 28 was photographed at Euston Station Bus Station at around 04.00 on Saturday morning 10 December 2011. *Philip Wallis*

Routes N1 (Barnet), N20

27/28 October 1989: Introduced. **Numbered N1.** Operated: **Victoria Bus Station** ***or*** **Aldwych – High Barnet Station** via *either* Victoria Street, Parliament Square, Bridge Street, Victoria Embankment, Temple Place, Surrey Street to Aldwych (outbound from Victoria Station only) *or* Whitehall, Parliament Square, Victoria Street (inbound from Trafalgar Square to Victoria Station only) then Trafalgar Square, Charing Cross Road, Tottenham Court Road (outbound), Gower Street (inbound), Euston, Camden Town, Kentish Town, Archway, East Finchley, North Finchley, Whetstone. Operator: **London Northern**. Allocation: Holloway Garage (joint N5) 5 M nightly, Fr-Sa allocation increased to 6 M from 16/17 November 1990.

17/18 July 1992: Section of route Aldwych – Trafalgar Square withdrawn. Victoria jnys revised to operate Trafalgar Square – Victoria Station via Whitehall in both directions of travel. Now operated: **Victoria Bus Station – High Barnet Station.** Allocation: Holloway Garage (joint N5) 5 M nightly.

By 26/27 March 1993: Use of S-type Scania N113s observed (discontinued by 3/4 December 1993). Official allocation to N1/N5 remained M-type Metrobus.

26 October 1994: Operated by **MTL London Northern**.

23/24 June 1995: **Re-numbered N20.** Section of route Victoria – Trafalgar Square withdrawn. Projected High Barnet Station – Potters Bar. Now operated: **Trafalgar Square – Potters Bar, Bus Garage** via Charing Cross Road, Tottenham Court Road (outbound), Gower Street (inbound), Euston, Camden Town, Kentish Town, Archway, East Finchley, North Finchley, Whetstone, High Barnet, Barnet Church, Hadley Highstone. Joint allocation with N5 dissolved, now: Holloway Garage 3 M, Potters Bar Garage 1 M/S nightly.

24/24 July 1998: LRT contract awarded to **First Group**, re-titled **First London** March 2001. Section of route High Barnet – Potters Bar withdrawn. Now operated: **Trafalgar Square – Barnet Church**. Allocation: Northumberland Park Garage 5 AE nightly, Fr-Sa allocation increased to 11 AE from 7/8 January 2000.

By 29/30 June 2002: Vehicle-type change to mixed Dennis Arrow and Volvo Olympian at Northumberland Park Garage 5 AE/VA/VN (Su-Th), 11 AE/VA/VN (Fr-Sa).

25/26 July 2003: LBSL contract awarded to **Metroline London Northern**. Allocation: Potters Bar Garage 6 TP (Su-Th), 12 TP (Fr-Sa).

1 January 2005: Reassigned to **Metroline Travel.**

4/5 Feb 2005: Allocation: Potters Bar Garage 6 TP (Su-Th), 12 TP (Fr-Sa), Holloway Garage 2 VP (Fr-Sa).

25/26 July 2008: Allocation: Potters Bar Garage 5 TP (Su), 4 TP (M-Th), 12 TP (Fr-Sa), Holloway Garage 2 VP (Fr-Sa).

6/7 February 2009: Allocation: Holloway Garage 1 VP (Su), 2 VP (M-Th), 6 VP (Fr), 7 VP (Sa), Potters Bar Garage 5 TP (Su), 4 TP (M-Th), 8 TP (Fr), 7 TP (Sa).

June 2012: Holloway Garage allocation all VW-type Volvo B9TL Gemini 2.

26/27 July 2013: Allocation: Holloway Garage 1 VW (Su-Th), 8 VW (Fr-Sa), Potters Bar Garage 5 TE/TP (Su-Th), 8 TE/TP (Fr-Sa).

Holloway garage's M 1284 was seen loading passengers at bus stop C outside the National Gallery in Trafalgar Square during the early hours of Sunday morning 29 October 1989. Route N1's association with the Underground's Northern Line is evident from the (slightly misaligned) route number and intermediate points blind display, but part of the wording on the MCW Metrobus's destination blind display is misleading since route N1 never reached Barnet Church. *Roy Waterhouse*

First London's Northern Counties Palatine I-bodied Volvo Olympian 207 was seen against the backdrop of Admiralty Arch whilst heading towards the bus stop on the eastern side of Trafalgar Square to take up a short-working route N20 journey to Finchley Central. This view dates from Saturday morning 5 July 2003, just three weeks before operation of the N20 passed to Metroline London Northern. *Philip Wallis*

Metroline's TransBus President-bodied Trident TP 452 was seen Tottenham Court Road Station in the early hours of Sunday morning 11 June 2006. Route N20 has operated a 30 minute frequency Sunday to Thursday night service since 23/24 June 1995 but its Friday and Saturday night frequency has been progressively increased to have become 10 minutes since 26/27 July 2013. *Philip Wallis*

Route N3

27/28 October 1989: Introduced. Operated: **Victoria Bus Station *or* Marble Arch – Beckenham Junction Station** via Hyde Park Corner to Marble Arch (outbound from Victoria Station only) then Oxford Circus, Trafalgar Square, Whitehall (double-run via Whitehall and then via Victoria Street to Victoria in respect of inbound jnys only which terminated at Victoria) then Millbank, Oval, Brixton, Herne Hill Station, West Dulwich, Crystal Palace, Penge. Operator: **London Central**. Allocation: Camberwell Garage 3 T nightly. Note: Replaced Trafalgar Square – West Dulwich section of N59.

17/18 July 1992: Victoria-terminating jnys re-routed to operate Trafalgar Square – Victoria via Oxford Circus, Marble Arch and Hyde Park Corner (as outbound jnys). Allocation unchanged.

By 26/27 March 1993: Vehicle-type change at Camberwell Garage to Optare Spectra 3 SP nightly.

8/9 October 1993: Projected Fr-Sa only Beckenham Junction – Chislehurst via Bromley. Now operated: **Victoria Bus Station – Chislehurst, Gordon Arms.** Joint allocation with N79 introduced from Camberwell Garage 5 SP nightly, Peckham Garage 1 T (Fr-Sa only).

25/26 November 1994: Allocation: Camberwell Garage 2 SP + 1 SP (joint N79) (Su-Th), 3 SP (Fr-Sa), Peckham Garage 1 T (Fr-Sa).

18 November 1994: Operated by Go-Ahead group t/a **London Central**.

28/29 July 1995: Allocation: Camberwell Garage 2 SP + 1 SP (joint N79) (Su-Th), 4 SP (Fr-Sa).

26/27 April 1996: Joint allocation with N79 dissolved. Re-routed Crystal Palace – Penge via Anerley Road (replaced section of N71). Allocation: Camberwell Garage 2 SP (Su-Th), 5 SP (Fr-Sa), increased to 3 SP (Su-Th), 6 SP (Fr-Sa) by 10/11 October 1997.

By 7/8 November 1997: Vehicle-type change to Volvo Olympian at Camberwell Garage 3 NV (Su-Th), 6 NV (Fr-Sa).

13/14 November 1998: Allocation: Camberwell Garage 6 NV nightly, Peckham Garage 3 T/NV (Fr-Sa).

4/5 February 2000: LRT contract awarded to **Connex Bus**. Sections of route Victoria – Oxford Circus, Bromley North Station – Chislehurst withdrawn. Now operated: **Oxford Circus – Bromley North Station** via Trafalgar Square, Whitehall, Millbank, Oval, Brixton, Herne Hill Station, West Dulwich, Crystal Palace, Penge, Beckenham. Allocation: Beddington Cross Garage 6 TA (Su-Th), 9 TA (Fr-Sa).

20/21 April 2001: Revised timetable to improve reliability. Oxford Circus – Bromley North journey time increased by up to 19 min. Allocation: Beddington Cross Garage 6 TA (Su-Th), 10 TA (Fr-Sa).

26 February 2004: Operated by **Travel London**.

1/2 December 2006: Allocation: Beddington Cross Garage 6 TA (Su-Th), 11 TA (Fr-Sa).

9/10 February 2007: Allocation: Battersea Garage 1 TA (Fr-Sa), Beddington Cross Garage 6 TA (Su-Th), 10 TA (Fr-Sa).

9 June 2009: Travel London acquired by Ned Railways. Operated as **Abellio** from 30 October 2009 and as **Abellio London** from 1 June 2010.

24/25 June 2011: Allocation: Beddington Cross Garage 6 TA (Su-Th), 10 TA (Fr-Sa).

11/12 February 2012: Re-allocated to Battersea Garage with associated vehicle-type change to AD E40H Enviro400H hybrid 7 EDH (Su-Th), 12 EDH (Fr), 13 EDH (Sa).

The first night's operation of route N3 was recorded in this study of Camberwell garage's Leyland Titan T 955 seen in Regent Street, just south of Oxford Circus, early on Saturday morning 28 October 1989. The N3 operated to a then-hourly frequency between Oxford Circus and Beckenham Junction Station with certain journeys extended to and from Victoria Station for drivers' relief-break purposes. *Roy Waterhouse*

London Central's DAF DB250/Optare Spectra SP 14 was photographed outside Canada House in Trafalgar Square on Tuesday morning 22 June 1993. Camberwell garage deployed Optare Spectras on routes N3, N79 and N176 at various times between 26/27 March 1993 and 6/7 November 1997. *Malcolm Papes*

Abellio London's hybrid-powered AD E40H Enviro400H 2416 was photographed in Whitehall in the early hours of Friday morning 30 March 2012. Route N3 has operated a nightly 30 minute frequency service between Oxford Circus and Bromley North Station, combined with an enhanced 15 minute frequency service between Oxford Circus and Crystal Palace on Friday and Saturday nights, since 4/5 February 2000. *Philip Wallis*

Route N5

27/28 October 1989: Introduced. Operated: **Victoria Bus Station *or* Aldwych – Edgware Station** via *either* Victoria Street, Parliament Square, Bridge Street, Victoria Embankment, Temple Place, Surrey Street to Aldwych (outbound from Victoria Station only) *or* Whitehall, Parliament Square, Victoria Street (inbound from Trafalgar Square to Victoria Station only) then Trafalgar Square, Charing Cross Road, Tottenham Court Road (outbound), Gower Street (inbound), Euston, Camden Town, Chalk Farm, Belsize Park, Hampstead, Golders Green, Brent Cross, Hendon Central, West Hendon, Colindale, Grahame Park, Burnt Oak. Operator: **London Northern**. Allocation: Holloway Garage (joint N1) 5 M nightly, Fr-Sa allocation increased to 6 M from 16/17 November 1990.

17/18 July 1992: Section of route Aldwych – Trafalgar Square withdrawn. Victoria jnys revised to operate Trafalgar Square – Victoria Station via Whitehall in both directions of travel. Now operated: **Victoria Bus Station – Edgware Station.** Allocation: Holloway Garage (joint N1) 5 M nightly.

By 26/27 March 1993: Use of S-type Scania N113s observed (discontinued by 3/4 December 1993). Official allocation to N1/N5 remained M-type Metrobus.

28/29 January 1994: Re-routed away from Brent Cross to operate directly between Golders Green and Hendon Central via Brent Street.

26 October 1994: Operated by **MTL London Northern.**

23/24 June 1995: Section of route Victoria Station – Trafalgar Square withdrawn. Now operated: **Trafalgar Square – Edgware Station** via Charing Cross Road, Tottenham Court Road (outbound), Gower Street (inbound), Euston, Camden Town,Chalk Farm, Belsize Park, Hampstead, Golders Green, Hendon Central, West Hendon, Colindale, Grahame Park, Burnt Oak. Joint allocation with N1 dissolved, now: Holloway Garage 2 M (Su-Th), 4 M (Fr-Sa).

By 10/11 October 1997: Allocation: Holloway Garage 2 M (Su-Th), 6 M (Fr-Sa), increased to 6 M nightly from 24/25 July 1998.

17 August 1998: Operated by **Metroline London Northern.**

By 2/3 February 2001: Vehicle-type change to low-floor Volvo B7TL from Holloway Garage 6 VPL nightly, increased to 8 VPL (Su-Th), 11 VPL (Fr-Sa) from 31 August/1 September 2001.

18 February 2000: Metroline acquired by DelGro group.

c. May 2002: Vehicle-type change to TPL-type Trident at Holloway Garage 8 TPL (Su-Th), 11 TPL (Fr-Sa), Fr-Sa allocation increased to 13 TPL from 25/26 July 2003.

29/30 August 2003: Allocation: Edgware Garage 3 VPL nightly, Holloway Garage 5 TPL (Su-Th), 10 TPL (Fr-Sa).

3/4 September 2004: Allocation: Edgware Garage 6 VPL nightly, Holloway Garage 2 TPL (Su-Th), 7 TPL (Fr-Sa).

1 January 2005: Re-assigned to **Metroline Travel.**

4/5 February 2005: Allocation: Edgware Garage 6 VPL (Su-Th), 8 VPL (Fr-Sa), Holloway Garage 2 VP (Su-Th), 5 VP (Fr-Sa).

13/14 April 2007: Allocation: Edgware Garage 8 VPL (Su-Th), 10 VPL (Fr), 11 VPL (Sa), Holloway Garage 3 VPL (Fr), 2 VPL (Sa).

25/26 July 2009: Allocation: Edgware Garage 9 VPL (Su), 8 VPL (M-Th), 12 VPL (Fr), 13 VPL (Sa), Holloway Garage 4 VPL (Fr-Sa).

c. June 2012: Edgware Garage allocation now TE-type, Holloway Garage VW-type.

Holloway garage's MCW Metrobus M 1082 was seen at Edgware Bus Station loading passengers early on Sunday morning 29 October 1989, the second night of route N5's operation. The N5 operated a then-hourly frequency service between Edgware and Trafalgar Square whence most journeys, such as this one, continued to Aldwych except for two journeys which diverted at Trafalgar Square and travelled via Whitehall to reach Victoria Station for drivers' relief-break purposes. *Roy Waterhouse*

Twenty years later Metroline's Plaxton President-bodied Volvo B7TL VPL 196 was seen at Edgware Bus Station in the early hours of Saturday morning 24 April 2010. Route N5 continues to operate in parallel with the Edgware branch of the Underground's Northern Line but that association is no longer shown on bus blind displays. The N5 has operated a 15 minute Sunday to Thursday night and 10 minute Friday and Saturday night frequency service over its entire route length between Trafalgar Square and Edgware Station since 25/26 July 2009. *Philip Wallis*

The inaugural night of route N6's operation was recorded in this view of London Forest's Leyland Titan T 553 in Oxford Street during the early hours of Saturday morning 28 October 1989. Upon its inception the N6 operated a nightly hourly frequency service between Ash Grove and Willesden bus garages with three journeys originating from Walthamstow Central Station and four journeys continuing beyond Ash Grove to terminate at Walthamstow. *Roy Waterhouse*

Routes N6, (N)6

27/28 October 1989: Introduced. **Numbered N6.** Operated: **Walthamstow Central Station – Willesden Garage** via Leyton, Hackney Wick, Hackney, Cambridge Heath, Shoreditch, Bishopsgate, Bank, Ludgate Circus, Fleet Street, Aldwych, Trafalgar Square, Piccadilly Circus, Oxford Circus, Marble Arch, Edgware Road, Maida Vale, Warwick Avenue, Queens Park, Kensal Rise. Operator: **London Forest**. Allocation: Ash Grove Garage 3 T nightly. Note: Replaced Hackney Wick, Eastway – Cambridge Heath section of N11 and Trafalgar Square – Willesden Garage section of N79.

22/23 November 1991: LRT contract awarded to **Metroline.** Re-allocated to Willesden Garage 3 M nightly.

17/18 July 1992: Section of route Walthamstow Central Station – Trafalgar Square withdrawn (replaced by new route N26). Now operated: **Trafalgar Square – Willesden Garage.** Allocation: Willesden Garage (joint N99) 4 M nightly.

28/29 January 1994: LRT contract awarded to **London Suburban Bus.** Section of route Kensal Rise – Willesden Garage withdrawn. Projected Trafalgar Square – Aldwych. Now operated: **Aldwych – Kensal Rise Station.** Allocation: Edmonton Garage 2 Volvo Olympians.

12 April 1995: London Suburban Bus acquired by MTL Trust Holdings. Operation placed under the control of **MTL London Northern** with continued operation from Edmonton Garage. Operation formally assigned to MTL London Northern t/a **MTL London** on 11 November 1995 and re-allocated to Holloway Garage 2 V nightly from 31 May/1 June 1996.

17 August 1998: Operated by **Metroline London Northern.**

23/24 July 1999: Reassigned to **Metroline Travel**. Re-allocated to Willesden Garage 2 AV nightly, increased to 3 AV (Su-Th), 4 AV (Fr-Sa) from 2/3 February 2001.

18 February 2000: Metroline acquired by DelGro group.

By 28/29 Sept 2001: Vehicle-type change to low-floor Volvo B7TL (started c. May 2001) completed at Willesden Garage: 3 VPL (Su-Th), 4 VPL (Fr-Sa), increased to 6 VPL (Su-Th), 7 VPL (Fr-Sa) from 11/12 October 2002.

26/27 March 2004: **Renumbered (N)6.** Allocation: Willesden Garage 8 VP nightly, Fr-Sa allocation increased to 10 VP from 11/12 July 2008.

London Suburban Bus's Northern Counties Palatine II-bodied Volvo Olympian 203 was seen in Cockspur Street, Trafalgar Square at 05.38 on Thursday morning 16 June 1994 working that night's last outbound journey on then-hourly frequency route N6. *Malcolm Papes*

Routes N12, (N)12

25/26 August 1986, 31 Aug/1 Sept 1987: Operated these nights only on occasion of the Notting Hill Carnival: **Numbered N12. Shepherd's Bush – Dulwich, Plough** (see Chapter 2).

27/28 October 1989: Regular service introduced. **Numbered N12**. Operated: **Shepherd's Bush Green *or* Victoria Station, Bus Station – Dulwich, Plough *or* Nunhead loop** via Notting Hill Gate, Marble Arch, Oxford Circus, Piccadilly Circus, Trafalgar Square, Whitehall, then *either* Victoria Street (Victoria Station jnys only – one inbound jny from Dulwich also double-ran via Whitehall to serve Trafalgar Square) *or* Elephant & Castle, Camberwell Green, Peckham, Peckham Rye then *either* Barry Road to Dulwich *or* uni-directional circular via Nunhead Station, Honor Oak Estate to Peckham. Operator: **London Central**. Allocation: Peckham Garage 3 T nightly + 1 T (joint N85) nightly, increased to 4 T + 1 T (joint N85) nightly from 26/27 April 1991.

8/9 October 1993: Bifurcations around Nunhead loop (incorporated into new route N84) and to Victoria Station withdrawn. Now operated: **Shepherd's Bush Green – Dulwich, Plough**. Allocation: Peckham Garage (joint N36/N71/N84) 6 T (Su-Th), 7 T (Fr-Sa).

By April 1994: One outbound jny operated Victoria, Bus Station – Shepherd's Bush Green via Victoria Street to Parliament Square and line of route.

18 October 1994: Operated by Go-Ahead group t/a **London Central**.

c. June 1995: Allocation: Peckham Garage (joint N36/N71/N84) 6 T/AV (Su-Th), 7 T/AV (Fr-Sa).

By 14 October 1995: Outbound jny from Victoria Station withdrawn. Allocation: Peckham Garage (joint N36/N71/N84) 9 T/AV (Su-Th), 13 T/AV (Fr-Sa).

26/27 April 1996: Allocation; Peckham Garage (joint N36/N84) 9 T/AV(Su-Th), 14 T/AV(Fr-Sa).

By 11/12 January 1997: Joint allocation dissolved, now: Peckham Garage 2 T/AV (Su-Th), 3 T/AV (Fr-Sa), Fr-Sa allocation increased to 7 T/AV from 11/12 July 1997.

23/24 July 1999: Shepherd's Bush Green – Notting Hill Gate section of route withdrawn (replaced by new route N94 and extant N207). Now operated: **Notting Hill Gate – Dulwich, Plough** via Marble Arch, Oxford Circus, Piccadilly Circus, Trafalgar Square, Whitehall, Elephant & Castle, Camberwell Green, Peckham, Peckham Rye, Barry Road. Allocation: Peckham Garage (joint N84) 6 T/AV (Su-Th), 7 T/AV (Fr-Sa).

4/5 February 2000: Vehicle-type change to low-floor Volvo B7TL and largely re-allocated to Camberwell Garage 4 AVL nightly, Peckham Garage (joint N84) 1 AV/AVL (Fr-Sa).

2/3 February 2001: Joint allocation with N84 dissolved, now: Camberwell Garage 4 AVL (Su-Th), 5 AVL (Fr-Sa), vehicle-type change to 4 PVL (Su-Th), 5 PVL (Fr-Sa) by June 2003..

23/24 January 2004: **Re-numbered (N)12.**

5/6 November 2004: Notting Hill Gate – Oxford Circus section of route withdrawn (replaced by projection of (N)390 and extant N207). Converted to operation by articulated low-floor single-deck Mercedes Benz Citaro bendy bus. Now operated: **Oxford Circus – Dulwich Library**. Allocation: Camberwell Garage 3 MAL (Su-Th), 4 MAL (Fr-Sa).

4/5 November 2011: Re-converted to double-deck bus operation using Volvo B9TL diesel and B5LH hybrid buses. Allocation: Camberwell Garage 3 WVL/WHV (Su-Th), 8 WVL/WHV (Fr-Sa).

Roy Waterhouse recorded the inaugural night of regular operation of route N12 when he took this view of Peckham garage's Leyland Titan T 942 in Regent Street, just south of Oxford Circus, at 23.27 on Friday night 27 October 1989. Route N12's initial timetable was rather complicated but gave an approximately hourly frequency service between Shepherd's Bush Green and Peckham Rye with four journeys projected to and from Dulwich combined with three outbound journeys and one inbound journey around the Nunhead loop. *Roy Waterhouse*

Route N19

31 Dec 1988/1 Jan 1989: Operated this New Year's Eve night only: **Victoria Bus Station *or* Trafalgar Square – Clapham Junction** *outbound only* via *either* Grosvenor Place (ex Victoria) *or* Piccadilly Circus (ex Trafalgar Square) to Hyde Park Corner then Sloane Square, Chelsea, Battersea. Allocation: Victoria Garage 1 M.

27/28 October 1989: Regular service introduced. Operated: **Finsbury Park Station – Clapham Junction, Northcote** via Highbury Barn, Highbury Corner, Islington, Bloomsbury, New Oxford Street, Charing Cross Road, Trafalgar Square, Piccadilly Circus, Hyde Park Corner, Sloane Square, Chelsea, Battersea. Operator: **London General**. Allocation: Victoria Garage 2 M nightly, re-allocated to Stockwell Garage 2 M nightly on 16/17 July 1993.

2 November 1994: London General acquired by management/ employee buy-out.

18/19 August 1995: Falcon Road – Northcote section of route in Clapham Junction withdrawn. Now operated: **Finsbury Park Station – Clapham Junction, Falcon Road.** Allocation unchanged.

24 May 1996: Operated by Go-Ahead group t/a **London General**.

26/27 June 1998: Re-routed Cambridge Circus – Piccadilly Circus via Shaftesbury Avenue. Continued to operate: **Finsbury Park Station – Clapham Junction, Falcon Road.** Allocation unchanged.

28/29 April 2000: LBSL contract awarded to **Arriva London South**. Allocation: Brixton Garage 6 M (Su-Th), 7 M (Fr-Sa).

February 2001: Completion of vehicle-type change (started 17/18 January 2001) to Leyland Olympian from Brixton Garage 6 L (Su-Th), 7 L (Fr-Sa).

c. December 2002: Completion of conversion to low-floor DAF DB250LF (started by July 2002) at Brixton Garage 6 DLA (Su-Th), 7 DLA (Fr-Sa).

30/31 January 2004: Clapham Junction terminus now St Johns Hill.

9/10 July 2004: Allocation: Brixton Garage 6 DW (Su-Th), 7 DW (Fr-Sa).

27 August 2010: Arriva acquired by Deutsche Bahn.

30/31 March 2012: LBSL contract awarded to **London General**. Re-allocated to Stockwell Garage with associated vehicle-type change to Volvo B5LH hybrid and Volvo B9TL diesel engine 4 WHV/ WVL (Su-Th), 8 WHV/WVL (Fr-Sa).

Top Yet another first night's regular operation of a Night Bus route was recorded by Roy Waterhouse with this view of Victoria garage's MCW Metrobus M 846 at Sloane Square taken in the early hours of Saturday morning 28 October 1989. Upon inception route N19 operated five nightly through northbound journeys between Clapham Junction and Finsbury Park between 23.51 and 05.20 but only two southbound journeys from Finsbury Park worked through to Clapham Junction since other southbound journeys were split in central London to facilitate drivers' relief-breaks. *Roy Waterhouse*

Centre T 1000, equipped with LED destination display, was one of London Central's three emergency stand-by Leyland Titans based at Camberwell garage. It had been deployed onto route N19 on New Year's Day 1993 to help move crowds of revellers away from Aldwych. *Roy Waterhouse*

Bottom Brixton garage's Wrightbus-bodied VDL DB250LF DW 93 was seen at Finsbury Park Station at around 4 o'clock in the morning on New Year's Day 2005. At this time route N19 operated a nightly 30 minute frequency service but its Friday and Saturday night frequency was increased to 20 minutes from 30/31 March 2012. *Philip Wallis*

Routes N53, (N)53

27/28 October 1989: Introduced. **Numbered N53**. Operated: **Victoria Bus Station – Erith, Bexley Road/Cross Street** via Victoria Street, Whitehall (Victoria jnys only), Trafalgar Square, Whitehall, Westminster Bridge, Elephant & Castle, Old Kent Road, New Cross, Deptford, Lewisham, Blackheath, Charlton Village, Woolwich, Plumstead Common, Lodge Hill, Upper Belvedere. Jnys Plumstead Garage to both Plumstead Common and to Woolwich. Jointly operated by **London Central** New Cross Garage 1 T + 1 T (joint N77) nightly and **Selkent** Plumstead Garage 2 L + 2 L (joint N77) nightly.

23/24 November 1990: Plumstead allocation now L/T-types.

28/29 April 1991: Allocation: London Central: New Cross Garage (joint N77) 1 T/L (Su-Th), 2 T/L (Fr-Sa), Selkent: Plumstead Garage 4 T/L nightly (2 joint N77 Fr-Sa).

8/9 October 1993: Allocation (joint N77): London Central: New Cross Garage 1 T/L (Su-Th), 2 T/L (Fr-Sa), Selkent: Plumstead Garage 5 T/L (Su-Th), 4 T/L (Fr-Sa).

6 September 1994: Plumstead Garage operated by **Stagecoach Selkent**.

18 October 1994: New Cross Garage operated by Go-Ahead group t/a **London Central**.

28/29 July 1995: LRT contract awarded to **Stagecoach Selkent**. Bifurcations Trafalgar Square – Oxford Circus, Plumstead Common – Thamesmead introduced. Plumstead Garage jnys withdrawn. Now operated: **Victoria Bus Station *or* Oxford Circus – Thamesmead, Town Centre *or* Erith, Bexley Road/Cross St** via *either* Victoria Street, Whitehall (Victoria jnys only) Station) *or* Piccadilly Circus (Oxford Circus jnys only) then Trafalgar Square, Whitehall, Westminster Bridge, Elephant & Castle, Old Kent Road, New Cross, Deptford, Lewisham, Blackheath, Charlton Village, Woolwich, Plumstead Common, then *either* Plumstead, Abbey Wood to Thamesmead (circular routeing via Bentham Road, Town Centre, Crossway) *or* Lodge Hill, Upper Belvedere to Erith. Allocation: Plumstead Garage 6 L/T nightly. Note: Replaced Plumstead – Thamesmead section of N77 (different routeing at Thamesmead).

3/4 November 1995: Allocation: Plumstead Garage 6 L/VN nightly, increased to 7 L/VN nightly from 28 February/1 March 1997. Vehicle-type changed to all Volvo Olympian 7 VN-type nightly by 25/26 June 1999.

7/8 January 2000: Bifurcations Victoria – Trafalgar Square, Plumstead Common – Thamesmead withdrawn. Now operated: **Oxford Circus – Erith, Cross Street.** Allocation: Plumstead Garage 6 VN (Su-Th), 9 VN (Fr-Sa). Note: Plumstead – Thamesmead section of N53 replaced by projection of N1.

By 28/29 September 2001: Completion of conversion to low-floor Dennis Trident (started c. November 2000). Allocation: Plumstead Garage 6 TA (Su-Th), 9 TA (Fr-Sa).

28/29 June 2002: Plumstead Common – Erith section of route withdrawn. Projected Plumstead Common – Plumstead Station. Re-routed Deptford – Blackheath, Royal Standard via Blackheath Hill (replaced N81). Now operated: **Oxford Circus – Plumstead Station.** Allocation: Plumstead Garage 6 TA (Su-Th), 9 TA (Fr-Sa). Note: Deptford – Blackheath via Lewisham section of N53 replaced by N89. The N89 also provided an all-night service to Erith via Bexleyheath but the Lodge Hill and Upper Belvedere areas lost all-night bus facilities.

14/15 February 2003: Section of route Oxford Circus – Whitehall withdrawn. Now operated: **Whitehall, Horse Guards – Plumstead Station.** Allocation: Plumstead Garage 7 TA nightly. Note: Oxford Circus – Whitehall section of N53 replaced by route N453 (and covered by extant Nighters). The N453 also supplemented the N53's service between Whitehall and Deptford.

19/20 March 2004: **Re-numbered (N)53.**

30 August 2006: Operated by Macquarie Bank Ltd t/a East London Bus Group. Fleetname: **Selkent**.

14 October 2010: Operated by Stagecoach Bus Holdings Ltd t/a **Selkent**.

1/2 July 2011: Vehicle-type change to AD E40D Enviro400 at Plumstead Garage 7 TE nightly.

Stagecoach Selkent's Alexander ALX400-bodied Dennis Trident TA 276 was seen loading passengers in Trafalgar Square on Sunday morning 14 July 2002. Southbound Night Bus routes which approached Trafalgar Square along Pall Mall East, such as the N53, completed a circuit around the Square to reach bus stop V outside Canada House. *Philip Wallis*

Route N62

27/28 October 1989: Introduced. Operated: **Victoria Bus Station – Orpington Station** via Whitehall, Trafalgar Square, Aldwych, Ludgate Circus, Blackfriars Bridge, Elephant & Castle, Camberwell Green, Peckham, New Cross, Lewisham, Lee Green, Eltham, Blackfen, Sidcup, Foots Cray, St Mary Cray, Ramsden Estate. Operator: **London Central**. Allocation: New Cross Garage 2 T/L nightly. Note: Co-ordinated timetable Trafalgar Square – Eltham with N72 (Su-Th) and N72/N82 (Fr-Sa).

18 October 1994: Operated by Go-Ahead group t/a **London Central**.

27/28 July 1995: Last night of operation. Note: Lewisham – Foots Cray section of N62 replaced by new route N21.

Orpington was first reached by LRT's Night Buses from 27/28 October 1989 when both a bifurcated extension to route N47 from Bromley South Station and route N62 were introduced. New Cross garage's Leyland Titan T 609 was seen outside Canada House in Trafalgar Square on Saturday morning 28 October 1989 awaiting departure time for one of three nightly N62 journeys to Orpington. *Roy Waterhouse*

Brixton garage's Leyland Fleetline DMS 2425 was in service of the first night of route N69's operation and was photographed outside Canada House in Trafalgar Square in the early hours of Saturday morning 28 October 1989 loading passengers for one of four nightly N69 journeys to Norwood Junction. *Roy Waterhouse*

Route N69 (Norwood Junction)
27/28 October 1989: Introduced. Operated: **Victoria Bus Station – Norwood Junction** via Whitehall, Trafalgar Square, Aldwych, Waterloo, Elephant & Castle, Kennington, Brixton, Streatham Hill, Streatham, Streatham Common, Green Lane, Thornton Heath High Street. Operator: **South London**. Allocation (joint N78): Brixton Garage 7 M nightly. Note: Streatham – Thornton Heath section of N69 previously served by N60 from 26/27 October 1984 to 5/6 February 1987.

20/21 July 1990: Re-allocated to Thornton Heath Garage (joint N78) 7 L nightly.

11/12 March 1994: Last night of operation. Note: Aldwych/ Trafalgar Square – Streatham section of N69 replaced by N109 (different intermediate routeing). Streatham – Norwood Junction section of N69 not replaced by an all-night service although Green Lane and Thornton Heath became served by N250 from 29/30 August 2003.

Below Brixton garage's MCW Metrobus M 175 was working what appears to have been a supplementary route N69 journey to Streatham when photographed in Aldwych during the early hours of New Year's Day 1990. *Roy Waterhouse*

Routes N70, N381

27/28 October 1989: Introduced. **Numbered N70.** Operated Fr-Sa only: **Trafalgar Square – Bromley South Station** via Aldwych, Ludgate Circus, Cannon Street, London Bridge, Jamaica Road, Rotherhithe, Salter Road, Redriff Road, Surrey Quays, Deptford, Lewisham, Catford, Bromley Road. Jnys Peckham Garage – Surrey Quays. Jointly operated by **London Central** Peckham Garage 1 T (Fr-Sa) and **Selkent** Catford Garage 1 T (Fr-Sa).

26/27 April 1991: Diverted Surrey Quays – Deptford via Pepys Estate.

8/9 October 1993: LRT contract awarded to **London Central**. Re-routed to form a unidirectional circular service: **Trafalgar Square – Trafalgar Square** via Whitehall, Westminster Bridge, York Road, Stamford Street, Southwark Street, Tooley Street, Jamaica Road, Rotherhithe, Salter Road, Redriff Road, Surrey Quays, Bermondsey, Rotherhithe New Road, St James's Road, Peckham Park Road, Peckham, Camberwell Green, Kennington Vauxhall, Victoria, Whitehall. Allocation: Peckham Garage 1 T (Fr-Sa).

18 October 1994: Operated by Go-Ahead group t/a **London Central**.

26/27 April 1996: Restructured to form a bidirectional service. St James's Road/Old Kent Road – Trafalgar Square section of route withdrawn. Projected Old Kent Road – Norwood Junction. Now operated: **Trafalgar Square – Norwood Junction** via Whitehall, Westminster Bridge, York Road, Stamford Street, Southwark Street, Tooley Street, Jamaica Road, Rotherhithe, Salter Road, Redriff Road, Surrey Quays, Rotherhithe New Road, Bermondsey, St James's Road, Old Kent Road, New Cross Gate, Brockley Rise, Forest Hill, Kirkdale, Penge, Anerley. Allocation: Peckham Garage 2 T (Fr-Sa). Note: Replaced Forest Hill – Anerley section of N71 and restored an all-night service to Norwood Junction, previously served by N69 until 10/11 March 1994.

By 25/26 June 1999: Vehicle-type change to Volvo Olympian at Peckham Garage 2 AV (Fr-Sa).

8/9 October 1999: **Re-numbered N381.** Old Kent Road – Norwood Junction section of route withdrawn. Projected St James's Road/Old Kent Road – Peckham. Nightly operation introduced: **Trafalgar Square – Peckham, Bus Station** via Whitehall, Westminster Bridge, York Road, Stamford Street, Southwark Street, Tooley Street, Jamaica Road, Rotherhithe, Salter Road, Redriff Road, Surrey Quays, Rotherhithe New Road, Bermondsey, St James Road, Peckham Park Road. Allocation: Peckham Garage 3 AV nightly. Note: Most withdrawn sections of N70 covered by other all-night bus routes (principally N171/N176) except for a small section of route around Forest Hill and Anerley – Norwood Junction.

By 18/19 July 2000: Allocation mixed step-floor Volvo Olympian and low-floor Volvo B7TL from Peckham Garage 3 AV/NV/AVL nightly.

31 Aug/1 Sept 2002: Truncated to terminate at Whitehall, Horse Guards. Now operated: **Whitehall, Horse Guards – Peckham, Bus Station.** Allocation unchanged.

By 4/5 July 2003: Allocation: Peckham Garage 3 NV/AVL/PVL nightly.

8/9 October 2004: LBSL contract awarded to **Travel London**. Allocation: Walworth Garage 4 V nightly.

9 June 2009: Travel London acquired by Ned Railways. Operated as **Abellio** from 30 October 2009 and as **Abellio London** from 1 June 2010.

By 27/28 July 2013: Allocation: Walworth Garage 4 V/ED/EDH nightly.

Top The first night's operation of Friday and Saturday nights-only route N70 would appear to have attracted good passenger numbers if the size of the crowd around Peckham garage's Leyland Titan T 730 seen outside Canada House in Trafalgar Square, loading for the first-ever outbound N70 departure at 00.36 on Saturday morning 28 October 1989, is any measure. *Roy Waterhouse*

Left Travel London's Wrightbus bodied Volvo B7TL V 5 was photographed on stand at Peckham Bus Station before working the 00.55 journey to Whitehall of 30 minute frequency route N381 on Tuesday morning 19 October 2004. *Philip Wallis*

Route N31

Introduced. **Night Arrow**. Operated Fr-Sa only: **Camden Town, Bayham Street – Fulham Broadway** via Chalk Farm, Swiss Cottage, Kilburn, Westbourne Park, Notting Hill Gate, Kensington High Street then *clockwise loop* via Earls Court, Fulham Road to Fulham Broadway then North End Road, Olympia to line of route at Kensington High Street. Operator: **Centrewest**. Allocation: Westbourne Park Garage 3 MA (Fr-Sa).

15/16 June 1991: Allocation: Westbourne Park Garage 3 DW (Fr-Sa).

17/18 July 1992: Nightly service introduced. Allocation: Westbourne Park Garage 1 DW (Su-Th), 3 DW (Fr-Sa).

2 September 1994: Centrewest acquired by management/employee buy-out.

26 March 1997: Operated by **First Bus**, re-titled **First Group** December 1997, **First London** March 2001.

1 /2 May 1998: Vehicle type change to low-floor Dennis Dart SLF at Westbourne Park 1 DM (Su-Th), 3 DM (Fr-Sa).

28/29 May 1999: Section of loop working Fulham Road – jct Kensington High Street/Earls Court Road withdrawn. Projected Earls Court – Clapham Junction. Now operated: **Camden Town, Bayham Street – Clapham Junction, Battersea Rise** via Chalk Farm, Swiss Cottage, Kilburn, Westbourne Park, Notting Hill Gate, Kensington High Street, Earls Court, Chelsea, Battersea. Allocation: Westbourne Park Garage 2 DM (Su-Th), 4 DM (Fr-Sa). Note: Fulham Broadway – jct Kensington High Street/ Earls Court Road section of N31 replaced by new route N28. Co-ordinated timetable Camden Town – Kensington High Street with N28.

30/31 January 2004: Clapham Junction terminus now St John's Hill.

By 27/28 August 2004: Allocation mixed low-floor single-deck/double-deck from Westbourne Park Garage 2 DM/TNA/VNW (Su-Th), 4 DM/TNA/VNW(Fr-Sa).

c. September 2004: Allocation now double-deck TNA/ VNW-type, all VNW-type by 8/9 May 2010.

30 Sept/1 Oct 2011: Re-allocated to Atlas Road Harlesden Garage 2 VNW (Su-Th), 4 VNW (Fr-Sa).

21/22 June 2013: Operated by **Tower Transit**.

Top Night Arrow route N31 was spawned from the success of Centrewest's daytime Gold Arrow routes 28 (Golders Green – Wandsworth) and 31 (Camden Town – Chelsea) over which midibuses, working high frequency services, had replaced double-deck buses from 4 March and 15 April 1989 respectively and increased passenger numbers and revenue according to Peter Hendy, Centrewest's Managing Director. Roy Waterhouse was in Bayham Street, Camden Town on the N31's first night of operation where he photographed Westbourne Park garage's 28-seat Alexander-bodied Mercedes-Benz 811D MA 15 in the early hours of Sunday morning 12 November 1989. *Roy Waterhouse*

Centre Route N31 had recently been upgraded to nightly operation when 26-seat Wright Handybus-bodied Dennis Dart DW 107 was seen in Bayham Street, Camden Town in the early hours of Saturday morning 1 August 1992. *Roy Waterhouse.*

Right Route N31 was fully converted to double-deck bus operation around September 2004. First London's Wrightbus-bodied Volvo B7TL VNW 32414 was nearing journey's end when seen in Falcon Road, Clapham Junction during the early morning hours of Sunday 30 September 2007. *Philip Wallis*

Route N67

5/6 January 1990: Introduced. Operated Fr-Sa only: **Victoria Bus Station (arr only)** ***or*** **Trafalgar Square – Staines, Bus Station** via *either* Whitehall, Victoria Street (to Victoria Station only) *or* Piccadilly Circus, Hyde Park Corner, Knightsbridge, Kensington High Street, Hammersmith, Stamford Brook, Turnham Green, Chiswick, Brentford, Isleworth, Hounslow, Hounslow Heath, Feltham, Lower Feltham, Ashford. Shepherd's Bush Garage jnys. Operator: **London United**. Allocation (joint N97): Hounslow Garage 6 M (Fr-Sa), Shepherd's Bush Garage 6 M (Fr-Sa).

17/18 July 1992: Su-Th service introduced Trafalgar Square – Lower Feltham. Projected Staines – Egham (Fr-Sa). Re-routed Lower Feltham – Ashford. Victoria terminating jny revised to operate from Hyde Park Corner. Now operated: **Victoria Bus Station (arr only)** ***or*** **Trafalgar Square – Egham, High Street** via *either* Grosvenor Place (to Victoria Station only) *or* Piccadilly Circus, Hyde Park Corner, Knightsbridge, Kensington High Street, Hammersmith, Stamford Brook, Turnham Green, Chiswick, Brentford, Isleworth, Hounslow, Hounslow Heath, Feltham, Lower Feltham, Sunbury Cross, Ashford, Staines. Shepherd's Bush Garage jny (Fr-Sa). Allocation (joint N97): Hounslow Garage 3 M (Su-Th), 5 M (Fr-Sa), Shepherd's Bush Garage 3 M (Su-Th), 5 M (Fr-Sa).

26/27 March 1993: Partially re-allocated (joint N97) to Stamford Brook Garage 3 L (Su-Th), 5 L (Fr-Sa), Hounslow Garage 3 M (Su-Th), 5 M (Fr-Sa). Shepherd's Bush Garage jny withdrawn.

24/25 February 1994: Last night of operation. Note: Trafalgar Square – Sunbury Cross section of N67 replaced by bifurcation of N97 (partially different intermediate routeing). Sunbury Cross – Egham section of N67 abandoned.

London United's MCW Metrobus M 902 was seen at route N67's outbound Trafalgar Square pick-up bus stop W in Cockspur Street during the early hours of Sunday morning 14 January 1990. *Roy Waterhouse*

Route N9 (Enfield)
9/10 February 1990: Introduced. Operated: **Victoria Bus Station – Enfield Town, Little Park Gardens** via Victoria Street, Whitehall, Trafalgar Square, Tottenham Court Road, Camden Town, Holloway, Finsbury Park, Manor House, Turnpike Lane Station., Wood Green, Palmers Green, Southgate Station, Oakwood Station. One inbound jny operated Palmers Green (05.00) to Turnpike Lane Station (05.42) via Edmonton, Lower Edmonton, Ponders End to line of route at Enfield Town. Return jny from Turnpike Lane Station (05.50) via line of route to Enfield Town then to Ponders End Garage (06.18). Operator: **Leaside Buses**. Allocation: Palmers Green Garage 1 M nightly. Note: Co-ordinated timetable with N29.

31 Jan/1 Feb 1992: Projected Enfield Town – Ponders End Bus Garage. Now operated: **Victoria Bus Station – Ponders End Bus Garage.** 05.00 jny from Palmers Green to Turnpike Lane Station via Edmonton continued to operate. Allocation: Palmers Green Garage 1 M (Su-Th), 2 M (Fr-Sa).

24/25 June 1993: Last night of operation. Note: Palmers Green Garage N9 bus allocation transferred to N29.

Route NX1
19/20 October 1990: Introduced. **Medway Night Express, Limited Stop Service.** Operated Fr-Sa only: **Trafalgar Square – Gillingham, Jeffery Street.** *Outbound* via New Cross Gate, Welling Corner, Bexleyheath, Crayford, Dartford, Gravesend, Strood, Rochester, Chatham. *Inbound* via Chatham, Rochester, Strood then ***non-stop*** to Bexley, Black Prince then ***non-stop*** to *either* Trafalgar Square *or* New Cross Gate. Operator: **London Central**. Allocation: New Cross Garage 1 L coach-seated (Fr-Sa). Note: Between Trafalgar Square and Dartford only observed listed stops. Between Dartford and Gillingham (outbound) and between Gillingham and Strood (inbound) observed all authorised bus stops.

25/26 January 1991: First outbound jny back-projected to start at Victoria. Now operated: **Victoria Bus Station – Gillingham, Jeffery Street.** Allocation unchanged.

5/6 July 1991: Additional pick-up stop for outbound jnys introduced at Strand, Charing Cross Station.

2/3 October 1993: Last night of operation. Note: Elements of NX1 incorporated into new route N81.

Top Palmers Green garage's single bus allocated to route N9 was photographed entering service at North Circular Road, Palmers Green at 23.29 on Saturday night 17 February 1990 when MCW Metrobus M 605 worked that night's first N9 journey to Victoria Station. *Roy Waterhouse*

Right London Central's coach-seated Eastern Coach Works-bodied Leyland Olympian L 261 was photographed at Welling Corner at 01.32 on Saturday morning 20 October 1990 when working the inaugural journey of Medway Night Express route NX1. *Roy Waterhouse*

Routes introduced 1992

Route N26

17/18 July 1992: Introduced. Operated: **Victoria Bus Station – Walthamstow Central Station** via Victoria Street, Whitehall, Trafalgar Square, Alwych, Ludgate Circus, Bank, Liverpool Street Bus Station (inbound only), Bishopsgate, Shoreditch, Cambridge Heath, Hackney, Hackney Wick, Leyton. Operator: **East London**. Allocation: Leyton Garage 2 T nightly. Note: Replaced Trafalgar Square – Walthamstow Central Station section of N6.

6 September 1994: Operated by **Stagecoach East London**.

14/15 July 1995: Section of route Victoria – Trafalgar Square withdrawn. Projected within Walthamstow. Now operated: **Trafalgar Square – Walthamstow, Fulbourne Road/Wadham Road.** Allocation: Leyton Garage 2 'T' nightly. Outbound buses to Fulbourne Rd/Wadham Rd displayed destination blinds set for 'Walthamstow Crooked Billet' and continued to that point. Allocation unchanged.

21/22 June 1996: Re-allocated to Bow Garage 2 T nightly.

3/4 August 1997: Completion of conversion to VA/VN-type Volvo Olympian (started 6/7 December 1996) at Bow Garage 2 VA/VN nightly, increased to 4 VA/VN nightly from 30/31 October 1998 and had become all VA-type by 21/22 January 2000.

28/29 April 2000: Inbound jnys no longer served Liverpool Street Bus Station.

26/27 April 2001: Section of route Walthamstow Central – Fulbourne Road withdrawn (not replaced). Projected Walthamstow Central – Chingford Station (replaced N38). Re-routed London Fields – Hackney Wick, Hackney Wick – Leyton. Now operated: **Trafalgar Square – Chingford Station** via Aldwych, Ludgate Circus, Bank, Bishopsgate, Shoreditch, Cambridge Heath, Well Street, Hackney Wick, Temple Mills Lane, Leyton, Walthamstow Central, Crooked Billet, Chingford Mount, The Ridgeway. Re-allocated to Stratford Garage 8 VA nightly.

c. September 2001: Completion of vehicle-type change to low-floor Dennis Trident at Stratford Garage 8 TA nightly.

30 August 2006: Operated by Macquarie Bank Ltd t/a East London Bus Group. Fleetname: **East London**.

16/17 July 2007: Re-routed to operate directly between Hackney Wick and Leyton via Ruckholt Road.

23/24 February 2008: Re-allocated to West Ham Garage 9 TA nightly, re-allocated to Leyton Garage 8 TA nightly on 30/31 May 2008.

14 October 2010: Operated by Stagecoach Bus Holdings Ltd t/a **East London**.

24/25 June 2011: LBSL contract awarded to **First London**. Converted to AD Trident Enviro400 from Lea Interchange Garage 8 DN nightly.

27/28 July – 12/13 August and 29/30 August – 9/10 September 2012: Allocation from Lea Interchange Garage temporarily increased for reliability during Olympic and Paralympic Games 9 DN nightly.

21/22 June 2013: Operated by **Tower Transit**.

Route N65 (Archway – Hounslow)

17/18 July 1992: Introduced. Operated Fr-Sa only: **Archway Station *or* Victoria Bus Station (dep only) – Kingston, Fairfield Bus Station** via *either* Holloway, Highbury Corner, Islington, Rosebery Avenue, Holborn, Aldwych (Archway jnys) *or* Victoria Street, Whitehall (from Victoria) then Trafalgar Square, Piccadilly Circus, Hyde Park Corner, Knightsbridge, Kensington High Street, Hammersmith, Putney Bridge, Putney, Upper Richmond Road, East Sheen, Richmond, Petersham, Ham. Operated jointly by **London Northern** Holloway Garage 1 M (Fr-Sa) and **London United** Shepherd's Bush Garage 1 M (Fr-Sa). Note: Co-ordinated timetable Trafalgar Square – Kingston with N92 (partially different intermediate routeing).

Upon its introduction route N26 provided a nightly hourly frequency service over its entire route length between Victoria and Walthamstow Central stations. Leyton garage's Leyland Titan T 557 was seen at Victoria Bus Station in the early hours of Saturday morning 25 July 1992. *Roy Waterhouse*

Holloway garage's MCW Metrobus M 1148 was seen on arrival at Kingston, Fairfield Bus Station (referred to by its previous designation as Cattle Market Bus Station on the destination blind) at 02.01 on Saturday morning 25 July 1992 on completion of the 00.35 route N65 journey from Archway Station. *Roy Waterhouse*

Dawn was breaking as Willesden garage's MCW Metrobus M 1425 arrived from Trafalgar Square onto route N99's bus stand at Queensbury Station at 04.41 on Sunday morning 26 July 1992. *Roy Waterhouse*

26/27 March 1993: One outbound jny projected Kingston – Hounslow via Hampton Court, Hampton, Hanworth. Now operated: **Archway Station *or* Victoria Station, Bus Station (dep only) – Hounslow, Bus Station.** Allocation: London United: Re-allocated to Hounslow Garage 1 M (Fr-Sa), London Northern: Holloway Garage 1 M (Fr-Sa),

19/20 February 1994: Last night of operation. Note: Largely replaced by new route N9.

Routes N99 (Stanmore), N98 (Stanmore)

17/18 July 1992: Introduced. **Numbered N99.** Operated: **Trafalgar Square – Queensbury Station** via Piccadilly Circus, Oxford Circus, Marble Arch, Edgware Road, Kilburn, Willesden, Neasden, Kingsbury. Operator: **Metroline**. Allocation: Willesden Garage (joint N6) 4 M nightly.

28/29 January 1994: LRT contract awarded to **Centrewest**. Projected Queensbury Station – Stanmore Station. Now operated: **Trafalgar Square – Stanmore Station**. Allocation: Alperton Garage 3 M nightly, one of which also operated on N139 M-Sa.

2 September 1994: Centrewest acquired by management/employee buy-out.

18/19 August 1995: **Re-numbered N98.** Allocation unchanged.

By 11/12 January 1997: Joint allocation with N139 dissolved, now Alperton Garage 2 M nightly.

26 March 1997: Operated by **First Bus**, re-titled **First Group** December 1997.

31 March/1 April 1999: Vehicle-type change to Volvo Olympian at Alperton Garage 2 VN nightly.

19/20 November 1999: Fr-Sa supplementary service intoduced using Metrobuses of **Metropolitan Omnibus Company (London) Ltd**, trading as **London Traveller**. Last operated Millennium Eve 31 December 1999/1 January 2000.

28/29 April 2000: Section of route Trafalgar Square – Oxford Circus withdrawn. Projected Oxford Circus – Holborn. Now operated: **Holborn, Red Lion Square – Stanmore Station** via New Oxford Street, Oxford Circus, Marble Arch, Edgware Road, Kilburn, Willesden, Neasden, Kingsbury. Allocation: Alperton 2 VN nightly.

2/3 February 2001: LBSL contract awarded to **Metroline Travel**. Allocation: Edgware Garage 4 M (Su-Th), 5 M (Fr-Sa).

By October 2001: Completion of vehicle-type change (started September 2001) to low-floor Volvo B7TL at Edgware Garage 4 VPL (Su-Th), 5 VPL (Fr-Sa).

11/12 October 2002: Allocation: Edgware Garage 4 VPL (Su-Th), 5 VPL (Fr-Sa), Willesden Garage 3 VPL (Su-Th), 4 VPL (Fr-Sa).

7/8 November 2003: Allocation: Edgware Garage 4 VPL (Su-Th), 8 VPL (Fr-Sa), Willesden Garage 3 VPL (Su-Th), 5 VPL (Fr-Sa).

26/27 March 2004: Allocation : Edgware Garage 4 VPL (Su-Th), 8 VPL (Fr-Sa), Willesden Garage 3 VP (Su-Th), 5 VP (Fr-Sa).

18/19 November 2005: Allocation: Edgware Garage 5 VPL (Su-Th), 8 VPL (Fr-Sa), Willesden Garage 3 VP (Su-Th), 5 VP (Fr-Sa).

By 27/28 July 2013: Edgware Garage TE/VPL-types, Willesden Garage VP/VPL-types.

Route N98 operates additional journeys on Sunday mornings to cover a later starting time of the Underground's Jubilee Line on that day of the week. Edgware garage's Plaxton President-bodied Volvo B7TL VPL 160 was seen at Stanmore Station at 07.45 on Sunday morning 26 June 2005 having worked the N98's penultimate 06.55 journey from Holborn. The final Sunday morning N98 journey left Holborn at 07.25 and on its arrival at Stanmore Station at 08.15 was the last Night Bus to go out of service across London at that time. *Philip Wallis*

Route N17

30/31 October 1992: Introduced. Operated Fr-Sa outbound only: **Trafalgar Square – Harrow Weald, Bus Garage** via Piccadilly Circus, Oxford Circus, Marble Arch, Paddington Station, Harrow Road, Harlesden, Stonebridge Park, Wembley, Sudbury, Harrow, South Harrow, Rayners Lane Station, North Harrow, Pinner, Northwood, Carpenders Park Station. Operator: **Metroline**. Allocation: Harrow Weald Garage 1 M (Fr-Sa). Note: Pinner – Harrow Weald section of route served only if passengers were already on board at Pinner, Love Lane.

22/23 January 1994: Last night of operation.

Route N66

30/31 October 1992: Introduced. Operated Fr-Su outbound only: **Cricklewood Broadway – Edgware Station** via Willesden, Craven Park, Harlesden, Stonebridge Park, Wembley, Preston Road, Kingsbury, Queensbury, Camrose Avenue. Operator: **Metroline**. Allocation: Edgware Garage 1 M (Fr-Su).

5/6 March 1993: Allocation: Cricklewood Garage 1 M (Fr, Su), Edgware Garage 1 M (Sa).

23/24 January 1994: Last night of operation.

Harrow Weald garage's MCW Metrobus M 993 was seen on layover at Aldwych prior to taking up service on its route N17 journey on New Year's Day 1 January 1993. *Roy Waterhouse*

Despite the large slipboard displayed in its windscreen there seemed to be little prospect of passengers from Ashton's night-club or indeed anywhere else materialising to board Edgware garage's MCW Metrobus M 1198 as it waited in a deserted Cricklewood Broadway for 02.20 departure time for its N66 journey to Edgware Station on Saturday morning 31 October 1992. *Roy Waterhouse*

Routes introduced 1993

Route N253

3/4 September 1993: Introduced. Operated: **Aldgate, Bus Station – Euston, Bus Station** via Whitechapel, Bethnal Green, Cambridge Heath, Hackney, Clapton, Stamford Hill, Manor House, Finsbury Park, Holloway, Camden Town. Operator: **Leaside Buses**. Allocation: Stamford Hill Garage 4 L nightly.

29 September 1994: Operated by **Cowie Leaside**.

25/26 November 1994: Projected Euston – Trafalgar Square via Gower Street (inbound), Tottenham Court Road (outbound), Charing Cross Road. Now operated: **Aldgate, Bus Station – Trafalgar Square**. Allocation: Stamford Hill Garage 5 L nightly.

12/13 May 1995: Re-allocated to Clapton Garage 5 L nightly, Fr-Sa allocation increased to 6 L from 26/27 April 1996.

2 April 1998: Operated by **Arriva London North**.

29/30 May 1998: Section of route Tottenham Court Road Station – Trafalgar Square withdrawn. Now operated: **Aldgate, Bus Station – Tottenham Court Road Station** (set-down: New Oxford Street, pick-up: Tottenham Court Road). Allocation: Clapton Garage 5 L (Su-Th), 6 L (Fr-Sa), became 5 L nightly from 16/17 February 2001.

19/20 July 2002: Vehicle-type change to low-floor DAF DB250LF at Clapton Garage 5 DLA nightly, increased to 6 DLA nightly from 30/31 May 2003 and to 8 DLA nightly from 13/14 January 2006.

31 March/1 April 2006: Re-allocated to Stamford Hill Garage 8 DLA/VLW nightly, increased to 11 DLA/VLW nightly from 18/19 April 2008.

2/3 January 2009: Tottenham Court Road Station set-down now St. Giles High Street.

4/5 September 2009: Allocation: Stamford Hill Garage 11 DLA/VLW (Su-Th), 13 DLA/VLW (Fr-Sa), had become all VLW-type Volvo B7TL by 8/9 May 2010.

27 August 2010: Arriva acquired by Deutsche Bahn.

By 29/20 June 2012: Allocation now all DW-type.

May 2013: Converted to Volvo B5LH hybrid. 14/15 June 2013: Allocation: Stamford Hill Garage 10 HV (Su-Th), 13 HV (Fr-Sa).

Stamford Hill garage's TransBus ALX400-bodied DAF DB250LF DLA 385 was seen loading passengers at Tottenham Court Road Station for then-20 minute frequency route N253 at around 2 o'clock on Sunday morning 11 June 2006. Garage running number 221 was displayed in both the windscreen and beside the SF garage code. *Philip Wallis*

Coincidentally Stamford Hill garage running number 221 applied to Wrightbus DB300 Gemini 2DL Integral DW 428 when it was photographed a t Euston Station Bus Station at around 03.45 on Saturday morning 11 December 2011. Route N253 has operated to a 15 minute Sunday to Thursday night and 12 minute Friday and Saturday night frequency since 4/5 September 2009. *Philip Wallis*

Routes N36, N136

25/26 August 1986, 31 Aug/1 Sept 1987: Operated these nights only on occasion of Notting Hill Carnival: **Numbered N36**. Operated: **Harrow Road, Prince of Wales – Lewisham** (see Chapter 2).

8/9 October 1993: Regular service introduced. **Numbered N36.** Operated: **Trafalgar Square – Grove Park Station** via Whitehall, Victoria Street, Victoria, Vauxhall, Kennington, Camberwell Green, Peckham, New Cross, Lewisham, Catford, Bromley Road, Downham Way. Operator: **London Central**. Allocation: Peckham Garage (joint N12/N71/N84) 6 T(Su-Th), 7 T (Fr-Sa). Note: Replaced Camberwell – Lewisham section of N82 and New Cross Gate – Grove Park section of N85.

18 October 1994: Operated by Go-Ahead group t/a **London Central**.

26/27 April 1996: Projected Trafalgar Square – Queens Park Station via Piccadilly Circus, Oxford Circus, Marble Arch, Paddington Station, Harrow Road. Now operated: **Queens Park Station – Grove Park Station.** Allocation: Peckham Garage (joint N12/N84) 9 T/AV (Su-Th), 14 T/AV (Fr-Sa).

By 12/13 January 1997: Joint allocation dissolved, now: Peckham Garage 6 T/AV (Su-Th), 9 T/AV (Fr-Sa).

11/12 July 1997: Allocation: Peckham Garage 6 T/AV (Su-Th), 10 T/AV (Fr-Sa), New Cross Garage 2 T (Fr-Sa).

By June 1998: Allocation: Peckham Garage 6 T/AV (Su-Th), 8 T/AV (Fr-Sa), New Cross Garage 4 T (Fr-Sa).

23/24 July 1999: Allocation: New Cross Garage 1 NV (Su-Th), 2 NV (Fr-Sa), Peckham Garage 4 T/AV (Su-Th), 6 T/AV (Fr-Sa).

By June 2001: Completion of conversion to low-floor Volvo B7TL (started 4/5 February 2000) from Peckham Garage 6 AVL (Su-Th), 10 AVL (Fr-Sa), increased to 7 AVL (Su-Th), 12 AVL (Fr-Sa) by November 2001.

20/21 February 2003: Allocation: New Cross Garage 2 PVL nightly, Peckham Garage 4 AVL (Su-Th), 10 AVL (Fr-Sa), Peckham Garage's allocation had become AVL/PVL-types by c. May 2003 and AVL/PVL/E-types by 21/22 June 2006.

8/9 February 2008: **Re-numbered N136.** LBSL contract awarded to Macquarie Bank's East London Bus Group t/a **Selkent**. Queens Park Station – Oxford Circus section of route withdrawn. Projected Grove Park Station – Chislehurst. Now operated: **Oxford Circus – Chislehurst, War Memorial** via Piccadilly Circus, Trafalgar Square, Whitehall, Victoria Street, Victoria, Vauxhall, Kennington, Camberwell Green, Peckham, New Cross, Lewisham, Catford, Bromley Road, Downham Way, Grove Park, Dunkery Road, Chislehurst High Street. Allocation: Catford Garage 6 TA (Su-Th), 10 TA (Fr –Sa). Note: Queens Park Station – Marble Arch section of N36 replaced by new route (N)36. (N)36/N136 shared common routeing Victoria – New Cross Garage. The N136 restored an all-night bus service to Chislehurst, previously served by N3 between 8/9 October 1993 and 29/30 January 2000 and by N21 between 7/8 November 1997 and 10/11 October 2002.

14 October 2010: Operated by Stagecoach Bus Holdings Ltd t/a **Selkent**.

By 29/30 March 2012: Vehicle-type AD E40D Enviro400 from Catford Garage 6 TE (Su-Th), 10 TE (Fr-Sa).

Top Peckham garage's Leyland Titan T 1109 outside Canada House in Trafalgar Square ready for the 05.20 departure of then-hourly frequency route N36 on Saturday morning 11 June 1994. *JGS Smith*

Left The last weeks of route N36's existence are represented by this view of Peckham garage's AD Trident Enviro400 E 29 seen in Terminus Place at Victoria Station on a short-working journey to Catford Bus Garage in the early hours of Sunday morning 20 January 2008. *Philip Wallis*

Route N51 (Woolwich)

8/9 October 1993: Introduced. Operated Fr-Sa only: **Trafalgar Square – Woolwich Arsenal Station** via Aldwych, Waterloo, Elephant & Castle, Bricklayers Arms, Bermondsey, Surrey Quays, Pepys Estate, Deptford, Lewisham, Lee Green, Eltham, Shooters Hill. Garage jny Deptford Broadway – New Cross Gate. Operator: **London Central**. Allocation: New Cross Garage 1 T/L (Fr-Sa). Note: Co-ordinated timetable with N61. Routes N51/N61 replaced Surrey Quays – Lewisham section of N70 and Lewisham – Eltham section of N82. N51 additionally replaced Eltham – Woolwich section of N82.

18 October 1994: Operated by Go-Ahead group t/a **London Central**.

22/23 July 1995: Last night of operation. Note: Sections of N51/N61 Trafalgar Square – Deptford replaced by N1 and Lewisham – Eltham by new route N21. The withdrawal of route N51 severed the long-established all-night bus link between Woolwich and Eltham which had been introduced with an all-night service on route 182 from 5/6 July 1952 and perpetuated by route N82 until 2/3 October 1993.

Route N61

8/9 October 1993: Introduced. Operated Fr-Sa only: **Trafalgar Square – Sidcup Station** via Aldwych, Waterloo, Elephant & Castle, Bricklayers Arms, Bermondsey, Surrey Quays, Pepys Estate, Deptford, Lewisham, Lee Green, Eltham, Mottingham, New Eltham. Operator: **London Central**. Allocation: New Cross Garage 1 T/L (Fr-Sa). Note: Co-ordinated timetable with N51.

18 October 1994: Operated by Go-Ahead group t/a **London Central**.

22/23 July 1995: Last night of operation. Note: Eltham – Sidcup Station section of N61 replaced by bifurcation of new route N21 (Fr-Sa). See also note on route N51.

Woolwich route N51 and Sidcup route N61 combined to give an hourly frequency service on Friday and Saturday nights-only between Trafalgar Square and Eltham via Bermondsey, Surrey Quays and Lewisham. New Cross garage's Leyland Titans T 1008 (top) and T 1056 (bottom) were seen outside Canada House in Trafalgar Square loading for one of two N51 journeys to Woolwich and for one of three N61 journeys to Sidcup respectively in the early hours of Sunday morning 5 February 1995. *Both Malc McDonald*

Routes N81 (via Bexleyheath), N89 (Erith)

8/9 October 1993: Introduced. **Numbered N81.** Operated: **Victoria Bus Station – Gillingham, Jeffery Street** via Victoria Street, Whitehall, Trafalgar Square, Whitehall, Westminster Bridge, Elephant & Castle, Old Kent Road, New Cross, Deptford, Shooters Hill, Welling, Bexleyheath, Crayford, Dartford, Gravesend then Fr-Sa only via Strood, Rochester and Chatham to Gillingham. One inbound jny operated Elephant & Castle – Trafalgar Square via Blackfriars Bridge, Ludgate Circus and Aldwych. Operator: **London Central**. Allocation: New Cross Garage 2 T/L nightly. Note: Replaced Welling – Dartford section of route N72 and Dartford – Gillingham section of route NX1. N81 also superseded NX1's Fr-Sa service between central London and Dartford, Gravesend and the Medway Towns.

18 October 1994: Operated by Go-Ahead group t/a **London Central**.

28/29 July 1995: Re-routed Trafalgar Square – New Cross Gate via Aldwych, Blackfriars Bridge, Elephant & Castle, Walworth Road, Camberwell Green, Peckham. Service beyond Crayford restricted to Fr-Sa operation. Continued to operate: **Victoria Bus Station – Gillingham, Jeffery Street.** Allocation: New Cross Garage (joint N1/N21) 8 T (Su-Th), 11 T (Fr- Sa).

26/27 April 1996: Additional Su-Th inbound jnys introduced Deptford (04.38, 05.38) – Victoria. Allocation supplemented by New Cross Garage 1 T/L (joint daytime 21 (Su-Th).

c. June 1996: Allocation became T/NV-types.

16/17 May 1997: Joint allocation largely dissolved, now: Bexleyheath Garage 1 NV (Fr-Sa), New Cross Garage 4 NV + 1 T/L (joint 21 Su-Th), 4 NV (Fr-Sa).

7/8 November 1997: Joint allocation re-introduced, now: Bexleyheath Garage (joint N1/N21) 2 NV (Su-Th), 4 NV (Fr-Sa), New Cross Garage 4 NV (joint N1) nightly + 1 NV (joint 21 Su-Th).

13/14 November 1998: Allocation: Bexleyheath Garage (joint N21) 2 NV (Su-Th), 4 NV (Fr-Sa), New Cross Garage 2 NV nightly + 1 NV (joint 21 Su-Th).

23/24 July 1999: Section of route Bexleyheath – Gillingham withdrawn. Now operated: **Victoria Bus Station – Bexleyheath, Shopping Centre.** Allocation (joint N21): Bexleyheath Garage 2NV (Su-Th), 5 NV (Fr-Sa), New Cross Garage 6 NV (Su-Th), 7 NV (Fr-Sa). Note. A replacement Fr-Sa service from central London to Crayford, Dartford, Gravesend and the Medway Towns was provided by London Central's new commercially-operated routes N80/N82 (see Chapter 8).

4/5 February 2000: Joint allocation dissolved, now New Cross Garage 2 NV nightly.

16/17 March 2001: Vehicle-type change to low-floor Volvo B7TL at New Cross Garage 2 PVL nightly.

28/29 June 2002: **Re-numbered N89.** Section of route Victoria – Trafalgar Square withdrawn. Projected Bexleyheath – Erith. Re-routed Deptford – Shooters Hill Road. Now operated: **Trafalgar Square – Erith, Cross Street** via Aldwych, Ludgate Circus, Blackfriars Bridge, Elephant & Castle, Walworth Road, Camberwell Green, Peckham, New Cross, Deptford, Lewisham, Blackheath, Shooters Hill, Welling, Bexleyheath, Barnehurst, Northumberland Heath, Slade Green. Allocation: Bexleyheath Garage 6 PVL nightly. Note: Replaced Deptford – Shooters Hill Road via Lewisham section of N53 with onward service to Erith (different intermediate routeing).

20/21 February 2009: Trafalgar Square pick-up now Duncannon Street.

3/4 September 2010: Allocation: Bexleyheath Garage 6 PVL (Su-Th), 9 PVL (Fr-Sa).

27/28 January 2012: Allocation: Bexleyheath Garage 6 E (Su-Th), 9 E (Fr-Sa). Had become all WVL-type by 27/28 July 2013.

Bexleyheath garage's Northern Counties Palatine I-bodied Volvo Olympian NV 22 was seen at bus stop V on the western perimeter of Trafalgar Square ready to set off on the 04.44 route N81 journey to Gravesend on Saturday morning 26 June 1999, within the last month of LRT-sponsored Night Bus operation into Kent. *Philip Wallis*

Bexleyheath garage's Plaxton President-bodied Volvo B7TL PVL 15 was photographed at 05.33 on Sunday morning 26 June 2005 having just crossed Blackfriars Bridge when working that night's last inbound journey of then-30 minute frequency route N89. *Philip Wallis*

Routes N84 (Nunhead), N343

8/9 October 1993: Introduced. **Numbered N84.** Operated: **Oxford Circus – Nunhead** via Piccadilly Circus, Trafalgar Square, Whitehall, Westminster Bridge, Elephant & Castle, Walworth, Albany Road, North Peckham, Southampton Way, Peckham, Peckham Rye then unidirectional circular via Nunhead Station, Ivydale Road back to Peckham Rye and line of route. Operator: **London Central**. Allocation: Peckham Garage (joint N12/N36/N71) 6 T (Su-Th), 7 T (Fr-Sa). Note: Replaced Nunhead loop section of N12.

28/29 January 1994: 01.24 dep ex Nunhead diverted at Westminster to run via Victoria Street to Victoria Bus Station nightly.

18 October 1994: Operated by Go-Ahead group t/a **London Central**.

c. June 1995: Allocation (joint N12/N36/N71): Peckham Garage 6 AV/T (Su-Th), 7 AV/T (Fr-Sa), increased to 9 AV/T (Su-Th), 13 AV/T (Fr-Sa) by 13/14 October 1995.

26/27 April 1996: Inbound Victoria jny withdrawn. Allocation (joint N12/N36): Peckham Garage 9 AV/T (Su-Th), 14 AV/T (Fr-Sa).

By 11/12 January 1997: Joint allocation dissolved, now: Peckham Garage 1 AV/T (Su-Th), 2 AV/T (Fr-Sa).

11/12 July 1997: 01.24 dep ex Nunhead again diverted at Westminster to run via Victoria Street to Victoria Bus Station (Su-Th). Allocation: Peckham Garage 3 AV/T (Su-Th), 2 AV/T (Fr-Sa).

23/24 July 1999: Sections of route Oxford Circus – Trafalgar Square and unidirectional circuit of Nunhead loop withdrawn. Projected Trafalgar Square – Victoria, Peckham Rye – New Cross Gate. Re-routed Trafalgar Square – Elephant & Castle. Now operated: **Victoria Station, Bus Station – New Cross Gate, Bus Garage** via Victoria Street, Whitehall, Trafalgar Square, Aldwych, Waterloo Bridge, Stamford Street, Southwark Street, London Bridge Station, Borough High Street, Elephant & Castle, Walworth, Albany Road, North Peckham, Southampton Way, Peckham, Peckham Rye, Ivydale Road, Brockley, Telegraph Hill, Jerningham Road (outbound), Pepys Road (inbound). Allocation (joint N12): Peckham Garage 6 T/AV (Su-Th), 7 T/AV (Fr-Sa).

4/5 February 2000: Progressive introduction of low-floor Volvo B7TL from Peckham Garage 2 AV/AVL (Su-Th), 2 AV/AVL + 1 AV/AVL (joint N12) (Fr-Sa).

2/3 February 2001: **Re-numbered N343.** Joint allocation with N12 dissolved, now: Camberwell Garage 2 AVL nightly, Peckham Garage 1 AV/AVL (Su-Th).

27/28 July 2001: Allocation: Camberwell Garage 4 AVL nightly, changed to 4 PVL nightly by June 2003.

3/4 February 2006: LBSL contract awarded to **Travel London**. Victoria – Trafalgar Square section of route withdrawn. Revised terminus at New Cross Gate. Now operated: **Trafalgar Square (Charing Cross Station) – New Cross Gate, Jerningham Road.** Allocation: Walworth Garage 4 V nightly.

20/21 February 2009: Trafalgar Square pick-up now Duncannon Street.

9 June 2009: Travel London acquired by Ned Railways. Operated as **Abellio** from 30 October 2009 and as **Abellio London** from 1 June 2010.

By 8/9 May 2010: Allocation: Walworth Garage 5 V nightly. ED/EDH-types by 27/28 July 2013.

Top Just two early morning route N84 journeys operated beyond Trafalgar Square to and from Oxford Circus. Peckham garage's Leyland Titan T 1057 was seen upon arrival at Oxford Circus's bus stand in Hollies Street at around 6 o'clock on Saturday morning 11 June 1994. *JGS Smith*

Above Abellio London's Wrightbus-bodied Volvo B7TL 9002 had stopped to pick-up a passenger for 30 minute frequency route N343 at London Bridge Station when this photograph was taken at around 4 o'clock on Friday morning 15 October 2010. *Philip Wallis*

Routes N52, (N)52

3/4 December 1993: Introduced. Operated: **Victoria Bus Station – Willesden, Roundwood Park** via Whitehall, Trafalgar Square, Piccadilly Circus, Hyde Park Corner, Knightsbridge, Kensington High Street, Notting Hill Gate, Ladbroke Grove, Kensal Green, Kensal Rise, Willesden. Operator: **London Coaches** (Pullman group). Allocation: Wandsworth Garage 6 Leyland Titan nightly.

5/6 August 1994: Re-assigned within Pullman group to **Atlas Bus and Coach Ltd** t/a **Atlas Bus**. Re-allocated to Harlesden Garage. Pullman group Bristol VRT double-deck buses were deployed on the N52 night 5/6 August 1994 whilst the Leyland Titans were being switched from Wandsworth to Harlesden Garage.

27 September 1994: Metroline M-type Metrobuses on hire to Atlas Bus. Atlas Bus and Coach Ltd acquired by Metroline group on 28 November 1994. Continued to trade as **Atlas Bus** with allocation from Harlesden Garage 6 T nightly.

31 March/1 April 1995: Section of route Willesden Garage – Roundwood Park withdrawn. Now operated: **Victoria Bus Station – Willesden Bus Garage.** Allocation unchanged.

24/25 November 1995: Re-allocated to Metroline's Willesden Garage and increasingly operated by M/T-types from Metroline's fleet. Continued to trade as Atlas Bus.

13/14 September 1996: Reassigned to **Metroline Travel**. Allocation: Willesden Garage 6 AV nightly from 29/30 November 1996.

18 February 2000: Metroline group acquired by DelGro group.

17/18 November 2000: Allocation: Willesden Garage 4 AV nightly, c. March 2001 vehicle-type changed to low-floor Volvo B7TL 4 VPL nightly.

26/27 June 2009: Victoria pick-up now Wilton Road, set-down now Terminus Place but reverted to Bus Station from 16/17 November 2011.

7/8 December 2012: **Re-numbered (N)52.** Re-routed Victoria – Hyde Park Corner via Grosvenor Place. Continued to operate: **Victoria Station, Wilton Road (dep)** ***or*** **Bus Station (arr) – Willesden Bus Garage.** Allocation: Willesden Garage 3 VPL nightly.

15/16 February 2013: Diverted via Ladbroke Grove Sainsbury's. Allocation: Willesden Garage 3 VW/VWH nightly.

London Coaches applied clear and effective route branding to its buses which took up operation of daytime route 52 and night-time N52 from 3/4 December 1993. Smartly presented former London Buses Leyland Titan T 518 was seen in Cockspur Street in the early hours of Saturday morning 22 January 1994. *Mike Harris*

Willesden garage's VPL 193 had paused at Notting Hill Gate's bus stop in Kensington Church Street when this view of the Plaxton President-bodied Volvo B7TL working 30 minute frequency route N52 in the early hours of Saturday morning 28 August 2004 was taken. *Philip Wallis*

Routes introduced 1994

Route N9 (via Hammersmith)

25/26 February 1994: Introduced. Operated: **Trafalgar Square – Kingston, Fairfield Bus Station** via Piccadilly Circus, Hyde Park Corner, Knightsbridge, Kensington High Street, Hammersmith, Putney, Lower Richmond Road, Barnes, Mortlake, East Sheen, Upper Richmond Road, Lower Mortlake Road, Richmond then *either* Twickenham, Fulwell, Teddington to Kingston *or* Petersham, Ham to Kingston. Operator: **London United**. Allocation: Stamford Brook Garage 5 L nightly. Note: Replaced Trafalgar Square – Kingston sections of N65/N92 (different intermediate routeing Putney – Richmond).

5 November 1994: London United acquired by management/employee buy-out.

30/31 August 1996: Allocation: Stamford Brook Garage 5 M nightly.

8/9 November 1996: Re-allocated to Hounslow Garage 5 M + 2 M (joint N11) nightly.

7/8 March 1997: Projected Trafalgar Square – Aldwych. Now operated: **Aldwych – Kingston, Fairfield Bus Station.** Allocation unchanged.

27/28 June 1997: Bifurcation Richmond – Kingston via Ham withdrawn. All jnys now via Twickenham. Continued to operate: **Aldwych – Kingston, Fairfield Bus Station.** Allocation unchanged. Note: Richmond – Kingston via Ham section of N9 served by new route N65 from 30/31 August 2002.

July 1997: Operated by Transdev group t/a **London United**.

By 16/17 October 1998: Joint allocation with N11 dissolved, now: Hounslow Garage 7 M nightly.

c. May 2000: Start of progressive conversion to low-floor Volvo B7TL at Hounslow Garage 7 VA/VP nightly, became 7 VA/VP (Su-Th), 10 VA/VP (Fr-Sa) from 29/30 September 2000.

24/25 November 2000: Re-routed Putney Bridge – Richmond town centre via Putney High Street and Upper Richmond Road. Allocation: Hounslow Garage 7 VA/VP (Su-Th), 11 VA/VP (Fr-Sa). Note: Putney – Richmond via Barnes and Mortlake section of N9 largely replaced by new route N22.

28/29 September 2001: Section of route Hammersmith – Kingston withdrawn. Projected Hammersmith – Heathrow Airport Central. Now operated: **Aldwych – Heathrow Airport Central** via Trafalgar Square, Piccadilly Circus, Hyde Park Corner, Knightsbridge, Kensington High Street, Hammersmith, Turnham Green, Brentford, Hounslow, Cranford, Heathrow Airport North. Allocation: Hounslow Garage 6 VA/VP (Su-Th), 10 VA/VP (Fr-Sa). Note: Replaced Hammersmith – Heathrow Airport section of N97. The N9's more direct routeing out of central London compared with route N97 reduced Trafalgar Square – Heathrow Airport jny time by up to 18 min. Hammersmith – Richmond section of N9 replaced by new route N10. Richmond – Kingston section of N9 replaced by projection of N22.

3/4 September 2004: Allocation: Hounslow Garage 6 VA/VP (Su-Th), 11 VA/VP (Fr-Sa), increased to 9 VA/VP (Su-Th), 16 VA/VP (Fr-Sa) from 11/12 November 2005.

4 April 2006: **Transdev** corporate logo adopted.

21/22 March 2008: Projected Heathrow Airport Central to Terminal 5 via Airport Tunnel, West Ramp, Northern and Western Perimeter Roads. Now operated: **Aldwych – Heathrow Airport, Terminal 5.** Allocation: Hounslow Garage 10 VA/VP (Su-Th), 16 VA/VP (Fr-Sa).

c. May 2010: Progressive vehicle-type change to Scania Omnicity at Hounslow Garage 10 SP (Su-Th), 16 SP (Fr-Sa), increased to 11 SP (Su-Th), 17 SP (Fr-Sa) from 4/5 February 2011.

3 March 2011: Operated by RATP DEV UK Ltd t/a **London United**.

24/25 February 2012: Re-routed Trafalgar Square – Piccadilly via Pall Mall, St James Street. Continued to operate: **Aldwych – Heathrow Airport, Terminal 5.** Allocation unchanged.

Upon introduction from 25/26 February 1994 route N9 operated a nightly 30 minute frequency service between Trafalgar Square and Kingston with alternate journeys forming bifurcations between Richmond and Kingston either via Twickenham or via Petersham. Stamford Brook garage's all-Leyland Olympian L 310, with local Riversidebus identity, was seen taking a layover on the north side of Trafalgar Square on Thursday morning 16 June 1994. This bus would then have moved to the south side of the Square to take up its outbound Kingston journey from Cockspur Street. *Malcolm Papes*

Route N91 (Cockfosters)

25/26 February 1994: Introduced. Operated: **Trafalgar Square – Hornsey Rise, Favourite** via Aldwych, Holborn Station, Russell Square, Euston Station, Euston Road, King's Cross, Caledonian Road, Holloway. Operator: **London Northern**. Allocation: Holloway Garage 1 M nightly. Note: Replaced Trafalgar Square – Holborn section of N92.

26 October 1994: Operated by MTL Trust Holdings t/a **MTL London Northern**.

23/24 June 1995: Projected Hornsey Rise – Potters Bar. Re-routed Trafalgar Square – Holborn. Now operated: **Trafalgar Square – Potters Bar, Bus Garage** via Piccadilly Circus, Shaftesbury Avenue, New Oxford Street, Holborn, Russell Square, Euston Station, Euston Road, King's Cross, Caledonian Road, Holloway, Hornsey Rise, Crouch End, Turnpike Lane, Wood Green, Bounds Green, New Southgate, Arnos Grove, Southgate, Oakwood, Cockfosters. Allocation: Potters Bar Garage 4 M/S (Su-Th), 5 M/S (Fr-Sa). Note: Absorbed much of route N21.

31 Jan/1 Feb 1997: LRT contact awarded to **Capital Citybus**. Section of route Cockfosters – Potters Bar withdrawn (not replaced with all-night service). Now operated: **Trafalgar Square, Northumberland Avenue** (pick-up)**, Whitehall** (set-down) – **Cockfosters Station.** Allocation: Northumberland Park Garage 4 VA (Su-Th), 5 VA (Fr-Sa).

16/17 May 1997: Re-routed Trafalgar Square – Cambridge Circus via Charing Cross Road.

8 July 1998: Operated by **First Group**, re-titled **First London** March 2001. By 25/26 June 1999: Allocation now VA/VN-types.

28/29 April 2000: Re-routed Trafalgar Square – Holborn via Aldwych. Continued to operate: **Trafalgar Square, Northumberland Avenue** (pick-up)**, Whitehall** (set-down) – **Cockfosters Station.** Allocation: Northumberland Park Garage 4 VA/VN (Su-Th), 5 VA/VN (Fr-Sa), increased to 5 VA/VN (Su-Th), 8 VA/VN (Fr-Sa) from 1/2 February 2002.

c. January 2004: Conversion to low-floor Dennis Trident completed (started October 2002) at Northumberland Park Garage 5 TN (Su-Th), 8 TN (Fr-Sa), increased to 6 TN (Su-Th), 10 TN (Fr-Sa) from 3/4 February 2006.

6/7 February 2009: LBSL contract awarded to **Metroline Travel**. No change to routeing, other than outbound jnys now served Oakwood Station forecourt and inbound jnys no longer served Euston bus station. Allocation: Holloway garage 3 TE (Su), 1 TE (M-Th), 5 TE (Fr), 7 TE (Sa), Potters Bar Garage 4 TE (Su), 5 TE (M-Th), 6 TE (Fr), 7 TE (Sa). Holloway Garage VW-type by 27/28 July 2013.

27/28 July – 12/13 August and 29/30 August – 9/10 September 2012: Frequency increased to 12 min nightly for duration of Olympic and Paralympic Games. Combined allocation from Holloway and Potters Bar Garages temporarily increased to 15 TE nightly.

Top Capital Citybus took up operation of daytime route 91 and night-time N91 from 31 January/1 February 1997. Alexander-bodied Volvo Olympian 226 was seen loading passengers outside the National Gallery in Trafalgar Square for the 05.12 N91 journey to Cockfosters Station on Saturday 26 June 1999. *Philip Wallis*

Centre First London's Plaxton President-bodied Dennis Trident TN 32839 was seen at Holborn Station bus stop in Kingsway early on Tuesday morning 6 December 2005. Route N91 had operated a 30 minute Sunday to Thursday night and 20 minute Friday and Saturday night frequency service since 1/2 February 2002. *Philip Wallis*

Bottom AD Trident Enviro400 TE 937 was taken at Euston Station Bus Station at around 4 o'clock on Saturday morning 10 December 2011. The Friday and Saturday night frequency of route N91 had been increased to 15 minutes coincident with Metroline taking up the LBSL contract from 6/7 February 2009 but the Sunday to Thursday night frequency had been retained at 30 minutes. *Philip Wallis*

Routes N134, (N)134

25/26 February 1994: Introduced. **Numbered N134**. Operated: **Trafalgar Square – North Finchley, Tally Ho Corner** via Charing Cross Road, Tottenham Court Road (outbound), Gower Street (inbound), Camden Town, Kentish Town, Archway Station, Highgate Station, Muswell Hill, Friern Barnet. Operator: **London Northern.** Allocation: Holloway Garage 2 M nightly.

26 October 1994: Operated by **MTL London Northern**. Allocation increased to 3 M nightly from 23/24 June 1995.

30/31 January 1998: Outbound jnys re-routed at Tottenham Court Road Station to serve Centrepoint bus stop. Allocation: Holloway Garage 4 M nightly.

17 August 1998: Operated by **Metroline London Northern**.

13/14 November 1998: Outbound jnys no longer served Centrepoint.

By 8/9 October 1999: Conversion to low-floor Dennis Trident completed (started August 1999) at Holloway Garage 4 TP nightly.

18 February 2000: Metroline group acquired by DelGro group.

28/29 April 2000: Section of route Trafalgar Square – Tottenham Court Road Station withdrawn. Now operated: **Tottenham Court Road Station, Centrepoint – North Finchley, Tally Ho Corner**. Allocation unchanged.

By 2/3 February 2001: Allocation: Holloway Garage 4 TP/VPL, increased to 6 TP/VPL (Su-Th), 8 TP/VPL (Fr-Sa) from 31 August/1 September 2001 and c. November 2002 had become TP/VP-types.

23/24 April 2004: **Re-numbered (N)134.**

By September 2004: Allocation: Holloway Garage 6 TPL (Su-Th), 8 TPL (Fr-Sa).

1 January 2005: Reassigned to **Metroline Travel**.

4/5 February 2005: Allocation: Holloway Garage 6 TPL (Su-Th), 10 TPL (Fr-Sa), had become VPL/TPL-types by 1/2 April 2005 and VPL/TPL/TE-types by 9/10 November 2007.

2/3 January 2009: Pick-up now Tottenham Court Road Station, set-down now St. Giles High Street.

By 29/30 May 2009: Allocation: Holloway Garage 6 VPL/TE (Su-Th), 10 VPL/TE (Fr-Sa).

c. April 2012: Allocation now AD Trident andVolvo B9TL from Holloway Garage 6 TE/VW (Su-Th), 10 TE/VW (Fr-Sa).

By 29/30 June 2012: Allocation now all VW-type.

Metroline's TransBus Trident TP 352 was seen at Tottenham Court Road Station working an outbound journey on then-15 minute frequency route N134 during the early hours of Saturday morning 7 June 2003. *Philip Wallis*

Right Route N50 was the only LBSL-contracted bus route, daytime or night-time, to serve any section of Victoria Embankment when the N50's outbound Embankment bus stop flag was photographed on Sunday morning 20 June 2004. Subsequently, daytime bus route 388 was projected beyond Blackfriars to Temple Station from 16 August 2008 and further extended to Embankment Station from 1 November 2008. This was to cover the Underground's Circle and District service whilst Blackfriars Underground Station was closed for rebuilding works. Upon completion of such works the 388's section of route between Blackfriars and Embankment Station was withdrawn after 23 March 2012. This left successor route N550 as the only daytime or night-time LBSL-contacted bus route to serve any section of Victoria Embankment. *Philip Wallis*

Far right Route N50 was split into routes N550 and N551 from 29/30 August 2008. The N550 covered the N50's Isle of Dogs loop routeing which allowed the N551 to achieve faster journey times between Gallions Reach and central London by virtue of more direct routeing through Poplar and along The Highway. Upton Park garage's TransBus Trident ALX400 17890 was seen at Canning Town Bus Station in the early hours of Sunday morning 14 September 2008 working an inbound journey on 30 minute frequency route N550. *Philip Wallis*

Upton Park garage's TransBus Trident ALX400 17842 was photographed at Gallions Reach Shopping Park before departure at 23.35 on Saturday night 28 June 2008 on that night's first inbound journey on 30 minute frequency route N50. *Philip Wallis*

Routes introduced 1995

Routes N50 (via Canning Town), N550

14/15 July 1995: Introduced. **Numbered N50.** Operated: **Oxford Circus – Ilford Broadway** via Piccadilly Circus, Trafalgar Square, Aldwych, Ludgate Circus, Bank, Aldgate, The Highway, Westferry, Isle of Dogs, Poplar, Canning Town, Newham Way, Tollgate Road, East Beckton, Movers Lane, Barking, Ilford Lane. Operator: **Stagecoach East London**. Allocation: Upton Park Garage 3 S nightly, increased to 4 S nightly by 11/12 January 1997. Note: Replaced Isle of Dogs loop of N8.

21/22 August 1998: LRT contract awarded to **First Group**, re-titled **First London** from March 2001. Sections of route Oxford Circus – Trafalgar Square, East Beckton – Ilford withdrawn. Re-routed Aldgate – Westferry, Canning Town – Tollgate Road. Now operated: **Trafalgar Square – East Beckton District Centre, Asda** via Aldwych, Ludgate Circus, Bank, Aldgate, Commercial Road, Limehouse, Westferry, Isle of Dogs, Poplar, Canning Town, Kier Hardie Estate, Prince Regent DLR Station, Tollgate Road. Allocation: Northumberland Park Garage 2 AE (Su-Th), 4 AE (Fr-Sa), had become AE/VA/VN-types by 7/8 August 1999.

23/24 March 2001: Re-routed Trafalgar Square – Mansion House via Northumberland Avenue, Victoria Embankment, Blackfriars, Queen Victoria Street.

29/30 August 2003: LBSL contract awarded to **Stagecoach East London.** Projected Beckton Asda – East Beckton via Woolwich Manor Way, Armada Way. Re-routed at Westferry to serve Canary Wharf. Now operated: **Trafalgar Square – East Beckton, Tesco.** Allocation: Upton Park Garage 6 TA nightly.

16/17 December 2005: Revised termini in central London and East Beckton. Now operated: **Haymarket (pick-up) *or* Trafalgar Square, Cockspur Street (set-down) – Gallions Reach Shopping Park.** Allocation unchanged.

30 August 2006: Operated by Macquarie Bank Ltd t/a East London Bus Group. Fleetname: **East London**.

29/30 August 2008: **Re-numbered N550.** Section of route Canning Town – Gallions Reach withdrawn (replaced by new route N551). Now operated: **Haymarket (pick-up) *or* Trafalgar Square, Cockspur Street (set-down) – Canning Town, Bus Station.** Allocation: Upton Park Garage 5 TA nightly.

14 October 2010: Operated by Stagecoach Bus Holdings Ltd t/a **East London**.

16/17 September 2011: Re-allocated to West Ham 5 TA nightly.

29/30 June 2012: Withdrawn from Haymarket, central London terminus now Trafalgar Square, Cockspur Street (pick-up and set-down). 21/22 June 2013: LBSL contract awarded to **Tower Transit.** Allocation: Lea Interchange Garage 4 DN + 1 DN (joint N551) nightly.

New Cross garage's PVL 193 was seen outside Canada House in Trafalgar Square working an end of night route N21 journey which would go out of service outside the Plaxton President-bodied Volvo B7TL's home garage on Sunday morning 14 July 2002. *Philip Wallis*

Route N21 (via Lewisham)

28/29 July 1995: Introduced. Operated: **Victoria Station, Bus Station – Foots Cray *or* Sidcup Station** via Victoria Street, Whitehall, Trafalgar Square, Aldwych, Ludgate Circus, Blackfriars Bridge, Southwark Street, Borough High Street (outbound), Marshalsea Road (inbound), Bricklayers Arms, Old Kent Road, New Cross, Lewisham, Lee Green, Eltham then *either* Blackfen, Sidcup to Foots Cray *or* Mottingham, New Eltham to Sidcup Station. Operator: **London Central**. Allocation: New Cross Garage (joint N1/N81) 8 T (Su-Th), 11 T (Fr-Sa). Note: Replaced New Cross/ Lewisham – Eltham sections of N51/N61/N62/N72, Eltham – Sidcup section of N61 and Eltham – Foots Cray section of N62.

7/8 November 1997: Mottingham – Sidcup Station section of route withdrawn. Projected Mottingham – Chislehurst. Re-routed Ludgate Circus – Borough High Street via Bank, London Bridge. Now operated: **Victoria Bus Station – Foots Cray *or* Chislehurst, War Memorial.** Allocation: Bexleyheath Garage (joint N1/N81) 2 NV (Su-Th), 4 NV (Fr-Sa), New Cross Garage 4 NV (Su-Th), 6 NV (Fr-Sa).

13/14 November 1998: Allocation: Bexleyheath Garage (joint N81) 2 NV (Su-Th), 4 NV (Fr-Sa), New Cross Garage 4 NV (Su-Th), 7 NV (Fr-Sa).

23/24 January 1999: Projected to terminate at Foots Cray Tesco. Allocation: Bexleyheath Garage (joint N81) 2 NV (Su-Th), 5 NV (Fr-Sa), New Cross Garage (joint N81) 6 NV (Su-Th), 7 NV (Fr-Sa).

4/5 February 2000: Joint allocation with N81 dissolved, now: New Cross Garage 5 NV (Su-Th), 8 NV (Fr-Sa), Peckham Garage 1 NV (Su-Th), 2 NV (Fr-Sa).

16/17 March 2001: Converted to low-floor Volvo B7TL. Allocation: New Cross Garage 5 PVL (Su-Th), 8 PVL (Fr-Sa), Peckham Garage 1 AVL (Su-Th), 2 AVL (Fr-Sa).

28/29 June 2002: Section of route Victoria – Trafalgar Square withdrawn. Now operated: **Trafalgar Square – Foots Cray, Tesco *or* Chislehurst, War Memorial.** Allocation unchanged.

11/12 October 2002: Eltham – Chislehurst bifurcation withdrawn. Now operated: **Trafalgar Square – Foots Cray, Tesco**. Allocation: New Cross Garage 5 PVL (Su-Th), 8 PVL (Fr-Sa), Peckham Garage 1 AVL nightly. Note: Chislehurst regained an all-night bus service with the introduction of route N136 from 8/9 February 2008.

21/22 February 2003: Allocation: Bexleyheath Garage 2 PVL (Su-Th), 4 PVL (Fr-Sa), New Cross Garage 3 PVL (Su-Th), 5 PVL (Fr-Sa). One New Cross bus became joint with (N)36 (Su-Th) from 8/9 February 2008.

20/21 February 2009: Trafalgar Square pick-up now Duncannon Street.

9/10 October 2009: Section of route Blackfen – Foots Cray withdrawn. Projected Blackfen – Bexleyheath. Now operated: **Trafalgar Square – Bexleyheath, Town Centre** via Aldwych, Ludgate Circus, Bank, London Bridge, Borough High Street, Bricklayers Arms, Old Kent Road, New Cross, Lewisham, Lee Green, Eltham, Blackfen, Blendon, Bexley Village. Allocation: Bexleyheath Garage 2 PVL nightly, New Cross Garage 2 PVL + 1 PVL(joint (N)36 (Su-Th), 3 PVL (Fr-Sa). Note: Sidcup – Foots Cray section of N21 replaced by new route (N)321 which also supplemented New Cross Gate – Eltham section of N21. Blackfen – Sidcup section of N21 not replaced.

13/14 November 2009: Joint allocation with (N)36 (Su-Th) dissolved, now Bexleyheath Garage 2 PVL nightly, New Cross Garage 3 PVL nightly. New Cross Garage had changed to 3 WVL-type by 8/9 May 2010. Bexleyheath Garage 2 WVL-type by 27/28 July 2013.

Route introduced 1996

Route N176, (N)176

26/27 April 1996: Introduced. **Numbered N176.** Operated: **Oxford Circus – Penge, Crooked Billet** via Tottenham Court Road Station, Charing Cross Road, Trafalgar Square, Aldwych (outbound only), Waterloo, Elephant & Castle, Walworth Road, Camberwell Green, East Dulwich, Dulwich, Forest Hill, Sydenham. Operator: **London Central**. Allocation: Camberwell Garage 3 SP nightly. Note: Replaced Camberwell Green – Forest Hill section of N79 and Forest Hill – Penge section of N71.

16/17 May 1997: Driver relief-break jnys activated to run *outbound only* from Victoria – Oxford Circus via Hyde Park Corner, Marble Arch. Now operated: **Victoria Bus Station (dep only) – Oxford Circus – Penge, Crooked Billet.** Allocation: Camberwell Garage 3 SP nightly, New Cross Garage 2 L/NV (Fr-Sa). Camberwell Garage allocation had become 3 NV by 7/8 November 1997.

13/14 November 1998: LRT contract awarded to **Arriva London South**. Section of route Victoria – Oxford Circus withdrawn. Now operated: **Oxford Circus – Penge, Crooked Billet**. Allocation: Norwood Garage 5 L nightly.

31 August/1 September 2001: Vehicle-type change to low-floor DAF DB250LF at Norwood Garage 5 DLA nightly.

14/15 November 2003: **Re-numbered (N)176.** Penge terminus now Pawleyne Arms. Allocation: Norwood Garage 7 VLA (Su-Th), 9 VLA (Fr-Sa).

2/3 January 2009: Section of route Oxford Circus – Tottenham Court Road Station withdrawn. Now operated: **Tottenham Court Road Station** (pick-up: St Giles High Street, set-down: New Oxford Street) – **Penge, Pawleyne Arms.** Allocation unchanged.

27 August 2010: Arriva acquired by Deutsche Bahn.

c. April 2012: Vehicle-type change to AD E40D Enviro400 at Norwood Garage 7 T (Su-Th), 9 T (Fr-Sa).

29/30 June 2012: Right-hand turn introduced Strand – Lancaster Place and Waterloo Bridge. Outbound jnys no longer served Aldwych.

Routes introduced 1997

Route N35

25/26 April 1997: Introduced: **Trafalgar Square – Clapham Junction, Meyrick Arms** via Aldwych, Holborn, Clerkenwell Green, Shoreditch, Bishopsgate, London Bridge, Borough High Street, Elephant & Castle, Camberwell Green, Loughborough Junction, Brixton, Clapham Common. Operator: **London Central**. Allocation: Camberwell Garage 2 SP/T nightly, vehicle-type had become Volvo Olympian 2 NV nightly by 10/11 October 1997.

28/29 April 2000: Section of route Trafalgar Square – Holborn withdrawn. Projected Holborn – Tottenham Court Road Station via New Oxford Street. Now operated:**Tottenham Court Road Station – Clapham Junction, Meyrick Arms.** Allocation unchanged.

26/27 April 2002: Clapham Junction terminus redesignated Grant Road. Allocation: Camberwell Garage 4 NV nightly.

c. July 2002: Vehicle-type change to low-floor Volvo B7TL at Camberwell Garage 4 PVL nightly, had changed to 4 WVL nightly by 29/30 September 2007 and Fr-Sa allocation increased to 8 WVL from 25/26 January 2008.

1/2 May 2009: LBSL contract awarded to **Travel London**. Allocation: Battersea Garage 7 ED (Su-Th), 9 ED (Fr-Sa).

9 June 2009: Travel London acquired by Ned Railways. Operated as **Abellio** from 30 October 2009 and as **Abellio London** from 1 June 2010.

20/21 May 2011: Allocation: Battersea Garage 7 ED (Su-Th), 12 ED (Fr-Sa).

22/23 June 2012: Re-allocated to Walworth Garage 7 ED (Su-Th), 15 ED (Fr-Sa).27/28 July – 12/13 August and 29/30 August – 9/10 September 2012: Frequency increased to 10 min nightly for duration of Olympic and Paralympic Games. Allocation from Walworth Garage temporarily increased to 21 ED nightly.

Top Norwood garage's Northern Counties-bodied Leyland Olympian L 551 was seen outside the National Gallery at Trafalgar Square in the early hours of Midsummer Day 21 June 2001 whilst working then-30 minute frequency route N176. *Philip Wallis*

Above Route N35 had operated a nightly 30 minute frequency service since 26/27 April 2002. The increased demand for Friday and Saturday night travel on central London-serving Night Bus routes is exemplified by route N35 over which its Friday and Saturday night frequency was increased to 20 minutes from 1/2 May 2009, further increased to 15 minutes from 20/21 May 2011 and yet further increased to 12 minutes from 22/23 June 2012 although the route's Sunday to Thursday night frequency has remained constant at 30 minutes. Abellio's AD Trident Enviro400 9453, with Battersea garage running number 328 prominently displayed in its windscreen, was photographed at the start of an outbound N35 journey in New Oxford Street early on Sunday morning 25 April 2010. *Philip Wallis*

Facing page New Cross garage's Wrightbus-bodied Volvo B9TL WVL 292 was seen at London Bridge working an inbound journey on 30 minute frequency route N21 in the early hours of Friday morning 15 October 2010. *Philip Wallis*

Routes N37, (N)37

25/26 April 1997: Introduced. **Numbered N37**. Operated: **Peckham, Bus Station – Putney Station** via East Dulwich, Herne Hill, Brixton, Clapham Common, Clapham Junction, Wandsworth. Operator: **London General**. Allocation: Stockwell Garage 2 M nightly.

16/17 June 2000: Vehicle-type change to low-floor Volvo B7TL at Stockwell Garage 2 PVL nightly, changed to 2 WVL-type c. May 2003.

2/3 April 2004: **Re-numbered (N)37**.

8/9 October 2004: Reassigned to **London Central**. Re-allocated to Peckham Garage 2 AVL/PVL nightly.

2/3 June 2006: LBSL contract formally awarded to **London Central.** Vehicle-type change to AD Trident Enviro400 from Peckham Garage 2 E nightly.

20/21 April 2007: Projected Putney Station – Putney Heath via Putney Hill. Now operated: **Peckham, Bus Station – Putney Heath, Green Man**. Allocation: Peckham Garage 4 E nightly.

The schedule of route N37 comprised just four nightly journeys from each terminus with departures at hourly intervals. Stockwell garage's Wrightbus-bodied Volvo B7TL WVL 77 was photographed at the route's Putney Station pick-up bus stop in Richmond Road (part of the South Circular Road) loading passengers for the 01.04 departure on Sunday morning 28 March 2004, just six nights before the route stopped displaying an 'N' route number prefix. *Philip Wallis*

Route (N)37's service still comprised just four nightly journeys at hourly intervals from each terminus when this photograph of Peckham garage's AD Trident Enviro400 E 36 was taken in Richmond Road, Putney at 02.04 on Friday morning 16 February 2007. The (N)37 was the last outer London Night Bus route with an hourly service until its frequency was increased to 30 minutes nightly coincident with the route's extension to Putney Heath from 20/21 April 2007. *Philip Wallis*

Routes introduced 1999

Route N68 (via Croydon)

26/27 March 1999: Introduced. Operated: **Trafalgar Square – Purley, Brighton Road** via Aldwych, Waterloo, Elephant & Castle, Walworth Road, Camberwell Green, Herne Hill, Tulse Hill, West Norwood, Upper Norwood, Thornton Heath, West Croydon, Croydon, South Croydon. Operator: **Arriva London South**. Allocation: South Croydon Garage 5 L nightly. Note: Restored an all-night bus service to Thornton Heath High Street, previously served by N69 until 11/12 March 1994.

28/29 April 2000: Section of route Trafalgar Square – Aldwych withdrawn. Projected Aldwych – Tottenham Court Road Station via Holborn Station, Purley – Old Coulsdon via Coulsdon. Re-routed to serve East Croydon Station. Now operated: **Tottenham Court Road Station – Old Coulsdon, Tudor Rose.** Vehicle-type change to low-floor DAF DB250LF at South Croydon Garage 8 DLA nightly. Note: Replaced Croydon – Coulsdon section of N159.

31 March/1 April 2006: LBSL contract awarded to **London Central**. Allocation: Camberwell Garage 6 WVL nightly.

2/3 January 2009: Tottenham Court Road pick-up New Oxford Street, set-down now St Giles High Street.

South Croydon garage's Alexander ALX400-bodied DAF DB250LF DLA 179 was photographed at Holborn Station bus stop in Kingsway when just into its 1¼ hour-long route N68 journey to Old Coulsdon on Tuesday morning 6 December 2005. *Philip Wallis*

Camberwell garage's Wrightbus-bodied Volvo B7TL WVL 242 was seen at East Croydon Station in the early hours of Friday 7 April 2006 whilst working an outbound journey on 30 minute frequency route N68. *Philip Wallis*

Route N28
28/29 May 1999: Introduced. Operated: **Camden Town, Bayham Street – Wandsworth, Arndale Centre** via Chalk Farm, Swiss Cottage, Kilburn, Maida Hill, Westbourne Park, Notting Hill Gate, Kensington High Street, Olympia, West Kensington, Fulham Broadway, Wandsworth Bridge. Operator: **First Centrewest,** re-titled **First London** in March 2001. Allocation: Westbourne Park Garage 2 DM (Su-Th), 4 DM (Fr-Sa) Note: Replaced Kensington High Street – Fulham Broadway section of N31. Co-ordinated timetable with N31 Camden Town – Kensington High Street.

By 27/28 August 2004: Allocation mixed low-floor single-deck/double-deck from Westbourne Park Garage 2 DM/TNA/VNW (Su-Th), 4 DM/TNA/VNW (Fr-Sa).

c. September 2004: Allocation now double-deck low-floor types from Westbourne Park Garage 2 TNA/VNW (Su-Th), 4 TNA/VNW (Fr-Sa), had become all VNW-type by 8/9 May 2010.

30 Sept/1 Oct 2011: Re-allocated to Atlas Road Harlesden Garage 2 VNW (Su-Th), 4 VNW (Fr-Sa).

21/22 June 2013: Operated by **Tower Transit**.

Routes N94 (Acton Green), (N)94
23/24 July 1999: Introduced. **Numbered N94**. Operated: **Piccadilly Circus, Charles II Street – Acton Green, Duke of Sussex** via Oxford Circus, Marble Arch, Lancaster Gate, Notting Hill Gate, Shepherd's Bush, Goldhawk Road, Turnham Green. Operator: **London United**. Allocation: Shepherd's Bush Garage 3 M + 1 M (joint N11) (Su-Th), 4 M (Fr-Sa). Note: Replaced Notting Hill Gate – Shepherd's Bush section of N12. The N94 was the first all-night bus service along Goldhawk Road since the withdrawal of LGOC's route 189 (Turnham Green – Ludgate Circus) after operation on 3/4 July 1934.

Dec 1999/Jan 2000: Single-deck low-floor DP/DPS-type Dennis Dart SLFs noted working N94.

c. March 2000: Vehicle-type change to low-floor Volvo B7TL at Shepherd's Bush Garage 3 VA + 1 DP/VA (joint N11) (Su-Th), 4 VA (Fr-Sa).

30/31 March 2001: Joint allocation with N11 dissolved, now Shepherd's Bush Garage 3 VA (Su-Th), 4 VA (Fr-Sa), became 3 VA nightly from 27/28 June 2003.

Single-deck bus operation on route N28 (and N31) had pretty well ended when Westbourne Park garage's Marshall-bodied Dennis Dart SLF DM 41208 was seen in Kensington Church Street at Notting Hill Gate on Saturday morning 28 August 2004. The author recalls that during an hour spent photographing Night Buses at Notting Hill Gate on that night this was the only single-deck bus seen in service on routes N28 and N31. *Philip Wallis*

First London's Wrightbus-bodied Volvo B7TL VNW 32388 was seen at route N28's Wandsworth pick-up bus stop in Garratt Lane about to start its 53 minute long journey to Camden Town at 03.15 on Sunday morning 20 January 2008. *Philip Wallis*

23/24 January 2004: **Re-numbered (N)94.** Vehicle-type change to Dennis Trident at Shepherd's Bush Garage 3 TLA nightly, Fr-Sa allocation increased to 6 TLA from 24/25 March 2006.

4 April 2006: **Transdev** corporate logo adopted.

4/5 November 2010: Vehicle-type change to AD Trident Enviro400H hybrid at Shepherd's Bush Garage 3 ADH (Su-Th), 6 ADH (Fr-Sa).

3 March 2011: Operated by RATP DEV UK Ltd t/a **London United**

Routes N72 (East Acton), (N)72

3/4 September 1999: Introduced. **Numbered N72**. Operated: **East Acton, Brunel Road–Roehampton, Bessborough Road** via Wormwood Scrubs, White City, Shepherd's Bush, Hammersmith, Barnes, Barnes Common, Roehampton Lane. Operator: **London United**. Allocation: Shepherd's Bush Garage 3 DR nightly.

December 1999: Progressive vehicle-type change to low-floor Dennis Dart SLF at Shepherd's Bush Garage 3 DPS nightly.

27/28 October 2000: Revised schedule, following re-opening of Hammersmith Bridge after repairs, allowed through jny times to be reduced by up to 10 min. Allocation reduced to 2 DPS nightly.

23/24 January 2004: **Re-numbered (N)72.**

4 April 2006: **Transdev** corporate logo adopted.

4/5 September 2009: Vehicle-type change to AD Dart Enviro200 from Shepherd's Bush Garage 3 DE nightly.

3 March 2011: Operated by RATP DEV UK Ltd t/a **London United**

Routes N24, (N)24

26/27 November 1999: Introduced. **Numbered N24**. Operated: **Pimlico, Grosvenor Road – Hampstead Heath, South End Green** via Belgrave Road, Wilton Road, Victoria, Whitehall, Trafalgar Square, Charing Cross Road, Tottenham Court Road (outbound), Gower Street (inbound), Camden Town, Chalk Farm. Operator: **Arriva London North East** (formerly Grey-Green). Allocation: Stamford Hill Garage 3 Volvo Citybus or Scania N113 nightly. Replaced Trafalgar Square – Hampstead Heath part of N2.

24/25 March 2000: Re-assigned to **Arriva London North.** Re-allocated to Tottenham Garage 3 VA (Volvo Citybus) nightly.

c. April 2001: Vehicle-type change to low-floor DAF DB250LF at Tottenham Garage 3 DLA nightly.

8/9 November 2002: LBSL contract awarded to **Metroline London Northern**. Allocation: Holloway Garage 3 VP (Su-Th), 6 VP (Fr-Sa), increased to 6 VP nightly from 31 January/1 February 2003 and Fr-Sa allocation further increased to 7 VP from 8/9 October 2004.

23/24 April 2004: **Re-numbered (N)24.**

1 January 2005: Re-assigned to **Metroline Travel**.

9/10 November 2007: LBSL contract awarded to **London General**. Allocation: Stockwell Garage 6 E (Su-Th), 7 E (Fr-Sa).

9/10 November 2012: LBSL contract awarded to **Metroline Travel**. Allocation: Holloway Garage 6 VW/VWH (Su-Th), 7 VW/ VWH (Fr-Sa).

22/23 June 2013: Vehicle-type change to LT. Allocation: Holloway Garage 6 LT (Su-Th), 7 LT (Fr-Sa).

Tottenham garage's Alexander ALX400-bodied DAF DB250LF DLA 305 was working that night's last northbound journey on then-30 minute frequency route N24 when photographed entering Trafalgar Square from Whitehall at 05.25 on Sunday morning 30 June 2002. *Philip Wallis*

CHAPTER 7
ROUTES INTRODUCED 2000 TO 2013

This chapter lists new routes introduced since 2000 and the subsequent changes to those routes up to 30/31 August 2013.

Routes introduced 2000

Routes N140, (N)140

31 March/1 April 2000: Introduced. **Numbered N140**. Operated: **Harrow Weald, Bus Garage – Heathrow Airport Central Bus Station** via Harrow & Wealdstone Station, Harrow, South Harrow, Northolt, Yeading, Hayes, Harlington Corner. Operator: **Metroline Travel**. Allocation: Harrow Weald Garage 4 TA nightly, became 4 TPL nightly from 1/2 February 2002.

16/17 April 2004: **Re-numbered (N)140.**

3/4 September 2004: Vehicle-type change to Volvo B7TL at Harrow Weald Garage 4 VP nightly.

Routes N149, (N)149

18/19 August 2000: Introduced. **Numbered N149**. Operated: **Victoria Bus Station – Edmonton Green** via Whitehall, Trafalgar Square, Aldwych, Ludgate Circus, Bank, Bishopsgate, Liverpool Street Station, Shoreditch, Dalston, Stoke Newington, Stamford Hill, South Tottenham, Tottenham. Jnys Enfield Garage – Edmonton Green. Operator: **Arriva London North**. Allocation: Enfield Garage 2 DLA/DLP nightly.

2/3 November 2001: Section of route Victoria – Trafalgar Square withdrawn. Now operated: **Trafalgar Square – Edmonton Green.** Allocation unchanged.

24/25 October 2003: Sections of route Trafalgar Square – Bishopsgate and Enfield Garage jnys withdrawn. Projected Bishopsgate – London Bridge Station. Now operated: **London Bridge Station – Edmonton Green** via London Bridge, Monument, Gracechurch Street, Bishopsgate, Liverpool Street Station, Shoreditch, Dalston, Stoke Newington, Stamford Hill, Tottenham. Re-allocated to Stamford Hill Garage 4 DLA nightly.

23/24 April 2004: **Re-numbered (N)149.** Vehicle-type change to low-floor articulated single-deck Mercedes-Benz Citaro bendy bus. Re-allocated to Edmonton Garage 4 MA nightly, further re-allocated to Lea Valley Garage 4 MA nightly from 18/19 February 2005.

2627 January 2007: Edmonton Green terminus now Bus Station.

27 August 2010: Arriva acquired by Deutsche Bahn.

15/16 October 2010: Re-converted to double-deck bus operation with Wrightbus DB300 Gemini Integral from Tottenham Garage 4 DW nightly.

27/28 July – 12/13 August and 29/30 August – 9/10 September 2012: Frequency increased to 15 min nightly for duration of Olympic and Paralympic Games. Allocation from Tottenham Garage temporarily increased to 8 DW nightly.

Opposite Route N93 is representative of Transport for London's expansion of 24-hour services which have formed fresh night-time links across the capital. 30 minute frequency N93 ran between common termini at Putney Bridge Station and North Cheam in parallel with established daytime route 93 when introduced from 30 November/1 December 2001. Sutton garage's East Lancs Vyking-bodied Volvo B7TL EVL 7 was photographed in Putney High Street on Sunday morning 28 March 2004, just six nights before N93 buses officially discontinued the display of the distinguishing 'N' route number prefix. *Philip Wallis*

Metroline's TransBus Trident TPL 200 was seen at Northolt Station when Heathrow Airport-bound on a 30 minute frequency route N140 journey in the early hours of Sunday 11 April 2004, six nights before the route discontinued use of its 'N' route number prefix. *Philip Wallis*

Metroline London Northern's Marshall Capital-bodied Dennis Dart SLF DMS 4 was seen on arrival in Liverpool Street Bus Station on then-15 minute frequency route N214 during the early hours of Saturday morning 1 November 2003. *Philip Wallis*

Routes N214, (N)214

1/2 September 2000: Introduced. **Numbered N214.** Operated: **Liverpool Street Bus Station – Highgate Village, North Road** via Moorgate, City Road, Islington, King's Cross Station, Pancras Road, Camden Town, Kentish Town, Parliament Hill Fields. Operator: **Metroline London Northern**. Allocation: Holloway Garage step-floor Dennis Dart 3 DNL nightly.

29/30 August 2003: Completion of conversion to low-floor Dennis Dart (started c. May 2003) from Holloway Garage 6 DMS/DLS nightly, vehicle-type changed to 6 DL nightly from 20/21 February 2004.

16/17 April 2004: **Re-numbered (N)214.**

1 January 2005: Re-assigned to **Metroline Travel**.

19/20 August 2005: Allocation: Holloway Garage 4 DL (Su-Th), 6 DL (Fr-Sa).

c. January 2006: Allocation: Holloway Garage 4 DLD (Su-Th), 6 DLD (Fr-Sa), Fr-Sa allocation increased to 8 DLD from 25/26 July 2008.

9/10 July 2010: Re-allocated to King's Cross Garage 4 DLD (Su-Th), 8 DLD (Fr-Sa).

9/10 September 2012: Section of route Moorgate – Liverpool Street withdrawn. Now operated: **Moorgate, Finsbury Square – Highgate Village, North Road**. Allocation unchanged. Note: (N)214 had previously terminated at Moorgate, Finsbury Square between 17/18 June and 15/16 September 2011 and between 24/25 February and 31 May/1 June 2012.

By 27/28 July 2013: Allocation: King's Cross Garage 4 DE/DLD (Su-Th), 8 DE/DLD (Fr-Sa). All DE-type by 30/31 August 2013.

Hammersmith Grove was the setting for Metroline's TP 400 when the TransBus Trident was photographed early on Sunday morning 11 April 2004 waiting departure time for its northbound journey on 30 minute frequency route N266. *Philip Wallis*

Routes N266, (N)266

21/22 September 2000: Introduced. **Numbered N266.** Operated: **Hammersmith Grove – Cricklewood Bus Garage** via Acton Vale, Acton, North Acton, Willesden Junction, Harlesden, Craven Park, Willesden, Willesden Green. Operator: **Metroline Travel**. Allocation: Cricklewood Garage 4 TA nightly.

25/26 July 2003: Projected Cricklewood – Brent Cross. Now operated: **Hammersmith Grove – Brent Cross Shopping Centre.** Allocation unchanged.

By 10/11 April 2004: Allocation: Cricklewood Garage 4 TP nightly, became 4 TA nightly from 20/21 May 2005.

16/17 April 2004: **Re-numbered (N)266.**

15/16 February 2008: Hammersmith terminus now Bus Station.

18/19 May 2012: LBSL contract awarded to **First London**. Allocation: Atlas Road Garage 4 VN nightly.

21/22 June 2013: Operated by **Tower Transit**.

Routes N236, (N)236

29/30 September 2000: Introduced. **Numbered N236.** Operated: **Finsbury Park Station – Hackney Wick, Eastway** via Highbury Barn, Canonbury, Newington Green, Dalston, London Fields, Hackney, Homerton. Operator: **First Capital**, re-titled **First London** in March 2001. Allocation: Hackney Wick Garage 4 DM nightly, had become 4 DM/DML by September 2001.

16/17 April 2004: **Re-numbered (N)236.**

14/15 January 2005: Allocation: Hackney Wick Garage 3 DM/DML nightly.

14/15 December 2007: Re-allocated to Lea Interchange Garage 3 DM/DML nightly, vehicle-type changed to AD E20D Enviro200 3 DMV nightly from 26/27 April 2012.

4/5 October 2012: Last night of operation.

Route N22

24/25 November 2000: Introduced. Operated: **Piccadilly Circus – Richmond, Bus Station** via Hyde Park Corner, Knightsbridge, Sloane Square, Chelsea, Putney Bridge Station (outbound only), Putney Bridge, Putney Common, Barnes, Mortlake. Operator: **London General**. Allocation: Putney Garage 4 NV (Su-Th), 5 NV (Fr-Sa). Note: Replaced much of N9's routeing between Putney Bridge and Richmond via Barnes.

28/29 September 2001: Projected Richmond – Kingston via Twickenham, Fulwell, Teddington. Now operated: **Piccadilly Circus – Kingston, Fairfield Bus Station**. Allocation: Putney Garage 5 NV (Su-Th), 6 NV (Fr-Sa). Note: Replaced Richmond – Kingston section of N9.

22/23 November 2002: Outbound jnys no longer served Putney Bridge Station. Vehicle-type change to low-floor Volvo B7TL at Putney Garage 5 WVL (Su-Th), 6 WVL (Fr-Sa).

2/3 June 2006: Section of route Fulwell – Kingston withdrawn (replaced by new route (N)281). Now operated: **Piccadilly Circus – Fulwell, Stanley Road** via Hyde Park Corner, Knightsbridge, Sloane Square, Chelsea, Putney Bridge, Putney Common, Barnes, Mortlake, Richmond, Twickenham. Allocation: Putney Garage 5 WVL nightly, Fr-Sa allocation increased to 8 WVL from 21/22 October 2007.

Putney garage's Northern Counties Palatine II-bodied Volvo Olympian NV 183 was seen at Hyde Park Corner working an end of the night inbound journey on then-30 minute frequency route N22 on Friday morning 5 July 2002. *Philip Wallis*

Route N41

1/2 December 2000: Introduced. Operated: **Archway Station – Tottenham Hale Station** via Hornsey Rise, Crouch End, Hornsey, Turnpike Lane, West Green Road, Seven Sisters. Operator: **Arriva London North**. Allocation: Tottenham Garage 2 M nightly, vehicle-type changed to low-floor DAF DB250LF 2 DLA nightly c. June 2001 and became 2 VLW nightly c. May 2003.

4/5 February 2005: Projected Archway Station – Trafalgar Square. Now operated: **Trafalgar Square – Tottenham Hale Station** via Charing Cross Road, New Oxford Street, Bloomsbury, Islington, Highbury Corner, Holloway, Archway, Hornsey Rise, Crouch End, Hornsey, Turnpike Lane, West Green Road, Seven Sisters. Allocation: Tottenham Garage 5 VLA/VLW nightly. Note: Replaced Trafalgar Square – Islington section of N43.

27 August 2010: Arriva acquired by Deutsche Bahn.

By 3/4 February 2011: Allocation: Tottenham Garage 5 DLA nightly, became 5 DW (Su-Th), 7 DW (Fr-Sa) from 1/2 February 2013.

Routes introduced 2001

Route N27 (Chalk Farm), (N)27

2/3 February 2001: Introduced. **Numbered N27**. Operated: **Turnham Green, Church – Chalk Farm, Safeway** via Hammersmith, Kensington High Street, Notting Hill Gate, Westbourne Grove, Paddington Station, Marylebone Road, Hampstead Road, Camden Town. Operator: **First Centrewest**, re-titled **First London** in March 2001. Allocation: Westbourne Park Garage 4 M nightly, vehicle-type changed to low-floor Dennis Trident 4 TN nightly c. March 2001.

19/20 March 2004: **Re-numbered (N)27**.

c. September 2004: Allocation: Westbourne Park Garage 4 VNW nightly

11/12 November 2005: LBSL contract awarded to **London United** from Hounslow Garage 4 VA/VP nightly.

4 April 2006: **Transdev** corporate logo adopted.

During 2006: Chalk Farm terminus re-designated 'Morrisons'.

By 8/9 May 2010: Vehicle-type change to Scania OmniCity at Hounslow Garage 4 SP nightly.

3 March 2011: Operated by RATP DEV UK Ltd t/a **London United**.

9/10 November 2012: Projected Turnham Green – Chiswick Business Park via Chiswick High Road. Now operated: **Chiswick Business Park – Chalk Farm, Morrisons**. Allocation unchanged.

Top Tottenham garage's Wrightbus-bodied Volvo B7TL VLW 128 had paused at the Centrepoint bus stop near Tottenham Court Road Station in the early hours of Saturday morning 19 February 2005 shortly after then-30 minute frequency route N41 had been extended to Trafalgar Square. *Philip Wallis*

Bottom First London's Plaxton President-bodied Dennis Trident TN 979 was seen at Kensington Church Street in Notting Hill Gate at 04.53 on Midsummer's Day 21 June 2003 bound for Chalk Farm on 30 minute frequency route N27. *Philip Wallis*

Route N137
16/17 March 2001: Introduced. Operated: **Oxford Circus – Crystal Palace, Parade** via Marble Arch, Hyde Park Corner, Knightsbridge, Sloane Square Chelsea Bridge, Battersea Park, Queenstown Road, Clapham Common, Clapham Park, Streatham Hill, Norwood. Operator: **London Central**. Allocation: Camberwell Garage 4 AVL nightly.

9/10 July 2004: LBSL contract awarded to **Arriva London South**. Allocation: Norwood Garage 5 DLA/VLA (Su-Th), 10 DLA/VLA (Fr-Sa).

27 August 2010: Arriva acquired by Deutsche Bahn.

By April 2012: Vehicle-type change to AD E40D Enviro400 at Norwood Garage 5 T (Su-Th), 10 T (Fr-Sa).

Route N55
27/28 April 2001: Introduced. Operated: **Oxford Circus – Whipps Cross, Roundabout** via New Oxford Street, Bloomsbury, Clerkenwell Green, Shoreditch, Cambridge Heath, Hackney, Clapton, Leyton. Operator: **Stagecoach East London**. Allocation: Leyton Garage 4 TA nightly.

25/26 June 2004: Projected Whipps Cross – Woodford Wells via Leytonstone, Wanstead, Snaresbrook, South Woodford. Now ran: **Oxford Circus – Woodford Wells, Horse & Well.** Allocation: Leyton Garage 5 TA nightly. Note: Replaced Wanstead – Woodford Wells section of N8.

30 August 2006: Operated by Macquarie Bank Ltd t/a East London Bus Group. Fleetname: **East London.**

2/3 March 2007: Allocation: Leyton Garage 5 TA (Su-Th), 11 TA (Fr-Sa).

14 October 2010: Operated by Stagecoach Bus Holdings Ltd t/a **East London.**

Routes N58, (N)58
27/28 April 2001: Introduced. **Numbered N58**. Operated: **Walthamstow Central Station – East Ham, White Horse** via Markhouse Road, Leyton, Leytonstone, Wanstead Park, Forest Gate, Upton Park. Operator: **Stagecoach East London**. Allocation: Leyton Garage 3 TA nightly.

26/27 March 2004: **Re-numbered (N)58.**

3/4 March 2005: Last night of operation.

Routes N69 (Walthamstow), (N)69
27/28 April 2001: Introduced. **Numbered N69.** Operated: **Walthamstow Central Station – London City Airport** via Leyton, Leytonstone, Stratford, Plaistow, Canning Town, Silvertown Way. Operator: **Stagecoach East London**. Allocation: Leyton Garage 3 TA nightly.

30 Apr/1 May 2004: **Re-numbered (N)69.**

16/17 December 2005: Section of route Canning Town – London City Airport withdrawn. Now operated: **Walthamstow Central Station – Canning Town, Bus Station**. Allocation: Leyton Garage 2 TA nightly. Note: Canning Town – London City Airport section of (N)69 served by new route (N)474 from 2/3 November 2007.

30 August 2006: Operated by Macquarie Bank Ltd t/a East London Bus Group. Fleetname: **East London**.

2/3 March 2007: Allocation: Leyton Garage 3 TA nightly.

14 October 2010: Operated by Stagecoach Bus Holdings Ltd t/a **East London**.

27/28 July – 12/13 August and 29/30 August – 9/10 September 2012: Frequency increased to 12 min nightly for duration of Olympic and Paralympic Games. Allocation from Leyton Garage temporarily increased to 6 TA nightly.

Top London Central's tenure as operator of then-30 minute frequency route N137 is represented by this view of Camberwell garage's Alexander ALX400-bodied Volvo B7TL AVL 6 seen at Hyde Park Corner early on Friday morning 5 July 2002. *Philip Wallis*

Bottom Stagecoach East London's TransBus Trident ALX400 17810 was photographed at Whipps Cross Roundabout when about to set off on then-30 minute frequency route N55's first inbound journey of the night at 00.10 on Sunday morning 6 June 2004. *Philip Wallis*

This picture of Stratford garage's Plaxton Pointer-bodied Dennis Dart SLF 34115m displaying route number N106 raises a number of questions. The view must date from post-January 2003 when Stagecoach re-numbered its national fleet into a five-digit numerical system (original fleet number was SLD 115). The official allocation for night-time N106 (and daytime 106) had changed to double-deck TAS-type Dennis Tridents around about October 2001. The only routeing difference between the 106 and N106 was that the N106 extended beyond Whitechapel to terminate at Aldgate Station. It seems likely that this was an early morning view taken at Finsbury Park Station when 34115m was substituting for a double-deck bus on daytime route 106 to Whitechapel and that the driver had set an incorrect route number display. *Capital Transport*

Stratford garage's 9.9 metre Alexander ALX400-bodied Dennis Trident 17522s was seen at Finsbury Park Station loading passengers for the 04.09 departure of 30 minute frequency route N106 on Saturday morning 29 January 2005. *Philip Wallis*

Route N101

27/28 April 2001: Introduced. Operated: **Wanstead Station – North Woolwich, Free Ferry** via Aldersbrook, Manor Park, East Ham, East Beckton, Cyprus. Operator: **Stagecoach East London**. Allocation: Upton Park Garage 3 SLW nightly.

By 24/25 April 2004: Vehicle-type change to Dennis Trident from Upton Park Garage 3 TA nightly.

16/17 September 2004: Last night of operation.

Route N106

27/28 April 2001: Introduced. Operated: **Finsbury Park Station – Aldgate Station** via Lordship Park, Stoke Newington, Clapton, Hackney, Cambridge Heath, Bethnal Green, Whitechapel. Operator: **Stagecoach East London**. Allocation: Stratford Garage 3 PD nightly.

c. October 2001: Vehicle-type change to low-floor double-deck Dennis Trident from Stratford Garage 3 TAS nightly.

30 August 2006: Operated by Macquarie Bank Ltd. t/a East London Bus Group. Fleetname: **East London**.

23/24 February 2008: Re-allocated to West Ham Garage 3 TAS nightly.

24/25 April 2008: Last night of operation.

First London's Plaxton President-bodied Dennis Trident TN 997 was photographed at Greenford Station loading passengers for the 00.30 departure of 30 minute frequency route N105 on Sunday morning 11 April 2004. *Philip Wallis*

Routes N105, (N)105

29/30 June 2001: Introduced. **Numbered N105**. Operated: **Greenford Station – Heathrow Airport, Central Bus Station** via Southall, Cranford, Harlington Corner, Compass Centre. Operator: **First London**. Allocation: Greenford Garage 4 TN nightly.

16/17 April 2004: **Re-numbered (N)105**.

1/2 July 2011: LBSL contract awarded to **Metroline Travel**. Section of route via Compass Centre at Heathrow Airport withdrawn. Continued to operate: **Greenford Station – Heathrow Airport, Central Bus Station.** Allocation: West Perivale Garage 3 VW nightly.

Routes N285, (N)285

29/30 June 2001: Introduced. **Numbered N285.** Operated: **Kingston, Cromwell Road Bus Station – Heathrow Airport, Central Bus Station** via Hampton Wick, Teddington, Hampton Hill, Hanworth, Feltham, Hatton Cross, Harlington Corner. Operator: **London United**. Allocation: Hounslow Heath Garage 4 DPS nightly.

30 Nov/1 Dec 2001: Diverted to serve Feltham Station Interchange.

December 2001, 24/25 January 2003 to 11/12 January 2004 and 5/6 March 2004 to 17/18 March 2005: During these three time periods routes N285/(N)285 were projected within Heathrow Airport beyond the Central Bus Station to terminate at Terminal 3.

23/24 January 2004: **Re-numbered (N)285.**

4 April 2006: **Transdev** corporate logo adopted.

c. September 2008: Vehicle-type change to AD Dart Enviro200 at Hounslow Heath Garage 4 DE nightly.

3 March 2011: Operated by RATP t/a **London United**.

London United's Plaxton Pointer-bodied Dennis Dart SLF DPS 537 was seen on stand at Heathrow Airport Central Bus Station on Tuesday morning 3 July 2001 during the fourth night of 30 minute frequency route N285's operation. *Philip Wallis*

Routes N10, (N)10

28/29 September 2001: Introduced. **Numbered N10**. Operated: **Archway Station – Richmond, Bus Station** via Tufnell Park, King's Cross, Euston, Gower Street (inbound), Tottenham Court Road (outbound), Oxford Circus, Marble Arch, Hyde Park Corner, Kensington, Hammersmith, Putney, East Sheen. Operator: **London United**. Allocation: Hounslow Garage 5 VA/VP (Su-Th), 6 VA/VP (Fr-Sa). Note: Replaced Hammersmith – Richmond section of N9.

3/4 September 2004: LBSL contract awarded to **First London**. Section of route Archway Station – King's Cross withdrawn. Now operated: **King's Cross Station – Richmond Bus Station.** Allocation: Alperton Garage 6 VTL nightly, reclassified VNL-type c. October 2004. Note: Archway – King's Cross section of N10 replaced by new route (N)390. Contracted operation of N10 by First London started one night late on 4/5 September 2004.

1/2 April 2005: Allocation: Alperton Garage 6 VNL (Su-W), 7 VNL (Th-Sa), had become mixed VNL/VNW/VNZ-types by June 2006.

22/23 June 2007: Re-allocated to Westbourne Park Garage 6 TNA (Su-W), 7 TNA (Th-Sa).

29/30 January 2010: **Re-numbered (N)10**. LBSL contract awarded to **Transdev London United.** Section of route Hammersmith – Richmond withdrawn. Now operated: **King's Cross Station – Hammersmith.** Allocation: Stamford Brook Garage 3 SP (Su-Th), 4 SP (Fr-Sa). Note: Replacement service Hammersmith – Richmond provided by new route (N)33 (different intermediate routeing).

3 March 2011: Operated by RATP t/a **London United**.

27/28 July – 12/13 August 2012: Frequency increased to 15 min nightly for duration of the Olympic Games. Allocation from Stamford Brook Garage temporarily increased to 6 SP (Su-Th), 8 SP (Fr-Sa).

22/23 March 2013: Vehicle-type change to AD E40H hybrid from Stamford Brook Garage 6 ADH (Su-Th), 8 ADH (Fr-Sa).

Alperton garage's TransBus President-bodied Volvo B7TL VNL 32210 was photographed outside Putney Station when Richmond-bound on 30 minute frequency route N10 during the early hours of Friday morning 16 February 2007. *Philip Wallis*

East Thames Buses' Caetano Compass-bodied Dennis Dart SLF DC 9 was seen on layover at the former Lewisham Bus Station between turns on 30 minute frequency route N108 during the early hours of Saturday morning 5 July 2003. *Philip Wallis*

Routes N108, (N)108

28/29 September 2001: Introduced. **Numbered N108.** Operated: **Stratford Bus Station – Lewisham Station** via Bromley-by-Bow, Blackwall Tunnel, North Greenwich, East Greenwich, Blackheath. Operator: **East Thames Buses**. Allocation: Belvedere Garage 3 Optare Excel nightly, had become mixed Optare Excel and DC-type Dennis Dart SLF by 4/5 July 2003 and had been increased to 4 DC by September 2003.

14/15 November 2003: **Re-numbered (N)108.**

c. July 2004: Vehicle-type changed to Volvo Merit 4 DWL from Belvedere Garage.

2 October 2009: East Thames Buses acquired by Go-Ahead group. Re-assigned to **London General**. Allocation unchanged.

30 April/1 May 2010: Re-assigned to **London Central**. Allocation: New Cross Garage 3 DWL nightly.

27/28 July – 12/13 August and 29/30 August – 9/10 September 2012: Frequency increased to 15 min nightly for duration of Olympic and Paralympic Games (between 02.00 and 04.00 reverted to 30 min). Allocation from New Cross Garage temporarily increased to 6 DWL nightly.

Routes N93 (North Cheam), (N)93

30 November/1 December 2001: Introduced. **Numbered N93**. Operated: **Putney Bridge Station – North Cheam, Priory Road** via Putney High Street, Putney Heath, Wimbledon Common, Wimbledon, South Wimbledon, Morden, Stonecot Hill. Operator: **London General**. Allocation: Sutton Garage 3 NV nightly, vehicle-type changed to low-floor Volvo B7TL 3 EVL nightly c. March 2002.

2/3 April 2004: **Re-numbered (N)93.**

c. March 2009: Vehicle-type change to AD Trident at Sutton Garage 3 DOE nightly.

Routes introduced 2002

Routes N75, (N)75

8/9 February 2002: Introduced. **Numbered N75.** Operated: **Lewisham Station, Loampit Vale – Croydon, Fairfield Halls** via Catford, Perry Vale, Sydenham, Penge, Anerley, Norwood Junction, Selhurst, West Croydon. Operator: **Stagecoach Selkent**. Allocation: Catford Garage 3 TAS nightly.

29/30 August 2003: Re-routed to serve East Croydon Station in both directions of travel (inbound via Dingwall Road, outbound via George Street).

19/20 March 2004: **Re-numbered (N)75.**

30 August 2006: Operated by Macquarie Bank Ltd t/a East London Bus Group. Fleetname: **Selkent**.

17/18 May 2007: Last night of operation.

Routes N75 and N108 both formed 24-hour services with daytime bus routes of equivalent route number and both night-time routes would soon drop the display of their distinguishing 'N' prefixes to their route numbers – at least officially. East Thames Buses' Optare Excel 320 and Stagecoach Selkent's TransBus Trident ALX400 17588s were on layover at the former Lewisham Bus Station when photographed early on Saturday morning 5 July 2003. *Philip Wallis*

London General's Wrightbus-bodied Volvo B7TL WVL 30 was seen on layover at Putney Bridge Station between turns on 30 minute frequency route N85 during the early hours of Sunday morning 28 March 2004.
Philip Wallis

Routes N345, (N)345
26/27 April 2002: Introduced. **Numbered N345.** Operated: **South Kensington Station – Peckham, Bus Station** via Chelsea, Battersea, Clapham Junction, Clapham Common, Clapham, Stockwell, Brixton, Loughborough Junction, Camberwell Green. Operator: **London General**. Allocation: Stockwell Garage 4 WVL nightly.

2/3 April 2004: **Re-numbered (N)345.**

1/2 May 2009: Allocation from Stockwell Garage increased to 5 WVL nightly, became 5 WVL/E nightly c. July 2009.

30/31 March 2012: Reassigned to **London Central**. Allocation: Camberwell Garage 4 WVL/E, had become all E-type by 30/31 August 2013.

Routes N85 (Kingston), (N)85
28/29 June 2002:
Introduced. **Numbered N85**. Operated: **Putney Bridge Station – Kingston, Fairfield Bus Station** via Putney High Street, Putney Heath, Roehampton, Alton East Estate (towards Putney), Kingston Vale, Norbiton. Operator: **London General**. Allocation: Putney Garage 2 WVL nightly.

2/3 April 2004: **Re-numbered (N)85.**

3/4 July 2009: Kingston terminus now Kingston Hall Road.

By 8/9 May 2010: Putney Garage increased to 3 WVL nightly.

Routes N88 (Camden Town), (N)88
28/29 June 2002: Introduced. **Numbered N88**. Operated: **Camden Town, Camden Gardens – Clapham Common, Old Town** via Hampstead Road, Portland Place, Oxford Circus, Piccadilly Circus, Trafalgar Square, Whitehall, Westminster, Marsham Street, Vauxhall Bridge, Vauxhall, Stockwell, Clapham. Operator: **London General**. Allocation: Stockwell Garage 4 PDL nightly, vehicle-type changed to 4 WVL nightly c. May 2003 and Fr-Sa allocation became 5 WVL from 12/13 December 2003.

2/3 April 2004: **Re-numbered (N)88.**

1/2 May 2009: Allocation: Stockwell Garage 5 WVL (Su-Th), 6 WVL (Fr-Sa). Fr-Sa increased to 7 WVL from 11/12 December 2010. Allocation had become mixed E/WVL-types by 30 June/1 July 2012.

Stockwell garage's Wrightbus-bodied Volvo B7TL WVL 78 was seen heading along Cockspur Street just before twenty past five on Thursday morning 5 June 2003 whilst working that night's last southbound journey on then-30 minute frequency route N88.
Philip Wallis

Routes N213, (N)213

28/29 June 2002: Introduced. **Numbered N213**. Operated: **Kingston, Fairfield Bus Station – Sutton Garage** via Norbiton, New Malden, Worcester Park, North Cheam, Cheam, St Nicholas Way (inbound), High Street (outbound). Operator: **London General**. Allocation: Sutton Garage 3 EVL nightly.

12/13 December 2003: Projected Sutton – West Croydon via Carshalton, Wallington, Roundshaw, Croydon. Now operated: **Kingston, Fairfield Bus Station – West Croydon, Bus Station.** Return jnys from West Croydon routed via Dingwall Road (for East Croydon Station). Allocation: Sutton Garage 5 EVL nightly. Note: Replaced Sutton – Wallington section of N44.

3/4 July 2009: **Re-numbered (N)213.** Section of route Sutton – West Croydon withdrawn. Now operated: **Kingston, Fairfield Bus Station – Sutton Garage.** Allocation: Sutton Garage 3 EVL nightly, 3 PVL nightly c. August 2009. 3 DOE nightly by 27/28 July 2013.

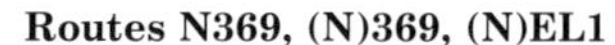

Routes N369, (N)369, (N)EL1

19/20 July 2002: Introduced. **Numbered N369**. Operated: **Ilford, Hainault Street – Thames View Estate, Abridge Way** via Ilford Hill, Ilford Lane, Barking Station, London Road, Movers Lane, Bastable Avenue. Operator: **Stagecoach East London**. Allocation: Barking Garage 2 TA nightly.

30 April/1 May 2004: **Re-numbered (N)369.**

30 August 2006: Operated by Macquarie Bank Ltd t/a East London Bus Group. Fleetname: **East London**.

19/20 February 2010: LBSL contract awarded to **Blue Triangle** (Go-Ahead group). **Re-numbered (N)EL1**, branded as **East London Transit**. Section of route Hainault Street – Ilford Hill withdrawn. Re-routed in Barking via pedestrianised Town Centre. Now operated: **Ilford, Ilford Hill – Thames View Estate, Abridge Way.** Allocation: Rainham Garage 2 WVL nightly.

The N213 was an elusive route with buses to be found in service anywhere along its route length for just over four hours of the night between around 1 o'clock and 5 o'clock in the morning. Sutton garage's East Lancs-bodied Volvo B7TL EVL 6 was photographed in the early hours of Friday morning 7 April 2006 following the N213's outbound routeing from Croydon along Dingwall Road in order to serve East Croydon Station. *Philip Wallis*

Stagecoach East London's Alexander ALX400-bodied Dennis Trident 17375, seen at Barking Station, was one of the two buses allocated from Barking garage to work route N369's 30-minute frequency service on Saturday night/Sunday morning 24/25 April 2004. *Philip Wallis*

Routes N65 (Ealing Broadway), (N)65

30/31 August 2002: Introduced. **Numbered N65**. Operated: **Ealing Broadway Station – Kingston, Brook Street** via South Ealing, Brentford, Kew Bridge, Richmond, Petersham, Ham. Operator: **London United**. Allocation: Fulwell Garage 3 TA nightly. Note: Richmond to Kingston via Ham previously served by the first route N65 (Archway – Hounslow) until 19/20 February 1994.

23/24 January 2004: **Re-numbered (N)65.**

4 April 2006: **Transdev** corporate logo adopted.

3/4 July 2009: Projected Kingston – Chessington via Surbiton, Hook, Copt Gilders Estate. Now operated: **Ealing Broadway Station – Chessington, World of Adventures.** Allocation: Fulwell Garage 4 TA nightly. Kingston and Chessington had previously been linked by route N14 between 26/27 April 1991 and 17/18 August 1995.

c. August 2009: Vehicle-type change to Scania OmniCity at Fulwell Garage 4 SP nightly.

3 March 2011: Operated by RATP DEV UK Ltd t/a **London United**.

14/15 June 2013: Allocation: Fulwell Garage 4 SP (Su-Th), 5 SP (Fr-Sa).

Routes N83 (Golders Green), (N)83

13/14 September 2002: Introduced. **Numbered N83**. Operated: **Ealing Hospital – Golders Green Station** via Hanwell, Ealing, Hanger Lane, Alperton, Wembley, Wembley Park, Kingsbury, West Hendon, Hendon. Operator: **First London**. Allocation: Alperton Garage 4 TN nightly, type change to Volvo B7TL 4 VTL nightly c. October 2002, VTL-type re-classified as VNL-type c. October 2004.

16/17 April 2004: **Re-numbered (N)83.**

c. November 2009: Vehicle-type change to Volvo B9TL at Alperton Garage 4VN nightly.

21/22 June 2013: Operated by **Metroline West** VW-type.

Routes N148, (N)148

4/5 October 2002: Introduced. **Numbered N148**. Operated: **Shepherd's Bush Green – Camberwell Green** via Notting Hill Gate, Lancaster Gate, Marble Arch, Hyde Park Corner, Victoria, Westminster, Westminster Bridge, Elephant & Castle, Walworth Road. Operator: **London United**. Allocation: Shepherd's Bush Garage 3 TA nightly, vehicle-type change to Volvo B7TL 3 VA nightly c. November 2002.

23/24 January 2004: **Re-numbered (N)148.**

4 April 2006: **Transdev** corporate logo adopted.

By 15/16 February 2007: Allocation: Shepherd's Bush Garage 3 VA/TLA, increased to 5 VA/TLA nightly from 11/12 May 2007.

By November 2007: Vehicle-type change to Scania N230UD and Scania OmniCity at Shepherd's Bush Garage 5 SO/SP nightly, became 5 SP nightly c. April 2008.

28/29 November 2008: Projected Shepherd's Bush – White City. Now operated: **White City, Bus Station – Camberwell Green.** Allocation: Shepherd's Bush Garage 5 SP (Su-Th), 6 SP (Fr-Sa).

3 March 2011: Operated by RATP DEV UK Ltd t/a **London United**.

27/28 July – 12/13 August 2012: Frequency increased to 15 min nightly for duration of Olympic Games. Allocation from Shepherd's Bush Garage temporarily increased to 7 SP nightly.

First London's 10.6 metre TransBus President-bodied Volvo B7TL VTL 1219 was photographed at the Ealing Hospital terminus of 30 minute frequency route N83 during the early hours of Sunday morning 11 April 2004, just six nights before that route would officially discontinue display of its 'N' route number prefix. *Philip Wallis*

Routes N189, (N)189

11/12 October 2002: Introduced. **Numbered N189.** Operated: **Oxford Circus – North Cricklewood, Tilling Road** via Oxford Street, Gloucester Place (outbound), Baker Street (inbound), Lisson Grove, Abbey Road, Kilburn, Cricklewood. Operator: **Metroline Travel**. Allocation: Cricklewood Garage 3 TA (Su-Th), 4 TA (Fr-Sa).

31 Jan/1 Feb 2003: Projected North Cricklewood – Brent Cross. Now operated: **Oxford Circus – Brent Cross Shopping Centre**. Allocation: Cricklewood Garage 3 TP (Su-Th), 4 TP (Fr-Sa).

23/24 April 2004: **Re-numbered (N)189.**

14/15 November 2010: Vehicle-type change to AD Trident Enviro400 at Cricklewood Garage 3 TE (Su-Th), 4 TE (Fr-Sa), further vehicle-type change to AD E40D Enviro400H hybrid 3 TEH (Su-Th), 4 TEH (Fr-Sa) by 29/30 June 2012.

Route N63

15/16 November 2002: Introduced. Operated: **King's Cross Station – Crystal Palace, Parade** via Farringdon Road, Ludgate Circus, Blackfriars Bridge, Elephant & Castle, Bricklayers Arms, North Peckham, Peckham, Peckham Rye, Honor Oak, Sydenham Hill. Operator: **London Central**. Allocation: Peckham Garage 4 AVL nightly, had become 4 AVL/PVL nightly by 17/18 July 2004. Fr-Sa allocation increased to 6 AVL/PVL from 30 November/1 December 2007 and to 8 AVL/PVL from 13/14 November 2009. c. December 2009: Allocation: Peckham Garage 4 WVL (Su-Th), 8 WVL (Fr-Sa).

27/28 July – 12/13 August and 29/30 August – 9/10 September 2012: Frequency increased to 20 min (Su-Th) and 12 min (Fr-Sa) for duration of Olympic and Paralympic Games. Allocation from Peckham temporarily increased to 6 WVL (Su-Th), 10 WVL (Fr-Sa).

Dawn was breaking as Cricklewood garage's 10.5 Metre Alexander ALX400-bodied Dennis Trident TAL 128 paused at the traffic lights between Baker Street and Marylebone Road when making an inbound journey on 30 minute frequency route N189 during Sunday morning 11 April 2004. *Philip Wallis*

Peckham garage's Alexander ALX400-bodied Volvo B7TL AVL 31 had attracted a good passenger loading as it crossed Blackfriars Bridge at 05.25 on Tuesday morning 6 July 2004 whilst working that night's last inbound journey on then-30 minute frequency route N63. *Philip Wallis*

Right Putney Garage's Wrightbus-bodied Volvo B7TL WVL 33 was seen in Baker Street at 04.40 on Sunday 11 April 2004 working that night's penultimate outbound journey on 30 minute frequency route N74. *Philip Wallis*

Centre South Croydon garage's AD Trident Enviro400 T 120 was seen on London Bridge working an inbound journey on 20 minute frequency route N133 during the early hours of Friday morning 15 October 2010. *Philip Wallis*

Route N74 (Roehampton)
22/23 November 2002 : Introduced. Operated: **Baker Street Station – Roehampton, Danebury Avenue** via Oxford Street, Marble Arch, Hyde Park Corner, Knightsbridge, South Kensington, Earls Court, West Brompton, Putney Bridge, Putney, Upper Richmond Road, Roehampton Lane. Operator: **London General**. Allocation: Putney Garage 4 WVL (Su-Th), 5 WVL (Fr-Sa). Note: Danebury Avenue previously served by route N14.

27/28 July – 12/13 August 2012: Frequency over entire route length increased to 15 min nightly for duration of the Olympic Games. Allocation from Putney Garage temporarily increased to 6 WVL nightly. Supplementary service West Brompton – Marble Arch operated over the Olympic Games period with allocation from Camberwell Garage 5 PVL (Su-Th), 4 PVL (Fr-Sa).

Routes introduced 2003

Route N133
24/25 January 2003: Introduced. Operated: **Liverpool Street, Bus Station – Tooting Broadway** via Finsbury Circus, Moorgate, Bank, London Bridge, Borough High Street, Elephant & Castle, Kennington, Brixton, Streatham Hill, Streatham, Southcroft Road. Operator: **London General**. Stockwell Garage 4 WVL nightly.

31 August/1 September 2007: Section of route Streatham – Tooting Broadway withdrawn (already covered by (N)57). Projected Streatham – Mitcham via Streatam Vale, Manor Road. Now operated: **Liverpool Street, Bus Station – Mitcham, Fair Green.** Allocation unchanged. Note: Streatham Vale previously served by N78 from 22/23 May 1987 to 11/12 March 1994.

2/3 November 2007: Re-allocated to Mandela Way Garage 4 WVL.

22/23 January 2010: LBSL contract awarded to **Arriva London South**. Allocation: Norwood Garage 6 T nightly.

27 August 2010: Arriva acquired by Deutsche Bahn.

27/28 August 2010: Re-allocated to South Croydon Garage 6 T nightly.

13/14 February 2011: Re-routed Liverpool Street – Bank via Old Broad Street and Threadneedle Street. Continued to operate: **Liverpool Street, Bus Station – Mitcham, Fair Green**.

27/28 July – 12/13 August and 29/30 August – 9/10 September 2012: Frequency increased to 12 min nightly for duration of the Olympic and Paralympic Games. Allocation from South Croydon Garage temporarily increased to 10 T nightly.

Route N76 (Northumberland Park)
31 January/1 February 2003: Introduced. Operated: **Waterloo, Baylis Road – Northumberland Park Station** via Waterloo Bridge, Aldwych, Ludgate Circus, Bank, Moorgate, Old Street Station, Hoxton, Dalston Junction, Stoke Newington, Stamford Hill, South Tottenham, Tottenham. Operator: **Arriva London North**. Allocation: Tottenham Garage 5 VLW nightly.

29/30 January 2010: Allocation from Tottenham Garage increased to 8 VLW nightly to allow for 'shoulder-period' running using buses off late night/early morning daytime routes.

27 August 2010: Arriva acquired by Deutsche Bahn.

17/18 January 2011: Vehicle-type DAF DB250LF diesel and Volvo B5LH hybrid at Tottenham Garage 8 DLA/HV nightly. DW/HV-types by 30/31 August 2013.

Ludgate Circus was an important focal point for an earlier range of London General Omnibus Company and London Transport all-night bus routes and Special Night Journeys. Arriva London North's Wrightbus-bodied Volvo B7TL VLW 129 was representative of Transport for London's modern Night Bus route network as it crossed the Circus at 05.42 on Sunday morning 18 July 2004 working that night's last outbound journey on 30 minute frequency route N76. *Philip Wallis*

Routes N242, (N)242

31 January/1 February 2003: Introduced. **Numbered N242.** Operated: **Tottenham Court Road Station – Homerton Hospital, Homerton Grove** via New Oxford Street, Holborn, Holborn Circus, Bank, Bishopsgate, Liverpool Street Station, Shoreditch, Dalston, Hackney, Millfields Road, Clapton Park. Operator: **Arriva London North**. Allocation: Clapton Garage 4 DLA nightly.

23/24 April 2004: **Re-numbered (N)242.**

4/5 March 2005: Homerton Hospital terminus now changed to Wardle Street.

2/3 September 2005: Allocation: Clapton Garage 5 DLA nightly, re-allocated to Stamford Hill Garage 5 DLA nightly from 31 March/1 April 2006.

31 Aug/1 Sept 2007: Allocation: Stamford Hill Garage 6 DLA (Su), 7 DLA (M-Th), 9 DLA (Fr), 10 DLA (Sa).

18/19 April 2008: Largely re-allocated to Tottenham Garage 6 DLA (Su-Th), 8 DLA (Fr), 9 DLA (Sa), Stamford Hill 1 DLA (M-Sa).

2/3 January 2009: Tottenham Court Road set-down now St Giles High Street, pick-up New Oxford Street.

13/14 November 2009: Re-allocated to Clapton Garage 6 T/DW/VLW (Su-Th), 9 T/DW/VLW (Fr-Sa).

27 August 2010: Arriva acquired by Deutsche Bahn.

By 27/28 May 2011: Allocation: Clapton Garage 6 DW (Su-Th), 9 DW (Fr-Sa).

14/15 June 2013: Allocation from Clapton Garage now 8 DW (Su-Th), 9 DW (Fr-Sa).

Routes N271, (N)271

31 January/1 February 2003: Introduced. **Numbered N271.** Operated: **Liverpool Street, Bus Station – Highgate Village** via Moorgate, City Road, Hoxton, Canonbury, Highbury Corner, Holloway Road, Holloway, Archway, Highgate Hill. Operator: **Metroline London Northern**. Holloway Garage 2 TP nightly.

16/17 April 2004: **Re-numbered (N)271.**

1 January 2005: Reassigned to **Metroline Travel**.

17/18 June 2011: Section of route Moorgate, Finsbury Square – Liverpool Street, Bus Station withdrawn. Now operated: **Moorgate, Finsbury Square – Highgate Village**. Allocation unchanged.

By 27/28 July 2013: Allocation: Holloway Garage 2 VW nightly.

Routes N274, (N)274

31 January/1 February 2003: Introduced. **Numbered N274.** Operated: **Lancaster Gate, Bayswater Road – Islington, Angel** via Marble Arch, Gloucester Place (outbound), Baker Street (inbound), St John's Wood, Regent's Park (London Zoo), Camden Town, Agar Grove, Caledonian Road, Copenhagen Street. Operator: **Metroline London Northern**. Allocation: Holloway Garage 3 DML nightly.

19/20 March 2004: **Re-numbered (N)274.**

1 January 2005: Reassigned to **Metroline Travel**.

4/5 February 2005: Re-allocated to King's Cross Garage 3 DLD nightly. Further re-allocated to Holloway Garage 3 DLD nightly from 3/4 February 2006 and re-allocated again to new King's Cross Garage in Freight Way 3 DLD nightly from 2/3 July 2010.

23/24 June 2011: Last night of operation.

Metroline London Northern's TransBus Trident TP 426 was photographed on arrival at Liverpool Street Bus Station when it was one of the two buses allocated from Holloway garage to 30 minute frequency route N271 on Friday night/Saturday morning 31 October/1 November 2003.
Philip Wallis

Routes N453, (N)453

14/15 February 2003: Introduced. **Numbered N453.** Operated: **Marylebone Station, Great Central Street – Deptford Broadway** via Marylebone Road, Great Portland Street (inbound), Portland Place (outbound), Oxford Circus, Piccadilly Circus, Trafalgar Square, Whitehall, Westminster Bridge, Elephant & Castle, Old Kent Road, New Cross Gate, New Cross. Operator: **Stagecoach Selkent**. Allocation: N453 (and daytime 453) were intended to be operated by new articulated single-deck Mercedes-Benz Citaro bendy buses but, due to late delivery of these vehicles, operation started using Volvo Olympian and Dennis Trident double-deck buses from Plumstead Garage 10 VA/VN/TA nightly. Note: Replaced Oxford Circus – Trafalgar Square section of route N53 and supplemented the N53's service onwards to Deptford Broadway.

14/15 March 2003: Progessive introduction of new articulated Mercedes-Benz Citaro bendy buses from early hours Saturday 15 March 2003. Allocation: Plumstead Garage 10 MA nightly.

19/20 March 2004: **Re-numbered (N)453.**

24/25 March 2004: Due to safety concerns following fires on three London Central Mercedes-Benz Citaros all such buses in London service were taken off the road for checks. Temporary replacement on (N)453 was provided by 10 TA/TAS-type Tridents from Plumstead and other Stagecoach garages.

5/6 April 2004: Full allocation of 10 MA-type Mercedes-Benz Citaros restored.

30 August 2006: Operated by Macquarie Bank Ltd t/a East London Bus Group. Fleetname: **Selkent**.

8/9 September 2006: Projected Deptford Broadway – Deptford Bridge. Now operated: **Marylebone Station, Great Central Street – Deptford Bridge DLR Station.** Allocation from Plumstead Garage reduced to 7 MA nightly due to elimination of lengthy 'dead-run' from the former Deptford terminus to reach the bus stand in Jerrard Sreet, Lewisham.

15/16 February 2008: LBSL contract awarded to **London General**. New articulated single-deck Mercedes-Benz Citaros to Euro 5 Enhanced Emission Vehicle standard introduced from Mandela Way Garage 6 MAL nightly.

23/24 September 2011: Converted to double-deck bus operation with AD Trident Enviro400. Allocation: Mandela Way Garage 6 E (Su-Th), 11 E (Fr-Sa).

Routes N277, (N)277

28 February/1 March 2003: Introduced. **Numbered N277.** Operated: **Highbury and Islington Station – Leamouth** via Balls Pond Road, Dalston, Hackney, Well Street, Victoria Park, Mile End, Burdett Road, Limehouse, Westferry, Canary Wharf. Operator: **Stagecoach East London**. Allocation: Bow Garage 3 TA nightly.

26/27 March 2004: **Re-numbered (N)277.**

30 August 2006: Operated by Macquarie Bank Ltd t/a East London Bus Group. Fleetname: **East London**.

28/29 August 2009: Re-allocated to West Ham 3 TA nightly.

14 October 2010: Operated by Stagecoach Bus Holdings Ltd t/a **East London.**

30/31 August 2013: Re-allocated to Bow Garage 3 TA nightly.

Routes N341, (N)341

25/26 July 2003: Introduced. **Numbered N341.** Operated: **Waterloo, County Hall – Northumberland Park, Tesco** via Waterloo Bridge, Aldwych, Fetter Lane, Holborn Circus, Grays Inn Road, Rosebery Avenue, Islington, Essex Road, Newington Green, Manor House, Harringay, West Green, Philip Lane, Tottenham, Northumberland Park Station. Operator: **First London**. Allocation: Northumberland Park Garage 4 VN nightly. Vehicle-type changed to low-floor Transbus Trident 4 TN nightly c. January 2004.

16/17 April 2004: **Re-numbered (N)341.**

29/30 June 2009: Waterloo termini now Baylis Road (pick-up), York Road (set-down).

15/16 October 2010: LBSL contract awarded to **Arriva London North.** Allocation: Lea Valley Garage 4 T nightly.

Route N7

29/30 August 2003: Introduced. Operated: **Russell Square – Northolt Station** via New Oxford Street, Oxford Circus, Marble Arch, Paddington Station, Westbourne Grove, Ladbroke Grove, Wormwood Scrubs, East Acton, Acton, Ealing Common, Ealing Broadway, Greenford, Yeading. Operator: **First London**. Allocation: Alperton Garage 7 VTL nightly, changed to 7 VNW/VNZ nightly c. April 2004. Replaced Ladbroke Grove – Northolt Station section of N23.

22/23 June 2007: LBSL contract awarded to **Metroline Travel**. Allocation: Perivale Garage 6 TP/TPL nightly.

By 29/30 May 2009: Allocation: Perivale Garage 6 SEL (Su-Th), 7 SEL (Fr-Sa), re-allocated to West Perivale Garage 6 SEL nightly from 22/23 June 2012.

Above left Plumstead garage's articulated Mercedes-Benz Citaro bendy bus 23024 was seen passing along Cockspur Street just before 5am on Thursday 5 June 2003 working that night's last outbound journey on then-20 minute frequency route N453. *Philip Wallis*

Left Over one hour's journey time lay ahead of First London's Wrightbus-bodied Volvo B7TL VNW 32357 as it loaded passengers in New Oxford Street for its Northolt-bound journey on 30 minute frequency route N7 in the early hours of Saturday morning 19 February 2005. *Philip Wallis*

Routes N119, (N)119

29/30 August 2003: Introduced. **Numbered N119.** Operated: **Croydon Airport, Purley Way – Bromley North Station** via South Croydon, Croydon, East Croydon, Shirley Park, Shirley, West Wickham, Hayes. Operator: **Metrobus**. Allocation: Orpington Garage 3 Scania OmniDekka nightly.

14/15 November 2003: **Re-numbered (N)119.**

By 6/7 April 2006: Croydon Airport terminus re-designated Croydon Colonnades.

Routes N250, (N)250

29/30 August 2003: Introduced. **Numbered N250.** Operated: **Brixton Station – Croydon, Fairfields Hall** (set-down)**, East Croydon Station** (pick-up) via Streatham Hill, Streatham, Green Lane, Thornton Heath, Brigstock Road, Thornton Heath Pond, West Croydon Station, Wellesley Road thence *inbound* via Dingwall Road (for East Croydon Station) to Fairfield Halls. *Outbound* journeys originated from East Croydon Station, George Street via Katharine Street to line of route in Wellesley Road. Operator: **Arriva London South**. Allocation: Brixton Garage 4 DLA nightly, became 4 DW nightly from 9/10 July 2004.

19/20 March 2004: **Re-numbered (N)250.**

27 August 2010: Arriva acquired by Deutsche Bahn.

27/28 August 2010: Croydon pick-up now Katharine Street with outbound jnys via George Street (for East Croydon Station) to line of route in Wellesley Road. Now operated: **Brixton Station – Croydon, Fairfields Hall** (set-down), **Katharine Street** (pick-up). Re-allocated to Thornton Heath Garage 4 T nightly.

Routes N264, (N)264 29/30 August 2003: Introduced. **Numbered N264.** Operated: **Tooting, St George's Hospital – Croydon, High Street Flyover** (set-down), **Katharine Street** (pick-up) via Tooting, Mitcham, Mitcham Common, Reeves Corner, West Croydon. Operator: **Arriva London South**. Allocation: Beddington Farm Garage 3 L nightly, vehicle-type changed to low-floor DAF DB250LF 3 DW nightly during November 2003.

19/20 March 2004: **Re-numbered (N)264.**

27 August 2010: Arriva acquired by Deutsche Bahn.

30/31 March 2012: Re-allocated to South Croydon Garage 3 DW nightly.

Routes introduced 2004

Route N86 (Harold Hill)

25/26 June 2004: Introduced. Operated: **Stratford, Bus Station – Harold Hill, Gooshays Drive** via Forest Gate, Manor Park, Ilford, Seven Kings, Chadwell Heath, Romford Market, Romford Station, Gallows Corner. Operator: **Stagecoach East London**. Allocation: Romford Garage 5 TA nightly. Note: Replaced Ilford – Harold Hill section of N25 and augmented the (N)25's service between Stratford and Ilford.

30 August 2006: Operated by Macquarie Bank Ltd t/a East London Bus Group. Fleetname: **East London**.

30/31 March 2007: Projected in Harold Hill to terminate at Dagnam Park Square.

14 October 2010: Operated by Stagecoach t/a **East London.**

By 27/28 July 2013: Allocation: Romford Garage 5 TE nightly.

Route (N)390

3/4 September 2004: Introduced. Operated: **Archway Station – Marble Arch** via Tufnell Park Station, Brecknock Road, York Way, King's Cross Station, Euston Station, Gower Street (inbound), Tottenham Court Road (outbound), Oxford Circus, Oxford Street. Operator: **Metroline London Northern**. Allocation: Holloway Garage 3 VPL nightly. Note: Replaced Archway Station – King's Cross section of N10.

5/6 November 2004: Projected Marble Arch – Notting Hill Gate via Bayswater Road. Now operated: **Archway Station – Notting Hill Gate**. Allocation unchanged.

1 January 2005: Reassigned to **Metroline Travel**.

31 August/1 September 2007: Allocation: Holloway Garage 3 VPL (Su-Th), 4 VPL (Fr-Sa).

By 30 June/1 July 2012: Allocation from Holloway Garage now 3 VW (Su-Th), 4 VW (Fr-Sa).

East London's AD Trident ALX400 18451 was displaying Romford North Street's garage running number 365 in its windscreen which indicated that it was one of five buses allocated to that night's operation of 30 minute frequency route N86 when photographed at Romford Station whilst working a Stratford-bound journey during the early hours of Tuesday morning 20 July 2010. *Philip Wallis*

***Route introduced* 2005**

Route (N)220
21/22 October 2005: Introduced. Operated: **Harlesden, Willesden Junction – Wandsworth, Garratt Lane** via Harlesden, College Park, Scrubs Lane, White City, Shepherd's Bush, Hammersmith, Fulham Palace Road, Putney Bridge, Putney. **London United**. Allocation: Shepherd's Bush Garage 3 VA nightly.

4 April 2006: **Transdev** corporate logo adopted.

By 19/20 January 2008: Allocation: Shepherd's Bush Garage 3 TLA nightly.

3 March 2011: Operated by RATP t/a **London United**.

16/17 March 2012: Vehicle-type change to AD Trident Enviro400H hybrid at Shepherd's Bush Garage 3 ADH nightly.

Routes introduced 2006

Route (N)281
2/3 June 2006: Introduced. Operated: **Hounslow Bus Station – Tolworth, Ewell Road** via Whitton, Twickenham, Fulwell, Teddington, Hampton Wick, Kingston, Surbiton. Operator: **Transdev London United**. Fulwell Garage 3 TA nightly, increased to 4 TA nightly from 3/4 July 2009. Note: Replaced Fulwell – Kingston section of N22 and Kingston – Tolworth section of N87.

3 March 2011: Operated by RATP t/a **London United**.

Route (N)344
10/11 November 2006: Introduced. Operated: **Clapham Junction, St John's Hill – Liverpool Street Station, Bishopsgate** via Battersea, Battersea Park Station, Nine Elms Lane, Vauxhall, Albert Embankment, Lambeth Palace, Elephant & Castle, Southwark Bridge Road, Southwark Bridge, Monument, Gracechurch Street. Operator: **Travel London**. Allocation: Battersea Garage 4 TA nightly. Note: Replaced Battersea Park Station – Lambeth Palace section of N44. (N)344 provided the first all-night bus service over Southwark Bridge since the withdrawal of route 182's Woolwich – Cannon Street Station jnys after operation on 13/14 June 1968.

During 2007: Projected Bishopsgate – Worship Street. Now operated: **Clapham Junction, St John's Hill – Liverpool Street Station, Worship Street.** Allocation unchanged.

9 June 2009: Travel London acquired by Dutch-owned Ned Railways. Operated as **Abellio** from 30 October 2009 and as **Abellio London** from 1 June 2010.

c. September 2009: Vehicle-type change to AD Trident Enviro400 at Battersea Garage 4 ED nightly. 4 ED/EDH by 27/28 July 2013.

Routes introduced 2007

Route (N)C2
13/14 April 2007: Introduced. Operated: **Oxford Circus – Parliament Hill Fields** via Great Portland Street, Albany Street, Camden Town, Kentish Town. Operator: **Metroline Travel**. Allocation: Holloway Garage 3 TP nightly.

26/27 June 2009: Projected Oxford Circus – Victoria Station via Berkeley Square and Piccadilly (replaced N8). Now operated: **Victoria Bus Station – Parliament Hill Fields.** Allocation unchanged.

16/17 November 2011: Victoria termini now Buckingham Palace Road (set-down), Grosvenor Gardens (pick-up).

27/28 April 2012: LBSL contract awarded to **Abellio London.** Allocation: Battersea Garage 4 ED nightly. 4 ED/EDH nightly by 27/28 July 2013.

Routes (N)205, N205
27/28 April 2007: Introduced. **Numbered (N)205**. Operated: **Paddington Station – Mile End Station** via Marylebone Station, Marylebone Road, Euston Road, Euston Station, King's Cross Station, Islington, City Road, Moorgate, Liverpool Street Station, Houndsditch (outbound), Bevis Marks (inbound), Aldgate, Whitechapel, Stepney Green. Operator: **Metroline Travel**. Allocation: Perivale Garage 4 TP nightly.

28/29 August 2009: LBSL contract awarded to **East London**. Projected Mile End – Bow. Now operated: **Paddington Station – Bow, Fairfield Road** (set-down), **Bow Church** (pick-up). Allocation: Bow Garage 4 SC nightly, Fr-Sa allocation increased to 5 SC from 27/28 August 2010.

14 October 2010: Operated by **Stagecoach** t/a East London.

13/14 July 2012: Allocation: Bow 5 SC (Su-Th), 6 SC (Fr-Sa).

30/31 August 2013: **Re-numbered N205**, Projected beyond Bow via Stratford City Bus Station, Temple Mills Lane to Leyton. Now operated: **Paddington Station – Leyton, Downsell Road**. Allocation: Bow Garage 6 SC (Su-Th), 7 SC (Fr-Sa).

Route (N)57
29/30 June 2007: Introduced. Operated: **Kingston, Fairfield Bus Station – Clapham Park, Atkins Road** via Norbiton, Coombe Lane West, Raynes Park, Wimbledon, South Wimbledon, Merton, Colliers Wood, Tooting Broadway, Southcroft Road, Streatham, Streatham Hill. Operator: **London United**. Tolworth 4 TA nightly.

3 March 2011: Operated by RATP t/a **London United**.

Route (N)188
27/28 July 2007: Introduced. Operated: **Russell Square – North Greenwich Station** via Holborn Station, Aldwych, Waterloo Bridge, Elephant & Castle, Bricklayers Arms, Bermondsey, Rotherhithe, Surrey Quays, Deptford, Greenwich, East Greenwich. Operator: **Travel London**. Allocation: Walworth Garage 5 V nightly.

9 June 2009: Travel London acquired by Ned Railways. Operated as **Abellio** from 30 October 2009 and as **Abellio London** from 1 June 2010.

3/4 December 2010: Allocation: Walworth Garage 4 V nightly, had become mixed Volvo B7TL and AD E40H Enviro400H hybrid 4 V/EDH nightly by 29/30 June 2012.

27/28 July – 12/13 August and 29/30 August – 9/10 September 2012: Frequency increased to 15 min nightly for duration of the Olympic and Paralympic Games. Allocation from Walworth Garage temporarily increased to 8 V/EDH nightly.

By 27/28 July 2013: Allocation: Walworth 4 ED/EDH nightly.

Route (N)102
31 August/1 September 2007: Introduced. Operated: **Edmonton Green Station – Golders Green, Finchley Road** via Edmonton, Silver Street, Palmers Green, Bounds Green, Muswell Hill, Fortis Green, East Finchley. Operator: **Arriva London North**. Allocation: Palmers Green Garage 4 VLW nightly. Vehicle-type changed to AD Trident Enviro400 4 T nightly c. April 2008.

Route (N)295
14/15 September 2007: Introduced. Operated: **Ladbroke Grove, Sainsbury's – Clapham Junction** via Latimer Road Station, Shepherds Bush, Hammersmith, Dawes Road, Fulham Broadway, Wandsworth Bridge, York Road, Plough Road. Operator: **First London**. Westbourne Park 4 TN/VNW nightly, had become 4 TNA nightly by 8/9 May 2010 and 4 TN/VN nightly by 29/30 June 2012.

21/22 June 2013: Operated by **Tower Transit** DN/VN-types.

Route (N)472
28/29 September 2007: Introduced. Operated: **North Greenwich Station – Thamesmead, Town Centre** via West Parkside, Charlton, Woolwich, Plumstead Station, Nathan Way, Woolwich Industrial Estate, Central Road, Crossway. Operator: **Stagecoach Selkent**. Allocation: Plumstead Garage 3 TA nightly.

By 29/30 June 2012: Allocation: Plumstead Garage 3 TA/SC, had become all SC-type by 27/28 July 2013.

Route (N)128
5/6 October 2007: Introduced. Operated: **Claybury Broadway – Romford Station** via Barkingside, Gants Hill, Ilford, Green Lane, Becontree Heath, Oldchurch Road, Romford Market. Operator: **Arriva London North**. Allocation: Barking Garage 5 VLA nightly. Note. Restored an all-night bus service between Gants Hill and Ilford via Cranbrook Road previously served by N25 until 24/25 June 2004.

27 August 2010: Arriva acquired by Deutsche Bahn.

8/9 June 2012: Re-routed Rush Green Road – Waterloo Road via Roneo Corner and Queen's Hospital.

By 27/28 July 2013: Allocation: Barking Garage 5 T nightly.

Route (N)474
2/3 November 2007: Introduced. Operated: **Canning Town, Hermit Road – Manor Park Station** via Silvertown Way, London City Airport, Silvertown, North Woolwich, Cyprus, Beckton, East Ham. Operator: **Docklands Minibuses Ltd** t/a **Docklands Buses** (Go-Ahead group). Allocation: Silvertown Garage 3 TL/SO nightly. Note: Canning Town – London City Airport previously served by (N)69 until 15/16 December 2005. North Woolwich – Manor Park previously served by N101 until 16/17 September 2004.

14 December 2007: Reassigned to **Docklands Buses Ltd.**

By 13/14 Sept 2008: Allocation: Silvertown Garage 3 SO/SOC nightly, vehicle-type changed to Volvo B7TL 3 WVL nightly from 29/30 April 2011.

Route (N)111
30 November/1 December 2007: Introduced. Operated: **Kingston, Cromwell Road Bus Station – Heathrow Airport, Central Bus Station** via Hampton Court, Hampton Station, Nurseryland, Hanworth, Hounslow, Heston, Cranford, Harlington Corner. Operator: **Transdev London United**. Allocation: Hounslow Garage 4 VA/TA nightly. Note: Kingston – Hampton Court previously served by N87 until 17/18 August 1995. One outbound Fr-Sa jny on N65 had operated Kingston (dep 05.01) to Hounslow along line of daytime route 111 between 26/27 March 1993 and 19/20 February 1994.

30 April/1 May 2010: Vehicle-type change to Scania OmniCity at Hounslow Garage 4 SP nightly.

3 March 2011: Operated by RATP DEV UK Ltd t/a **London United**.

Routes introduced 2008

Route (N)36
8/9 February 2008: Introduced. Operated: **New Cross Garage – Queens Park Station** via Peckham, Camberwell Green, Kennington, Vauxhall, Victoria, Hyde Park Corner, Marble Arch, Paddington Station, Harrow Road. Operator: **London Central**. Allocation: New Cross Garage 1 PVL (joint N21 (Su-Th), Peckham Garage 4 AVL/PVL/E (Su-Th), 6 AVL/PVL/E (Fr-Sa). Note: Replaced Queens Park Station – Marble Arch section of N36.

13/14 November 2009: Joint allocation N21 dissolved, now Peckham Garage 4 PVL/E (Su-Th), 6 PVL/E (Fr-Sa). By 27/28 July 2013 had become 4 WVL (Su-Th), 6 WVL (Fr-Sa).

Route (N)297
6/7 October 2008: Introduced. Operated: **Willesden Bus Garage – Ealing Broadway, Haven Green** via Neasden, Wembley Park, Wembley, Alperton, Perivale, Scotch Common, Castlebar Road. Operator: **Metroline Travel**. Allocation: Perivale Garage 3 TP (Su-Th), 4 TP (Fr-Sa). Note: Replaced Wembley Central – Scotch Common section of N11.

6/7 March 2009: Re-allocated to West Perivale Garage 3 TE (Su-Th), 4 TE (Fr-Sa), had become 3 VW (Su-Th), 4 VW (Fr-Sa) by 29/30 June 2012.

The LBSL-contract for route (N)474 was originally awarded to then-independent Blue Triangle, operator of daytime route 474 since 1 May 1999, with a planned introduction date of 18/19 May 2007 which was subsequently deferred. Blue Triangle was acquired by the Go-Ahead group on 29 June 2007. Operation of route (N)474 started on 2/3 November 2007 by Docklands Minibuses Ltd, owned by the Go-Ahead group since 18 September 2006, and that company was renamed Docklands Buses Ltd on 14 December 2007. There was much interchange of buses between the Blue Triangle and Docklands Buses fleets under Go-Ahead's ownership. East Lancs Lolyne-bodied Dennis Trident TL 923 displayed some evidence on its front panels of its Blue Triangle fleet origin when it was photographed in High Street, Manor Park at 02.42 on Sunday morning 29 June 2008 whilst working a Canning Town-bound journey on 30 minute frequency route (N)474. *Philip Wallis*

Route N551
29/30 August 2008: Introduced. Operated: **Haymarket** (pick-up), **Cockspur Street** (set-down) – **Gallions Reach Shopping Park** via Trafalgar Square, Aldwych, Ludgate Circus, Bank, Cornhill, Leadenhall Street, Aldgate, Tower Gateway, The Highway, Butcher Row, Limehouse, East India Dock Road, Poplar, Canning Town, Kier Hardie Estate, Custom House, Prince Regent, Tollgate Road, Beckton, Armada Way. Operator: **Docklands Buses** (Go-Ahead group). Allocation: Silvertown Garage 6 SOC nightly. Note: Replaced Canning Town – Gallions Reach section of N50.

By 29/30 March 2012: Vehicle-type now Scania OmniCity and Volvo B7TL from Silvertown Garage 6 SOC/WVL nightly.

29/30 June 2012: Withdrawn from Haymarket, central London terminus now Trafalgar Square, Cockspur Street.

By 8/9 July 2013: Allocation: Silvertown Garage 6 WVL nightly.

30/31 August 2013: LBSL contract awarded to **Tower Transit**. Allocation: Lea Interchange Garage 5 DN + 1DN (joint N550) nightly.

Route (N)365
27/28 September 2008: Introduced. Operated: **Havering Park, Hunters Grove – Mardyke Estate** via Collier Row, Romford Market, Romford Station, Roneo Corner, Abbs Cross Lane, Elm Park, Mungo Park Road, South Hornchurch. Operator: **First London**. Allocation: Dagenham Garage 3 TN nightly, vehicle-type changed to AD Trident Enviro 400 3 DN nightly c. December 2008.

21/22 June 2013: Operated by **First Capital East**.

Route introduced 2009

Route (N)321
9/10 October 2009: Introduced. Operated: **New Cross Gate – Foots Cray, Tesco** via New Cross, Lewisham, Lee Green, Eltham, New Eltham, Sidcup. Operator: **London Central**. Allocation: New Cross Garage 3 PVL nightly. Note: Replaced Sidcup – Foots Cray section of N21.

By 27/28 July 2013: Allocation: New Cross Garage 3 PVL/WVL nightly. All WVL-type by 30/31 August 2013.

Routes introduced 2010

Route (N)33
29/30 January 2010: Introduced. Operated: **Hammersmith, Bus Station – Fulwell, Stanley Road** via Barnes, East Sheen, Richmond, Twickenham, Teddington. Operator: **Transdev London United.** Allocation: Twickenham Garage 3 Dart SLF nightly, vehicle-type change to AD Dart Enviro200 3 DE nightly from 12/13 November 2010. Note: Replaced Hammersmith – Richmond section of N10 (different intermediate routeing).

25/26 June 2010: Reassigned to **London United.**

3 March 2011: Operated by RATP DEV UK Ltd t/a **London United**.

1/2 February 2013: Re-allocated to Fulwell Garage 3 DE nightly.

Route N64
27/28 August 2010: Introduced. Operated: **Thornton Heath Pond – New Addington, Homestead Way** via West Croydon, East Croydon Station, Park Hill Road, Croham Road, Selsdon, Addington Village, Lodge Lane, Fieldway, Headley Drive, King Henry's Drive. Operator: **Metrobus**. Allocation: Croydon Garage 3 Scania OmniCity nightly. Note: Replaced Thornton Heath – New Addington section of N159 (different intermediate routeing between East Croydon and Addington Park).

Route (N)159
27/28 August 2010: Introduced. Operated: **Paddington Basin – Streatham, Old Bus Garage** via Paddington Station, Marble Arch, Oxford Circus, Piccadilly Circus, Trafalgar Square, Whitehall, Westminster Bridge, Kennington, Brixton, Streatham Hill. Operator: **Arriva London South**. Allocation: Brixton Garage 7 VLA (Su-Th), 8 VLA (Fr-Sa). Note: Replaced Paddington Basin – Regent Street section of N15 and Marble Arch – Streatham Garage section of N159.

By 27/28 May 2011: Vehicle-type change to mixed Wrightbus Gemini 2DL integral and Volvo B7TL at Brixton Garage 7 DW/VLA (Su-Th), 8 DW/VLA (Fr-Sa).

15/16 August 2012: Streatham terminus now Streatham Station Hub.

By 8/9 July 2013: Allocation: Brixton Garage 7 DW/DLA (Su-Th), 8 DW/DLA (Fr-Sa). All DW-type by 30/31 August 2013.

Routes introduced 2012

Route N113
29/30 June 2012: Introduced: Operated: **Trafalgar Square, Cockspur Street** (pick-up), **Northumberland Avenue** (set-down) – **Edgware, Bus Station** via Piccadilly Circus, Oxford Circus, Gloucester Place (outbound), Baker Street (inbound), St John's Wood, Swiss Cottage, Hendon Way, Brent Cross, Hendon Central, Watford Way, Mill Hill Circus, Apex Corner, Edgware Way. Operator: **Metroline Travel**. Allocation: Edgware Garage 4 TE nightly. Note: Augmented Trafalgar Square – Finchley Road section of N13. Route N59 had previously operated along the route axis Hendon Way, Brent Cross, Hendon Central, Watford Way to Mill Hill Circus, with onward service via Mill Hill Broadway Station to Edgware and Watford Junction Station, between 20/21 June 1986 and 24/25 September 1987.

Route (N)238
27/28 July – 12/13 August and 29/30 August – 9/10 September 2012: 20 min frequency all-night service introduced over extant daytime route 238 for duration of the Olympic and Paralympic Games. Numbered **(N)238**. Operated: **Stratford – Barking Station** via Plashet Grove and East Ham. Allocation: West Ham Garage 3 TA nightly.

Docklands Buses' Scania OmniCity SOC 7 was photographed at Canning Town Bus Station whilst working an outbound journey on 30 minute frequency route N551 during the early hours of Sunday morning 14 September 2008. *Philip Wallis*

London Buses Night Bus and 24-hour Route Network 30/31 August 2013

Readers seeking greater route detail are recommended to consult
The Greater London Night Bus Map – 27th April 2013
published by Mike Harris

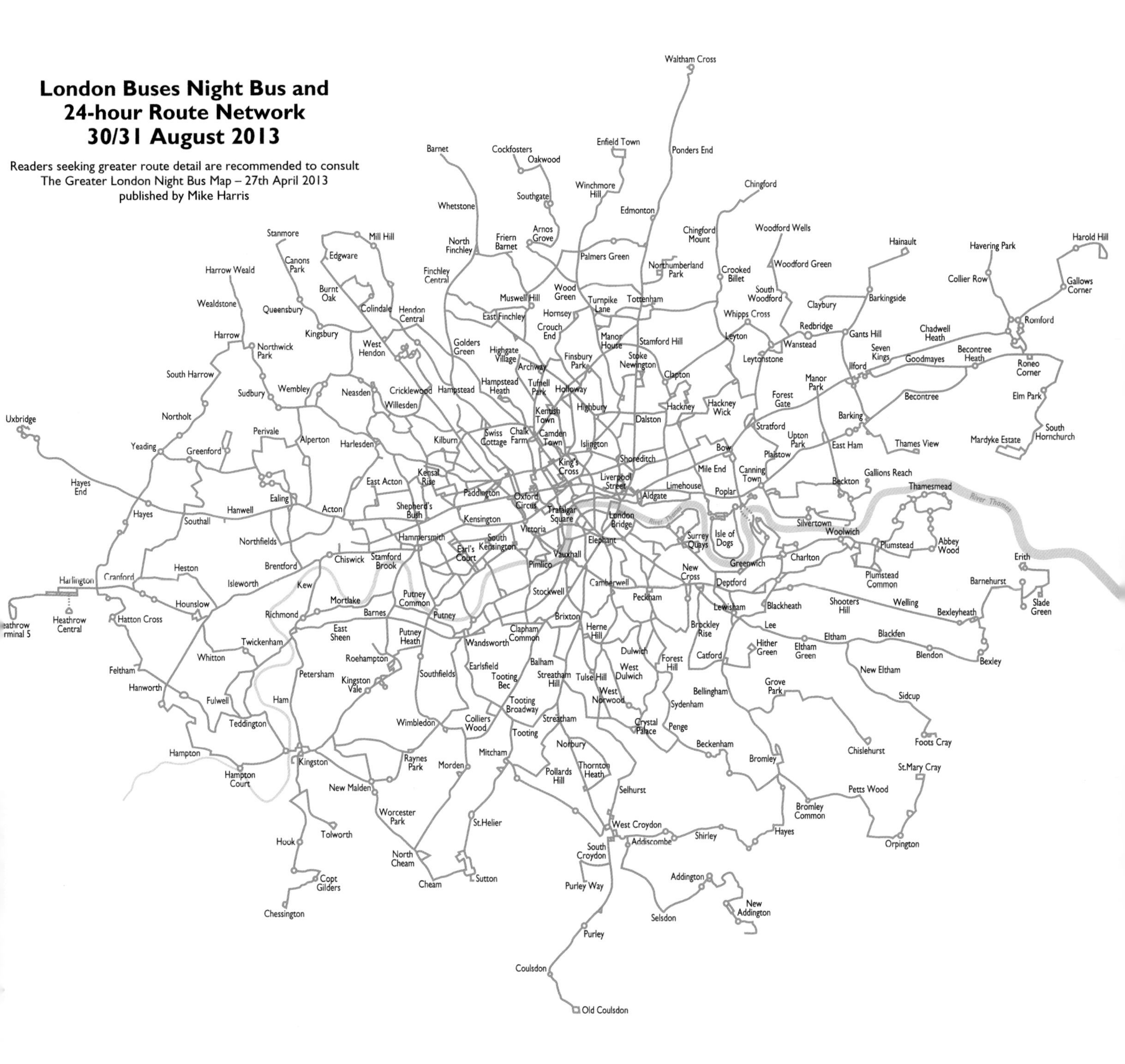

CHAPTER 8
COMMERCIAL SERVICES

Uno's Caetano Nimbus-bodied AD Dart 153 was seen in Edgware Bus Station ready to work the 23.50 route 614N departure on Friday night 23 April 2010. Edgware garage's Volvo B7TL VPL 205 was waiting time to take up service on route N98. *Philip Wallis*

Over the period reviewed in this Volume certain operators have provided commercial all-night bus services around London and its environs which operated outside the remit of London Regional Transport or Transport for London. In some cases, local authority or police funding supported such services.

In the context of this volume only those routes which offered travel opportunities within Greater London, or which operated from towns once reached by London Regional Transport's all-night bus routes, are chronicled.

Central Parking Systems Ltd trading as **Centra Passenger Services**, Unit 18, Heathrow International Trading Estate, Green Lane, Hounslow, TW4 6HB

In 2004 Centra introduced a number of night bus services in Surrey from Staines (N100, N200), Epsom (N300, N400, N500), and Camberley (N600, N700). Only route N200 marginally entered the Greater London area 'on request' to serve Feltham. Centra's entire night bus network was withdrawn after operation on 27/28 August 2005.

Profile: Route N100

6/7 February 2004: Introduced. Operated Friday and Saturday nights only. Journeys departed **Staines (Blue Anchor)** at 23.30, 00.50 and 02.10 to *set down only* at Egham, Royal Holloway College, Virginia Water, Addlestone, Chertsey and Pooley Green as required by passengers who had boarded at Staines. Operated in association with Spelthorpe Crime and Disorder Reduction Partnership.

27/28 August 2005: Last night of operation.

Profile: Route N200

6/7 February 2004: Introduced. Operated Friday and Saturday nights only. Journeys departed **Staines (Blue Anchor and Post Office)** at 00.10, 01.30 and 02.50 to *set down only* at Stanwell, Ashford, Upper Halliford, Shepperton and Laleham as required by passengers who had boarded at Staines. The 02.50 departure also served Feltham 'on request'. Operated in association with Spelthorpe Crime and Disorder Reduction Partnership.

27/28 August 2005: Last night of operation.

FirstGroup plc, 395 King Street, Aberdeen, AB24 5RP

First Capital Connect

Vital engineering work on the Thameslink Programme to increase the capacity of the Thameslink railway line across central London necessitated the closure of that line every night, and on most weekends, for nearly 3½ years between 15 December 2008 and 18 May 2012. A nightly rail replacement bus service was provided between St Pancras International and London Bridge stations from approximately 22.30 to 04.30 on Sunday nights/Monday mornings to Friday nights/Saturday mornings, along with a more limited service on Sunday mornings. All journeys called at Blackfriars station and certain journeys also called at Farringdon and City Thameslink stations. Buses for the service were allocated from First London's Dagenham garage.

This operation was purely a long-term railway replacement service primarily intended to provide a cross-London link for rail passengers making through journeys, such as between Luton Airport Parkway and Gatwick Airport stations. Railway fares applied and TfL bus tickets were not valid on it but the service could have been used by any holder of a valid Oyster card or Travelcard. At weekends, for the duration of the railway line closure, train tickets were also accepted on London Buses' daytime route 17 between St Pancras International and London Bridge stations and between St Pancras International and Blackfriars stations on daytime routes 45 and 63, as well as on all-night route N63.

The Thameslink railway line across central London was re-opened to service from Saturday 19 May 2012 and the nightly rail replacement bus service was withdrawn.

First London's Plaxton President-bodied Dennis Trident TNL 33036 was seen at London Bridge Station working First Capital Connect's night-time railway replacement service to St Pancras International Station in the early hours of Friday morning 15 October 2010. *Philip Wallis*

Travel with Hunny Bus and Coach Services, Langston Road, Loughton, IG10 3TQ.
This operator introduced Monday – Friday daytime bus route 55 between Harlow and Debden via Epping and Loughton on 8 September 2008 and Saturday daytime route L55 between Harlow and Lakeside vis Loughton on 13 September 2008. Complementary evening and night bus route N55 was introduced on Friday night/ Saturday morning 10/11 October 2008 but its service did not last for long, with the N55 being withdrawn after operation on Saturday night/Sunday morning 27/28 December 2008. Since then, the operator has continued with the provision of daytime bus services in west Esssex, along with private hire activities.

Profile: Route N55
10/11 October 2008: Introduced. Operated **Harlow, Bus Station – Harlow, Bus Station** via Potter Street, Tylers Green, North Weald, Epping, Old Orleans Roundabout, Goldings Hill then anticlockwise loop via Church Hill, Loughton, Borders Lane, Debden to Goldings Hill, then Old Orleans Roundabout, Epping, North Weald, Tylers Green, Potter Street.

Frequency: Friday and Saturday nights only = Five journeys: 20.25* ex Church Hill to Harlow, arrive 21.18, then 21.30*, 23.30* and 01.30 ex Harlow, arrive back in Harlow at 22.52, 00.48 and 02.48 respectively, then 03.00 ex Harlow to Debden, Rectory Lane, arrive 03.50. Key: * Also served Epping Station (23.30 journey inbound only).

Allocation = One single-deck bus.

27/28 December 2008: Last night of operation.

London Central Bus Company Ltd, 25 Raleigh Gardens, Mitcham, London, CR4 3NS
London Buses Ltd subsidiary company London Central was a thrusting operator on the all-night bus scene following expansion of the network from 13/14 April 1984 and quickly built-up a strong portfolio of tendered LRT all-night bus routes. The company's enthusiasm for involvement in all-night bus operations extended to operation of the LRT-sponsored quasi-commercial route NX1 between London and Gillingham in Kent upon that route's introduction on 19/20 October 1990. Route NX1's part limited stop service became incorporated into LRT-sponsored normal stopping route N81 (Victoria – Gillingham) from 8/9 October 1993 with continued operation by London Central (see Chapter 6). London Central was acquired by the Go-Ahead group on 18 October 1994.

London Central's commercial all-night bus route operation, which developed to become the most extensive and sustained of such operations during the LRT era, was inaugurated with the introduction of Friday and Saturday nights-only route N60 (Victoria Station – Hemel Hempstead) on 25/26 October 1996. Six months later the N60 was substantially revised to operate between Victoria Station and St Albans.

London Regional Transport withdrew its sponsorship for that section of Gillingham route N81 beyond the Greater London boundary after operation on 17/18 July 1999. One week later London Central commenced commercial all-night bus route operation into Kent with routes N80 (Gravesend) and N82 (Gillingham). These two routes were linked operationally with a revised N60 to give a through, linked service across central London between Watford Junction and Gravesend and Gillingham with an allocation of four buses on Friday and Saturday nights. Commercial fares were applied although holders of LRT Bus Passes and period Travelcards could travel at half price within the Greater London area, subject to a minimum fare of £1.

London Central's commercial all-night bus route operations entered a decline from 12/13 May 2000. Watford Junction route N60 was withdrawn after operation on 27/28 January 2001 whilst Gravesend and Gillingham routes N80/N82 ran for the last time on 18/19 May 2002.

London Central's Optare Spectra SP 8 was photographed on arrival at St Albans City Station on Sunday morning 29 June 1997. *JGS Smith*

Profile: Route N60

25/26 October 1996: Introduced. Operated: **Victoria Bus Station – Hemel Hempstead Bus Station. Limited Stop Service.** *Outbound* via Trafalgar Square*, Piccadilly Circus*, Oxford Circus*, Bond Street Station*, Marble Arch*, Kilburn High Road Station*, Cricklewood Broadway*, Edgware High Street, Stanmore Station, Bushey, Watford (Beechen Grove, Kudos Club), Garston Bus Garage, Abbots Langley, Redmond, Leverstock Green, Adeyfield to Hemel Hempstead. *Inbound either* via Scratchwood Services#, Marble Arch# to Victoria *or* via Adeyfield, Leverstock Green, Scratchwood Services#, Cricklewood Broadway#, Kilburn High Road Station#, Marble Arch#, Hyde Park Corner# to Victoria. Key: * Stopped to pick-up only, # Stopped to set-down only.

Frequency: Friday and Saturday nights only. *Outbound:* Two journeys depart Victoria 00.50 and 03.30, arrive Hemel Hempstead 02.30 and 05.10. *Inbound:* One journey departs Hemel Hempstead 02.35 via Scratchwood Services and Marble Arch to Victoria, arrive 03.25, and one journey departs Hemel Hempstead 05.15 via full inbound route designated above; arrives Victoria 06.10. Allocation: Camberwell Garage = 1 SP (Fr-Sa).

25/26 April 1997: Substantially revised to operate: **Victoria Bus Station – St Albans City Station. Limited Stop Service.** *Outbound* via Trafalgar Square*, Piccadilly Circus*, Oxford Circus*, Bond Street Station*, Portman Square*, Gloucester Place*, North Acton (Western Avenue, Horn Lane), Hanger Lane Station, Alperton Bus garage, Sudbury (Swan), Harrow Bus Station, North Harrow, Hatch End Station, Oxhey Lane, Watford Heath, Bushey Station, Watford (Beechen Grove, Kudos Club), Garston Bus garage, Chiswell Green, St Albans (St Peters Street) to St Albans City Station. *Inbound:* Reverse of outbound journeys *except* after Hanger Lane Station operated via Baker Street Station#, Orchard Street#, Marble Arch#, Hyde Park Corner#, Victoria (Vauxhall Bridge Road)#, to Victoria, Wilton Road. Key: * Stopped to pick-up only, # Stopped to set-down only.

Frequency: Friday and Saturday nights only. *Outbound:* One journey departs Victoria 01.25 to Watford, Beeechen Grove, Kudos Club), arrives 02.30, one journey departs Victoria 03.35 to St Albans City Station, arrives 05.03. *Inbound:* One journey departs Watford, Beechen Grove, Kudos Club at 02.35 to Victoria, Wilton Road, arrives 03.30, and one journey departs St Albans City Station 05.10 to Victoria, Vauxhall Bridge Road, arrives 06.29.

Allocation: Camberwell Garage = 1 SP (Fr-Sa).

7/8 November 1997: Re-allocated to New Cross garage with associated vehicle-type change to 1NV-type Volvo Olympian (Fr-Sa). Reduced running time over section of route between Watford and St Albans. Departure from St Albans City Station retarded to 05.18.

23/24 July 1999: Sections of route Victoria – Trafalgar Square (outbound), Orchard Street – Victoria (inbound) and Watford – St Albans withdrawn. Revised in Watford to terminate at Watford Junction Station. Outbound service revised to commence at Elephant & Castle, inbound service revised to terminate at Baker Street. Now operated: **Limited Stop Service.** *Outbound:* **Elephant & Castle – Watford Junction Station** via Trafalgar Square, Piccadilly Circus, Oxford Circus, Portman Street, Gloucester Place, North Acton (Western Avenue, Horn Lane), Hanger Lane Station, Alperton Bus Garage, Sudbury (Swan), Harrow Bus Station, North Harrow, Hatch End Station, Oxhey Lane, Bushey Station to Watford Junction Station. *Inbound:* **Watford Junction Station – Baker Street** via reverse routeing of outbound journeys as far as Hanger Lane station thence to Baker Street.

Frequency: Friday and Saturday nights only = Hourly (four journeys to/from Watford). Allocation: New Cross Garage (joint routes N60/N80/N82) = 4 NV (Fr-Sa).

Note: Formed linked service at Elephant & Castle with route N80 from Gravesend. Formed linked service at Baker Street with route N80 to Gravesend, with one such journey continuing to Gillingham as route N82.

4/5 February 2000: Camberwell garage allocation introduced, allocation now (joint routes N60/N80/N82 Fr-Sa): Camberwell Garage = 2 NV, New Cross Garage =2 NV.

12/13 May 2000: Reduction in frequency from four to two journeys to/from Watford. One outbound journey formed linked service at Elephant & Castle with inbound route N80 journey from New Cross Gate and one outbound journey formed linked service at Elephant & Castle with inbound route N80 journey from Gravesend. One inbound journey formed linked service at Baker Street with outbound N80 journey to Gravesend, which continued as route N82 to Gillingham, and one inbound journey formed a linked service at Baker Street with outbound N80 journey to Dartford. Allocation (joint routes N60/N80/N82 (Fr-Sa): Camberwell Garage = 1 NV, New Cross Garage = 2 NV.

27/28 January 2001: Last night of operation.

Profile: Route N80

23/24 July 1999: Introduced. **Limited Stop Service.** Operated: *Outbound:* **Baker Street – Gravesend, Clock Tower** via Oxford Circus, Piccadilly Circus, Trafalgar Square, Elephant & Castle, New Cross Gate, Deptford Broadway, Blackheath, Shooters Hill, Welling Corner, Bexleyheath, Crayford, Dartford Station, Swanscombe. *Inbound:* **Gravesend, Clock Tower – Elephant & Castle** via Bexley (Black Prince), Blackheath, Deptford Broadway, New Cross Gate. Frequency: Friday and Saturday nights only = Hourly (four journeys to/three journeys from Gravesend). Allocation: New Cross Garage (joint routes N60/N80/N82) = 4 NV (Fr-Sa only). Formed linked service at Baker Street with route N60 from Watford Junction. One journey formed linked service at Gravesend with route N82 to/from Gillingham. Formed linked service at Elephant & Castle with route N60 to Watford Junction.

4/5 February 2000: Camberwell garage allocation introduced, allocation now (joint routes N60/N80/N82 (Fr-Sa): Camberwell Garage = 2 NV, New Cross Garage = 2 NV.

12/13 May 2000: Numerical joint allocation reduced commensurate with frequency reduction on route N60. Allocation now (joint routes N60/N80/N82 (Fr-Sa): Camberwell Garage = 1 NV, New Cross Garage = 2 NV. Existing frequency maintained.

Note. Number of cross linked journeys formed at Baker Street with route N60 from Watford Junction and at Elephant & Castle with route N60 to Watford Junction reduced from four to two in each case. One journey continued to form linked service at Gravesend with route N82 to/from Gillingham.

2/3 February 2001: Joint allocation involving route N60 dissolved upon the withdrawal of that route. Continued to operate: *Outbound:* **Baker Street – Gravesend, Clock Tower,** *Inbound:* **Gravesend, Clock Tower – Elephant & Castle.** Frequency now: *Outbound:* Baker Street (1 departure) – Trafalgar Square (4 departures) – Gravesend. *Inbound:* 1 journey New Cross Gate – Elephant & Castle, 2 journeys Gravesend – Elephant & Castle, 1 journey Gravesend – New Cross Gate. Allocation now (joint routes N80/N82 (Fr-Sa): Camberwell garage = 1 NV, New Cross garage = 1 NV.

18/19 May 2002: Last night of operation.

Profile: Route N82

23/24 July 1999: Introduced. **Limited Stop Service.** Operated: **Gravesend, Clock Tower – Gillingham, Jeffrey Street** via Higham, Strood, Rochester, Chatham. Frequency: Friday and Saturday nights only = 1 journey. Allocation: See routes N60/N80.

Note. Formed linked service at Gravesend with outbound route N80 journey from Baker Street and with inbound N80 journey to New Cross Gate.

2/3 February 2001: Outbound route N80 journey, which formed linked service at Gravesend with route N82, now originated from Trafalgar Square.

18/19 May 2002: Last night of operation.

Routemaster Travel Ltd trading as **Routemasters**
Routemaster House, 47 Bruce Road, Willesden, London NW10 8RE

Appropriately named operator Routemasters restored RM-type Routemaster bus operation to the Nighters from 24/25 April 1992 with commercially-operated route H29, which provided a weekend-nights travel facility between Hatfield Heath (in Essex) and Trafalgar Square. It seems likely that the 'H' route number prefix was allied to the route's Harlow connection whilst '29' bore a strong numerical affinity with LRT routes 29/N29, with which the H29 shared a lengthy common section of routeing between Wood Green and Cambridge Circus as well as an onward service to Trafalgar Square. Service and route revisions followed until Routemasters' most comprehensive timetable came into force, from 7/8 January 1993, which incorporated a linked through-vehicle service between Watford Junction and Trafalgar Square via Hoddesdon. RMs 1571, 1959 and 2156 were all recorded as having been used by the company prior to the abrupt cessation of its services after operating on 29/30 May 1993.

Profile: Route H29

24/25 April 1992: Introduced. Operated: **Hatfield Heath, White Horse – Trafalgar Square, Pall Mall East** (inbound), **Charing Cross Station** (outbound) via Sheering, Old Harlow, Harlow, Stanstead Abbots, Hundred Acre Estate, Hoddesdon, Broxbourne, Wormley, Cheshunt, Great Cambridge Road, Edmonton, White Hart Lane, Wood Green, Turnpike Lane Station, Manor House, Finsbury Park, Holloway, Camden Town, Hampstead Road, Gower Street (inbound), Tottenham Court Road (outbound), Cambridge Circus, Shaftesbury Avenue, Piccadilly Circus. Frequency: *Inbound:* Saturday evening only one journey depart Hatfield Heath 19.37. *Outbound:* Friday night/Saturday morning and Saturday night/Sunday morning one journey departs Charing Cross Station 02.40. Allocation: 1 RM-type Routemaster.

20/21 August 1992: Section of route between Hatfield Heath and Harlow withdrawn. Projected beyond Harlow Bus Station to Potter Street. Re-routed between Cheshunt and Great Cambridge Road via Waltham Cross. Now operated: **Potter Street, Red Lion – Trafalgar Square, Pall Mall East** (inbound), **Charing Cross Station** (outbound) via Bush Fair, Harlow, Stanstead Abbots, Hundred Acre Estate, Hoddesdon, Broxbourne, Wormley, Cheshunt, Waltham Cross, Great Cambridge Road, Edmonton, White Hart Lane, Wood Green, Turnpike Lane Station, Manor House, Finsbury Park, Holloway, Camden Town, Hampstead Road, Gower Street (inbound), Tottenham Court Road (outbound), Cambridge Circus, Shaftesbury Avenue, Piccadilly Circus. Frequency: *Inbound:* 19.48 ex Potter Street (Fr-Sa), 01.21 ex Hundred Acre Estate (Th-Sa). *Outbound:* 00.01 ex Charing Cross Station to Hundred Acre Estate (Th-Sa), 02.40 ex Charing Cross Station to Hoddesdon with onward service to Potter Street 'by request' (Th-Sa). Allocation: 1 RM.

29/30 October 1992: Two additional journeys introduced. One outbound journey (Th-Sa) continued beyond Hoddesdon as route 624 via Ware, Hertford, Hatfield and St Albans to Watford Junction Station. Allocation: 2 RM.

4/5 December 1992: Inbound route 624 journey introduced on Friday/Saturday evenings from Watford Junction Station to St Margarets which thence continued as route H29 to Trafalgar Square.

5/6 December 1992: Section of route between Potter Street and Hoddesdon withdrawn after operating on this night.

Christmas 1992 and New Year's Eve 1993. Proposed operation on night of 24/25 December 1992 reported, but exact details of service unconfirmed. Definitely operated night of 31 December1992/1 January 1993.

7/8 January 1993: Revised timetable, with cross linked journeys at Hoddesdon between route H29 and route 624 to/from Watford Junction via Hertford, Welwyn Garden City, Hatfield and St Albans. Frequency now: Thursday nights/Friday mornings: *Inbound:* Two journeys depart Hoddesdon 23.43* and 01.25* to Trafalgar Square. *Outbound:* Two journeys depart Charing Cross Station at 01.40# and 02.40# to Hoddesdon. Friday nights/Saturday mornings and Saturday nights/Sunday mornings: *Inbound:* Three journeys depart Hoddesdon 20.20*, 23.43* and 01.25 to Trafalgar Square. One journey departs Great Cambridge Road, Halfway House at 02.45 to Trafalgar Square. *Outbound:* One journey departs Charing Cross Station at 00.01 to Hoddesdon, Hundred Acre Estate, one journey depart Charing Cross Station at 01.40 to Great Cambridge Road, Halfway House, two journeys depart Charing Cross Station at 02.40# and 03.40# to Hoddesdon. Allocation: 2 RM (Th-Sa).

Key. * Journey originated from Watford as route 624, # Journey continued to Watford as route 624.

29/30 May 1993: Last night of operation.

Routemaster Travel's RM 1571 had attracted a full capacity passenger load for its H29 journey to Carterhatch when photographed outside the Waldorf Hotel in Aldwych in the early hours of New Year's Day 1993. *Roy Waterhouse*

ROUTEMASTERS

H29

IMPROVEMENTS TO YOUR
LOCAL NIGHTBUS SERVICE

COMMENCING 20th AUGUST 1992

Front cover of Routemasters timetable.

Sullivan Bus and Coach Ltd trading as **Sullivan Buses**
Deards House, St Albans Road, Potters Bar, EN6 3NE

The concept of Watford area Night Bus routes N1 and N2 originated in 1999 as an element of a strategy to combat crime and disorder in that town centre at night. They were intended to help with the dispersal of clubgoers and other late night revellers, predominantly of the younger generation, some of whom might otherwise engage in loutish behaviour in the early morning hours, particularly at weekends. Route detail was devised by the Passenger Transport Unit of Hertfordshire County Council, who were mindful that London Central's commercially-operated route N60 from Watford Junction Station, which had its frequency increased from 23/24 July 1999 to give four departures on weekend nights, already provided a southbound night service from Watford via Bushey Station and Watford Heath *en route* to central London. The Passenger Transport Unit invited 'expressions of interest' in operating the routes from 20 local bus and coach operators, four of whom responded. A subsidy based contract, initially for a six month period and funded by Hertfordshire County Council, Watford Town Council and Hertfordshire Constabulary, was awarded to Sullivan Buses. Operation of Watford Night Bus routes N1, a unidirectional service which served communities to the north of Watford and Abbots Langley, and N2, to Rickmansworth, was inaugurated on Friday night/Saturday morning 26/27 November 1999. At that time Watford's largest night club, Destiny, was near to the Rickmansworth Road so that both routes started and terminated in that road, with buses standing in the lay-by opposite Watford Town Hall, facing west.

The local taxi trade put up stiff opposition to the introduction of the routes, complaining that public money was being used to undermine their trade, although a shortage of taxis at times during the night had previously exacerbated instances of disorder. Initially, police assistance was given to prevent taxi drivers from obstructing or touting for business from the bus stand, as well as to ensure that orderly behaviour was maintained.

A flat fare of £2 was charged, with both routes departing at the same time. A total of 31 passengers were carried on the first night of operation, just five of whom used route N1. As word spread, passenger numbers increased and loadings increased to around 150 passengers, across both routes, on a Saturday night. Rickmansworth route N2 proved to be the most popular, especially on a Saturday night, when it often carried more than 100 passengers, which required the use of a double decker. Former London Buses Leyland Titans T 85, T 890 and MCW Metrobus M 276 were regularly used on the N2, whilst Routemaster RM 1069 was also sometimes deployed. Route N1, usually operated by former London Buses Dennis Dart DT 4 (G504 GYE), struggled to attract reasonable custom, particularly on Friday nights when journeys often ran empty, and eventually followed a fairly loose route around the North Watford area, according to demand. Initially, a third 'spare' bus was provided as part of the contract in order to give back-up and to cope with any surge in demand. In practice, this bus often supplemented the service on route N2, giving a 30 minute headway.

A 'short-hop' fare of £1 was later introduced. The N1 and N2 also operated an earlier service, which started at around 20.00, on both Christmas Eve 24/25 December 1999 and Millennium Eve 31 December 1999/1 January 2000. These additional journeys, which were operated commercially by Sullivan Buses, were poorly patronised and failed to cover their operating costs. On Millennium Eve the normal flat fare of £2 was applied on journeys up to midnight, with a £4 fare being applied after that time. However, many passengers expected the Watford night bus routes to be free on Millennium Eve, as was the established practice in London.

Additional council support to extend operation of the Watford night bus routes beyond the initial six month period was forthcoming, but during summer 2000 it became clear that further public funding for the routes was in jeopardy. Such support ebbed away, with Hertfordshire County Council funding ceasing after operation after 14 July 2000 and Watford Town Council's support ceasing at the end of August 2000.

Sullivan Buses decided to revise both routes and to run them commercially from 18/19 August 2000. The N1 had its frequency increased to 40 minutes and was shortened to travel directly between North Watford and Garston, as well as within Abbots Langley. The N2 was withdrawn from the Berry Lane Estate in Rickmansworth, where there had been instances of anti-social behaviour, instead being revised to terminate at Rickmansworth Station. The N2 was also re-routed to better serve residential areas in Croxley and Croxley Green and speeded up by being routed directly out of Watford along the Rickmansworth Road. These route changes enabled an enhanced 30 minute frequency to be maintained on the N2 by just one bus. First journeys on each route were revised to start from the Woodside Cinema Complex.

Unfortunately these route changes failed to attract sufficient custom and, with no prospect of further funding from the public purse, Sullivan Buses reluctantly withdrew routes N1 and N2 after operation on Saturday night/Sunday morning 14/15 October 2000. The company took the view that Rickmansworth route N2 was viable, and had potential for growth, but the operator was not willing to risk a lone member of staff working for most of the night without additional support.

Profile: Route N1
26/27 November 1999: Introduced. Operated: **Watford, Rickmansworth Road – Watford, Rickmansworth Road.** Unidirectional service via Town Centre, Watford Junction Station, North Watford, Bushey Mill Lane, Meriden, Garston, Horseshoe Lane, Abbots Langley (Tibbs Hill Road, High Street, Hazlewood Lane, Upper Highway, South Way), Leavesden, Legatts Way, The Harebreaks, North Watford. Frequency: Friday and Saturday nights only = Four departures at 00.15, 01.15, 02.15. and 03.15 (did not serve Watford Junction Station). Allocation = One single-deck bus.

Note: On night of 26/27 November 1999 only, route terminated at Watford, Beechen Grove.

24/25 December 1999 and 31 December/1 January 2000: On these nights only, an hourly frequency commercially-operated evening service ran with departures from Watford at 20.15, 21.15, 22.15, 23.15, after which the contracted service commenced at 00.15.

18/19 August 2000: Intermediate routeing revised to operate via Watford Junction Station, North Watford, St Albans Road, Garston, Horseshoe Lane, Abbots Langley (Tibbs Hill Road, High Street, Trowley Rise, Langley Lane), Sheepcot Lane, Woodside Cinema Complex, Garston, St Albans Road, North Watford. Frequency: Friday and Saturday nights only = Six departures at 23.59, 00.45, 01.30, 02.10, 02.50 (did not serve Abbots Langley), 03.15 (did not serve Watford Junction Station and after Woodside continued in service to terminate at Garston, Three Horseshoes public house). Additional journey at 23.45 from Woodside Cinema Complex to Watford. Allocation = One single-deck bus.

14/15 October 2000: Last night of operation.

Profile: Route N2
26/27 November 1999: Introduced. Operated: **Watford, Rickmansworth Road – Rickmansworth, Berry Lane Estate, Oakfield** via Town Centre and Whippendell Road (both outbound only), Rickmansworth Road (inbound only), Croxley Station, New Road, Croxley Green, Rickmansworth High Street and Rickmansworth Station (both outbound only), Park Road (inbound only), Uxbridge Road, Church Lane, Tudor Way, Berry Lane.

Frequency: Friday and Saturday nights only = Four outbound departures at 00.15, 01.15, 02.15 and 03.15. Four inbound departures at 00.38, 01.38, 02.38 and 03.38.

Allocation = One double-deck bus.

24/25 December 1999: On this night only, an hourly frequency commercially-operated service ran between Watford Junction Station and Rickmansworth Station, with outbound departures from Watford Junction Station at 20.10, 21.10, 22.10, 23.10 and inbound departures from Rickmansworth Station at 20.35, 21.35, 22.35 and 23.35 (to Watford Town Centre only). The contracted service commenced at 00.15.

31 December 1999/1 January 2000: On this night only, a commercially-operated service was combined with the contracted service to give a scheduled 30 minute frequency evening and night-time service over a route extended to commence and terminate at Watford Junction Station. Frequency: *Outbound* from Watford Junction Station at 20.40, then every 30 minutes until 05.10, *Inbound* from Rickmansworth, Berry Lane Estate at 21.06, then every 30 minutes until 05.36.

18/19 August 2000: Revised to operate: **Watford, Rickmansworth Road – Rickmansworth Station** via Rickmansworth Road, Croxley Station, Croxley Green (outbound via Barton Way, Baldwins Lane, The Green, inbound via Watford Road), Rickmansworth High Street (outbound only), Park Road (inbound only). Frequency: Friday and Saturday nights only: *Outbound* = 30 minutes between 00.15 and 03.15, *Inbound* = 30 minutes between 00.27 and 03.27 (this last journey continued in service beyond Watford via North Watford to Garston, Three Horseshoes public house). Additional journey at 23.59 from Woodside Cinema Complex via North Watford to Watford, where it formed the 00.15 departure to Rickmansworth. Allocation = One double-deck bus.

14/15 October 2000: Last night of operation.

UniversityBus Ltd trading as **Uno**, Gypsy Moth Avenue, Hatfield, AL10 9BS

With origins in the 1970s providing transport for students and staff at the then-Hatfield Polytechnic, UniversityBus has developed into a substantial operator of bus services in central Hertfordshire. Uno's bus services continue to meet the needs of students and staff at the University of Hertfordshire and have also expanded to include commercial operations.

A few, largely daytime, Uno routes have entered the Greater London area under TfL London Local Service Agreements or Permits and continue to do so under TfL London Service Permits. The 614N was one such route, introduced on 30 September/1 October 2009. It provided three return journeys between Hatfield, University of Hertfordshire Campus and Edgware Bus Station on Wednesday, Thursday and Friday nights, during term time only, with departures from Hatfield Campus at 22.21, 23.31 and 00.21 and corresponding return journeys from Edgware Bus Station at 22.50, 23.50 and 00.50. The earliest journey from Hatfield Campus originated at Uno's Hatfield garage at 22.10 and the last journey from Edgware continued past the campus to terminate at the garage at 01.23. The service provided a convenient connectional facility at Edgware Station with late trains on the Underground's Northern Line. Route 614N operated for the last time on 28/29 May 2010 (end of 2009/10 academic year at the University of Hertfordshire) and was not subsequently reinstated.

Arriva the Shires and Essex's tri-axle 63 seat Van Hool T917 Acron 4384 was photographed at Green Line 757's outbound coach stop in Gloucester Place at 04.15 on Friday morning 24 February 2012. *Philip Wallis*

All-night coach services

A considerable number of bus and coach services enter, or operate within, Greater London under London Service Permits issued by Transport for London. Such services, most of which operate in the daytime only, are not part of the TfL network but local journeys within London can be made on many of them. TfL fares and ticket availability, such as use of Oyster card or Travelcard, do not generally apply on these services. Six coach services offer opportunities to make night-time, as well as daytime, journeys entirely within Greater London. Such services in operation at 30/31 August 2013 comprised:

Arriva the Shires and Essex Ltd, 487 Dunstable Road, Luton, LU4 8DS

Green Line Route 757: Victoria, Buckingham Palace Road - Luton

A night-time service, comprising five outbound departures from Victoria between midnight and 05.30 and three inbound departures from Luton Airport at 00.15, 03.20 and 04.20, was added to existing daytime Green Line route 757 from Thursday 1 July 1999. The night-time frequency was increased to hourly from 23 January 2005 and further increased to 30 minutes from 1 May 2005. In original form most 757 journeys were routed through Luton town centre to and from the airport. The service was re-routed from 17 February 2008 so that the 757 operated directly between Victoria and Luton Airport with some journeys continuing to Luton town centre. The night-time frequency was boosted on both 8 February 2009 and 21 May 2010 after which the outbound service from Victoria ran every 20/30 minutes and the inbound service at 30/60 minute intervals.

A blow was dealt to Green Line 757 from 1 May 2013 when Abertis, the Spanish-owned contractor-operator of Luton Airport, revoked the 757's right of access to the airport in favour of new National Express route A1. The 757 maintained its then-existing frequency service for a further two months but coaches had to call at Eaton Green Road long-stay car park on Luton Airport's periphery from where a shuttle service connected with the airport.

The 757 was re-routed away from Luton Airport from midnight on 30 June 2013 to terminate in Luton town centre with a shuttle service connection to and from the airport. The night-time service frequency was much reduced from that date to comprise departures from Victoria at midnight, 01.00, 02.30, 03.30 and 04.00 – after which the 757 ran every 30 minutes. Inbound departures from Luton town centre were at 01.05, 02.05 and 04.05. The 757 will terminate at the new Bus Interchange at Luton Station when it opens and it is planned that the route's night-time element will run hourly from that time.

Fare stages within Greater London are at Buckingham Palace Road, Hyde Park Corner, Marble Arch, Gloucester Place (outbound) or Baker Street (inbound), St John's Wood, Finchley Road 02 Centre, Hendon Way and Brent Cross. Single fares allow intermediate travel between any of those fare stages whilst return fares to Victoria are available from Brent Cross, Hendon Way and Finchley Road.

National Express Ltd, Birmingham Coach Station, Digbeth, Birmingham, B5 6DD

Route A1: Victoria Coach Station – Luton Airport

This 24-hour service was introduced from 1 May 2013. The night-time outbound service from Victoria runs at between 10 and 60 minute intervals. The inbound night-time service from Luton Airport operates every 30 minutes. Route A1 has a fare stage between Victoria and Golders Green.

Route A3: Victoria Coach Station – Gatwick Airport, North Terminal.

This 24-hour service was introduced from 5 December 2011. The night-time element comprises an hourly frequency outbound service from Victoria throughout the night, starting at 00.30. The first night-time inbound journey departs from Gatwick Airport, North Terminal, at 00.15 but there is then a gap in service until the next departure at 02.00, after which an hourly frequency is maintained. Intermediate stops, within the Greater London Area, are at Vauxhall, Stockwell, Streatham, Mitcham, Sutton and Belmont. The National Express website indicates that fares are available for intermediate travel between any of the London area stops on the A3's line of route.

Route A6: Victoria Coach Station – Stansted Airport.

This 24-hour service was introduced on Sunday 2 April 2000 as a constituent route of National Express' contemporary Airlinks network. The service was branded as 'Airbus' and worked by double-deck Volvo Olympians. In original form, within London, the A6 travelled along the Finchley Road and Hendon Way to reach the North Circular Road, calling *en route* at Hendon Central Station. One year later it was re-routed, from 2 April 2001, to travel along the the full length of Finchley Road to reach the North Circular Road, at which time a stop at Golders Green Bus and Tube Station replaced that at Hendon Central. From the same date, the A6 absorbed the service of route A7, which had operated between Victoria and

Between 3 November 2003 and 21 May 2006 outbound journeys on National Express routes A6 and A7 were routed to pick-up at stop 1 in Bulleid Way one minute after leaving Victoria Coach Station. This was in response to competition with Terravision's 24/7 non-stop coach service between Victoria and Stansted Airport which terminated at Bulleid Way. National Express' Plaxton Panther-bodied Volvo B7R V42 was seen in Bulleid Way in the early hours of Sunday morning 19 September 2004. *Philip Wallis*

Stansted Airport via Stratford. The night-time A6 frequency ranged from 30 to 60 minutes in both directions of travel. Double-deck operation was superseded by single-deck coaches around March 2002 and the Airbus branding was replaced by the familiar white National Express livery, at that time adorned with 'National Express Airport Coach Services' branding, from 7 April 2003.

From the night of 2/3 November 2003, certain night-time journeys were routed via Stratford, designated by revived route number A7, and the frequency of the A6's night-time service via Golders Green became irregular, ranging from 15 to 40 minutes outbound from Victoria, with inbound departures from Stansted Airport at 00.15, 00.45, 01.15 and 01.45, followed by a long gap in service until 04.30, although route A7 departures left Stansted Airport bound for Victoria during this interval.

A profound change to the operation of route A6 occurred from 21 May 2006 when its service was revised to no longer call at Golders Green Bus Station, even though it remained routed along the Finchley Road. Instead, a daytime and part-evening service between Golders Green and Stansted Airport was provided by newly-introduced route A4. However, during the late evening and part of the night, when the revised A6 did not operate, this new route A4 was extended to Victoria, thus maintaining a service between Victoria and Stansted Airport, which called at Golders Green, at such times. Route A4 departures from Victoria operated at 15 to 30 minute intervals between 21.10 and 02.25 nightly whilst A4 joureys left Stansted Airport at 10 to 30 minute intervals between 20.00 and 04.00 nightly. Timings were modified from 21 January 2008 to give an earlier-starting A4 service, with first departures at 20.10 from Victoria and at 19.20 from Stansted Airport.

Route A4 was withdrawn after operating on 1 June 2008 and route A6 was revised, from 2 June 2008, to once again form a 24-hour service between Victoria and Stansted Airport via Golders Green. The current night-time service comprises 30 minute frequency outbound departures from Victoria between midnight and 03.00, after which time the frequency increases to 15 minutes. Inbound night-time departures leave Stansted Airport at 15 minute intervals between midnight and 02.00, then at 30 minute intervals until 04.00, after which time the frequency increases to 20 minutes. The route has a fare stage between Victoria and Golders Green.

The City of Oxford Motor Services Ltd, Cowley House, Watlington Road, Oxford, OX4 6GA.
Route X90: Victoria Coach Station – Oxford, Gloucester Green.
The X90 was developed from the Oxford Bus Company's established daytime and evening CityLink 190 motorway express service which linked the two cities. Additional evening journeys were added to the 190's schedule from 6 June 1993, including a later last departure from Victoria at 01.20 nightly. The Oxford Bus Company was acquired by the Go-Ahead group on 1 March 1994. Under new management, the 190 was rebranded as CityLink X90 just over one year later, from 9 April 1995. At this time a stop was introduced at Hillingdon Station, on the line the X90's westerly approach to London along Western Avenue and the elevated Westway. The last departure from Victoria was further retarded to 02.10 from 31 October 1995, coincident with which date all outbound departures from Victoria, between 20.40 and 02.10, became routed via Trafalgar Square, with a pick-up point in Cockspur Street, for the benefit of those returning from a night out in the West End.

The X90 became a 24-hour service from 30 November 1997, with 30 minute frequency night-time outbound departures from Victoria between 00.10 and 02.40, after which an hourly frequency prevailed until 06.40. Evening and night-time outbound journeys from Victoria between 21.10 and 05.40 were routed via Trafalgar Square nightly. The inbound night-time service from Oxford operated hourly.

The frequencies of both the inbound and outbound night-time services were reduced to become two hourly for much of the night from 15 October 2000 and the diversion of outbound evening and night-time journeys via Trafalgar Square ceased from 2 September 2002. The Sunday to Thursday night-time X90 service was withdrawn from 29 January 2006. A full Friday and Saturday night-time service contined to operate for a further 14 months before being modified, from 1 April 2007, to give a last outbound departure from Victoria at 02.30 and a last inbound departure from Oxford at 00.30. Sunday to Thursday night-time operations were altered, from the date, to have the similar last journey times. This level of night-time service has been maintained by the X90 since that date, with 30 minute frequency outbound departures from Victoria from midnight up until 02.30, followed by a four hour gap until the daytime service starts at 06.30. The last inbound departure leaves Oxford at 00.30, after which there is a four hour gap in service until the first daytime journey at 04.30.

The X90 has been re-branded three times since the service's inception as CityLink X90. It became designated the 'Oxford Express' from 21 May 2000, which was tweaked to become 'Oxford Espress' in March 2004. Most recently, from 5 March 2012, the service has been prominently branded as 'X90 Oxford – London' and worked by a fleet of refurbished Plaxton Panther-bodied Volvo B12B coaches sporting a distinctive silver and grey livery. Although the X90 has intermediate stops in Buckingham Palace Road, at Marble Arch and in Marylebone Road (outbound) or Baker Street (inbound), the only fares available entirely within the Greater London Area are to and from Hillingdon Station.

Thames Transit Ltd, Horspath Road, Cowley, Oxford, OX4 2RY
Oxford Tube: Victoria, Buckingham Palace Road – Oxford, Gloucester Green.
The Oxford Tube was introduced by Harry Blundred's Thames Transit as a daytime and evening service on Saturday 7 March 1987, in competition with the the Oxford Bus Company's CityLink 190. The Oxford Tube approached London via Western Avenue and the West Cross Route, Shepherd's Bush and Notting Hill Gate to reach its original London terminus at Marble Arch. Its service was extended to Victoria, Grosvenor Gardens on 23 November 1987. The frequency of the daytime and evening service was progressively increased and the last outbound departure from Victoria was retarded to leave at 01.05 from 13 October 1991.

The Oxford Tube became a 24-hour service from 4 April 1993 when an hourly frequency night-time service was introduced. The night-time service was quickly enhanced, from 31 October 1993, to give 30 minute frequency outbound departures from London up until 03.10, after which an hourly headway was applied until 06.10. The inbound service from Oxford retained an hourly night-time frequency. Thames Transit was acquired by the Stagecoach group on 21 July 1997. The route was extended at Victoria, from 20 September 2003, to terminate in Buckingham Palace Road, close to both Victoria Coach Station and the termini of Green Line and other long distance coach operators' services in Buckingham Palace Road and Bulleid Way. The current night-time schedule comprises a 30 minute frequency outbound service from Victoria between 00.05 and 03.05 (02.05 on Sunday nights), after which an hourly headway prevails until 06.05. The inbound service from Oxford operates hourly during the night. The operational fleet comprises twin-deck Van Hool Astromega coaches, new in 2009.

Fare stages, within the Greater London Area, are at Hillingdon Station, Shepherd's Bush, Notting Hill Gate, Marble Arch and Victoria, former fare stages at South Greenford and Park Royal having been discontinued at earlier dates. Single fares allow intermediate travel between any of those fare stages whilst return fares, as well as 12 trip, 4 week, 13 week and annual season tickets, are available between Hillingdon and London.

APPENDIX 1

Fare Policies

London Regional Transport

London Regional Transport assumed operating powers from 29 June 1984 and initially maintained the fares policy of its predecessor, the London Transport Executive, with parity of daytime and all-night bus fares over equivalent fare zones. In the penultimate month of that Executive's existence, the night-time Railair Link service had been introduced, on 13/14 May 1984, with a 40p fare from Euston to Victoria, whilst journeys to Heathrow Airport cost £2.50, the same as the daytime Airbus service. Travelcards were not valid on the Railair Link.

The Inter-Station Route, which ran non-stop between main line railway termini, had maintained a flat-fare policy since LPTB operation began on 1 October 1936. The adult fare had progressively increased from an original cost of one shilling to £1.00 when the route operated for the last time on 25/26 April 1985. From the following night, elements of the Inter-Station Route's service were incorporated into new routes N50 and N51 which were stopping services (on request) on which ordinary fares were applied. LRT's contemporary publicity material highlighted the fact that the N50/N51s fares – 25p, 40p, or 55p, according to distance travelled – were considerably cheaper than £1.00 flat fare which had previously applied on the Inter-Station Route and that Travelcards – not valid on the Inter-Station Route – could now be used. The Railair Link service was incorporated into new route N56 coincident with the introduction of routes N50/N51 on 26/27 April 1985. The N56's section of route between King's Cross and Hyde Park Corner was fully integrated into the all-night bus network and had the same stopping and fare arrangements as routes N50/N51, with which it interworked, to provide a combined hourly frequency. Journeys to and from Heathrow Airport maintained a premium fare of £3.00, the same as the contemporary daytime Airbus fare, and Travelcards remained invalid over the N56's non-stop sections of route to and from Heathrow Airport.

London Regional Transport brought in a hefty increase to all-night bus route fares, of up to 67%, from Sunday morning 10 January 1988. This increase was considerably higher than that which was applied to daytime bus routes at the same time and created a premium fares structure for the Nighters. In contrast to London Transport Executive's earlier attempt, in 1972, to impose premium fares on the Nighters, London Regional Transport's application of such fares proved to be enduring. The nature of the Nighters, as well as their passenger profile, had changed markedly between 1972 and 1988, by which latter date burgeoning demand, particularly at weekends, had encouraged LRT to plan the introduction of many more all-night bus routes. Separate fare scales were applied to those sections of all-night bus routes which operated beyond the Greater London boundary to destinations in Essex, Hertfordshire, Kent and Surrey.

Use of the Travelcard, which had originally been introduced in weekly, monthly and annual forms on 22 May 1983, became more extensive when a One-Day Travelcard went on sale in 1984. The Travelcard was joined by a period Capitalcard, first available from 6 January 1985, which additionally allowed travel on British Rail trains in the Greater London area. From their inceptions both the Travelcard and Capitalcard had allowed travel on all-night bus routes until 03.00 on the day following the date of issue. The Capitalcard was subsumed by the Travelcard, with validity extended to British Rail in the Greater London area, from 8 January 1989 but from that date use of the One-Day Travelcard on all-night bus routes was revoked, although period Travelcards continued to remain valid on the Nighters. A Weekend Travelcard was introduced from 10 May 1996 which was also valid on the Nighters during the night following the first day of validity.

From Saturday morning 6 February 1993, daytime route 207 fares and conditions became applied beyond Shepherd's Bush to all outbound route N89 journeys that were timed to arrive at Uxbridge at 06.00 or later. From 21/22 May 1993, daytime route 23 fares and conditions became applied to the last inbound journey route N23 journey over its section of route between Ladbroke Grove and Aldwych (daily) or Liverpool Street Station (Monday to Friday mornings). From 14/15 July 1995, daytime fares and conditions (applicable to routes 25 and 86, according to section of route) became applied from Aldgate Station and beyond to outbound route N25 journeys timed to depart Aldgate at 05.58, 06.18 and 06.35 bound for Romford Station via Chadwell Heath.

Daytime fares started to be charged from 04.30 on all N-prefixed all-night bus routes from Saturday morning 18 May 1996. This applied also to all-night route journeys scheduled before 04.30 if the bus was running late.

London Regional Transport brought in its last fares increase from 9 January 2000 with Night Bus fares costing up to 50% more than equivalent zonal daytime fares, as detailed:

<u>Zone</u>

Including Zone 1 (Central) : £1.00 (daytime), £1.50 (Night Bus)

Outside Zone 1 : £0.70 (daytime), £1.00 (Night Bus)

Transport for London

Transport for London's assumption of powers from 3 July 2000 heralded, *inter alia*, a massive expansion of the all-night bus route network, particularly during the first three years or so of its existence. In order to encourage use of the Nighters, validity of the One-Day Travelcard (and other one-day cards and passes) was extended to all N-prefixed all-night bus routes from midnight on 18/19 November 2000, after which date such cards could be used up to 04.30 in the morning on the day following their date of issue.

Much of TfL's all-night bus route expansion has been achieved with the introduction of 24-hour 'seamless' services and the prolonged maintenance of separate daytime and all-night fare structures would have confused passengers and increased operational difficulties. Accordingly, separate fare

The Inter-Station route was replaced by King's Cross Station to Ladbroke Grove routes N50 (westbound journeys) and N51 (eastbound journeys) from 26/27 April 1985. Shepherd's Bush garage's MCW Metrobus M 960 was seen outside the National Gallery in Trafalgar Square at 5 o'clock on Sunday morning 21 July 1985. Route N51 was absorbed into route N50 from 20/21 June 1986 when the N50 became a bidirectional service. *JGS Smith*

structures for daytime and all-night bus routes were replaced from 29/30 September 2001 when Night Bus fares were reduced to £1.00 (Zone 1) or £0.70 (outside Zone 1), which brought parity between Night Bus and daytime fares.

Development of smart card technology for fare payment had been initiated by London Regional Transport, as the LT Prestige Ticket Project, on 14 August 1998, and came to fruition when TfL launched selected sale of Oyster cards to the public on 26 June 2003. Validity of Oyster cards was extended to include TfL's bus network from 16 May 2004.

A 100% differential between cash fares and 'Pay As You Go' Oyster cards when used on the buses, created with the fares rise of 2 January 2007 when the cash fare became £2 and the Oyster card fare £1, was intended to encourage take-up of Oyster cards and clearly has succeeded. Concessionary Passes have also contributed to the great reduction in cash fares taken on London's buses. The London Freedom Pass for the elderly and disabled was introduced on 1 April 1998. The English National Concessionary Bus Pass was launched on 1 April 2006 but one of its conditions, which restricted use to between the hours of 09.30 and 23.00 on Mondays to Fridays, meant that it could only be used on London's Nighters at weekends. As a result of a pledge made by London's Mayor, Boris Johnson, time restrictions on the use of both the London Freedom Pass and the English National Concessionary Bus Pass on London's buses were lifted on 1 April 2009, from which date they could be used at anytime of the day or night. Free travel for the over 60s was introduced from 1 November 2012. 'Wave and Pay' contactless payment by credit, debit and charge card was launched on all TfL buses from 13 December 2012.

Despite the sea-change in methods of payment across TfL's network it was still possible, at the date of writing this book, to board a London bus, pay a cash fare to the driver and be issued with a bus ticket. The contemporary cash fare of £2.40, effective from 2 January 2013, for a journey of any distance on the bus boarded, whilst expensive for short hops, represented very good value on London's lengthier all-night bus routes. The Oyster card 'Pay As You Go' fare of £1.40 for such a journey was better value still.

Ash Grove garage's Leyland Titan T 420 was seen departing from Euston Bus Station at 04.57 on Monday morning 6 July 1987 working the once nightly outbound route N56 journey to Heathrow Airport. This journey originated at Paddington Station and was scheduled to arrive at Euston Station nine minutes earlier to provide a connection with an overnight train from Liverpool and Manchester. *JGS Smith*

The passenger beside the recently installed ticket machine at Embankment Station had boarded Upton Park Garage's TransBus Trident ALX400 17838 expecting to pay his fare to the driver. The driver had directed the passenger to the ticket machine and patiently waited for him to purchase a ticket and re-board the bus before continuing with this N50 journey on Sunday morning 20 June 2004. *Philip Wallis*

The core service of route N23 operated hourly between Aldwych and Ealing Broadway Station when this view of Westbourne Park garage's MCW Metrobus M 1054 was taken at 00.43 on Saturday morning 29 January 1994 at Charing Cross Station. *Philip Wallis*

Cashless methods of payment have done much to reduce bus boarding times and speed up services. When this view of Stagecoach East London's Alexander ALX400-bodied Dennis Trident TA 67 was taken in Duncannon Street on Sunday morning 14 July 2002 many passengers paid cash fares on London's buses with resultant queues to pay the driver and long dwell times at bus stops. *Philip Wallis*

A kerbside ticket machine may be seen to the right of Arriva London North's hybrid-powered Wrightbus Eclipse Gemini 2-bodied Volvo B5LH HV 65 when photographed at route N253's Tottenham Court Road outbound pick-up stop on Wednesday morning 10 July 2013. It was still a requirement for cash paying passengers to buy a ticket from a kerbside ticket machine before boarding a bus in central London at 30/31 August 2013. *Philip Wallis*

APPENDIX 2

Changing the Clock

The practice of putting the clocks forward to British Summer Time (BST), one hour ahead of Greenwich Mean Time (GMT), in the spring and backwards one hour to GMT in the autumn was first adopted in Britain and Ireland on 21 May 1916, during the First World War. It has been maintained over successive years, with the exception of a period during the Second World War when clocks were moved forward by two hours, as well as between 1968 and 1971 when year-round BST applied.

British Summer Time allows more daylight during the evening and is considered to benefit the retail trade, tourist industry, sporting activities and outdoor pursuits generally. The clock change is made on a Sunday morning, at 01.00 GMT in the spring (forward to 02.00 BST) and at 02.00 BST in the autumn (back to 01.00 GMT). The moment of change can sometimes complicate the operation of time-sensitive computers and machinery, as well as cause disruption to timekeeping and schedules.

The London General Omnibus Company, London Passenger Transport Board and London Transport (Executive and Board) always operated services on the night of any clock change as if the clock had not changed. In the spring all-night bus routes ran to GMT throughout the night, which had the potential to give an over-provision of service since daytime routes started their service at BST timings. The opposite effect arose in the autumn, with a one hour gap in service provision, since all-night routes ran to BST throughout the night whilst daytime routes started their service at GMT timings. No great problems arose with Special Night Journeys, all finished their service by 02.30 or earlier.

The overlap of all-night and daytime services in the spring caused no great difficulties for passengers, provided that they had not put their personal clocks or watches forward before setting out on a night bus journey. The one hour gap in service provision on the night of the autumn clock change did create a difficulty for passengers. This gap was theoretically covered by 'local arrangement' made by any appropriate night route's garage. However, that delightful turn of phrase, always a good coverall for senior management when faced with an ambiguous situation, gave scope for wide interpration or misinterpretation, action or inaction.

In fact, for many years the scale of the problem was not that great. Prior to the Second World War, only route 298, of the mainstream all-night bus routes, ran a Saturday night and Sunday morning service, between Romford Garage and Aldgate. The Inter-Station Route featured Saturday night and Sunday morning upon its reinstatement from 20/21 December 1943 and a handful of other Nighters gained a service on that night of the week after the Second World War. However, most Nighters continued to operate 'Saturday night/Sunday morning Excepted'. The same crews usually worked all-night bus routes and would have got to recognise their regular passengers, so it is possible that crews would have advised their regulars about special arrangements, if any, for clock-change nights. Those passengers who did shift work were likely to have started and finished their shifts at the 'old' time, so were probably ready to travel as if the clocks had not changed. All the routes involved had irregular frequencies, so it would have been very difficult to arrange additional crew cover.

The scope for potential problems would have increased upon the adoption of universal Saturday night and Sunday morning operation across the all-night bus route network from 29/30 October 1983, and intensified further as that network entered a sustained period of exponential growth, following its expansion from 13/14 April 1984. However, adjustments, if any, to all-night bus route's schedules on clock-change nights continued to be made by 'local arrangement' throughout the entire London Regional Transport era, between 29 June 1984 and 2 July 2000.

Transport for London assumed powers from 3 July 2000. The long established practice of covering clock-change nights by 'local arrangement' has since been progressively replaced by a contract process which, *inter alia*, requires contractor-operators to prepare specific schedules to be applied on clock-change nights. The need to formalise arrangements has been partially driven by the number of buses and drivers which link between daytime and all-night bus routes and the growth of the number of 24-hour service routes. The development of iBus technology now allows TfL to monitor most aspects of 'on the road' operations and the potential to apply penalties to operators for any unplanned variances.

An example of how one operator, Metroline, scheduled additional buses to cover the autumn clock-change night in 2004 was contained in *The London Bus* issue 483 (November 2004) and is reproduced by kind permission of David Stewart, Managing Editor.

'.....how do bus operators cope with the movement of our clocks in the Spring and Autumn? And especially the latter, when the clocks go back and we gain an extra hour in the night. For an insight we look at one company, Metroline, to observe how they dealt with this matter this year.

In order to maintain the advertised service, with the 01.00 to 02.00 time period occurring twice, for the night of Saturday 30th October / morning of Sunday 31st October (2004), Metroline used a total of nine more buses than usual on its night services as follows:

One extra bus on each of routes N5 (Edgware Garage), N20, (N)24, N43, N98 (Willesden Garage), (N)134, (N)214, (N)271 and (N)274. These extras used the next number in the running number sequence, except for the N20 where 891 was not available so 878 was used. There were also some odd buses swapped between routes, so unusual running numbers appeared on some routes (for example AC734 (from route (N)6) on the route N52).'

In 2004 the normal weekend nights allocation to route N98 (Holborn – Stanmore Station and second-time use of this route number) comprised eight buses from Edgware garage and five from Willesden garage. Having entered service in that same year, Metroline's TransBus President-bodied Volvo B7TL VP 533 was displaying Willesden garage's running number 751 in its windscreen when photographed in Oxford Street on Sunday morning 18 July 2004. *Philip Wallis*

Demand for night-time travel has led to progressive frequency increases on many routes. Route N73 operated a nightly hourly frequency service between Victoria Station and Walthamstow Central Station upon the introduction of a regular service from 22/23 September 1989. The N73's frequency has been progressively increased such that it operated a 30 minute Sunday to Thursday night and 12 minute Friday and Saturday night frequency service between the same termini at 30/31 August 2013. Tottenham garage's Wrightbus Eclipse Gemini-bodied Volvo B7TL VLW 119 was photographed heading up a line of Night Buses in New Oxford Street during the early hours of Saturday morning 24 April 2010. Route N73 was re-allocated to Stamford Hill garage from 2/3 September 2011 coincident with the start of its progressive conversion to operation by HV-type hybrid-powered Volvo B5LH buses. *Philip Wallis*

Route N5 operates in parallel with the Edgware branch of the Underground's Northern Line and provides an overnight service when the Underground is closed. Holloway garage running number 802 indicated that Metroline's TransBus President-bodied Trident TPL 293 was one of eleven buses allocated at weekends to maintain the N5's then-15 minute frequency service between Trafalgar Square and Edgware Station when photographed at Tottenham Court Road Station in the early hours of Saturday morning 7 June 2003.
Philip Wallis

BIBLIOGRAPHY

Harris, M. *The Greater London Bus Map, various editions including Night Bus Maps dated 19 March 2011, 28 April 2012 and 27 April 2013* (M. Harris, various dates)

London Historical Research Group. *London Bus and Underground Timetables* (The Omnibus Society, 1998)

Weinreb, Ben, and Hibbert, Christopher. *The London Encyclopaedia* (Macmillan Reference Books, 1995)

Chronicle of Britain (Chronicle Communications Ltd, 1992)

London Operators' Route Working Indexes (The PSV Circle, London Omnibus Traction Society, various dates)

London Vehicle Type Histories (Joint The Omnibus Society and The PSV Circle, The PSV Circle, various dates)

Journals and Magazines (Various dates according to title)

Buses (Ian Allan Publishing Ltd)

London Bus, The (London Omnibus Traction Society)

London Bus Magazine (London Omnibus Traction Society)

London Historical Research Group Bulletin (The Omnibus Society)

Omnibus Magazine, The (The Omnibus Society)

ALL-NIGHT BUS ROUTE NUMBER CHRONOLOGY AND INDEX 13/14 APRIL 1984 – 30/31 AUGUST 2013

London Transport Executive, London Regional Transport (directly-operated and contracted) and Transport for London contracted Night Bus Routes and night-time elements of 24-hour service routes which have operated between 13/14 April 1984 and 30/31 August 2013.

The Index is intended to help readers to trace the development of all-night bus services along particular route corridors.

N21 (via Wood Green)	Extant 13/14 April 1984 (as route number 221)	22/23 June 1995	13, 14, 28, 32, 41, 46, 49, 55, 86, 101, 105, 149
N27 (Richmond)	13/14 April 1984	25/26 April 1985	13, 14, 18, 46, 55, 56, 106
N74 (Bromley North)	13/14 April 1984	31 Oct/1 Nov 1985	13, 14, 46, 55, 56, 106, 117
N76 (via Leytonstone)	13/14 April 1984	13/14 July 1995	13, 14, 41, 46, 55, 106, 121
N77 (Thamesmead), N1 (Thamesmead)	13/14 April 1984		13, 14, 25, 26, 30, 41, 42, 43, 46, 49, 55, 58, 71, 106, 117, 132, 144, 145, 152
N78, N109, N159, N109	13/14 April 1984		13, 14, 19, 20, 25, 26, 33, 40, 42, 46, 49, 52, 55, 56, 58, 62, 76, 108, 110, 134, 155, 172, 178
N79	13/14 April 1984	25/26 April 1996	13, 14, 28, 41, 46, 55, 57, 71, 74, 111, 126, 129, 153
Railair Link	13/14 May 1984	25/26 April 1985	26, 27, 47, 55, 111, 116, 190
N60	26/27 October 1984	5/6 February 1987	56, 108, 111, 134
N50 (Ladbroke Grove), N23, (N)23	26/27 April 1985		19, 25, 27, 30, 39, 42, 46, 47, 49, 50, 51, 56, 67, 82, 83, 113, 114, 115, 116, 174, 190
N51 (Ladbroke Grove)	26/27 April 1985	19/20 June 1986	19, 27, 46, 47, 50, 56, 67, 113, 115, 116, 190
N56	26/27 April 1985	20/21 May 1993	27, 47, 56, 67, 111, 113, 114, 115, 116, 190
N47	1/2 November 1985		30, 56, 58, 74, 106, 107, 111, 117
N72 (via Welling)	1/2 November 1985	27/28 July 1995	41, 47, 56, 61, 71,118, 133, 145, 162
N54	20/21 June 1986	21/22 May 1987	47, 56, 79, 118
N59, N139, (N)139	20/21 June 1986		24, 42, 45, 49, 50, 51, 56, 57, 104, 118, 119, 126, 140, 178
N99 (Cranham)	8/9 August 1986	7/8 September 1991	24, 48, 57, 120
279/279A	25/26 September 1987	30/31 January 1992	46, 57, 59, 85, 120
N8	12/13 August 1988		23, 25, 26, 30, 41, 47, 56, 58, 61, 64, 92, 94, 106, 121, 122, 152, 163, 176
Special Service	31 Dec 1988/1 Jan 1989	31 Dec 1989/1 Jan 1990	36
N73*	22/23 September 1989		23, 25, 30, 39, 57, 72, 85, 123
N1 (Barnet), N20	27/28 October 1989		19, 28, 30, 32, 41, 43, 47, 49, 50, 52, 57, 87, 124, 128, 194
N3	27/28 October 1989		25, 41, 42, 47, 57, 119, 126
N5	27/28 October 1989		19, 25, 30, 32, 41, 47, 50, 52, 57, 119, 124, 128, 143, 194
N6, (N)6	27/28 October 1989		24, 30, 41, 47, 50, 51, 57, 100, 111, 129, 139, 140, 194
N12*, (N)12	27/28 October 1989		39, 42, 43, 44, 50, 51, 57, 73, 74, 130, 143, 146, 156
N19#	27/28 October 1989		28, 30, 38, 47, 57, 131
N53, (N)53	27/28 October 1989		41, 51, 57, 71, 106, 107, 132, 145, 174
N62	27/28 October 1989	27/28 July 1995	41, 47, 58, 71, 133, 152
N69 (Norwood Junction)	27/28 October 1989	10/11 March 1994	58, 108, 134, 135, 155
N70, N381	27/28 October 1989		30, 41, 43, 49, 58, 62, 63, 74, 111, 135
N31	11/12 November 1989		26, 33, 42, 58, 64, 136, 156
N67	5/6 January 1990	24/25 February 1994	59, 93, 137
N9 (Enfield)	9/10 February 1990	24/25 June 1993	59, 138
NX1	19/20 October 1990	2/3 October 1993	48, 59, 61, 138, 145, 182
Central London Link	31 Dec 1990/1 Jan 1991	31 Dec 1991/1 Jan 1992	36
Victoria Express	31 Dec 1990/1 Jan 1991	31 Dec 1990/1 Jan 1991	36
N26	17/18 July 1992		23, 25, 60, 92, 129, 139
N65 (Archway – Hounslow)	17/18 July 1992	19/20 February 1994	47, 60, 86, 139, 148, 177
N99 (Stanmore), N98 (Stanmore)	17/18 July 1992		24, 30, 32, 43, 47, 48, 49, 50, 60, 119, 121, 126, 140, 194
N17	30/31 October 1992	22/23 January 1994	24, 60, 61, 141
N66	30/31 October 1992	23/24 January 1994	24, 47, 61, 141, 170
N100	31 Dec 1992/1 Jan 1993	31 Dec 1998/1 Jan 1999	36, 37, 48

N253	3/4 September 1993		30, 33, 48, 61, 142
N36*, N136	8/9 October 1993		26, 39, 42, 52, 61, 64, 71, 73, 74, 130, 143, 146, 152, 177
N51 (Woolwich)	8/9 October 1993	22/23 July 1995	47, 50, 61, 71, 107, 144, 152
N61	8/9 October 1993	22/23 July 1995	47, 61, 71, 107, 144, 152
N81 (via Bexleyheath), N89 (Erith)	8/9 October 1993		29, 30, 48, 49, 50, 59, 61, 63, 73, 107, 118, 132, 138, 145, 152, 182
N84 (Nunhead), N343	8/9 October 1993		30, 42, 48, 49, 50, 61, 74, 130, 143, 146
N52, (N)52	3/4 December 1993		41, 52, 61, 147, 194
N9 (via Hammersmith)	25/26 February 1994		30, 32, 60, 61, 86, 93, 100, 140, 148, 161, 166
N91 (Cockfosters)	25/26 February 1994		23, 25, 28, 32, 41, 49, 85, 86, 98, 105, 149
N134, (N)134	25/26 February 1994		30, 42, 50, 51, 61, 98, 150, 194
N50 (via Canning Town), N550	14/15 July 1995		19, 25, 26, 41, 43, 50, 52, 62, 121, 151, 178
N21 (via Lewisham)	28/29 July 1995		29, 30, 62, 107, 118, 133, 143, 144, 145, 152, 177, 178
N176, (N)176	26/27 April 1996		41, 51, 62, 74, 111, 135, 153
N35	25/26 April 1997		23, 25, 30, 33, 62, 153
N37, (N)37	25/26 April 1997		33, 50, 51, 62, 65, 154
N68 (via Croydon)	26/27 March 1999		25, 30, 62, 110, 155
N28	28/29 May 1999		26, 33, 42, 62, 64, 136, 156
N94 (Acton Green), (N)94	23/24 July 1999		30, 42, 45, 50, 51, 62, 100, 130, 156, 157
N72 (East Acton), (N)72	3/4 September 1999		33, 42, 44, 51, 62, 100, 157
N24, (N)24	26/27 November 1999		45, 50, 51, 62, 98, 157, 194
2000	31 Dec 1999/1 Jan 2000	31 Dec 1999/1 Jan 2000	37
N140, (N)140	31 March/1 April 2000		33, 42, 50, 51, 63, 159
N149, (N)149	18/19 August 2000		23, 25, 43, 44, 51, 64, 72, 159
N214, (N)214	1/2 September 2000		25, 42, 43, 44, 51, 64, 65, 72, 85, 160, 194
N266, (N)266	22/23 September 2000		51, 160
N236, (N)236	29/30 September 2000	4/5 October 2012	23, 26, 42, 44, 51, 161
N22	24/25 November 2000		42, 148, 161, 176
N41	1/2 December 2000		51, 87, 162
2001 A/B/C	31 Dec 2000/1 Jan 2001	31 Dec 2000/1 Jan 2001	37,
N27 (Chalk Farm), (N)27	2/3 February 2001		28, 51, 162
N137	16/17 March 2001		163
N55	27/28 April 2001		122, 163
N58, (N)58	27/28 April 2001	3/4 March 2005	26, 51, 163
N69 (Walthamstow), (N)69	27/28 April 2001		23, 51, 163, 177
N101	27/28 April 2001	16/17 September 2004	26, 42, 51, 164, 177
N106	27/28 April 2001	24/25 April 2008	26, 42, 164
N105, (N)105	29/30 June 2001		51, 165
N285, (N)285	29/30 June 2001		42, 44, 51, 165
N10, (N)10	28/29 September 2001		23, 25, 33, 52, 85, 148, 166, 175, 178
N108, (N)108	28/29 September 2001		23, 25, 26, 42, 44, 51, 167
N93 (North Cheam), (N)93	30 Nov/1 Dec 2001		51, 167
A, B	31 Dec 2001/1 Jan 2002	31 Dec 2003/1 Jan 2004	37
N75, (N)75	8/9 February 2002	17/18 May 2007	25, 26, 51, 167
N345, (N)345	26/27 April 2002		51, 168
N85 (Kingston), (N)85	28/29 June 2002		51, 168
N88 (Camden Town), (N)88	28/29 June 2002		28, 51, 168
N213, (N)213	28/29 June 2002		25, 52, 79, 169
N369, (N)369, (N)EL1	19/20 July 2002		26, 51, 169
N65 (Ealing Broadway), (N)65	30/31 August 2002		51, 52, 148, 170
N83 (Golders Green), (N)83	13/14 September 2002		51, 170

N148, (N)148	4/5 October 2002		23, 28, 50, 51, 170
N189, (N)189	11/12 October 2002		51, 171
N63	15/16 November 2002		23, 25, 171
N74 (Roehampton)	22/23 November 2002		23, 103, 172
N133	24/25 January 2003		23, 25, 108, 172
N76 (Northumberland Park)	31 Jan/1 Feb 2003		172
N242, (N)242	31 Jan/1 Feb 2003		25, 51, 173
N271, (N)271	31 Jan/1 Feb 2003		25, 51, 173, 194
N274, (N)274	31 Jan/1 Feb 2003	23/24 June 2011	23, 26, 42, 44, 51, 173, 194
N453, (N)453	14/15 February 2003		43, 44, 51, 64, 132, 174
N277, (N)277	28 February/1 March 2003		51, 174
N341, (N)341	25/26 July 2003		51, 174
N7	29/30 August 2003		114, 174
N119, (N)119	29/30 August 2003		25, 51, 175
N250, (N)250	29/30 August 2003		25, 51, 134, 175
N264, (N)264	29/30 August 2003		25, 51, 175
N86 (Harold Hill)	25/26 June 2004		52, 64, 94, 175
(N)390	3/4 September 2004		28, 52, 85, 130, 166, 175
(N)220	21/22 October 2005		176
(N)281	2/3 June 2006		69, 161, 176
(N)344	10/11 November 2006		79, 176
(N)C2	13/14 April 2007		122, 176
(N)205, N205	27/28 April 2007		23, 52, 176
(N)57	29/30 June 2007		172, 176
(N)188	27/28 July 2007		23, 51, 176
(N)102	31 August/1 September 2007		176
(N)295	14/15 September 2007		176
(N)472	28/29 September 2007		176
(N)128	5/6 October 2007		94, 177
(N)474	2/3 November 2007		26, 163, 177
(N)111	30 Nov/1 Dec 2007		177
(N)36	8/9 February 2008		28, 64, 143, 152, 177
(N)297	6/7 June 2008		100, 177
N551	29/30 August 2008		52, 151, 178
(N)365	26/27 September 2008		26, 178
(N)321	9/10 October 2009		152, 178
(N)33	29/30 January 2010		33, 44, 166, 178
N64	27/28 August 2010		33, 52, 108, 110, 178
(N)159	27/28 August 2010		23, 64, 110, 178
N113	29/30 June 2012		23, 26, 52, 101, 119, 178
(N)238	27/28 July 2012	9/10 September 2012	23, 178

Key. * Routes N12 (Shepherd's Bush – Dulwich), N36 (Harrow Road – Lewisham) and N73 (Shepherd's Bush – Tottenham) had earlier operated on occasions of the Notting Hill Carnival on 25/26 August 1986 and 31 August/1 September 1987.
Route N19 (Victoria/Trafalgar Square – Clapham Junction) had earlier operated on New Year's Day 31 December 1988/1 January 1989.